# Washington State

# Washington State

## Charles P. LeWarne

*Third Edition*

**UNIVERSITY OF WASHINGTON PRESS** *Seattle & London*

## ABOUT THE AUTHOR

Charles LeWarne taught in the Edmonds School District for over thirty years. He earned his doctorate in history at the University of Washington in 1969. He has published numerous articles on Northwest history and is the author of *Utopias on Puget Sound, 1885–1915*, and coauthor, with Robert E. Ficken, of *Washington: A Centennial History* (1988). Dr. LeWarne was named Washington State Teacher of the Year in 1987.

*Library of Congress Cataloging-in-Publication Data*
LeWarne, Charles Pierce, 1930–
      Washington State / Charles P. LeWarne.—3rd ed.
          p. cm.
      Includes bibliographical references and index.
      ISBN 978-0-295-98288-5
      1. Washington (State)—History.   2. Washington
      (State)—Description and travel.   I. Title.

F891.L43 2003
979.7—dc21                              2002026644

The paper used in this publication meets the minimum requirements of American National Standard for Information Sciences—Permanence of Paper for Printed Library Materials, ANSI Z39.48–1984.

# Contents

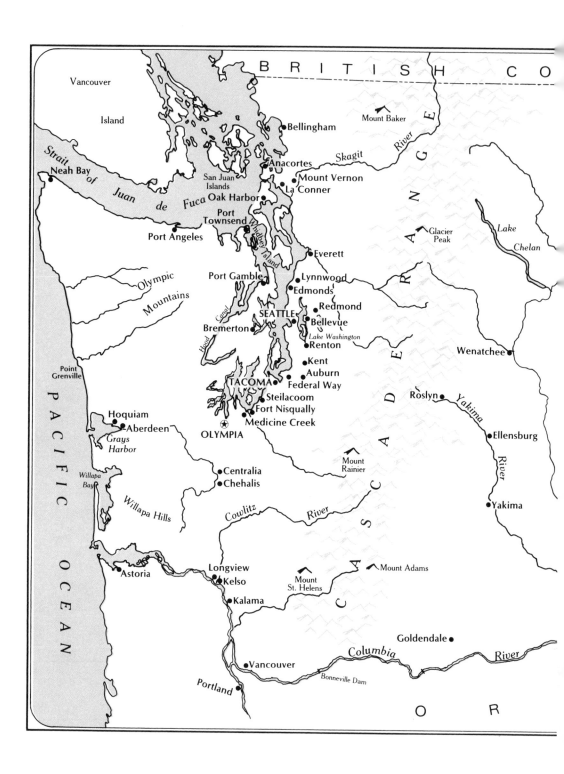

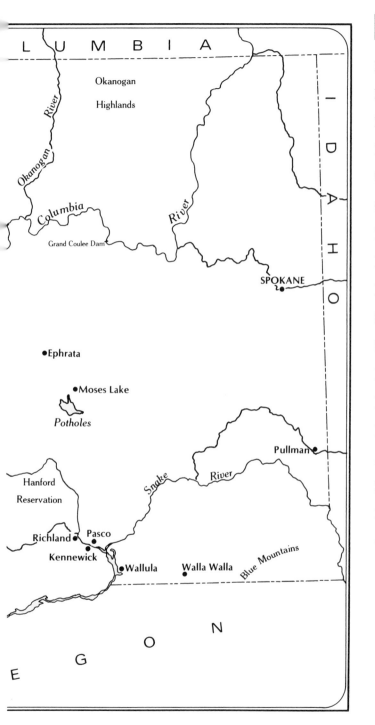

# The State Called Washington

The varied geography of Washington: rock outcrops on the Pacific coast; Moses Coulee; the Cascade Mountains

Mount Rainier, August 17, 1870. It is 6 A.M. Hazard Stevens and Philemon Beecher Van Trump leave their campsite just above timberline. They climb toward a massive rock ridge that they hope will lead to the summit of the 14,410-foot peak that is called Takhoma by local Indians. They carry alpenstocks, climbing irons, a long rope, an ice ax, a large canteen, and a brass plate with their names inscribed. No one has yet climbed this highest and grandest peak in the Northwest.

An Indian named Sluiskin, climbing higher than any other of his people, guided them up a winding route from the base of the mountain. But yesterday he had refused to continue. Takhoma, he said, is an ancient mountain, inhabited by an evil spirit who dwells in a fiery lake on its summit. No human being can ascend it, or even attempt its ascent, and survive. His own grandfather had once turned back after evil spirits sent falling rocks and cold winds to warn him. Stevens and Van Trump go on without him.

These two men are experienced mountaineers. Stevens, son of Washington Territory's first governor, Isaac Stevens, is twenty-eight years old. He has spent most of his life in Washington Territory. A former Civil War general and now surveyor-general of Washington, he is an outdoorsman and a close observer of nature. Van Trump, also a hardy pioneer, has long been eager to climb this mountain.

Since early yesterday morning the two men have trekked from a broad valley near southern Puget Sound, following the Nisqually River until it turned into a creek. They have watched giant firs and hemlocks give way to gnarled and thinly spaced trees. They have passed peaceful mountain lakes and crossed rocky ridges.

At present they are traversing a great ridge called Gibraltar. Glaciers have carved deep canyons out of the volcanic rock, and the canyon sides reveal different layers, or strata. Creeping along snowfields that resemble waves in a choppy sea, the men cross deep crevasses. Ice and rocks fall around them. The top of the mountain is still a mile above. They lean on their alpenstocks to rest, bracing themselves against the freezing wind.

By 5 P.M. they are chilled by a cold, bitter gale. Exhausted, they must spend the night near the summit of the mountain though they have little food and few supplies. Plodding along the narrow crest, they climb a ridge and discover a round crater, two hundred yards across and bedded with snow. Smelling sulfur, they notice steam jutting from cracks in the snow. Warmth!

Deep in a cavern under ice, in a shelter built from rocks, they spend a "most miserable night."

Morning comes cold, with wind howling ever wilder. A hint of blue sky suggests that it is time to descend. They place their brass name plate on the highest summit, proof of their feat.

In later years, the mountain on which Stevens and Van Trump stand will be called Mount Rainier. If we could join the two climbers on this day in 1870 and clear away the clouds, we would look upon changing land forms that stretch in every direction. To the south the perfect cone of Mount St. Helens and the rounded hulk of Mount Adams are surrounded by forested hills. The ever-broadening Columbia River cuts through the land, making giant curves on its route to the Pacific Ocean. West and north are the inland waters of Puget Sound, a mass of channels and inlets, of islands and peninsulas in variegated blues and greens. The snowcapped Olympic peaks are clustered to the northwest. To the east, green hills give way to brown plateaus and deserts that stretch beyond sight. Smaller mountain ranges appear in the distant northeast.

Mountains, deserts, forests, lakes, rivers, glaciers, streams, plateaus—Stevens and Van Trump could see all of them in one glance. During their climb they could observe how natural forces have shaped this land.

The land itself is full of records that tell us what it is and how it came to be that way. Records contained in the earth and records written by men and women combine to tell us much about the state called Washington.

# Over Ages of Change

The land formations and climate in Washington State are not the same today as they were in ages past. Changes have occurred slowly, over many millions of years. These changes are part of this state's geological history.

Stretch your imagination back 50 million years. Imagine a shoreline, many miles inland from the present coast, lush with tropical vegetation. Large rivers meander to the sea across sandy deltas with marshes and swamps. Fossil plants and coal from this era are preserved in sandstone formations. Over thousands of years the scene changes, and changes again.

The climate warms; the sun beats down and the land becomes drier. Water slowly evaporates. Picture now muddy areas, brown, thick, and slushy. As the mud dries, cracks appear. Wide and deep crevices shoot across the earth in sharp, irregular patterns. Edges break and crumble. The once lush land turns sandy, parched, and desolate under the scorching sun.

## Geologic Forces

Now feel a slight tremble, a quiver underfoot. The earth shifts—and shifts again. Once in a while it shakes wildly and then calms before the process starts once more. Even slight movements change the earth. Earthquakes repeated again and again and again create cracks and ridges. Layers of earth and rock fold over and pile up on older ridges and layers. Cracks widen and deepen to become canyons, and ridges become hills. Some rocks that are forced up by folding earth are especially high, rugged, and sharp. Canyons, hills, cliffs, and mountain ranges take shape.

Ever so slowly air and earth grow cool, then cold. Snow blankets the land and accumulates in high valleys and on slopes. In time the land is covered with a huge sheet of packed snow and ice. As new snow falls upon old, glaciers are built. We cannot observe what is happening beneath this heavily packed snow, but its shifting weight constantly reshapes the earth. Glaciers creep down to lower elevations and south from cold northern regions. They carry large boulders, pebbles, and sand, which scrape out new shapes across the land.

Over more thousands of years the edges of the glaciers begin to melt and draw back, making room for new plants and trees. Only then do we become aware that changes have occurred beneath the ice pack. The effect of the melting glaciers, on the other hand, is instantly obvious. Along glacier edges, snow turns to water that trickles down the hillside, finding paths along the ground. These paths become stream beds. Tiny streams merge to form large rivers cutting great areas across the land. These rivers carry silt and mud, rounded rocks and pebbles, tree trunks and limbs. They cut through vulnerable patches of earth and create new riverbeds and canyons. During this constant movement, the rolling rocks are ground smoother and rounder.

In time other changes occur. Intense heat and pressure from deep within the earth cause molten magma to form. Much as toothpaste is squeezed from a tube, this hot, liquid substance is pushed to the surface, where narrow cracks or fissures appear. Steam rises from them. Black and bubbling lava oozes out of the earth. As this lava cools, it forms layers to create new ridges and patterns of hard, shiny, black basalt rock.

Such volcanic activity builds mountains. A small mound spews out lava. The mound becomes a large hill as lava flows outside, cools, and hardens. Sometimes spectacular fireworks displays send glowing rock fragments and pulverized rock out of the earth and through the air. Such eruptions may build up a large mountain, filling slopes and craters with layers of volcanic ash and rock debris.

Volcanic activity pauses. Outpourings of lava and ash slow as the earth becomes calmer. The climate evolves into a moderate one familiar to us in the Pacific Northwest today. Vegetation reappears, watered by rain and by rivers fed by melting mountain snows. Grass and low bushes appear. Elsewhere huge trees flourish, hung with moss and surrounded by ferns and undergrowth.

Over the ages the face of the earth in this corner of North America comes to be as we know it in Washington State today.

But the landscape never stops changing. Winds continue to work upon its surface. Snow feeds glaciers that constantly scour out riverbeds. Lakes fill with silt and become dry land. Earthquakes shift the ground and volcanoes spout to life. Sun,

people are concerned about El Niño's long-term effects. An opposite occasional occurrence is La Niña, a movement of cold water that tends to bring wetter than normal conditions to the Pacific Northwest.

Our capsule picture has covered millions of years and different kinds of forces that have changed the Pacific Northwest. These forces carved out geographical features we take for granted: mountains, plains, valleys, streams, rivers, meadows, prairies, hills, islands, cliffs, peninsulas, and channels. The events creating these features did not necessarily occur in the order or the exact manner in which we imagined them. Sometimes various forces were working at the same time, aiding or challenging one another as they battled over the land.

Columns of basalt rock formed by lava flows

wind, water, snow, movements within the earth all continue to work their wonders on the land.

Even today the climate changes from year to year. El Niño, the periodic warming of the Pacific Ocean surface, raises local water temperatures by several degrees. Immediate effects may be hard to determine, but the usual sources of food for coldwater fish are threatened and some birds disappear from regular feeding spots. Several creatures from warmer areas have appeared in Northwest waters: barracuda in the Strait of Juan de Fuca and sea turtles off Westport. Many

Geologists—people who study the earth and its formation—can trace rocks back 3 billion years with some certainty, but the earth itself is about 4.6 billion years old.

People have always tried to explain how the land around them was formed. Modern geologists use the plate tectonic theory to explain the formation of the earth's continents and ocean basins. They view the outer skin of the earth as a jigsaw puzzle of rigid rock layers averaging fifty miles thick that float on hotter, more plastic rock beneath. When these layers or plates move, the earth's surface changes. When plates collide or rub together, or when substances are squeezed up or down between them, the vibrations may cause earthquakes, the folding or bending of rock layers, or volcanic eruptions.

Most of the Pacific Ocean rests on top of a giant plate that is slowly moving westward, only one to two inches a year. This helps explain the number of earthquake faults and the volcanic "Ring of Fire" that surround the entire Pacific.

Off the Washington shore the small Juan de Fuca plate is thought to be wedged between two larger plates. When these collide, local earthquakes and volcanic actions occur. A major earthquake centered near Olympia in April 1949 killed eight people and damaged many buildings. Another large quake in April 1965 was felt in several states and killed seven people. In the late morning of February 28, 2001, residents all around Puget Sound were jolted by a quake that registered 6.8 on the Richter seismic scale. Centered near Tacoma, it damaged many buildings, bridges, and highways. Yet because it was thirty miles beneath the surface, and because of strict building regulations in recent years, this event caused less damage than it might have. A few months later, Spokane residents were surprised to have several small quakes along a little-known fault in the area. Small earthquakes rattle windows somewhere in the state almost every year.

Mount St. Helens erupted in 1842 and again in May 1980. Other Cascade volcanoes, like Mount Rainier and Mount Baker, are dormant but not dead. Someday they will erupt again. Earthquakes and eruptions are dramatic evidence that the plates are always moving and modifying the earth's surface.

## THE LAND AS WE KNOW IT

All about us are vivid reminders of the changes in climate and earth that have shaped the land where we live.

## A Walk through Time

Let's take a make-believe walk through time, starting 200 million years ago, to watch how nature put together our part of the country.

Let's imagine that a mile represents 200 million years and that we're at the beginning point, even if this part of the country was nothing but open sea that long ago.

A strange process was beginning, a creeping movement of the Pacific Ocean floor that was to deliver land masses from far to the southwest and jam them up against the western edge of the ancient continent.

So our first walk, or swim, is for half a mile, representing 100 million years. By now, the long-distance delivery system has pushed huge land masses against the coastline, including one big one that was pushed up into what we know as the North Cascades.

Trudge on for another 1,584 feet—not quite a third of a mile. It is 40 million years ago and the Olympic Mountains have arrived, formed of lava erupted underwater far to the southwest and pushed into the continent by creeping seafloor.

Walk on another 633 feet, a little more than the length of two football fields. It is 16 million years ago and a great outpouring of lava begins that will repeatedly cover much of what is now central Washington. . . .

A shorter walk, only 343 feet, to a period three million years ago. We are within 80 feet of the end of our mile walk and the ice age is just beginning.

Toward the end of the ice age about 36,000 years ago, in the southern Cascades, a volcano is born. Millennia later, it would be named Mount St. Helens.

*Now we are only inches from the end of our mile walk through time and the ice sheet, once half a mile thick over what we know as Seattle, has retreated.*

*About then, somewhere within the last four inches of our time walk, a new creature appears in the Pacific Northwest, walking on two legs, moving onto land freshly uncovered by melting ice, hunting ice age game. Humans have arrived in the new, raw country.*

*At first the people are insignificant in numbers and in their effect on the land. That will change, but at this point in our time walk nature was in charge, still dealing harshly with the new arrivals.*

*There was the greatest flood known to have occurred on earth, unleashed over central Washington by the dying glaciers about 13,000 years ago. The land bears scars to this day. The flood lasted only about a week, but if humans had been in the area by then—and they could have been— much of the small population must have been destroyed.*

*Mount Rainier's biggest mudflow slid off the volcano 5,800 years ago and reached an arm of Puget Sound. We know the flow covered at least one Indian campground.*

*From there, less than two inches remain in our mile walk, and then we are there—or here— where the past becomes the present.*

Hill Williams, "The Forces at Work," *Seattle Times, May 29, 1983*

• Gaze up at Washington's mountains. In the Olympic and Cascade ranges, tectonic forces have pushed portions of rock up out of the earth. Volcanic peaks in the Cascades have been built up and torn down. The lands around them have been shaped by lava and mud flows.

• Observe currents and tides. Regular visitors to Washington's beaches notice how wind and water constantly change shorelines, cliffs, channels, and islands.

• Look at the great Columbia River. Its twisting course has changed several times. It has cut through hills and left dried riverbeds and empty channels that are now wide valleys or coulees in eastern Washington.

• Observe the changed landscape in the Toutle River Valley left by the 1980 eruption of Mount St. Helens.

• Touch the smooth, rounded rocks created by glaciers in numerous creek bottoms and riverbeds.

• Sift through the sandy soil in much of eastern Washington.

• Feel the force of a driving wind upon your face and body along an ocean shore or a mountain slope. Realize that these same winds helped shape the spot where you stand.

All of these forces that were at work in the past continue today to create the geography of Washington State.

## The Regions of Washington

Washington State is divided by the Cascade Mountains into two distinct parts: western Washington and eastern Washington. Each has its own clear features and personality.

The Cascades are more than just a noticeable division. They force wet winds from the Pacific Ocean to rise and cool, dropping moisture on the land below. This brings luxuriant greenness

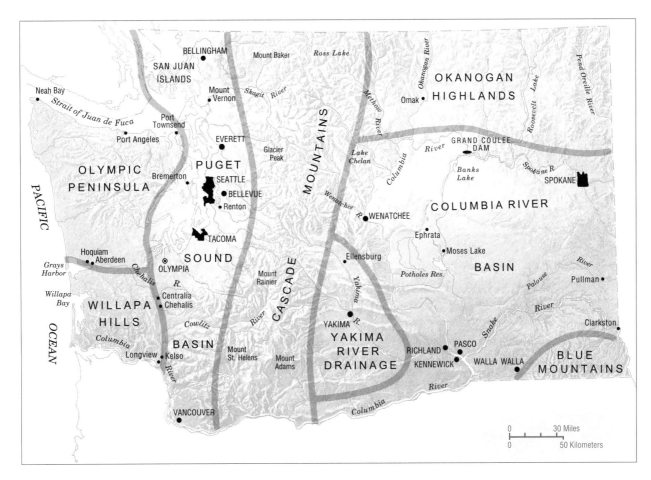

Regions of Washington State

to the western, or ocean, side of the mountains, while the eastern side receives less rainfall. Much of eastern Washington was desert land until the early 1900s when irrigation brought moisture. The eastern part of the state has greater extremes of hot and cold than the western.

## THE WESTERN PORTION

### The Olympic Peninsula

The Olympic Peninsula is framed by the Pacific Ocean on the west, by the Strait of Juan de Fuca on the north, by Puget Sound on the east, and by the valleys stretching between Puget Sound and Grays Harbor on the south.

The core of the peninsula is a rugged cluster of mountains called the Olympics. This range was pushed up from the sea floor by tectonic folding and further shaped by glaciers. The mountains are a series of high ridges, separated by meadows, deep valleys, and canyons. Some peaks remain snowcapped all year. The highest, 7,965-foot Mount Olympus, is surrounded by so many peaks of similar height that it scarcely stands out. Great stands of Douglas fir, Sitka spruce, white pine, western hemlock, and western red cedar grow in the Olympics.

Clouds moving in from the ocean drop so much water on the western slopes of the peninsula that dense rain forests of evergreens, moss, and ground cover fill several valleys. The interior of the Olympics is so thickly forested that most of the world was explored before these mountains. No transportation routes pass through the Olympics. They are crossed only by several days of arduous backpacking across ridge after ridge.

Olympic National Park, which contains the bulk of the mountains, was created in 1938 after a long struggle between timber companies and preservationists. Animal life in the park ranges from the often seen marmot to the black bear and herds of once nearly extinct Roosevelt elk.

U.S. Highway 101 loops around the mountains. Here, with mountains on one side and water on the other, travelers get a clear picture of what the peninsula is like. The valleys on the eastern side lead into Hood Canal or other bays of Puget Sound. Fishing, logging, and recreation abound.

Along the Strait of Juan de Fuca, small farms rest amid rolling hills. Large stands of timber await cutting next to areas where clear-cut logging has already taken place. Logging trucks roll past. Most towns reflect an economy related to forest products.

The largest town is Port Angeles with 19,000 people. It lies directly across the Strait from Victoria, British Columbia. Along with its lumber mills, seafood processing plants, and a U.S. Coast Guard station, Port Angeles offers business and commercial services to the entire northern peninsula.

Port Townsend, an early rival of Port Angeles, guards the point where the Strait joins Puget Sound. In the late 1800s Port Townsend dreamed of becoming the major city of Washington. Stately brick business buildings and elaborate mansions built then have become recent tourist attractions.

The farming and retirement community of Sequim, between Port Angeles and Port Townsend, lies in the "rain shadow" of the Olympic Mountains and has a dry climate. The Makah Indian fishing village of Neah Bay and the log-ging town of Forks are other major towns of the peninsula.

The ocean shore along the western portion of the peninsula is generally rocky and in places rugged. Cliffs and promontories jut into the water, separating sandy beaches. Many people come to fish, hike, and camp. One long stretch of ocean beach is part of Olympic National Park.

Three large Indian reservations—the Makah, Quileute, and Quinault—occupy portions of the coast; the fishing village of La Push is in one of them. Small fishing and resort towns, such as Moclips, Copalis, and Ocean Shores, also dot the shore. Logging is heavy in portions of the interior.

The southern boundary of the peninsula blends into the Willapa Hills. Lower hills, accessible and rich in timber, are interspersed with farmland. Shelton, located on an inlet of Puget Sound, is the most prominent town in this part of the peninsula.

*The Willapa Hills*

At first the Willapa Hills, the southwest region, seems like a small imitation of the Olympic Peninsula. Its center is a cluster of mountains, but they are lower than those to the north. The highest peak reaches less than three thousand feet. Snow-covered only in winter, the timbered hillsides provide logs for mills in nearby towns. To the northwest is Grays Harbor, one of the few excellent natural harbors on the entire Pacific Coast. Here, Aberdeen, Hoquiam, and Cosmopolis have carried on logging, lumbering, seafood processing, and trade for almost a century. A few miles south, Raymond and South Bend process timber from the Willapa region. Willapa Bay empties into the ocean and is separated from the coast by a narrow thirty-mile-long peninsula with sandy beaches and weathered resort towns. Oysterville, now almost a ghost town, reminds visitors of a time when seafood was abundant and the com-

Pounding waves shape the rocky coastline near La Push at the northwest tip of Washington.

munity had a prosperous oyster industry. Today cranberries grow in sandy bogs near the bay.

A stretch of the Columbia River forms the southern boundary of the Willapa Hills region. At its mouth the river is five miles wide. Ocean-going ships navigate the mouth, heading for distant ports or for cities upriver. Winds, shifting currents, and sandbars create hazards that mariners fear and respect, and specially trained pilots guide ships across the Columbia Bar.

In November of 1805 Meriwether Lewis and William Clark, the first Americans to cross the continent, ended their westward journey here. From a small cove near the mouth of the river, they viewed the ocean and explored the area. Then, despairing because of the dampness that rotted their food and leather clothing, they crossed the Columbia to present-day Oregon and camped for the winter on higher, drier ground.

### The Puget Sound Basin

Western Washington is dominated by the arm of the Pacific Ocean called Puget Sound. Puget Sound itself refers only to the waters south of Everett. But the Puget Sound *Basin* includes the whole mass of waterways, bays, inlets, and channels between Canada and Olympia as well as the broad valley south to Oregon. Over four million people live there, most of them in or near large cities, but many in small towns and on farms.

The economy of the region is rich and varied. Fishing, lumbering, and farming have been important from the earliest days of white settlement. Industrial development includes aluminum and steel production, food processing, and the manufacture of aircraft, paper products, computer software, and motor vehicles. Trade and shipping are vital. Seattle, with over half a million people within its city limits and more in surrounding areas, is a commercial and cultural center for much of the western United States.

In the far northern portion of the Puget Sound Basin, the San Juan Islands are magnets for tourism and recreation. More than 170 green and rocky islands support a small permanent population and thousands of seasonal visitors. Larger islands to the south are Whidbey, Camano, Bainbridge, and Vashon.

Seattle, Tacoma, Bellingham, Everett, Bremerton, and Olympia all have good saltwater harbors.

The first Tacoma Narrows Bridge was blown down by winds in 1940 . . .

Bellevue, Kent, Renton, Federal Way, and Mount Vernon are among the cities lying slightly inland, but still dependent upon the traffic of the Sound. Various suburbs—small towns on the outskirts of cities—dot the region.

Many government functions are centered around the Sound. Olympia is the state capital. Bremerton is the site of the Puget Sound Naval Shipyard. Other federal installations include Fort Lewis, McChord Air Force Base, the nuclear submarine base at Bangor, a naval carrier home port in Everett, and the Whidbey Island Naval Air Station. A state penitentiary occupies much of McNeil Island. The University of Washington in Seattle is the largest of many colleges and universities in the region.

Transportation about the Sound is aided by one of the nation's largest ferry systems and several impressive bridges, including the Tacoma Narrows Bridge and floating bridges that cross Lake Washington and Hood Canal.

To the south of Puget Sound, a wide inland trough separates the Cascade Mountains from the Willapa Hills. This is farming and logging country. Centralia and Chehalis are located in the central part of this Puget Sound trough.

At the bend of the Columbia River, Kelso and Longview have lumber and pulp mills. Border-

. . . it was replaced by the present bridge.

ing the Columbia is Vancouver, a port and manu-facturing town. In the early 1800s it was head-quarters for the powerful Hudson's Bay Company. Then Vancouver was the center of government, social, and economic activity for a whole north-western region much larger than present-day Washington.

### The Cascade Mountains

The Cascade Mountains run in a north-south direction and divide western and eastern Wash-ington. Created by both tectonic plate folding and volcanic eruptions, they include five volcanic peaks. Mount Rainier, which local Indians called

Takhoma, is the largest, rising 14,410 feet above sea level. Mount Baker, Glacier Peak, Mount St. Helens, and Mount Adams all reach above 8,000 feet.

All five peaks rise distinctly above the rugged skyline like solitary sentinels. Constantly snow-covered, they have ice packs year-round. Mount Rainier has the largest glacial system in the conti-nental United States, and Washington mountains have record snowfalls. In the winter of 1998–99, Mount Baker received 1,140 inches of snow, sur-passing a national record set at Mount Rainier twenty-seven years earlier.

Indications of volcanic activity remain at Rai-

The Nisqually Glacier on Mt. Rainier

Pass are near cities on Puget Sound and are usually passable in winter. They provide the leading highway and rail routes between east and west. Along with timber, the mountains provide a variety of minerals and ores. Coal mining has been important around Cle Elum and Roslyn and near Bellingham.

Recreational opportunities are great because the mountains are close to urban centers. Each year, hiking, camping, fishing, hunting, skiing, and other activities attract thousands of people into the Cascades. Tourism and recreation contribute significantly to the economy. The North Cascades and Mount Rainier National Parks preserve large portions of the mountains for public use. Most other areas are managed by the U.S. Forest Service.

Rapidly flowing mountain rivers have been harnessed to provide electric power. An impressive system of dams and hydroelectric plants is operated by Seattle City Light on the upper Skagit River in the North Cascades.

## THE EASTERN PORTION
### The Columbia River Basin

Just as Puget Sound is the dominant feature in western Washington, the Columbia River and its tributaries dominate eastern Washington. The 1,400-mile-long river emerges from Columbia Lake just north of the Canadian border. It moves north and then hooks south through British Columbia before it enters the northeastern corner of Washington. It continues to wind through the state, following the Cascade foothills. Sweeping southeast, it forms an area known as the Big Bend Country. The river makes another grand curve south and then west before it heads through the Cascades to the Pacific Ocean.

Along the way the Columbia picks up the waters of large tributaries with their own river systems. Together they pour two million gallons of water into the ocean every second. The Spo-

nier and Baker. Steam poured out of fissures in Mount Baker in the 1970s, suggesting a possible eruption that might cause mud slides and flooding in areas below. However, after several months, Mount Baker became dormant once more. On May 18, 1980, Mount St. Helens erupted dramatically, spewing volcanic ash almost twelve miles into the air and killing fifty-nine people. Resulting avalanches, mud flows, and floods permanently changed the face of the immediate area.

The Cascade Range is traversed by several mountain passes. Snoqualmie Pass and Stevens

kane, Okanogan, Wenatchee, Yakima, and Snake Rivers are major tributaries east of the Cascades. The winding, twisting Columbia, with its winding, twisting tributaries and the old, dry riverbeds left from ages past, create the Columbia River Basin.

Much land that once was considered desert has become rich farmland. Sagebrush has given way to wheat. Some wheat is grown on lands irrigated by river water; elsewhere, dry land farming uses plowing and planting practices that retain water in the ground. Other grains

Wheat harvest near Pomeroy in the Palouse Hills

and crops, notably alfalfa, peas, lentils, soy beans, and wine grapes, grow in the basin.

Washington's reputation as an apple capital rests on the vast orchards along and near the Okanogan, Wenatchee, and Yakima Rivers. Peaches, pears, cherries, and other fruits are also raised.

But the Columbia River Basin is not devoted entirely to agriculture. Rivers provide hydroelectric power used within and outside the region. Grand Coulee Dam, one of the largest structures ever built, is one of eleven dams on the river in Washington. Indeed, little of the Columbia flows freely today; it has become a series of lakes behind dams. These dams provide irrigation water for farms and electricity for towns, businesses, industries, and farms. In the center of what was once desert, Ephrata and Moses Lake have grown because of irrigation and electric power.

Dams have made possible aluminum processing and other manufacturing in the basin. The nuclear energy plant at Hanford also used river water as a cooling agent. The Hanford plant was responsible for the rapid growth of the Tri-Cities area. Richland, Kennewick, and Pasco have relied upon the nuclear industry, agriculture, and research to become a major urban center. East of the Tri-Cities is the wheat country of the Palouse, where Pullman is the site of Washington State University.

Spokane is the great city of the Columbia River Basin and the second largest city in the state. Wealth from Idaho mines helped build Spokane; lumbering and flour milling aided its prosperity. Today Spokane is an essential trading, financial, and cultural center for what is called the Inland Northwest, including eastern Washington, the panhandle of Idaho, westernmost Montana, and part of British Columbia.

There are a number of private and public colleges in the Columbia River Basin, several of them in Spokane, and a state university in Cheney.

Grand Coulee Dam dominates the arid landscape in eastern Washington. This photograph shows the dam under construction.

Artificial lakes, such as Franklin D. Roosevelt Lake behind Grand Coulee Dam, and natural ones, such as Lake Chelan, attract vacationers for water sports. Hunting and fishing are popular resident and tourist attractions.

### The Yakima River Drainage

Between the eastern slopes of the Cascades and the Columbia River, the Kittitas and Yakima River valleys form a region rich in agriculture. This drainage area is sometimes considered part of the Columbia River Basin because the Yakima River eventually enters the Columbia River near Richland. Yet the valleys have a distinct setting and are separated from the Columbia by several ridges.

In the dry, broad Kittitas Valley, Ellensburg, a center for raising livestock, has a state university. Forty miles south, Yakima was originally a rail center. Today it remains the commercial hub of an entire region that produces apples, other fruits, hops, and mint.

As the Yakima River winds southeasterly, its fertile valley is the setting for orchards, farms, and vineyards. Here were some of the first large irrigation projects in the state. Sunnyside, Grandview, Toppenish, and other towns meet the needs of the widely spread population in the valley. West toward the Cascades is the Yakama Indian Reservation, with over seven thousand tribal members.

### The Okanogan Highlands

The Okanogan Highlands is a large mountainous area that stretches across northern Washington between the Cascade Mountains and the Idaho border. Its mountains are not as high as the Cascades and are not always snow-covered. They are really a series of ranges that run north and south and are separated by rivers flowing into the Columbia. Pine stands support a logging industry.

The variety of minerals and ores in these highlands, including gold, silver, and copper, make mining important. Hunting and fishing are recreational additions to the economy. There are few large towns. Okanogan and Omak serve orchard-ists, alfalfa growers, and ranchers. Republic, Kettle Falls, and Newport are important towns in their respective valleys.

The Colville Reservation, the largest Indian reservation in the state, occupies 1.3 million acres north of the Columbia River.

### The Blue Mountains

The Blue Mountains extend into the southeastern corner of Washington and on into neighboring Oregon. The Snake River circles the northern boundary of this region. Walla Walla is the nearest large town, and the Walla Walla Valley, one of the state's oldest settled areas, is rich in farming. Dayton, Pomeroy, and Clarkston are wheat-

## Ahtanum

*As a boy growing up in Yakima and as an adult, U.S. Supreme Court Justice William O. Douglas loved hiking and camping in the wilderness of Washington. Here he recalls the sights, sounds, smells, and healing effect he found on the north fork of the Ahtanum River above Yakima:*

*"When I left the road at Soda Springs, I was at once in a deep forest that no ax had ever touched. Great yellow pine reached to the sky one hundred, two hundred feet. This was the dry, eastern slope of the Cascades. There was little underbrush; the woods were open, not dense. The sun came streaming in, as if it were pouring through long narrow windows high in a cathedral. The soft notes of some bird—a thrush, I believe—came floating down from the treetops. As I listened it was as though the music came from another world.*

. . . .

*"It was so silent I could almost hear my heart beat. No moving thing was in sight. The quiet was so deep that the breaking of a twig underfoot was startling. I was alone, yet I felt that dozens of animals must be aware of my presence and watching me—hawks, flycatchers, hummingbirds, camp robbers, bear, cougar, deer, porcupine, squirrels. But when I looked I could see nothing but trees and sky.*

*"Then I became aware of the fragrance of the trees. The ponderosa pine towered over all the others. But I began to see the scatterings of other conifers: black pine and whitebark pine, white and red fir, and the tamarack or larch. I stopped, looked up, and breathed deep. Then I realized I was experiencing a great healing.*

*"In Yakima I had been suffering from hay fever. Now it was gone. My nose wasn't stuffy. My eyes were clearing. I breathed deeply of the fragrant air again, as I lifted my face to the treetops. And I realized what had happened. I had lost my allergy."*

*From William O. Douglas, Of Men and Mountains (New York: Harper & Brothers, 1950)*

and vegetable-growing centers on the edges. The region is characterized by pine-laden hills and a dry climate; it supports little industry.

## Characteristics of Washington State

Washington State has a remarkable variety of climates, land formations, natural resources, and economic activities. The scenery constantly changes as one moves east and west, north and south, and from sea level to mountain summit.

### WASHINGTON TODAY

What is Washington today? Let us consider a few facts that should help to describe it.

- It is the most northwesterly state of the forty-eight contiguous, or connected, states.

- It is home to six million people, most of whom live in or near large cities. The population continues to increase.

- It occupies a little more than 68,000 square miles, including inland waters. It is much larger than most states along the eastern seaboard of the United States but is the smallest of the western states, except for Hawaii.

- It has a variety of climates and land forms, rising quickly from sea level to 14,410 feet. The state has salt waterways, rivers, lakes, deserts, canyons, mountains, and islands.

- It ranks among leading states in growing apples and wheat and other fruits and grains, in manufacturing airplanes and computer software, and in generating hydroelectric power.

- It is nicknamed the Evergreen State. State symbols include a state bird, the goldfinch; a state flower, the coastal rhododendron; a state tree, the western hemlock; and a state motto, "Alki," an Indian word meaning "by and by," which looks to the future greatness of the state.

Coastal rhododendron (*Rhododendron macrophyllum*), state flower; western hemlock (*Tsuga heterophylla*), state tree; willow goldfinch, state bird

## Chapter 1 Review

**I.** Define the following words and terms. Relate each one to Washington State.

Lava
El Niño
Geology and geologists
Plate tectonic theory
Puget Sound trough
Suburbs
Tourism
Tributaries
Agriculture
Hydroelectric power
Irrigation

**II.** Give an example of how each of the following activities has affected the geography of Washington.

Folding                  Volcanic action
Glaciers                 Wind erosion
Currents                 Water erosion
Tides

**III.** Each of the following questions should call your attention to factual information in the chapter. Try to answer each one. Then look back in the reading to check your answers and find any answers you do not know.

1.  What action within the earth creates columns of black basalt?

2.  What action creates the small, rounded rocks found in many riverbeds?

3.  What three kinds of trees are found on the Olympic Peninsula?

4.  What is the highest altitude in the Willapa Hills?

5.  About how many people live in the Puget Sound Basin?

6.  Name at least six cities in the Puget Sound Basin.

7.  Give two methods of transportation that are important for crossing Puget Sound.

8.  Name the five volcanic peaks in the Cascade Mountains of Washington.

9.  Name the two national parks in the Cascades.

10.  What important crop is raised on the land of the Columbia Basin that was once desert?

11.  What has made the dry areas of the Columbia Basin usable for agriculture?

12.  What is the name generally given to the area that includes Richland, Pasco, and Kennewick?

13.  Where is the Okanogan Region?

14.  Which tree grows throughout the Blue Mountains?

15. What is the population of Washington State?

16. What is the highest point in Washington? How many feet above sea level is it?

**IV.** Think about, discuss, and answer the following questions.

1. What is a region? Think of several ways to define the word. What is the difference between a geographical region and a political region? Which of the following are geographical regions? Which are political?

Washington State
Pacific Northwest
United States
North America
Cascade Mountains
Tacoma
Okanogan County
Okanogan Highlands
Columbia River
Columbia River Basin
Olympic Peninsula
Olympia

2. (a) Do you think that it is important for a state to have such things as a nickname, a state flower, a state tree, a state bird, and a state motto? Explain your reasons.

(b) Is "The Evergreen State" an appropriate nickname for Washington? Discuss.

3. Define each of the terms below. Locate examples on a map of Washington. Draw a map of an imaginary place that includes these features. Because some of the terms are similar to one another, be careful to explain distinctions between them (valley and canyon, for instance).

| | |
|---|---|
| Island | Prairie |
| Peninsula | Stream |
| Strait | Canyon |
| Lake | Inlet |
| River | Bay |
| Valley | Basin |
| Plain | Promontory |

# Chapter 2  The Earliest Settlers and How They Lived

This finely carved club was uncovered during the excavation of Ozette Village.

Ozette Village, Cape Alava. A spring day in the early 1500s. The sky is heavy with dark clouds. Rain pounds down upon this Makah Indian coastal village as it has for many days.

The village of Ozette is well set for sealing, whaling, and fishing. Indeed, the village has existed on this very spot for more than one thousand years. The broad beach is a continuing source of clams and mussels; fish are caught just offshore. Forests that slope behind the houses are thick with red cedar, spruce, and hemlock, smaller trees and bushes, roots, berries, and ferns. Such abundance provides a good life for the villagers.

Whales are an important resource too. No cape along the Washington coast juts farther into the ocean toward the path of the migrating whales. Yet this site is safe from all but the harshest winter storms. A sand spit that leads to an island just offshore creates a sheltered shore where canoes are easily beached and where whales can be towed ashore.

The whalers are the most honored of the village people. Sent on their way with rituals, preparation, and prayers, they paddle sturdy eight-man canoes miles beyond the surf in search of prey. Whaling is difficult and dangerous work. Sometimes a harpooned whale breaks toward open water or smashes the canoe with its great tail. But skilled hunters, aided by careful ritual and incoming tides, can bring even large whales ashore. There, ceremonies honor the animal's spirit. Beached while villagers sing and pray, the whales are stripped of their blubber. Meat is cut out and divided among families. Bones, blubber, and oil are preserved for a multitude of uses.

Many whales can be killed during the whaling season, which each year brings additional Makahs to this village. One of their five major sites along the coast, its population during whaling season can swell from 300 to over 500 people.

Cedar plank houses at Ozette cluster on a terrace above the shore. Measuring as much as thirty-five by seventy feet, they each shelter several related families—probably up to about forty people. Benches for sitting and sleeping line interior walls. Baskets woven from strips of cedar bark and cedar and spruce boughs seem to be everywhere. They hold dried fish and clams, fishhooks, woodworking tools, weaving materials, and harpoon blades protected by folded strips of cedar bark.

In front of each family living area within the large houses is a fire pit where food is cooked. The fire also provides warmth and more than a little smoke, although most of the smoke escapes through spaces between movable roof planks. Boxes and bowls differ according to purpose. Some are made of cedar, others of hardwoods obtained from the forest behind the village or gained in trade along the coast.

A woman who is making a mat skillfully threads a wooden needle. Another weaves at a loom. Babies sleep. Older children bat a feathered shuttlecock up and down with wooden paddles. Men cut wood, prepare harpoons and wooden arrows, repair nets, and carve boxes. They use tools with blades of shell, bone, stone, and even metal, which most likely drifted across the Pacific on wrecked ships from Asia.

The Ozette people are skilled artists. They carve and paint designs of seals, fish, whales, human faces, and other images onto everything from wall plaques and storage chests to tool handles, hunting and fishing equipment, and personal items such as combs. Much of this activity—both play and work—takes place in the large houses because the weather is cold and wet.

Then, unexpectedly, an avalanche of mud rushes down the hillside. It buries several houses in the center of the village. People have no time to comprehend what is happening. For them, time stops.

*

Waves still break upon the coast. The rain continues. But many houses are silent.

Makah whalers and fishermen will build new houses on the soil that buried their ancestors. The village will remain a sealing, whaling, and fishing site into the early 1900s. Later inhabitants are archaeologists, including Makahs, who unearth remains of the buried houses. Ozette village will become one of the richest archaeological finds in all of North America.

# Studying Washington's Past

**A**rchaeology is the study of the past based on the record within the earth, not on the pages of books and reports. Archaeologists investigate the remains of animals that people hunted, plants they gathered, soils they disturbed, and artifacts they made and used—any evidence left by ancient people. This way they learn what life was like in the past. By skillfully gathering information, interpreting clues, and using sophisticated laboratory techniques, archaeologists make some surprisingly clear and complete discoveries. They have worked at sites in both western and eastern Washington.

## THE OZETTE DIG

The uncovering of the Ozette village on the Washington coast illustrates how archaeologists work. Attracted by layers of ancient refuse on the hillside near Cape Alava, Professor Richard Daugherty of Washington State University (WSU) studied the spot in the late 1960s. In 1970 a winter storm ate away part of the bank, uncovering house planks and other artifacts. The Makah called Daugherty back, and he returned convinced that Ozette would widen knowledge of early Indian life.

He obtained support from the Makah Nation, from WSU, and from the federal government. The only land approach was a three-mile hike through the woods. Yet, a base was set up with buildings of driftwood and lumber flown in by helicopters, along with other supplies and laboratory equipment. Archaeologists, geologists, zoologists, botanists, and other specialists were joined by graduate students, Makahs, and occasional visitors, all working together.

In order to protect the discoveries it was necessary to uncover them carefully. Digging with hand trowels could damage artifacts. Instead, ocean water was pumped through hoses to wash mud away gently. House timbers, baskets, boxes, tools, fishing equipment, mats, pieces of clothing, and various other artifacts were slowly unearthed from the wet sand and mud deposits.

Objects made of wood, plant fibers, and other materials would ordinarily decompose or disintegrate quickly when exposed to air, but the buried houses had been waterlogged for nearly four centuries. No air had reached the artifacts. Archaeologists carefully recorded exactly where each item lay in the deposit so that the objects' relationships to each other would always be known. Such relationships are as important as the objects themselves. Once uncovered, the artifacts were preserved in chemical solutions and helicoptered to a laboratory in nearby Neah Bay.

Over 50,000 artifacts were uncovered in eleven years. Five houses buried by the mud slide were found. Archaeologists found traces of yet another house perhaps 800 years old. After several years of work the dig was closed. The artifacts from Ozette are displayed at a museum in Neah Bay, the last remaining Makah village.

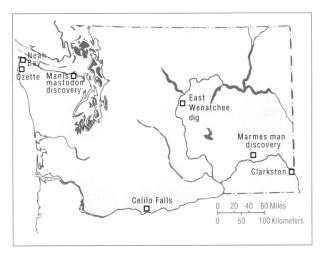

Major archaeological sites in Washington State

## MARMES MAN

In the lava country of southeast Washington, the Palouse River drops over a canyon wall and flows into the Snake River. For centuries, families that lived on the sunny sagebrush flat where the rivers meet caught and dried salmon.

Many people lived in pithouses that dominated the Columbia Plateau for at least 5,000 years. A pithouse typically consisted of a circular pit sunk three or four feet into the ground and topped by a pole framework covered with brush or mats. Easy to build, it could be any size and used materials, tools, and skills that were close at hand. A pithouse was well insulated. It could be made warm in winter by adding materials or cool in summer by reducing the covering to a single layer of mats. Today, concern with energy conservation has revived interest in such building, but the concept is old.

Pithouses were not the only places where early people lived. To fully use the varied resources in the area—fish, roots, berries, deer, and antelope—people had to move season by season. Sometimes they set up temporary shelters. Other times they stayed in small caves or natural overhangs beneath ledges that had been created by successive lava flows. One such overhang is the Marmes Rockshelter, named for the ranch family that owned the land. There, WSU archaeologists found human bones 10,000 years old.

Dr. Daugherty directed excavations near the Marmes Rockshelter and investigated other sites along the Snake River and its tributaries. Archaeologists found fragments of baskets and mats, or plant fibers finely twisted into cordage. In one rockshelter a stone knife still lay with its wooden handle. Most often, however, fragile materials had disappeared. Artifacts preserved within the dry deposits offered fewer clues to the past than those in the clay mud at Ozette.

Outside the rockshelters, archaeologists most often found only implements of stone or bone, or fish bones or hard seeds left from an ancient dinner, or mammal bones split open. Cooking hearths, charcoal, and rocks cracked by ancient fires also indicated that humans had been present.

Yet even small clues helped archaeologists piece together knowledge of the people who had inhabited the plateau century after century. They proved that this area had been occupied for thousands of years. But the Lower Monumental dam was about to be constructed twenty miles down the Snake River. Its reservoir would flood the remnants of a pithouse village on the Palouse and flood the Marmes Rockshelter. Investigation would cease.

For one final check, WSU geologist Roald Fryxell asked Roland Marmes to bulldoze a trench from the rockshelter down to the floodplain of the river. As he walked behind the dozer, Fryxell found fragments of a human skeleton. This was an important new find, but scientists who wanted to learn more had to race against completion of the dam.

Bones moved by bulldozers could tell them little. Only material still in place, lying undisturbed, could tell about the ancient people and how they lived. Quickly but carefully, searchers uncovered additional human bones. These bones rested twelve feet below the surface of the floodplain in a layer of earth 9,000 to 13,000 years old.

For more than 10,000 years, Marmes Man, as these finds became known, had lain buried and undisturbed. In a short time the archaeologists found partial remains of at least ten people, one a teenager. The deposits also contained other items: stone weapons and tools, the butchered remains of an elk larger than any alive today, bone needles the size of modern embroidery needles, and an owl-claw amulet that may have belonged to a shaman, or "medicine man."

Archaeologists work at the site where "Marmes Man" was discovered near the Palouse River.

What did these ancient people look like? Quite certainly their hair was black and their eyes brown, like present-day Indians and Asians. Their skeletal structure was modern. Dressed in current fashions, the Marmes people would appear very much like people of today.

These discoveries represented the earliest evidence of human life in all the Americas that could be related to the environment. This relation is important, for humans do not live in a vacuum. They depend on their surroundings and interact with them. Thus the WSU team could pose questions about how the environment has changed during the 12,000 years since the last ice age. What was the climate like at different periods? Has the Marmes Rockshelter area always been a land of sagebrush and grass, or was it once partly forested? What resources were available to people who existed at different times? Teams of archaeologists, geologists, and other scientists seek to answer such questions by investigating areas like that where Marmes Man was found.

## THE MANIS MASTODON

In August 1977, another chance discovery carried the story of humans in Washington back another two thousand years. Clare and Emanuel Manis had retired to Sequim, on the Strait of Juan de Fuca. While digging a pond in a low, marshy corner of their farm, Mr. Manis hit a hard object with his backhoe. He carefully raised it above ground. It was chalky white, with a smooth, polished appearance under its dirt covering. About six inches in diameter and four feet long, it was curved and tapered at one end—most unusual for a log! Minutes later Manis uncovered a similar object over six feet long. They looked like huge elephant tusks.

The Manises invited experts to inspect the finds. WSU archaeologists determined that the tusks were from an ancient mammoth or mastodon, an elephant-like creature that lived in the area when the last major ice age ended about 12,000 years ago.

A week after the first discovery came an even more remarkable one. Zoologist Carl Gustafson found a rib that was apparently from the same animal. Embedded in the rib was a bone point, the tip of a weapon that could have been thrust only by a human hunter.

For months the scientists carefully hosed deposits to uncover ancient objects and bones without damaging them. They precisely marked the locations and positions of each item, inspecting and preparing them for preservation. They learned a great deal about the creature, the site, the climate, the vegetation, and the human hunters.

Mammoths, an extinct grass-eating species, were already known to have inhabited the area. But a molar proved that this creature had been a mastodon that chewed brush. The teeth of the two species differed with their distinct feeding habits.

The long forelimb of the Manis mastodon is analyzed by an archaeologist in the laboratory.

Using methods that permit dating, the scientists determined that seeds and pollen grains in the pit where the mastodon lay were between 12,000 and 14,000 years old. They also learned that plants growing in the area then were typical of a cold climate, much like that of the subarctic today. The mastodon must have lived during a period when glacier ice was drawing back.

The spear point in the mastodon's rib had been hurled or thrust with enough force to penetrate the thick hide. But the blow did not kill the animal. Healing had taken place around the wound, suggesting that death had not come immediately. It appears that early humans deliberately hunted mastodons for food.

## CLOVIS POINTS

Ten years after the Manis bones were found, another remarkable discovery was made, this time in an apple orchard just above the Columbia River in East Wenatchee. Moises Aguirre was digging an irrigation trench when his shovel touched something hard. He had uncovered a translucent stone deftly fashioned into a long spear point. He and the orchard foreman soon turned up nineteen unusual stone tools. Six of them seemed to be ancient spear points, as large as eight and one half inches long with sharp, fluted edges. The workers and ranch owner Mark Richey wisely covered the site with a great concrete slab until archaeologists could investigate further. Later that year more artifacts were uncovered in a two-square-meter area.

The workers had found a great cache of Clovis points. Named for the New Mexico town where similar spear points had been uncovered earlier, Clovis points have appeared elsewhere in North America including Idaho and Oregon. They were made and used by the earliest inhabitants who hunted mammoth and other mammals.

Other tools had been found earlier in the

This ancient Indian petroglyph—a carving on rock—is located above the lower Columbia River.

Northwest, but this East Wenatchee find was unique. Testing of soil layers dated them to the end of the ice age 11,000 to 12,000 years ago. Moreover, they were the largest Clovis points ever found and the only ones found in the same site and position in which they had been left. *National Geographic* magazine thought the spot could have been "a simple tool cache, a habitation, the last resting-place of a Clovis chief, a flint knapper's hut, a hunting shrine, even a shaman's tent."

The uncovering of the tools marked an exciting new phase in efforts to understand the earliest humans on the continent. Their interpretation also underscores a growing awareness of Native American claims to the past.

## KENNEWICK MAN

Another discovery illustrates how important such findings are and how controversy can surround them. One July afternoon in 1996, two college students were among the thousands watching hydroplane races on the Columbia River at Kennewick. While wading at the edge of the river, one stumbled across a round, smooth "rock," which proved instead to be a skull. They turned it over to local police. A search turned up additional bones, and authorities called in a local archaeologist, Dr. James Chatters. He found a stone spear point several thousand years old embedded in one of the bones. Investigations indicated that the bones were approximately 9,300 years old; recent erosion along the river-bank had apparently dislodged them from their ancient resting place. It was a startling discovery, because this was thought to be the most complete ancient skeleton ever found in the Pacific North-west.

Controversy soon erupted over these prehis-toric bones. Individuals and groups disagreed about their origin, who should own them, and what should be done with them. The Army Corps of Engineers first took possession because the bones had been found on their property. Scientists wanted to study them in greater detail so as to learn more about the origins of humans in the area and on the North American continent. Native American groups were disturbed that the bones had been removed from their resting spot and wanted them reburied. A federal law requires that Indian remains held by other groups must be returned to tribes for burial. Disagree-ments could easily arise between such tribes. Yet five Northwest tribes cooperated in an effort to reclaim these bones.

Interestingly, however, the long, narrow shape of the skull was unlike the skull shape of known Indians. Perhaps this human was not related to them. Rather, perhaps this person was related to humans recently found to have lived in South America centuries before Native Americans were believed to have arrived. This threw into doubt theories that the Americas had originally been settled only by people who had crossed a land bridge from Siberian Asia at the end of the ice age. On the other hand, perhaps the unusual shape is not important: differences exist in the appearance and bone structure of known Indian groups. Or, possibly, the land bridge was crossed earlier than scientists have believed.

In 1999 a federal judge ordered the bones sent to the Thomas Burke Museum at the University of Washington in Seattle for safekeeping. A panel of scientists studied them. A few months later they announced that these were the remains of "an ancient man who lived most of his life and died in the Pacific Northwest more than 9,000 years ago. . . . Kennewick Man is Native American." Attempts to make a DNA analysis were not successful because of the age and condition of the bone. Meanwhile, authorities reviewed the anthropology and cultural history of Northwest tribes. In September 2000, U.S. Secretary of the Interior Bruce Babbit agreed that Kennewick Man was culturally related to the five Northwest tribes who claimed the bones. Then in 2002, a federal judge ruled the bones should go to scientists for further study.

The issue is complex, but discussions about Kennewick Man should help anthropologists learn more about early humans. Perhaps more important, they may help us iron out questions about the rightful possession and treatment of ancient bones. Meanwhile, it is obvious that ancient remains are all around us. In 2000, Kirkland middle school students were excited when construction workers on their school grounds uncovered bones that proved to be the 6,300-year-old remains of a mammoth.

## Native Americans

The mastodon hunters, Marmes Man, the Palouse villagers, the Ozette people, the Clovis hunters, and Kennewick Man are part of the state's archaeological story. Efforts to find and save evidence of the human past continue. No written record exists of life during the thousands of years before white people arrived. Archaeology and the traditions of today's Native Americans can tell something about that time.

When Christopher Columbus landed in the New World, he thought he was in India, so he called the local people "Indians." Today many people prefer the term "Native American" because it describes those present on this continent before Europeans arrived.

In Washington, native people were living in many distinct cultural groups before European and American explorers arrived. Their Indian descendants today include coastal tribes such as the Makah, Hoh-Quileute, Quinault, Lummi, and Nisqually-Puyallup, and interior groups such as the Yakama, Colville, and Wanapum.

Present state boundaries have nothing in common with the groupings of these people. Groups along the Pacific coast from northern California to southeastern Alaska had enough similarities to be considered as one large culture area. People east of the Cascade Mountains lived much as did others on the dry plateaus and basins to the north and south.

These Native Americans did not think of themselves as belonging to "tribes." They had relatives who spoke similar languages, practiced the same major customs, and cherished similar beliefs and values. But individual family groups and villages were largely responsible for their own economic and political lives. They also knew about and traded with people who lived and spoke in ways different from their own.

Estimates of how many Native Americans there were when white people arrived vary widely. Early census records are not accurate, and by the time the counts were made, many native people had died in epidemics. By the late 1800s, diseases entirely new to them—such as smallpox, measles, flu, and tuberculosis—had wiped out as much as 90 percent of many groups.

### ARRIVAL IN AMERICA

The people known as Native Americans may have originated in the northeastern part of Asia (Siberia or Mongolia) and migrated to the Americas. A long-held theory has been that Indians crossed to Alaska from Asia late during the last worldwide ice age. At that time the sea level fell 300 feet below its present level, and a bridge of land hundreds of miles wide connected the two continents at the Bering Strait. Only twenty-five miles wide today, the shallow floor of the Bering Strait once stood above water.

It was home for a variety of plants and animals. Humans could live there and pass from Asia to America in small groups, unaware of making a major migration. People simply moved as conditions and opportunities dictated. They must have

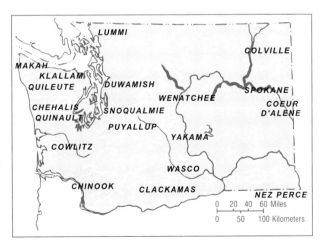

Major Indian groups

## Native Plant Medicines

*Indians from every part of Washington State have traditionally made use of plants for medicine as well as for food and for making canoes, totem poles, baskets, sleeping mats, and many other articles of daily life. Here are some examples of native medicines:*

*Cedar. "The Lummi chew the buds of cedar and swallow them for sore lungs, while the Cowlitz chew them for toothache, and the Skokomish boil them for a gargle. The Skagit boil the ends of the leaves for coughs. The Cowlitz boil the tips and mix them with some roots . . . for a cold medicine. . . . The Quinault make an infusion of the bark and twigs for kidney trouble. The seeds of cedar are steeped with the ends of the limbs and the infusion drunk to break a fever."*

*Nettle. "The medicinal value of this plant seems to be as great as its power of irritation. The Chehalis and Quileute take the whole stalk and whip a person having rheumatism, while the Quinault count that as a help for paralysis. For the same illness, the Cowlitz crush the sprout and use it as a poultice. Rubbing with nettles is also good for colds, according to the Snohomish. Perhaps less drastic and also less specific, baths are taken by the Samish and Swinomish in an infusion made of the entire nettle plant and the white fir (Abies grandis), pounded together and boiled. It serves as a general tonic."*

*Honeysuckle. "The leaves are pounded fresh and put on an abscess or boil by the Makah. The Cowlitz grind the leaves and put them on a sore joint to reduce the swelling. They also dip the bark in hot water and apply it to a swelling. The Squaxin mash the leaves and, after dipping the pulp in water, apply it to an area infected with blood poisoning."*

*From Erna Gunther, Ethnobotany of Western Washington: The Knowledge and Use of Indigenous Plants by Native Americans (Seattle: University of Washington Press, 1973 rev. ed.)*

hunted woolly mammoths and other large animals and small game like lemmings and muskrats. Surely they also gathered plant fibers and foods and fished along the coast and on lakes and rivers.

Even while ice blanketed most of the north, some livable areas were free of ice. One corridor probably reached from the interior of Alaska into central Canada and the United States. At times parts of the coast were also free of ice.

On the other hand, some scientists believe that people lived in the Americas before the land bridge. The physical appearance of Kennewick Man, for instance, is similar to certain Asian peoples, so perhaps his people had arrived and spread throughout parts of the Americas before there was a land bridge. Or perhaps they came by a different route—such as from the South Pacific to South America.

## LIVING ON THE LAND

In the Pacific Northwest, families and small bands settled where they found plentiful game, fish, or plants. Fresh water and winter shelter were also important. The people lived in small villages or extended family households and led lives that might differ from others a few miles away. Yet the land and its resources provided similarities.

Generation by generation, distinct ways of life developed as each group adapted to its own particular environment. People on the rainy Olympic Peninsula lived very differently from those within the windy gorge of the Columbia River or on the grassy or pine-forested plateaus. Traditions of ancient days are kept alive in the stories, songs, and art of today's Indians.

Life on both sides of the Cascade Mountains was reasonably comfortable. Near the coast, abundant salmon and seafood, sea mammals and land mammals, berries and edible roots assured ample food. The climate was mild. Huge western red cedars supplied material for canoes, houses, clothing, and household items.

East of the mountains, the environment was less friendly, and it probably took more time to obtain the necessities of life. Few people lived in the central desert area. Most were based along rivers and in the higher plains to the north and east. They traveled frequently in search of food or trade goods. But even inland Indians found living conditions easier than those in many other regions of the continent.

Native Americans did not recognize a larger government or tribal connection. They spoke many different languages and had different customs and beliefs. But they were not isolated from each other. Nearby communities were linked by marriages, and people gathered together for feasts, potlatches, and the winter season of stories and dances. Groups east of the mountains met coastal peoples for trade; arrowheads from one corner of the state might be exchanged many times to reach a village on the opposite side.

Native communities faced the same concerns that all societies have: food, shelter, transportation, communication, government, raising children. The solutions they arrived at served them well for many generations.

### Food

All people have staple foods, those items around which they plan their diet. Northwest Indians ate fish, particularly salmon. Among some, the word for salmon was the same as the word for fish. People developed rituals to show respect for this creature that sustained them.

Hatched far up rivers and streams, young salmon make their way to the ocean where they live for several years before returning to their birthplace to breed and die. As they travel back up the river, they are so abundant that they can be caught with ease—or so it was in early times.

Northwest Indians developed numerous fishing techniques. Nets dipped into streams brought large numbers ashore. Some Indians used a harpoon-like stick with a point that separated upon entering the fish but could be drawn in by a long cord. Some tribes built fence-like structures called weirs across the stream, channeling fish into traps. Large fishing platforms were built out over rapids at special fishing spots, such as Celilo Falls on the Columbia River.

The salmon was more than food; it was important in the cultural life of the people. Every year when the salmon first appeared, one was caught and brought back to the village with ceremony. It was laid out with its head upstream, pointing the direction other fish should go. Then it received special preparation for cooking and was eaten at a feast, while prayers were sung for its well-being. Bones and other remains were carefully laid in the river so the current could return them to the salmon country. Then the first salmon could tell others how he had been honored and urge them to follow his route upriver. Care was taken that the salmon, with its supernatural powers, not be offended in any way.

While men fished, women dried or cooked the catch. They boned and scraped the fish and then cut the meat lengthwise into strips, which they placed on large racks for smoking or drying. The fish might be smoked over a smoldering fire of alder wood for a week or longer. When the smoking was finished, the fish was stored in large baskets for winter.

Salmon was the most significant seafood, but the tiny eulachon was prized for its oil, and great sturgeon were important in the Columbia River region. Halibut and cod were hooked deep in the ocean, and freshwater fish were plentiful. Along the ocean coast, skilled Makah, Quileute, and Quinault whalers hunted from huge dugout canoes. The sighting of a whale meant a chase that might end with a harpooning.

Along the coast and the shores of Puget Sound,

These Indians use spears to fish in their traditional manner at Celilo Falls on the Columbia River; the spot has since been flooded by the construction of The Dalles Dam.

shellfish were abundant. Women and children gathered and prepared clams. Often a fire was built in a hole with rocks placed on top. When the fire burned down to coals, clams were laid on a layer of seaweed above the hot rocks and covered with seaweed or dirt to steam. Some might be dried later. Mussels, oysters, barnacles, and crabs were also plentiful.

Women gathered food on land. They filled baskets with various wild berries, nuts, crab apples, and roots. Special hard, pointed wooden tools were used to dig out roots—often hard work in the packed earth. Especially important was the camas root, which resembled a sweet potato and grew in large clumps with beautiful blue blooms during the growing season. The bulb was tasty when cooked. Camas could be ground and used like flour.

Along the coast, but especially in valleys and foothills near Puget Sound, hunting yielded bear and deer and smaller game. The successful hunter was an honored tribal member, and teenaged boys underwent much training to prepare themselves as hunters.

Along with spears and bows and arrows, Indian hunters devised traps and nets. Large game was often butchered on the spot because a carcass was difficult to carry out. Strips of meat were dried or broiled over a fire. Often several families went together to hunting camps where the women gathered berries and roots and then cooked the meat. Hunters also went after birds and fowl such as ducks.

The ability to preserve food for future use assured the continuing well-being of coastal Indians.

Indians east of the Cascades sought and ate many of the same foods as those on the west, but the variety was not as great. Food was also more difficult to obtain. Much of eastern Washington is a dry plateau cut through by the winding Columbia and Snake Rivers and smaller tributaries. Rivers provided water, fish, and transportation, so people usually clustered in the occasional green and damp valleys.

Large numbers of salmon swam up these rivers, and that fish was as vital to the Indians east of the Cascades as to those in the west. The Columbia was the world's greatest salmon-producing river, and tribes throughout the Northwest shared in the bounty of the returning runs.

Hunting was important east of the Cascades, and it forced Indians into a semi-nomadic life, moving frequently and far. They could not easily gather foods by staying in one place like coastal Indians. Deer was the chief object of the hunt, but elk, bear, and small game, such as rabbits and ground squirrels, were sought.

Gathering berries and digging roots required the women to go out for long periods because plants grew sparsely. The camas root was even more important than it was west of the mountains. Bitterroot was also dug in great quantities and was eaten or traded for dried clams from the coast.

By the mid-eighteenth century, the arrival of the horse in eastern Washington from the South-

This Colville woman is digging for bitterroot, using a stick with an elkhorn handle. Bitterroot was a staple food for eastern Washington Indians.

west made hunting much easier. Hunters could travel great distances and bring heavy game back to their encampments. They began to seek new prey, such as the bison to the east.

On both sides of the mountains, food was frequently smoked or broiled on sticks or racks over a fire. Sometimes it was baked in hot rocks or ashes. Boiling by adding hot rocks to water in boxes or water-tight baskets was also a common method of cooking. Dried food often had to be soaked and sometimes pounded before it was cooked. Baskets were specially shaped to use in preparing particular foods.

Especially on the west side of the mountains, carved wooden utensils included trays, buckets,

## A Tale of Whaling

*An elderly Makah Indian once described the ancient whaling methods of his people:*

*"Well within my lifetime, Indians were frequently employed in whaling. The killing of a whale meant a great celebration in the village at Neah Bay. The capture of these immense mammals was attended with great danger, and only the Indians skilled in casting the harpoon or in rowing the large canoes were permitted to engage in the hunt. One of the most successful hunters was 'Lighthouse Jim' who at the end of his life had established the reputation of having killed fifty-nine whales.*

*"The method of killing whales, although primitive, was well worked out, and usually successful. Harpoons were made with a long lance of wood, tipped with a removable bone point, to which was attached a rope made of twisted kelp and about 300 feet long. Hides of hair seal, well tanned and with the fur inside, were made into balloons which were blown up and carried in the sealing canoe.*

*"When a whale was sighted, the canoe was maneuvered into a position within six feet of the mammal, the harpooner cast his lance into the whale, and the oarsmen, with one strong sweep, carried their canoe out of danger of the whale's lashing tail. The whale immediately dived and then swam rapidly toward the open sea, dragging the canoe behind,*

*sometimes at great speed. When the animal rose to spout, other lances were driven into its body, and these were attached to the balloons which made it impossible, or at least difficult, for the whale to dive. When enough of the balloons had been attached to prevent the animal from diving, its body was penetrated again and again with lances until it was dead. Cruel the method must have been, but the Indians had no method of killing their prey quickly—it was simply stabbed again and again until it died from loss of blood. Its cries and moans of pain were almost like those of an agonized human being.*

*"The dead animal was kept afloat by the balloons and towed by canoes as close as possible to shore, where it was carried by the incoming tide, assisted by the entire village, to a point on the beach where receding tides would permit the men and squaws to cut it up. Great strips of blubber were cut off, some to be rendered into oil, some to be smoked like bacon and preserved for winter use. The smoking method was evidently a thorough one, as this smoked blubber could be kept for years. Probably, only a people who had developed a taste for this food would find it palatable."*

*From Washington Pioneer Project,*
*Told by the Pioneers, vol. 2*

spoons, and ladles. Food was usually served and eaten in a clean and formal manner. Smoking might follow the meal. Although most Northwest Indians did not raise tobacco, they obtained it in trade or used kinnikinnik and other wild plants in their pipes.

### Housing

The abundance of food and other necessities allowed coastal Indians to remain in one area much of the year. Their homes and villages reminded some early white arrivals of Indian villages in eastern states.

Houses were constructed of split cedar planks and had plank roofs. Some had gabled roofs but the shed roof style was more widespread. Appropriately called longhouses, some were 100 feet long and 40 feet wide and housed several families. Often they were clustered near saltwater beaches at the mouth of a stream or a river. Here Indians could hunt, gather, and fish in both salt and fresh water. Coastal Indians also set up seasonal camps near fishing grounds, summer hunting areas, berry gathering sites, and trading centers.

Red cedar was easily split into long straight boards. These would last many years, even on the rainy ocean coast. The huge trees were felled by a combination of burning and cutting. Tools were primitive and the process took time. Felled trees were floated downstream to the desired homesite and then split with hardwood wedges and stone hammers. The adze was similar to the hand-plane of today's carpenter; its smooth, hardened rock blades scraped and shaped the wood.

To build a longhouse the Indians first constructed a frame of upright poles and crosspieces. They skillfully used leverage to raise and place heavy timbers. Boards were cut to fit exactly into place and then tied together with cords made of twisted cedar root. Cracks were chinked with mud or moss and later covered with mats. There was no chimney but smoke rose through holes left in the roof above the fire pit. A few remaining cracks in walls and roofs allowed air to circulate and helped smoke escape.

The house's main door faced the river, but there were no windows. The floor was usually hard-packed earth with woven cattail or cedar bark mats placed about. Here adults worked and children played.

Most often, several related families occupied a single house, each with its own compartment separated from others by walls or mats. Platforms for sleeping and storing goods lined interior walls, and shelves held possessions. These shelves, cedar storage boxes, the baskets and mats, and a few utensils were the only furnishings. All served varied uses. Temporary hunting camps often were a framework of poles covered with cattail or cedar bark mats. Sweathouses (like modern saunas) and other temporary structures were also made of mats. Inland Indians faced a different situation. Sparse local vegetation did not provide enough building materials and the Indians had to move about to find necessities. Many took advantage of caves or natural rock shelters. Some were used by hunters on the move; some must have been permanent dwellings.

Archaeologists have found remains of pithouses in eastern Washington. Pithouses were well insulated and protected from the wind, which was important in the more extreme inland climate. Like longhouses, some were large enough to hold several families. A pit structure near Clarkston is over five thousand years old. A village near the mouth of the Snake River contained at least one hundred pithouses.

Indians on the move usually carried extremely light, portable houses made of poles and coverings woven from cattails, twigs, and other fibers. The materials were stretched upon the poles, which were stuck in the ground and tied together at the tops. Furnishings were also light: a few mats and some baskets. The Indians of Washington did not use hides or teepees as those in the central United States did until the horse altered their way of life.

*Clothing*

Clothing differed on the two sides of the Cascades. The moderate, damp climate on the west called for light clothes that would shed water. East of the mountains, winter cold required sturdier, warmer clothing.

The ever-present cedar bark was used for clothes on the west. After being softened by

Cattail mat lodge at a Skokomish fishing camp

beating, its long fibers were combed out and then woven into a light and flexible fabric that shed water. A person could move freely and work in it. Women wore cedar skirts or aprons; men wore ponchos and leggings of cedar. In warmer weather the men wore nothing and women usually went bare above the waist.

Rain hats were made from cedar roots. These hats were woven tightly to make them watertight and were cone-shaped to shed rain. Cattails and other fibers were also used for clothing. Feet were usually left bare.

Coastal Indians wore robes that signified wealth as much as they provided warmth. Grand ones were made of bear, sea otter, marten, or marmot pelts; plainer ones came from such animals as the hair seal or the raccoon. Wealthy chiefs might own several robes used for different occasions.

Salish women wove brightly colored blankets on simple looms. They supplemented scarce mountain goat wool with fireweed or other vegetable fibers. Some groups used the hair of dogs raised for that purpose. Birdskin capes and hats were an added finery.

Hunters on both sides of the mountains wore special clothing for protection against weather and scraping by underbrush. These included buckskin and other animal skin shirts, skirts, leggings, and sometimes moccasins.

Indians enjoyed ornamentation and jewelry. Depending upon their status and occupation, they wore earrings, nose rings, necklaces, and bracelets made of shell, bone, or stones. Often these were finely polished and beautiful. Indians painted their faces and bodies for special occasions and had tattoos. They rubbed oils on their skin and hair for cleanliness and beauty.

On the coast, along the Columbia River, and in southeastern Washington, some Indians flattened the heads of babies for attractiveness. They bound the child's head between a cradleboard and a pad of hardened animal skin so as to shape a high slanted forehead.

Clothing styles in eastern Washington changed rapidly after the horse appeared in the early 1700s. Earlier, clothing consisted of little more than breech cloths, simple skin garments, and fur capes and leggings in cold weather. But the horse allowed greater travel and trade, and these Indians were influenced by practices of coastal Indians and those to their east as contacts increased. Garments were more carefully styled and decorated with beads, pieces of shell, and elk teeth.

## TRANSPORTATION AND COMMUNICATION

The many waterways in western Washington provided transportation routes for fishing, hunting, visiting, and, especially along the lower Columbia River, trading. Coastal Indians were highly skilled canoe makers. Although sizes and shapes varied according to their use, all Northwest Indian canoes were made of cedar. Specialists in each community made their living building canoes.

Not only did the lengths and widths of canoes

A Wishram bride wears full wedding regalia.

differ, but the bow and stern had quite different shapes. Pointed bows could cut through rough water during heavy winds and waves. Flat, shovel-nosed boats were better in smooth water. Most canoes had sitting boards. Paddles differed; some were rounded, some narrow and flat, some pointed, and some crescent-shaped. Some had notches so they could pass over ropes.

Canoes were essential for coastal Indians on the ocean, on the many arms of Puget Sound, and on lakes and rivers. War canoes were unusual among the generally peaceable Indians, but the large war boats of the Haida and other northern tribes aroused fear when their carved and painted prows appeared on the horizon.

Along the Columbia River the canoe was used as far as the rapids at The Dalles, which stopped most travel upriver. Above that spot canoes were rare. Here the nomadic life meant traveling on

This young Nez Perce mother carries her infant in an elaborately decorated cradleboard.

foot, usually in large bands, to favored hunting areas. Horses were first used by the Nez Perce and Cayuse tribes and then spread to others. With horses, inland people could roam over wider areas and hunt or trade. Contact with new tribes brought conflict over territory. The horse became as vital to most inland Indians as the canoe was along the coast. The Nez Perce became skilled horse breeders and are credited with establishing the Appaloosa type.

Trade among Northwest Indians was common long before whites arrived. Regular canoe routes followed broad coastal waterways, with foot trails following inland streams and valleys. As items were exchanged up and down the coast, the Chinook Indians near the mouth of the Columbia River became expert middlemen.

Coastal canoes traveled up the Columbia to the annual trade fair at The Dalles where goods were exchanged with inland tribes. It was a festive occasion. Indian families came from all over the Northwest to visit, dance, gamble, tell stories,

To build his canoe, this Makah carver first carefully selected the best cedar tree and felled it. He hollowed out the log by burning and chopping out the core. Then he heated water in the canoe by adding hot rocks. This softened the wood so that he could shape it with an adze. Finally, he will grease it with whale oil to make it watertight and paint it. The hull will be sanded with dogfish oil to reduce friction.

gossip, and exchange goods. Thus furs, animal hides, elk teeth, bear claws, and other treasures of the interior found their way to the coast. Dried clams, fish oil, baskets, carved wooden tools, and dentalium shells from the coast moved inland. Dentalium shells were highly prized and were sometimes accepted as money. Slaves were also bought and sold.

But more than goods were traded. News was passed by word of mouth. Northwest Indians were not isolated from the world around them.

There were no written languages among these people, and the various spoken languages differed greatly. A trade language developed. Based on the Chinook language, it used simple grammar, and the vocabulary included words from several Indian languages. Thus, even before the arrival of the whites, a universal language existed in

A Cowlitz coiled basket made by Mary Kiona

the Northwest. English and French words were added later to this mix of Indian tongues and created the Chinook Jargon, a trading language many Indians knew. This permitted contacts that would not have been possible otherwise.

## GOVERNMENT

Coastal Indians lived in villages where several related families occupied a few houses. A short distance along a stream, there might be a similar village, and further on another. Many Indians knew only such close-by villages or others near fishing and hunting spots. Yet trade, potlatch celebrations, and other contacts made them aware of other groups and the geography of their region.

Loosely linked by similar language and customs, marriage, and defense alliances, Indians had some tribal ties. But tribes were not firm, fixed political units. Early whites in the region often assumed or forced tribal connections and leadership roles that did not actually exist.

Abundant food and other supplies and the permanence of the village helped establish the role of the chief. The chief had overall responsibility for the tribe's survival. He had real importance among his people. He did not usually have strong political power but was responsible for preserving and distributing fish, berries, game, and other products. His prestige came from handling this wealth. As the symbolic head of the community, he was honored. Almost always, the chief was the wealthiest man in the village. He owned a fine house, the most canoes, and possibly the fishing weir. To lose wealth might also mean losing power and authority.

Wealth and social rank were important. Each individual, from the chief to the lowliest person, had a clear position within the community. This was based upon age, wealth, the importance of the work performed, and approval by the chief. Rank and status might be displayed at banquets or formal gatherings by giving lavish gifts and providing food and songs. At the same time, they greatly feared ridicule or loss of face.

The potlatch provided an opportunity to display wealth and prestige. These great celebrations were held once or several times during the life of a chief, usually to honor a special event such as the birth of a child, a death, a marriage, or the presence of a spirit helper. Preparations might take years and involve the entire village.

At the chosen time, canoes arrived from all around Puget Sound and the northern coast. Guests spent several days eating, playing games, holding athletic contests, dancing, and socializing. The climax was a great feast when the chief distributed gifts to his guests. Here was proof of wealth so great that he could afford to lose it.

Villages might have several slaves, usually women or children captured from other tribes in raids. Wealthy villages at river mouths or on coastal beaches had significant numbers of slaves; upriver villages had few or none. Slaves did menial jobs and provided evidence of their owner's wealth and prestige. They had no power or rights. Occasionally slaves were exchanged or bartered away. Sometimes their own people ransomed them.

Moral codes were strict. Stealing was a serious offense. Killing, whether intentional or not, was usually punished by taking property from the offender or his family. This practice created misunderstandings and difficulties after white settlers arrived.

East of the Cascades, arrangements of government were even looser. Each village or traveling group was likely to have one leader or headman, but he had little power. Typically, the headman was the oldest member of the tribe or had inherited his position, but he could only try to direct the affairs of his people. He might advise them, argue with them, or try to persuade them to follow a certain course, but he could do no more. Each individual was likely to go his own way.

Villages might honor the elders, but they had little power beyond personal prestige and could only advise. There were exceptions. Indians in eastern Washington depended upon finding game, and the greatest hunter assumed authority during the hunt. Eastern Indians were frequently threatened by war parties or raiders from afar. At such times, military leaders might take control. The individual who displayed heroic courage or battlefield success was likely to be honored in the manner of a chief. Yet, such prestige was easily lost, and tribal arrangements and strong leadership never lasted over long periods of time.

## RELIGION

Indians believed that in the beginning, the earth was very different from what it is today. Then the Changer came. Some accounts portray him as heroic, but more frequently he was both a hero and a humorous trickster full of practical jokes.

Stories about Coyote, for example, show him reshaping laws of nature and human society through a series of comic episodes. The Changer fixed the earth in its present form and made the sea, mountains, and valleys. He gave animals and people their present forms and powers and laid down many rules of Indian life.

Indians saw the natural world populated with spirits whose help was necessary for success in any venture—hunting, house building, basket making, and other daily activities. The voices and actions of these spirits could be heard in the creaking of trees, the hum of the wind, and the ripple of water. Every individual might seek a spirit helper who could confer a particular skill. Individuals received special songs and dances from their spirits. Some Indians believed that the soul would return in the body of a newborn child after death.

Each village had a shaman, a man or sometimes a woman, whose spirit helper gave special curing powers. Each also had one or more storytellers who dramatically and humorously told tales of the Changer and other spirits. The storyteller repeated these again and again using different voices for persons and events. The stories became well known to everyone and were handed down to later generations.

### Life and Death

The Northwest Indians' way of life was based upon the family and upon hereditary social rank. "Family" went beyond parents and children to include several generations of parents, grandparents, aunts, uncles, and cousins. Usually such families lived together in a single longhouse or village. High-ranking and wealthy members were responsible for their poorer relatives.

The birth of a baby was important. Children were well cared for and protected. Coastal Indians strapped the baby onto a cradleboard where it could not move. For a year this board was its

## *A Clackamas Chinook Legend*

### COYOTE BUILDS WILLAMETTE FALLS AND THE MAGIC FISH TRAP

*Coyote came to that place [around Oregon City] and found the people there very hungry. The river was full of salmon, but they had no way to spear them in the deep water. Coyote decided he would build a big waterfall, so that the salmon would come to the surface for spearing. Then he would build a fish trap there too.*

*... Where the Willamette Falls are now he found just the right place, and he made the Falls high and wide. All the Indians came and began to fish.*

*Now Coyote made his magic fish trap. He made it so it would speak, and say Noseepsk! when it was full. Because he was pretty hungry, Coyote decided to try it first himself. He set the trap by the Falls, and then ran back up the shore to prepare to make a cooking-fire. But he had only begun when the trap called out, "Noseepsk!" He hurried back; indeed the trap was full of salmon. Running back with them, he started his fire again, but again the fish trap cried "Noseepsk! Noseepsk!" He went again and found the trap full of salmon. Again he ran to the shore with them; again he had hardly gotten to his fire when the trap called out, "Noseepsk! Noseepsk!" It happened again, and again; the fifth time Coyote became angry and said to the trap, "What, can't you wait with your fish-catching until I've built a fire?" The trap was very offended by Coyote's impatience, and stopped working right then. So after that the people had to spear their salmon as best they could.*

*From Jarold Ramsey, Coyote Was Going There (Seattle: University of Washington Press, 1977)*

home. The infant was carried while parents went about their daily tasks. Frequently the baby was taken from the board, played with, massaged with dogfish or whale oil, and shown love and affection.

Small children played about the house or village, becoming increasingly aware of what adults were doing. They learned by watching older persons work. By the time they were five or six, children knew what would be expected of them as whalers, hunters, fishers, gatherers, basket makers, or the like. More formal training began at the age of twelve or thirteen. Necessary skills were learned through observation, practice, and repetition. At puberty a youth might go into the woods on a spirit quest to seek spirit powers or guidance.

Families usually arranged their children's marriages. This maintained a family's wealth and position and cemented loose alliances between villages. The marriage ceremony included formal negotiations and feasts and festivities. The husband's family paid a bride price for the woman; her family was expected to return gifts of equal value.

The new couple usually wed in the house of the groom's parents. The bride became a sister in the household, sharing women's chores while her husband worked with the men. A man might have several wives, usually a sign of wealth and rank since he had to be able to support them. Divorce occurred among Northwest Indians; sometimes it was only the simple, quiet departure of the woman from the house.

Men and women played distinctly different roles and had different tasks. Men were hunters, fishers, carpenters, and village leaders, and they generally dominated affairs. Women gathered plants and berries, dug roots, prepared fish and game for storage, made baskets and blankets, cooked family meals, and kept house. Both men and women could develop strong spiritual powers, and both served as shamans and healers.

Makah mother Mary Butler rocks her baby in a traditional cradle.

During sickness, a shaman might call on spirit powers to diagnose and treat illnesses. Because shamans had the power to kill as well as cure, they were often blamed if a patient died.

Old age was honored. Older people gradually let their duties fall to younger adults, yet continued to be respected. They taught responsibilities and skills to the young. The old were also storytellers who kept family and village traditions and legends alive.

Death caused deep mourning. The deceased was laid out in a comfortable position for burial during ceremonies and rituals. The actual means of burial varied. Coastal Indians were often placed in canoes above ground or in the forks of trees, while Indians along eastern rivers were sometimes buried under mounds of rocks or with their heads pointed downstream. Private possessions were buried alongside. The memory of the deceased was preserved, but the name was not spoken aloud or given to another person for a long time afterward.

Most Northwest Indians believed that the dead went to another land, a comfortable and well-deserved resting place where they continued the activities of earthly life. Sometimes the dead returned to trouble the living; many groups had special rituals to placate them and return them to their rightful place.

## The Indian Heritage in the Northwest

Long before an actual encounter, Northwest Indians heard rumors that light-skinned men with beards had entered lands to the south or were trading along rivers beyond eastern mountains. Unfamiliar trade items appeared: iron hatchets, knives, and guns.

Stories circulated about a few persons who had actually met whites. One elderly Nez Perce woman told of being captured when in her teens and passed along through several tribes until she was sold to a white man. Although he treated her well, she escaped and made her way back to her own people. William Clark of the Lewis and Clark expedition may have met her.

Even before white persons appeared among them, Indians felt the effects of diseases that whites had brought to the continent. Smallpox had left its scars on Puget Sound Indians before Captain George Vancouver's ships arrived in 1792. Smallpox and other new diseases caused great loss of Indian lives and helped to dispossess Indians of their traditional lands and way of life.

Along the coast, the great boats of the whites began to appear. Indians reacted differently. The first Europeans to come ashore on the Olympic Peninsula were hastily killed by Quileutes. On the other hand, curious natives anxious to trade approached Robert Gray's crew when they entered Grays Harbor and the Columbia River. On Puget Sound, Indians trailed the small launches of Peter Puget. Worried that the new-

This restaurant at Blake Island State Park illustrates how Indian designs and architecture are used in a present-day setting.

comers would interfere with their fishing grounds, the Indians pondered what action to take. Finally a show of force from the whites led to trading and a peaceful outcome.

As whites became more common, these first encounters settled into new relationships. The Chinooks found whites eager to engage in trade, and their own power increased. The threat of white dominance helped some Indian leaders to increase authority among their people.

Along with new tools and ways of doing things, new attitudes and values began to alter a way of life that had endured for centuries. Soon the diseases of whites brought widespread epidemics and virtually destroyed some communi-

ties. Indians had adapted to changes in the past and certain practices had evolved over the centuries. But nothing could have prepared them for the changes that were about to occur.

Northwest Indians had much to offer in those earliest encounters with white men. Indians taught early settlers how to fish for salmon and dig clams. They introduced smoking and drying methods, and they pointed out edible foods, including the camas and wapato roots, wild celery, and berries. Some pioneers owed their survival to this help. Indian fishing techniques were copied by whites.

Northwest architecture and construction has followed patterns found in Indian houses, including the use of cedar and long vertical planks. Indian designs and themes enhance Northwest sculpture, paintings, weaving, and carving.

But despite all the contributions from Indians, what the whites really wanted was their most important possession—the land itself.

## Chapter 2 Review

**I.** Define the following words and terms. Relate each one to Washington State.

| | |
|---|---|
| Archaeology | Staple foods |
| Artifacts | Longhouses |
| Marmes Man | Chinook Jargon |
| Pithouse | Potlatch |
| Manis mastodon | The Changer |
| Kennewick Man | Spirits |
| Land bridge theory | Shaman |
| Native Americans | Heritage |

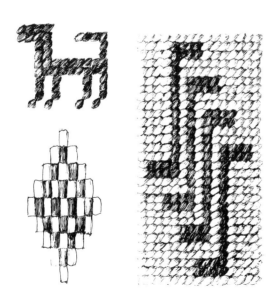

Traditional basket designs from western Washington often used geometric patterns such as these.

**II.** Each of the following questions should call your attention to factual information in the chapter. Try to answer each one. Then look back in the reading to check your answers and find any answers you do not know.

1. What natural event preserved the village of Ozette?

2. Why was it necessary to bring out the bones of "Marmes Man" in a hurry?

3. Why do archaeologists believe that hunters killed the Manis mastodon?

4. What was the basic staple food in the diet of Washington Indians? In what other ways did Indians use this food?

5. What bulb was an important food for the Native Americans?

6. Why did the Indians east of the Cascades lead a semi-nomadic life?

7. What different roles did men and women play in obtaining and preparing food?

8. Why were the hats of coastal Indians cone-shaped?

9. What did the robes of coastal Indians signify?

10. How did Indians decorate their possessions?

11. What means of travel was introduced to eastern Washington Indians in the 1700s?

12. What particular role did the Chinook Indians play among other tribes?

13. What might determine who would be selected chief of a village?

14. What was the basic group that bound Indians together?

15. How did a small Indian child learn the ways of the people?

16. How were older people treated?

17. List at least four things that Indians taught early white settlers.

**III.** Think about, discuss, and answer the questions below.

1. Prepare a grid in two columns under the headings "western Washington Indians" and "eastern Washington Indians." On the left side divide the grid into the categories of "Food," "Shelter," "Clothing," "Transportation," "Leadership," "Religion," "Social Organization," and "Art." Contrast the two groups of Indians by giving two examples in each category of how they met their needs.

2. Study the cedar tree in detail. List some of the many ways that Indians in western Washington used the cedar. Why was that tree adaptable to so many different uses? Obtain some pieces of cedar and make some of the same things the Indians made.

3. List counties, towns, rivers, lakes, mountains, streets, and other features in Washington that have Indian names. Try to learn which Indian groups contributed these names. Start your lists without using maps or books. After you have listed as many names as you can, turn to references that will help you add to the list.

4. Many schools use Indian names or words for team names, yearbooks, or newspapers. What examples do you know about? Professional sports teams and other organizations also use Indian names and symbols. What characteristics do such names and symbols seem to suggest? Is this a compliment to Indians or is it offensive? Particularly if you are of Indian descent, how do you feel about this? What other national or racial groups are characterized in such ways? How do you feel about the ways that people of your national background are characterized or stereotyped?

5. For several recent seasons, members of the Makah tribe on the Olympic Peninsula resumed the traditional whale hunts they had not engaged in for many years. They stated that whaling was a part of their way of life, their cultural heritage, and their religious beliefs. Many persons, including a few tribespeople, denounced it as a needless destruction of elegant creatures. Gather as much information as you can from both sides of the debate. What are your views?

# Explorers by Sea, Explorers by Land

Title page of Robert Haswell's journal; Haswell was third mate on the *Columbia Rediviva* under Captain Robert Gray.

At the mouth of the Columbia River, May 11, 1792. The sailing ship **Columbia Rediviva** rests off shore in the morning mist. From its stern flies an unfamiliar flag, the stars and stripes of the young United States of America. Captain Robert Gray of Boston walks the deck. A naval veteran of the recent Revolutionary War, Gray is no stranger to these waters. He is commanding his second voyage to the coast of northwest America. At age thirty-seven he is the first American to have circled the globe.

Gray has traded Northwest Coast furs in Asia with a shrewd business sense that is typical of his Yankee countrymen. He has come near to being shipwrecked in violent storms, has faced being captured and held hostage by Spaniards in California, has watched his men become ill with scurvy, and has seen a crew member stabbed to death by Indians at Tillamook Bay, which he named Murderers' Bay.

On an earlier trip to the coast, Captain Gray had noticed something curious about the spot where his ship is now anchored. Discolored water rushes from shore to meet the breakers. What would cause this? he wonders. A river. Perhaps a very big river. Could this be the great river of the Northwest that all explorers hoped to find?

Spain's Juan Pérez, Bruno de Heceta, and Juan Francisco de la Bodega y Quadra, England's James Cook and his successor George Vancouver, Gray's former partner John Kendrick, and others had passed this same spot. In 1775 Heceta had also noticed the discolored water. He had wondered if it could be a river, but because his crewmen were sick with scurvy, he did not explore. No one else had even suspected the existence of a river there. Perhaps they had been out too far, perhaps clouds had been too heavy or breakers too strong.

But Captain Gray's curiosity had been aroused and he had come back for another look.

The **Columbia** had arrived at dusk last evening. As morning light breaks through the mist, Gray makes his decision. Shortly after eight o'clock he sets sail and heads east-northeast between the breakers. His excitement is greater than is shown by the simple words he writes in his log: "When we were over the bar we found this to be a large river of fresh water, up which we started."

He records that the bars at the entrance are tricky, but the distance between them seems about ten miles. On the north bank is a Chinook Indian village. Some villagers row out to greet him and follow his boat. They offer fresh water, which he takes. After four hours he stops to camp at a sheltered spot that will ever after be known as Gray's Bay.

For the next nine days he will camp here and trade with the Indians. He will not explore farther up the river, but he does give it a name, the Columbia, after his ship.

May 11, 1792, is one of the momentous days in the history of the Pacific Northwest. An American, Robert Gray, has entered the river that others have only dreamed of finding. From this day on his young nation will have a claim to these lands as great as that of England or Spain. His discovery this day will affect the future of the Northwest Coast.

# Exploring the Northwest

Robert Gray's discovery of the Columbia River in 1792 was but one of many discoveries along the Northwest coast over three centuries beginning in the mid-1500s. Early explorers came by sea, often during voyages to other parts of the world. Later, land explorations linked the Pacific coast with eastern, settled portions of North America.

The earliest visitors left little evidence. Coastal Indian legends describe strangers from Japan or China or Pacific islands who fished Northwest waters or were shipwrecked along the coast. Spanish galleons sailing the South Pacific may also have passed by.

A Greek named Juan de Fuca claimed he had sailed from the Pacific to the Atlantic coast in 1592 along an inland route that became known as the Northwest Passage. Later explorers seeking this legendary passage found an opening with a location and appearance much like Juan de Fuca had described, and Charles Barkley named this the Strait of Juan de Fuca. De Fuca was right; it did lead into an inland sea, but the Northwest Passage remained a myth.

But such explorers did not travel alone. Expeditions were sent out, financed, and often directed by government officials, companies, and businessmen. Large amounts of money were needed to pay for ships, equipment, supplies, and the salaries of crew members. Nations and merchants supplied these necessities, hoping to profit from their efforts.

Navigators, astronomers, natural scientists, map makers, and artists, as well as ordinary seamen, were necessary. Explorers often compared notes with men from other ships even though their countries were rivals. Gray, for instance, ran into the commanders of the Spanish and English expeditions and told them that he had found the entrance to the Columbia River.

The interior of a Chinook lodge

## The Fabled Northwest Passage

*Famous, but of doubtful reliability, is the story of the Greek who sailed under the Spanish name of Juan de Fuca in the 1590s. He claimed to have sailed in an inland sea across North America to the Atlantic coast and back to Europe. His story was passed on by a European merchant and traveler, who reported that Juan de Fuca sailed a course*

*"... all alongst the coast of Nova Spania and California and the Indies, now called North America (all of which voyage he signified to me in a great map, and a sea chart of mine owne, which he laid before me), untill he came to the latitude of 47 and 48 degrees.*

*"There finding that the land trended north and northeast, with a broad inlet of sea ... he entered thereinto, sayling therein more than twentie days, and found that land, trending still sometimes northwest and northeast and north, and also east and southeastward, and very much broader sea than was at the said entrance, and that he passed by divers ilands in that sayling....*

*"And he said that he went on land in divers places and that he saw some people on land clad in beasts skins, and that the land is very fruitfull, and rich in gold, silver, pearle and other things, like Nova Spania.... Finding the sea wide enough everywhere, and to be about thirtie or fortie leagues wide in the mouth of the Straits where he entered, he thought he had now well discharged his office and done the thing which he was sent out to doe.... Not being armed to resist the force of the savage people ... he therefore set sayle and returned homewards againe towards Nova Spania, where he arrived at Acapulco, anno 1592, hoping to be rewarded greatly of the Viceroy for his service done in this said voyage."*

*Quoted in W. Storrs Lee, Washington State: A Literary Chronicle*

## Why the Explorations?

Why do people explore? Why do nations and businesses sponsor large expeditions? How does the exploration of a region help a country to acquire that region as its own?

Some explorations seek to increase knowledge. In the eighteenth and nineteenth centuries, people wanted to know more about plants and animals and about different cultures. Current missions expand our knowledge of outer space.

Countries often explore to gain national power. The first explorers at a particular place usually claim it for their nation. Certain spots are especially strategic. Discovering the mouth of a river, for instance, encourages the finder to claim all the territory drained by that river.

Individual explorers often had personal motives. Some sought adventure, or were curious, or wanted personal wealth or power, or were fleeing a difficult home life. Some hoped for sudden riches from gold or silver or diamonds. Others favored a slower route: the steady, reliable wealth that came from acquiring goods needed by many people over a long period of time, such as lumber or spices.

Wealth develops not only from possessing products but also from transporting and marketing them. Thus, merchants sought trade routes that were shorter, surer, or safer than the ones already known. This helps to explain the interest in Juan de Fuca's tales of a shortcut between the Pacific and Atlantic Oceans. Later explorers searched for that nonexistent Northwest Passage. Before the Panama Canal was completed in 1914, ships had to sail clear around South America to get from New York to the Pacific coast.

## Exploration by Sea

For the most part, explorers came to the Northwest Coast during the last twenty-five years of the eighteenth century, between 1775 and 1800.

Ships flying the flags of several nations were often anchored in the harbor at Nootka Sound.

During this time the thirteen colonies were separating from England, fighting the Revolutionary War, and establishing the United States of America. It had been almost three hundred years since Columbus, Magellan, Balboa, Cortés, and others had made the first recorded explorations in the Americas. During that time period, large parts of North and South America were explored and settled by Europeans. Spanish provinces were founded in Central and South America. British colonies along the Atlantic coast and French settlements in eastern Canada were started a century later. By the late 1700s, the North Ameri- can West remained the only great expanse of unrecorded and sparsely settled land.

Four countries did major sea explorations of the Northwest Coast during the late eighteenth century: Spain, Russia, the United States, and England. Each had its own motives and each came with different expectations.

## SPAIN

During the 1500s, Spain was the greatest and wealthiest nation in Europe. After the voyages of Columbus, Spanish adventurers established the first provinces in the New World. Spain had the strongest navy in the age of sea power. Gold and silver from the Americas made Spain rich and powerful. Spanish artists, writers, and architects set standards for the Western world for many decades.

But by the late 1700s, Spain's time of glory had ended. Its power and wealth had diminished. Rival nations pirated the galleons carrying riches across the ocean and weakened Spain's hold on the wealth of the New World. Other nations challenged its prominence.

Thus, Spain saw Northwest coastal explorations as a way to regain its former position. Spanish leaders also hoped to spread the Catholic religion and add to geographical knowledge.

Spanish explorers sailed to the Northwest from their naval base at San Blas on the western coast of Mexico. In 1774 Juan Pérez set out for the 60th parallel, far into present-day Alaska. But storms, sickness, and his own cautiousness caused him to turn back. He anchored in the Queen Charlotte Islands, off northern Vancouver Island. Pérez's crew was the first to describe the Northwest shoreline including mountains that must have been the Olympics.

Pérez's reports encouraged Spain to outfit a larger expedition with two ships led by Bruno de Heceta and Juan Francisco de la Bodega y Quadra. On July 14, 1775, Heceta went ashore at Point Grenville just north of Moclips. This was the first recorded landing by Europeans on the Washington coast, and he claimed the whole Northwest for Spain. A few miles north, Bodega y Quadra sent seven men ashore for fresh water and watched helplessly as Indians killed them. The ships continued a bit farther north before they returned to San Blas.

In 1790 Francisco Eliza led three ships north from Mexico to help strengthen the Spanish hold on the Northwest coast. From their settlement at Nootka Sound on Vancouver Island, Spanish ships explored in all directions. Three men in particular—Eliza, Salvador Fidalgo, and Manuel Quimper—investigated the waters surrounding Vancouver Island. Their crews explored the San Juan Islands and the Strait of Juan de Fuca, naming many features. They established a fort and village near the entrance to the strait, at what is now Neah Bay. Their maps, charts, and journals provided valuable information, but they failed to enter Puget Sound. Years later a large scientific expedition commanded by Alejandro Malaspina sailed along the Washington coast but did not touch shore.

## RUSSIA

Russia had spurred the interest of Spain and other nations in the Northwest. Stretching from the eastern edge of Europe to the Pacific, Russia was huge, undeveloped, and isolated in the 1700s. Nevertheless, Peter the Great and other rulers tried to advance the country and involve it in world affairs.

In the middle 1700s, Russian influence was moving along the Asian coast toward the North Pacific. Vitus Bering, a Danish-born sailor in the service of Russia, led two expeditions in the North Pacific. He hoped to learn whether a land bridge connected Russia and North America, where the Bering Sea and the Bering Strait now share his name. Many geologists think such a bridge had existed long before Bering's voyage. Bering's ships sailed as far south as the Columbia River.

Russians later established prosperous fur-trading posts in present-day Alaska. In the early 1800s, the Russian-American Company controlled the seal fur trade of the Far North working out of New Archangel (now Sitka).

Russians also looked south along the Pacific coast, establishing a post at Fort Ross in northern California in 1812. Other nations feared the expansion of Russia's vigorous fur-trading empire along the Northwest coast.

## THE UNITED STATES

The United States was the youngest country interested in the Northwest coast. At the beginning of the nineteenth century, most settled parts of this new nation were confined to a long, narrow strip between the Atlantic coastline and the Appalachian Mountains. Little was known of the vast interior of the continent west of the Appalachians. In the late 1770s, Americans were fighting to gain independence from England and struggling to start a new nation.

Many American colonists had grown wealthy trading in distant parts of the world, including China and other lands across the Pacific. During the American Revolution, old British trading centers in the Atlantic—the West Indies, for example—were closed to the rebelling Americans. The Pacific area became even more important. Ships sailed to the Pacific from New England ports such as Boston and Salem. Yankee sea captains were rugged, vigorous men, eager to compete in the quest for land and wealth.

Robert Gray was just such a person. His interest in exploration came second to his interest in trade. Along the Northwest coast he stopped for furs at Nootka Sound. This broad bay on the western coast of what is now Vancouver Island was rapidly becoming the busiest and most important stopping place on the entire North Pacific coast.

From Nootka Sound, Gray slowly moved south along the Olympic Peninsula. Spotting an opening among the beautiful low hills, he ventured into a wide bay which became known as Grays Harbor. For three days he anchored in this bay, and then a day farther south he entered the Columbia River. Gray camped nine nights near the mouth of the river, trading with the Chinook Indians. Then he sailed out to sea once more. Back at Nootka Sound, he told Bodega y Quadra and Vancouver of his discoveries before returning home to Boston.

Captain Robert Gray

Other Americans also appeared along the coast. But few would have guessed that the young United States would eventually possess most of this region.

## ENGLAND

A gambler would have bet that England, which controlled the British Empire, would someday control the Northwest coast. As Spain lost power in the world, England's influence grew. With few natural resources, this small island off the coast of Europe became prosperous by sending trading ships all over the world. England established colonies on several continents, controlled trade routes, and plundered Spanish galleons for gold.

Sir Francis Drake, the famous pirate and navigator, probably touched northern California in 1579 and may have come as far north as Washington or beyond. After Drake, little happened for two centuries. But by the 1700s, about to lose its American colonies and fearful of Spanish and Russian ventures in the North Pacific, England

Captain James Cook

made its move. English navigators especially wanted to find the Northwest Passage, that mythical channel that would allow ships to pass straight through the Americas.

In 1776 Captain James Cook was ordered to explore the North Pacific. In his late forties, Cook was a veteran of French wars and Canadian coastal surveys and famous for leading two scientific expeditions in the South Pacific. Among other accomplishments, Cook had reduced the dangerous effects of scurvy among his crews. Scurvy, which weakened resistance to wounds and disease, had spread death among seamen who had no fresh fruits and vegetables on long voyages. Cook stocked his ships with lemon juice and pickled cabbage. This diet spared most of his men from the disease.

Cook's third trip was to concentrate farther north, to seek trade routes and to claim land for England. Spanish and Russian claims were either not known or ignored in Cook's orders.

With two ships, the *Discovery* and the *Resolution*, and 170 men, he left England in 1776. He

discovered the Hawaiian Islands, naming them the Sandwich Islands after his chief sponsor, the Earl of Sandwich. The native inhabitants seemed friendly. (When he returned years later, however, Cook was killed by the islanders in a fight over a boat stolen from the *Discovery*.)

From Hawaii Cook proceeded to North America. He spent part of March 1778 off Oregon before heading north. Remaining well out to sea, he noted neither the Columbia River nor the Strait of Juan de Fuca. He finally touched land at Nootka Sound. He claimed the whole area for England, traded with Indians for sea otter pelts, and charted the land. Cook's men later recognized a great demand for sea otter furs in China, which started a new trade.

Cook charted the coast from Oregon to the Bering Sea. After his death in 1779, the crew returned home with more information about the North Pacific than had been gathered by any other expedition. Furthermore, Cook advanced the ability to sail great distances because he used new navigational instruments and took measures that improved the health and diet of his crew.

In the next few years, Englishmen, some of whom had sailed with Cook, added to the knowledge of the Northwest Coast. Charles Barkley, accompanied by his wife, Frances, who was the first white woman on the coast, entered and named the Strait of Juan de Fuca in 1787.

In 1788 John Meares named many features along the Olympic Peninsula, including Mount Olympus. Although Spain had already claimed the area, he secured land at Nootka from Indians, built a house, and launched the first ship built on this Pacific shore. Meares then headed to China with furs.

When his ship returned to Nootka Sound in 1789, a Spanish settlement and fort had been built there. Don Esteban José Martínez, commander of the fort, seized Meares's ships and other vessels. But the Spanish government wanted to avoid war and ordered them released. Nevertheless, England protested and relations between the two countries worsened.

## THE NOOTKA SOUND CONTROVERSY

The seizure of these ships led to the first international conflict in the Northwest. England and Spain each believed its cause to be just and considered war. Neither genuinely wanted to fight, however, and they reached an agreement. England promised not to fish near Spanish settlements; Spain agreed not to interfere with British activities elsewhere in the region. In other words, the whole Northwest was opened to the ships of both countries, but Spanish settlements were to be respected.

To work out the details, each country agreed to send to Nootka a representative who was skilled in negotiations and familiar with the area. The Spanish chose Bodega y Quadra, and the English sent George Vancouver, a member of Cook's last expedition. The two men planned to meet in the fall of 1792. Meanwhile, both nations sent ships into the Northwest to firm up their claims.

The autumn of 1792 was festive and busy at Nootka. Seamen of several nations rested, repaired ships, traded with Indians, and enjoyed a few comforts before sailing on. Twenty-seven ships of various descriptions were in the harbor, flying the flags of five nations (Spain, England, France, Portugal, and the United States). There was even finery. At their banquets the negotiators enjoyed silver service and dined well.

But despite pleasant surroundings and personal friendliness, the two negotiators settled little. Neither nation would give up its claims to the region. Yet both agreed to allow other countries' ships to stop at Nootka. When Vancouver and Bodega y Quadra parted, they agreed to name the island jointly after themselves: Quadra's and Vancouver's Island. (The cumbersome name did not last; eventually British occupation assured that it would bear the name of Vancouver alone.)

The problems the two men failed to settle at Nootka were never fully resolved. Actual events along the coast had more permanent results. When wars burst out between England and France in Europe, some Spaniards hoped that Spain might strengthen its hold on the northern Pacific coastline. But that government chose to concentrate on firmly held settlements and missions in California, which was under Spanish control, rather than to compete for more distant northern lands. Russian interests generally remained around Sitka and islands in the north. Thus the coast between Russian America and Spanish California was left to Britain and the United States.

For several more years, Nootka remained the most important outpost along the coast. The maritime fur trade grew. Its object was the playful sea otter, found on the rocky shoreline from Alaska to northern California. Its fine, thick fur of mingled white, silver, and brown tones was highly prized. Early traders found that pelts obtained from Indians could get one hundred dollars apiece in China. In return, the Indians gladly accepted all sorts of metal objects, including knives, tools, and nails, along with buttons, snuff, and sometimes glass beads.

For a decade or more traders from England, the United States, and other nations sailed the Pacific and made great profits. These traders explored and kept journals as they charted sea routes and mapped coastal areas. Over-hunting of the sea otter eventually led to its near extinction. As the animal became scarce, trade for inland beavers rose. The beaver trade assured that inland rivers would be explored.

## TWO EXPEDITIONS THAT STRENGTHENED BRITISH AND AMERICAN CLAIMS

By 1793 most of the coastal area had been explored and mapped. Two sea explorations were particularly important. One was British, under the command of George Vancouver; a later American one was commanded by Charles Wilkes.

### George Vancouver

England's George Vancouver had two assignments. In addition to negotiating with Bodega y Quadra, he was instructed to explore the coast and its inland waters in search of the Northwest Passage. His ships entered the Strait of Juan de Fuca in May of 1792. From Discovery Bay, named for his command ship, he surveyed the waters, forested foothills, and mountains beyond. He named one mountain Baker after a crew member. The large cone on the southeast horizon (known to Indians as Takhoma) became Rainier for his longtime friend, Commander (later Admiral) Peter Rainier.

Suspecting that the inland sea he had entered was extensive, he divided his expedition. He kept command of one ship and placed two small open boats under his chief lieutenants, Peter Puget and Joseph Whidbey. Each had a particular area to chart and describe. Rowing, and sailing when the wind allowed, the men carefully investigated all inlets and waterways that might be navigable. They produced a thorough, detailed, and often well-written description accompanied by charts

Vancouver's ship *Discovery* on the rocks near the Queen Charlotte Islands

and drawings. The crew, mostly young men in their teens and twenties, also described the friendly but cautious Indians who watched them.

By the time Vancouver's crews left, the inland waters were thoroughly and accurately charted. Vancouver named almost every outstanding feature: Puget Sound, Whidbey Island, Mount Baker, Mount Rainier, Hood Canal, Bellingham Bay, Vashon Island, Port Orchard, Admiralty Inlet, the Georgia Strait, Birch Bay, Port Gardner. On a beach north of present-day Everett, Vancouver went ashore on June 4, 1792, and claimed the whole region for Great Britain.

Vancouver had pretended to lack interest when he learned that Gray had discovered the Columbia River. Yet he quietly dispatched William Broughton to investigate farther up the river. Moving across sandbars and breakers beyond Gray's anchorage spot, Broughton's ship went as far up the river as it could. Broughton and his men explored the river to a point east of present-day Portland, Oregon, strengthening British claims in the region.

### Charles Wilkes

Decades later, in 1841, an American naval expedition under Charles Wilkes ventured up the Columbia and then into Puget Sound during a round-the-world scientific expedition. Wilkes spent several days in the Sound, some at the Hudson's Bay Company post of Fort Nisqually. His report urged the United States to pursue its own claim to this valuable region, particularly Puget Sound. He added details and names to

Members of the Wilkes expedition measured timber in the Northwest forest.

existing charts. His contributions include Bainbridge Island, Anderson Island, Elliott Bay, and McNeil Island. Vendovi Island was named for a captured Fiji native aboard his ship and Viti Rocks for the prisoner's home.

But long before Wilkes arrived, overland exploration of the Northwest was overshadowing sea exploration. British and American explorers were anxious to learn more about the expanse of land between the settled United States and the Pacific shore.

## Exploration by Land

The heart of North America remained blank on maps. Its edges had been touched by Spanish explorers in the Southwest, by French-Canadian trappers following streams out from the Great Lakes, and by other fur traders venturing up the Missouri River.

The first crossing of North America was made by Alexander Mackenzie, a trader from the British-owned North West Company who was seeking a route to the Pacific. In his first effort he mistakenly selected a river—now called the Mackenzie—that took him north to the Arctic Ocean.

On a second trip, in 1792–93, he guessed better. From the Canadian Rockies he followed one river until canyons and rapids forced him to cross to another stream. This was the Bella Coola River, which he descended to its mouth just north of Vancouver Island. Mackenzie thus was the first person to cross North America north of Mexico; he proved once and for all that there was no Northwest Passage. He believed that the threatening rapids he had avoided were on the Columbia, recently discovered by Gray. They proved instead to be on the Fraser River, in what is now southern British Columbia.

Two Americans and another Englishman completed the exploration of the Columbia River.

## THE OVERLAND EXPEDITION

By 1800 a few Americans were seriously curious about the lands west of the Mississippi River, the western border of the United States. That year Thomas Jefferson, a man greatly interested in natural science, geography, agriculture, and many other subjects, was elected president. He wanted to increase trade along the Northwest coast and interior rivers.

Three years later the United States doubled its size when it bought from France the 827,000 square miles known as the Louisiana Purchase. This was the first piece of territory that the United States acquired after independence. Suddenly the young nation stretched all the way from the Atlantic Ocean to the Rocky Mountains.

Long before acquiring Louisiana, President Jefferson had considered sending men to investigate the West. The great land purchase aroused interest in expansion and assured support. A scientific expedition was planned. Experts were to study the land, the geology, the animal and plant life, and the native inhabitants. Accurate records were to be kept and specimens gathered. Possible trade routes would be charted on western rivers.

Meriwether Lewis and William Clark led that first American crossing of the continent in 1804–6. Their maps, journals, notes, and specimens provide our earliest knowledge of the interior of the American West.

Lewis was twenty-nine years old, a military officer who was President Jefferson's personal secretary. A scholar, he was interested in engineering and intellectual matters as well as the outdoors. Clark was thirty-three and a personal friend of Lewis. He had spent years among Indians on the earlier frontier. His brother, George Rogers Clark, was a frontier hero of the American Revolution.

Each man was talented in ways the other was not. William Clark was more outgoing and friendly than the quiet Lewis; his ease among

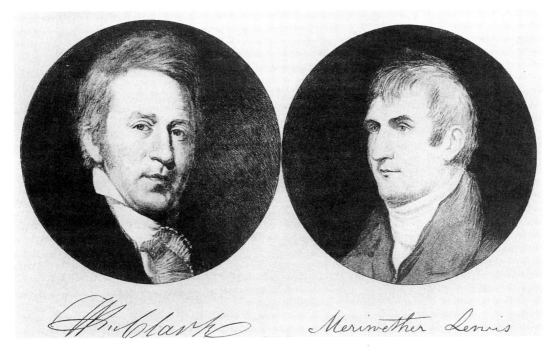

Meriwether Lewis and William Clark are Northwest legends. Along their route and elsewhere, counties, cities, lakes, rivers, parks, caves, colleges, and streets have been named for them. In 1905, the 100th anniversary of their journey, Portland, Oregon, hosted a World's Fair: the Lewis and Clark Exposition.

frontiersmen and Indians helped the project. Partnerships often work best when members are different enough to complement one another's talents and still get along well. So it was with Lewis and Clark, and their expedition stayed together through two years of hardship, uncertainty, and danger. The two men acted equally as co-leaders, although Lewis, an army captain, outranked his companion. In January of 2001, President Bill Clinton belatedly awarded William Clark with the rank of captain, which had been recommended almost two centuries earlier.

The mix of members included frontier guides, interpreters, trappers, naturalists, geographers, astronomers, artists, and map makers. They had uncommon abilities, skills, and interests, with long experience in rugged outdoor life. Several persons kept journals and took notes.

Sacajawea, the Shoshone wife of an interpreter hired in the Dakotas, became almost as famous as Lewis and Clark. Indians along the route interpreted the presence of this woman and her baby, Jean-Baptiste, as a sign of peace. Clark's black servant, York, was a source of support and a curiosity to Indians, who were impressed with his color, size, and strength.

### The Journey West

The expedition started out from Saint Louis. The first stretch of the trip, up the Missouri River to the Mandan Indian villages in present-day North Dakota, crossed land that was already known. The first winter was spent among friendly Mandan Indians. There was time to organize the party, modes of travel, and supplies.

On April 7, 1805, thirty-four persons including baby Jean-Baptiste left the Mandan villages. Lewis wrote: "Our vessels consisted of six small

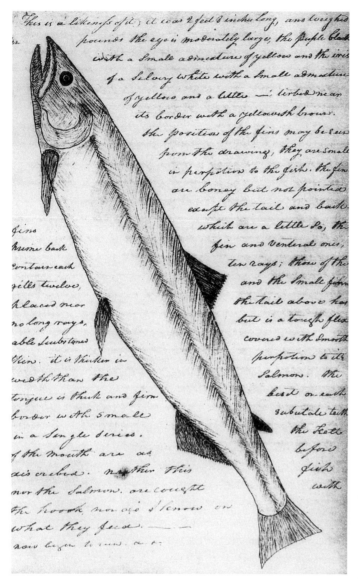

*This is a likeness of it; it was 2 feet 8 inches long, and weighed pounds the eye is moderately large, the pupil black with a small admixture of yellow and the iris of a silvery white with a small admixture of yellow and a little turbid near its border with a yellowish brown.*

A sketch of a Columbia River trout was included in this page from Clark's journal of his overland trip.

canoes, and two large perogues. This little fleet altho' not quite so respectable as those of Columbus or Capt. Cook, were still viewed by us with as much pleasure as those deservedly famed adventurers ever beheld theirs; and I dare say with as much anxiety for their safety and preservation. We were now about to penetrate a

country at least two thousand miles in width, on which the foot of civilized man had never trodden."

The route followed the Missouri River west across the plains. They portaged around the spectacular Great Falls of the river. At Three Forks, in present-day Montana, where three rivers join to form the Missouri, scouts were sent to determine which to follow into the Rocky Mountains. Naming the rivers the Jefferson, the Madison, and the Gallatin, after the president and his secretaries of state and treasury, the scouts correctly chose the Jefferson.

Leaving their boats behind, the explorers tramped through snow in the Rockies, crossed the range at Lemhi and Lolo passes, and searched for the best route to the Columbia River. They descended the Clearwater River.

Sacajawea proved her value when she obtained aid from her former tribespeople, including her brother, among the western Shoshone. Drawing maps on pieces of elk hide, they pointed out travel routes and provided horses. The Clearwater met the Snake River near the present eastern border of Washington State. At a Nez Perce village, the party, which had nearly starved since leaving the buffalo country east of the Rockies, received further help. They headed down the canyons and rapids of the Snake River.

On October 16, they became the first whites to view the Columbia River east of the Cascades. Going downriver in dugout canoes, they encountered Indians fishing, great rapids, and a deep passage through the mountains. "A cloudy, rainey, disagreeable morning," Lewis wrote on October 31. Almost every journal entry carried a similar thought. Overly impressed by the broad river that we know as the Willamette, they incorrectly guessed that it could lead far into the Southwest.

Downstream, the Columbia turned and grew wider. On November 7, the party made camp at a bay on the north side of its mouth. A short dis-

## An 1805 Christmas

*Even in difficult situations, people often try to observe special customs and holidays. At the makeshift Fort Clatsop near the Oregon coast, William Clark described Christmas day, 1805, in his diary:*

*"At day light this morning we we[re] awoke by the discharge of the fire arm[s] of all our party & a Selute, Shouts and a Song which the whole party joined in under our windows, after which they retired to their rooms. were chearful all the morning. after brackfast we divided our Tobacco which amounted to 12 carrots one haf of which we gave to the men of the party who used tobacco, and to those who doe not use it we make a present of a handkerchief. The Indians leave us in the evening, all the party Snugly fixed in their huts. I recved a pres[e]nt of Capt. L. of a fleece hosrie [hosiery], Shirt, Draws, and Socks, a pr. Mockersons of Whitehouse, a Small Indian basket of Gutherich, two Dozen white weazils tails of the Indian woman & some black root of the Indians before their departure. Drewyer informs me that he saw a Snake pass across the parth today. The day proved Showerey wet and disagreeable.*

*"we would have Spent this day the nativity of Christ in feasting, had we any thing either to raise our Sperits or even gratify our appetites, our Diner concisted of pore Elk, so much Spoiled that we eate it thro' mear necessity, Some Spoiled pounded fish and a fiew roots."*

*Quoted in The Journals of Lewis and Clark, B. DeVoto, ed. (Boston: Houghton Mifflin, 1953)*

tance from here came their first view of the Pacific, gray and rough in stormy weather. "Great joy in camp," wrote Clark, whose talents didn't include spelling, "we are in view of the Ocian, this great Pacific Ocean which we have been so long anxious to See. and the roreing or noise made by the weaves brakeing on the rockey Shores (as I suppose) may be heard distictly."

### Fort Clatsop and Home

The excitement of reaching their destination was lessened by wind, pounding rain, cold, and constant dampness. The lack of small game limited their diet to dried fish and roots, which had little appeal. They spent ten days exploring around Baker Bay just inside the river's mouth, Cape Disappointment, and nine miles of the coast before the expedition's leaders decided to let the members decide whether to move their campsite. This first democratic vote taken in the Northwest included an Indian woman, Sacajawea, and a black slave, York. The party elected to seek better weather and more protected ground. They moved south of the river and selected a winter campsite above a sheltered stream.

By Christmas they had built Fort Clatsop, a small stockade with living quarters, storage rooms, and workshops lining four sides. Fish and game were plentiful. The Clatsop Indians were helpful. On a beach men boiled ocean water to obtain salt for preserving food on the return trip. The winter stayed cold and rainy; life was monotonous and marred by sickness.

In early spring the Lewis and Clark party headed up the Columbia River for their return trip. Later, the two leaders split up. While Lewis followed the previous route and added a few side explorations, Clark explored to the south along the Yellowstone River. On August 12, 1806, they met up again near North Dakota. They revisited their Mandan friends, now threatened by attack and near annihilation from stronger Indian foes. They arrived back at Saint Louis on September 23, 1806. They had been gone for twenty-eight months, and some townspeople had feared that the party was lost and might never return.

The two leaders were keen observers, and their descriptions provided invaluable information. Specimens from the expedition included plants and stuffed birds and animals. These became the basis of some of the nation's first natural history collections.

Clark was appointed governor of Missouri Territory and lived many years in Saint Louis. A friendly, hospitable man, he shared his knowledge and experience with people going west when Saint Louis became a major outfitting place for the mountain fur trade. When he died at age sixty-eight in 1838, he was the city's most honored celebrity. His expedition partner was less fortunate. A moodiness that Lewis had sometimes displayed on the expedition increased as he suffered financial troubles. He was appointed governor of Louisiana Territory in 1807 and died a mysterious death either by his own hand or by murder in a backwoods settlement in 1809. He was only thirty-four.

## WILSON PRICE HUNT
## CROSSES THE CONTINENT

One explorer whom Clark advised was Wilson Price Hunt, a partner in the fur-trading venture of John Jacob Astor. In 1811 Hunt led the second American crossing of the continent. He traveled well south of the Lewis and Clark routes, along the north fork of the Platte and then the Snake River. The party experienced great hardships, including quarrels, sickness, starvation, unbearable weather, the desertion of a key member, and the death of a week-old baby born on the trail to the interpreter's wife.

The journey extended into the winter. Discouraged and in poor physical shape, the party reached the mouth of the Columbia River early

in 1812. With other members of their company who had arrived on the ship *Tonquin*, they established a fort called Astoria. The sea journey had been even worse than the overland trip. Several members had died in a shipwreck near the river mouth, others in an Indian attack. And after all that, their fur-trading efforts failed to prosper.

One morning the Astorians were surprised by the arrival of a fur trader some of them knew. David Thompson, an Englishman, had just followed the entire course of the Columbia River.

## DAVID THOMPSON
## TRACES THE COLUMBIA RIVER

David Thompson was more than a fur trader. Born in London in 1770, he apprenticed himself to the Hudson's Bay Company at age fourteen and sailed to Canada. He was seventeen when he made his first long wilderness expedition, and it left him with a passion for exploration and geography. He dreamed of exploring and mapping the Columbia River from its source to the mouth. He moved to the rival North West Company in 1797 and became its chief geographer.

He traveled the rivers and lakes of the Canadian Rocky Mountains as if they were his own backyard, always sure and competent, with a keen eye for things around him. Often taking his half-Indian wife and their children, he explored over 50,000 miles. Most of the time he worked from his base at Kootenai on Lake Windermere. Even as competition in the fur trade grew sharp, tracing the Columbia remained his chief goal.

On the first phase of his journey, he traveled north from Kettle Falls to the lakes that form the Columbia. Returning by way of the Spokane River, he assembled boats and headed downriver to the mouth of the Columbia. His trip was uneventful and successful. But he was disappointed to learn that Americans had already established a post at Astoria. Americans, not British, would claim the mouth of the river.

Thompson eventually retired in Quebec. There he gathered notes and sketches to complete a huge map showing the entire route of the Columbia from its upper reaches in Canada to Astoria. It was so detailed and accurate that fur traders and travelers relied on it for many years.

By this time the outline of the coast of the Pacific Northwest and the bodies of water in its interior were known. Now only gaps and details remained to be filled in.

## Chapter 3 Review

**I.** Identify the following people. Tell why each is important to Washington State.

*Exploration by sea*

| | |
|---|---|
| Robert Gray | Francis Drake |
| Juan de Fuca | Frances Barkley |
| Juan Pérez | John Meares |
| Bruno de Heceta | Don Esteban José |
| Juan Francisco de la | Martínez |
| Bodega y Quadra | George Vancouver |
| Francisco Eliza | William Broughton |
| Vitus Bering | Charles Wilkes |
| James Cook | |

*Exploration by land*

| | |
|---|---|
| Alexander Mackenzie | Sacajawea |
| Thomas Jefferson | York |
| William Clark | Wilson Price Hunt |
| Meriwether Lewis | David Thompson |

**II.** Define the following words and terms. Relate each one to Washington State.

| | |
|---|---|
| *Columbia Rediviva* | Nootka Sound |
| Northwest Passage | controversy |
| Territorial claim | International conflict |
| Scurvy | Sea otter |
| Journal | Scientific expedition |

**III.** Many places of importance in the history of the Pacific Northwest have been discussed in this chapter. Find the following locations on a map.

1. Locate each of the following places on a map, and tell why each is important in the history of the Pacific Northwest.

| | |
|---|---|
| Columbia River | Vancouver Island |
| Fort Ross | San Juan Islands |
| Strait of Juan de Fuca | Mackenzie River |
| Grays Harbor | Neah Bay |
| San Blas | Fraser River |
| Nootka Sound | Sitka |
| Point Grenville | Astoria |

2. Locate on a map these places along Lewis and Clark's route:

| | |
|---|---|
| Saint Louis | Snake River |
| Lemhi Pass | Three Forks |
| Mandan Indian | Columbia River |
| villages | Lolo Pass |
| Jefferson, Madison, | Fort Clatsop |
| and Gallatin Rivers | Seaside |
| Clearwater River | Missouri River |

3. Locate these places along the route of David Thompson:

| | |
|---|---|
| Kootenai | Astoria |
| Columbia River | Spokane River |
| Kettle Falls | |

**IV.** Each question below should call your attention to factual information in the chapter. Try to answer each one. Then look back in the reading to check your answer, correct your understanding, and find any answers you do not know.

1. What caused Robert Gray to suspect that a river was emptying into the ocean at the mouth of the Columbia?

2. What groups of people in Europe and the

United States supported explorations along the western coast of North America?

3. Describe the kinds of persons most likely to sail on these expeditions.

4. What important part of a river might an exploring party wish to claim on behalf of its nation?

5. What events were occurring on the eastern coast of North America at the time of major discoveries on the western coast?

6. By the 1500s Spain had become the richest and most powerful nation in Europe. Why?

7. What three results did Spain hope to achieve by its explorations along the Northwest coast?

8. What fur was most important to the seagoing fur trade?

9. Name the Russian company that carried on a fur trade out of Sitka.

10. What was Robert Gray's major purpose in sailing on the Northwest coast?

11. Tell two ways that Captain James Cook advanced the science of exploration.

12. What agreements did Vancouver and Bodega y Quadra reach during their meetings at Nootka Sound?

13. What did George Vancouver accomplish in Puget Sound?

14. What did Charles Wilkes recommend in his report to the United States government?

15. What was the major purpose of the Lewis and Clark expedition?

16. How did Sacajawea aid Lewis and Clark?

17. What event occurred on October 16, 1805?

18. How did the Lewis and Clark expedition preserve food during their winter in the Pacific Northwest?

19. How did the route of Wilson Price Hunt differ from that of Lewis and Clark?

20. What disappointment faced David Thompson at the end of his journey? What was his major contribution to the Pacific Northwest?

V. Think about, discuss, and answer the questions below.

1. Along the left side of a sheet of paper, list the four major countries that explored in the Pacific Northwest (Spain, Great Britain, Russia, the United States). Divide the paper into five columns headed "Reasons for Exploring," "Direction of Explorations," "Major Explorers," "Specific Events," "Results." Under each heading, write the major information for each of these countries.

2. Explorers often "claim" newly discovered land for their countries. Which countries do you believe had established the strongest claims to the Pacific Northwest? Justify your reasons. What country had the strongest claim to Puget Sound? To the mouth of the Columbia River? To the main course of the Columbia River? To Vancouver Island? To the Pacific coastline?

3. List and locate on a map the places named by Spanish explorers. Translate their meanings. List and locate places named by members of the Vancouver expedition, including Peter Puget and Joseph Whidbey. Explain these names. Find biographical information about some of the people for whom places were named, such as Mount Rainier, Mount Baker, and Hood Canal.

# Fur Traders and Missionaries

A diorama at Fort Vancouver National Monument depicts the Whitmans and Spaldings being welcomed by Dr. John McLoughlin.

*F*ort Vancouver, Oregon Country, September 12, 1836. Three married couples visit in a spacious Fort Vancouver living room. It is the most comfortable setting—possibly the only comfortable setting—that Narcissa Whitman and Eliza Spalding have seen during the 1,900 miles and four and one half months since the missionaries left Saint Louis.

They had not expected to find such pleasant surroundings, the soft couch and fine furnishings, or tasty and plentiful food, or cultivated companions. They enjoy talking with the three women whose husbands are officials for the Hudson's Bay Company. And their hostess is as gracious as her husband, Chief Factor John McLoughlin.

The missionary couples had arrived tired but relieved. Eliza, a quiet homebody, was ill much of the trip; gloomily, she accepted each hardship as God's will. But during these last weeks her spirits rose among green hillsides and smooth rivers and a growing fondness for the Indians they met. Narcissa, on the other hand, had been healthy, buoyant, and optimistic when she started this, her honeymoon trip. Cheerfully she had made the best of difficult traveling over little-known prairies. Then a change had crept over her. The tiny body growing inside her own caused her discomfort. She questioned whether she could be a good missionary, noticing that shy Eliza somehow got along better with these strange Indians than she did. She worried that the growing antagonism between their husbands might hinder their efforts to perform God's work.

The sight of Fort Vancouver reassured them all. From the river, they saw the British flag flying above the stockade and surrounding houses, fields, and orchards. Then Dr. McLoughlin rushed to welcome them, his long white hair flowing behind.

McLoughlin greeted the party warmly, praised these first women to endure the overland trail, and led them to the large house that befitted the most prominent person in the Northwest. Proudly he introduced his wife. If prudish Narcissa was bothered that her hostess was half Cree Indian and not formally married, Marguerite McLoughlin

Dr. John McLoughlin and his wife, Marguerite

soon overcame any doubts. She was an important influence on the temperamental McLoughlin and would prove a warm companion to Narcissa.

Over the next several weeks the two women will walk the grounds of the fur-trading headquarters together, shop its storerooms for supplies for the Whitman mission, and ride several miles outside the stockade to company farms, gardens, and dairy. Marguerite McLoughlin will provide seeds and sprouts for the intended mission grounds. Her guest will tutor the McLoughlins' daughter and teach stories and songs to all the children. Narcissa's affection for her new friend will become stronger than her feelings for her traveling companion, Eliza Spalding.

*

The two missionary women remain at Fort Vancouver while their husbands scout for possible mission sites. Six weeks later, they must leave to start their work in separate valleys beyond the great river bend. Their future days will be satisfying at times, but frustrating, lonely, and, finally, tragic.

But all that lies ahead. Today these couples dine and talk together, sharing a friendly interlude on this harsh and lonely frontier. The McLoughlins, Whitmans, and Spaldings; British, Indian, American; fur traders, missionaries; men and women. They will go different ways and meet different fates.

# New Visitors to the Northwest

Explorers came, charted and claimed the land, and then left; years later white settlers would arrive, take possession of the land, and remain. Between them others came who stayed only briefly and moved on. They used the knowledge left by explorers and they gathered knowledge that would aid settlers. Chief among such itinerant groups were inland fur traders and missionaries.

## Fur Traders

Two countries engaged in the inland trade of the Northwest: Britain, including its Canadian provinces, and the United States. Two British companies competed with one another until they merged in 1821. They were the North West Company and the Hudson's Bay Company. American traders included two large companies and several small ones along with freelancers who operated on their own.

They trapped and traded pelts of several animals, but the main interest was the beaver. High fashion made beaver pelts valuable: fur hats were stylish in Europe. These were not frontier hats with tails but elegant top hats and stovepipe hats. Fur capes and other garments were also popular. Softness was achieved by pulling out the coarse outer hairs, leaving fine, tiny hairs close to the skin. After demand far exceeded European supplies, merchants looked to North America.

### THE NORTH WEST COMPANY

The first fur company in the Pacific Northwest was the North West Company; its traders were known as Nor'westers. Founded in Montreal, Quebec, in the 1780s, it was a loose arrangement of merchants who organized to compete against the powerful Hudson's Bay Company (HBC), which controlled trade in eastern North America.

Nor'westers included English and Scottish traders as well as French Canadians who had been active near the Saint Lawrence River and the Great Lakes when France owned that area before 1763. Energetic young traders knew they could be promoted to better jobs within the company. Their drive and zeal pushed the North West Company into the West.

In 1807 David Thompson led company traders into regions drained by the Columbia River, where they established strategic posts along lakes and rivers. They acquired furs from local Indians and company men and dispatched them to Montreal. The posts supplied company traders with traps, packhorses, and supplies. The wide range of these expeditions is evident from David Thompson's maps of western Canada, all prepared while trapping. Similarly, Alexander Mackenzie had trapped his way across the entire continent.

When Thompson arrived at the mouth of the Columbia River in 1812, he found Americans had already established Fort Astoria there. Surrendered to the British during the War of 1812, Astoria was returned to the Americans afterward. Shortly thereafter, Astor's fur company sold the fort to the North West Company. Renamed Fort George, it remained the Pacific center of their enterprises for a decade. A large settlement was built; supply ships came in and furs went out.

Other posts included Spokane House, Fort Thompson at Kamloops, Kootenai House, Fort Alexander, and Fort Nez Perce at the mouth of the Walla Walla River. Fort Okanogan, established by Americans, also became part of the North West Company system during the War of 1812.

But the North West Company became too large and top-heavy with officers. Trade with Asia never materialized. Furthermore, their success in the Pacific Northwest could not offset the overall power of the Hudson's Bay Company throughout the continent.

The bitter rivalry between these two companies brought ruthless warfare. Halfway across the continent the Hudson's Bay Company brought settlers into the North West Company's trapping areas in the Red River Valley. Nor'westers killed the governor of the colony and twenty other settlers. The intense rivalry increased, and trading methods grew more cutthroat as the HBC extended into the Pacific Northwest. Eventually, the British government pressured the companies to merge. In 1821, all North West Company trading posts became Hudson's Bay Company posts.

Nevertheless, the North West Company had an immense impact. Alexander Mackenzie and David Thompson were only two of many traders whose explorations added to the knowledge of the Pacific Northwest. Nor'westers ventured along streams, through valleys, and across mountain passes and held lonely posts on lakes and at river mouths, building up a detailed picture of the region's geography.

## THE HUDSON'S BAY COMPANY

Chartered in London in 1670, the Hudson's Bay Company still exists, one of the world's oldest companies. Because French traders controlled the Saint Lawrence River, the main inland waterway in eastern North America, British traders had to find their own region if they wished to trade on the continent. This company was created to tap the resources of the great region around Hudson's Bay in northeastern Canada.

In the 1820s George Simpson, who headed all North American operations, determined to expand westward. Including the posts of its former competitor, the HBC locations were accessible to rivers and to areas where Indians lived. This ensured a source of furs and a market for company products and trade goods. Large storehouses held supplies, such as food and tools, which Indians, traders, and settlers could buy.

This logo on the Hudson's Bay Company journal shows how the company continued to use symbols from its early history.

Although the Hudson's Bay Company acquired Astoria in the merger, the company sought a new headquarters site farther up the Columbia River. Land south of the river seemed likely to become American, but the HBC expected the north side to remain British.

In 1823 a temporary headquarters was established about one hundred miles up the Columbia River opposite the mouth of the Willamette. George Simpson came to dedicate the new fort, which was named Vancouver as a reminder of English explorations and claims in the region. A stockade on the bank enclosed shops and housing. Fort Vancouver quickly became the center of most activities in the Northwest.

Dr. John McLoughlin presided over the fort as chief factor. Trained as a medical doctor, McLoughlin was a strong personality who dominated the Northwest for over twenty years. Six feet four inches tall and hot tempered, he ran company affairs with an iron hand. But he could also be polished and gracious. He was a company official rather than a government officer, but McLoughlin represented government and law for British subjects and others in the area including Americans. Recognizing that Americans might someday control much of the Northwest, he saw that they were treated courteously and received good service.

Fort Vancouver became headquarters for the whole Northwest, a social, political, and economic

## A Hudson's Bay Trading Post

*Fur-trading posts continued in some parts of the region long after the big trading days ended. Alex McLeod recalled his boyhood at Fort Colville in the 1850s.*

"*The trading post proper was a square inclosure. The store and warehouses were on the north side and Chief Trader McDonald's house was on the east side. The married employees, like my father, lived outside the inclosed post yard on the south and west sides.*

"*As early as I can remember, white placer miners were mining gold along the Columbia river bars above and below the trading post. They traded principally with Marcus Oppenheimer, who opened a store in one of the old British boundary barrack buildings. The trade at the Hudson's Bay post was mostly with Indians.*

"*A man named 'Squaw' Brown also had a little store on this side of the present town of Marcus, some 300 or 400 yards from Marcus Oppenheimer's store. When the best part of the bars had been worked out some years later, Chinamen replaced the white miners. I recall a Chinese mining camp at China bar, some six miles above Marcus, and another Chinese mining camp down the river near the present town of Peach.*

"*The Hudson's Bay Company trading post did quite a big business when I was a boy. The store was usually full of Indians and mixed bloods. Marten, mink, muskrat, coyote, bear and other skins were brought in, in large quantities and traded in for merchandise.*

"*Tobacco was then handled and sold in the form of a twisted rope. Two or three inches of this was cut off and traded in exchange for muskrat skin. Buffalo robes and buffalo meat were quite often traded in by the local Indians returning from hunting in the buffalo country.*"

*From Washington Pioneer Project, Told by the Pioneers, vol. 1*

center with influence beyond its role as a major fur-trading post. Traders and trappers went out in all directions, furs were brought in for shipment overseas, and most supplies and mail passed through Vancouver. Appalled that the North West Company had imported salmon from Scotland for dinners, Director Simpson insisted that the HBC be self-sufficient.

Simpson and McLoughlin encouraged agriculture. Crops and orchards were planted: legend holds that people saved seeds from their dinner fruit to start new trees. Wheat and apples, two crops that later became important in Washington, were first planted at Fort Vancouver. Livestock provided meat and hides. Shipping and fishing flourished and a sawmill was built.

In time, probably five hundred people lived in the area of the fort. They spoke a variety of languages. Besides the British and Americans, there were French Canadians and members of several Indian groups. Hawaiians, called Kanakans, were brought in to do manual labor; they lived in a village of their own. A Hawaiian (Owyhee) church was built inside the stockade with a Kanaka chaplain.

As company activities expanded, other HBC posts became small replicas of Fort Vancouver. Nisqually was built on southern Puget Sound, Okanogan at the mouth of the Okanogan River, and Spokane farther east. Near the present town of Chehalis a large farm was started, where Indians worked as cowboys. Thus, the HBC helped open up areas for settlement.

### THE NEW FORT VANCOUVER

The success of Fort Vancouver assured its role as Northwest headquarters for the Hudson's Bay Company. In 1829 officials moved to a better site on a grassy, flat area closer to the Columbia River. A new stockade, eventually 450 feet by 750 feet, was built. The fort and two bastions had no military purposes, however, because local Indians

Vancouver became a center for many activities. The stockaded fort on the low ground near the Columbia River was surrounded by farms, orchards, and houses. U.S. Army buildings were later built on the bluff above.

were friendly and Americans posed no military threat.

Inside the fort were workshops and storerooms, a well, a bakery and flour mill, Protestant and Catholic churches, and other evidences of a thriving, busy village. Here also was the big house for McLoughlin and his assistant James Douglas, and their families.

In 1836 the company brought the first steam-powered boat into the Pacific Northwest. Appropriately named the *Beaver*, it was 100 feet long and 40 feet across the decks. It had a large, noisy paddlewheel and a narrow, single funnel, but it also had masts and could let sails. For five decades the little boat hauled workers, furs, equipment, food, and traps along the Columbia River, up the coast, and in Puget Sound.

Fort Vancouver became the customary stopping place for visitors to the Northwest, providing good food, provisions, information, and gossip. Travelers and prospective settlers purchased supplies, repaired equipment, or sought advice and help. McLoughlin often advised missionaries and prospective settlers where to find good valleys, farmlands, and fresh streams. Later some of his countrymen criticized McLoughlin for helping Americans, even though he generally encouraged them to remain south of the Columbia River, where England had more or less given up its claim.

Prominent guests at Fort Vancouver included the Whitmans and the Spaldings, botanist David Douglas (for whom the Douglas fir is named), explorer John Charles Frémont, Lieutenant Robert

Peel (son of the Prime Minister of Great Britain), and numerous scientists, artists, explorers, traders, and travelers. Guests were received hospitably and put up comfortably. The McLoughlins' table was a gracious outpost on the frontier.

By the late 1830s more and more Americans were arriving in the Northwest. The HBC treated American fur traders as competitors, but settlers posed a greater threat. Trappers and settlers wanted to use the land for opposite purposes. Fur traders hoped the area would remain wild and generally unpopulated; settlers wanted more people, farms, and fences. The two groups could not co-exist for long.

As a result of more people and fewer beavers, in 1842 the HBC decided to move its headquarters north to Fort Victoria on Vancouver Island. Americans viewed this move as a clue that the British intended to give up their interests near the Columbia River. The HBC did not leave the Northwest, but its onetime dominance was gone.

McLoughlin himself acquired property among the Americans south of the Columbia River, where Oregon City is today. Following disagreements with his superiors, he resigned from the company in 1846. He built a large home and became an American citizen. Despite all his years spent directing British interests in the Northwest, he fell out of favor with the English. Nor was he ever thoroughly accepted by American settlers. He experienced severe financial difficulties and died in Oregon City in 1857.

## ASTORIA AND THE PACIFIC FUR COMPANY

The Pacific Fur Company (PFC) was part of the larger American Fur Company owned by John Jacob Astor. Astor was a successful fur merchant in upper New York State during its frontier days. As the supply of fur-bearing animals diminished there, he started the PFC to compete along the Pacific Coast. He had backing from President

Thomas Jefferson, who was eager to establish American influence in the region.

Two separate PFC parties were sent to start a post near the mouth of the Columbia River. Wilson Price Hunt led one group overland, while the ship *Tonquin* sailed around Cape Horn. Although the Hunt expedition met hardships and the *Tonquin* voyage ended tragically, the company persisted. Using many former employees of the North West Company, it built a post on a hillside near the mouth of the Columbia. This was named Fort Astoria.

Within a few months word came that the United States and England were at war: the War of 1812. The Americans at Astoria were manipulated into selling the fort to their rivals. After the war ended, a treaty returned the fort to the United States, but Astor soon sold it to the North West Company. The American Fur Company continued to prosper elsewhere but not in the Northwest. Renamed Fort George during its brief British ownership, Astoria remained the most important fur-trading post along the coast until Fort Vancouver was built.

The dramatic Astoria adventure interested

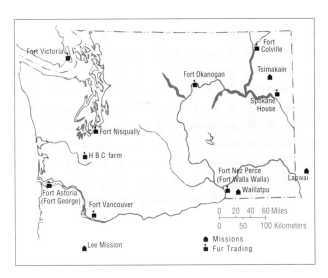

Fur trading posts and missions

New York storyteller Washington Irving, author of "Rip Van Winkle" and "The Legend of Sleepy Hollow." Irving's book *Astoria* was published in 1836. It gave many Americans their first glimpse of the Pacific Northwest.

Another American venture had more success in the western mountains and a great effect on settling the Northwest.

## THE ROCKY MOUNTAIN FUR COMPANY

American fur traders were active along the Missouri River and its tributaries during the 1820s, but few ventured into the Pacific Northwest. Companies and individuals followed the Missouri into Rocky Mountain foothills and returned with pelts secured from Indians or by their own efforts. Most were small enterprises, but the Rocky Mountain Fur Company, which was founded in Saint Louis in 1822, was larger.

Indian attacks had forced partners William Ashley and Andrew Henry to give up a post on the Missouri River. They determined to move farther into the Rocky Mountains and to maintain only a few scattered posts. But they added a new feature. Their employees and Indian allies did not simply establish posts and exchange goods for pelts brought to them. Instead, Rocky Mountain Fur Company men lived alone in the mountains for years at a time, wandering through the wilderness, trapping. They met once each summer to sell their catches and receive rewards. Called "mountain men," they led rugged, isolated lives, and often experienced sickness, maiming, and violent death.

These men adapted their lives to mountains and forests, making trails, building shelters and huts, hunting and eating what foods the wilderness allowed, and keeping few possessions. They came to live much like the Indians, and many had Indian wives.

Summer brought the rendezvous of the mountain men. At such locations as the Green Valley

An old-time mountain man with his ponies

or Jackson Hole in present-day Wyoming, they brought in furs from their winter's work and congregated for a week or ten days.

This colorful encampment brought together mountain men, company representatives, old-time French-Canadian trappers, traders from rival companies, and Indians bringing teepees. Furs were sold, goods and trinkets exchanged, and salaries paid. Then the rendezvous became a raucous, brawling party. Men who had been alone in the wilderness for many months suddenly had money, companions, and time. Liquor, dancing, women, and gambling were all at hand. Spectacular fights often broke out.

Before this wild fling ended, the site of the next

rendezvous was selected. The valley regained its natural quiet as the men headed back into the mountains for another year.

Some mountain men, like Jim Bridger, Jedediah Smith, Kit Carson, and Joe Meek, became famous. As they traveled and trapped and hunted, they came to know the woods, mountains, rivers, and valleys intimately. They crossed mountain passes and ridges, followed streams, and roamed through valleys to places no white men had seen before. Indians sometimes showed the way. John Colter described a spot where steam shot high in the sky and hot, colorful mud bubbled forth. His fellows ridiculed the fantastic tales and called the place "Colter's Hell." We know it as Yellowstone Park.

Mountain men entered the Grand Canyon of the Colorado River, already known to Pueblo Indians and Spanish explorers. Others found the gradual slope through the Rockies in present-day Wyoming that they called South Pass. Later, this pass made possible the Oregon Trail and the westward movement of settlers. Jedediah Smith discovered a route across the Sierra Nevadas into California, and others found the pass north through the Siskiyou Mountains into Oregon. Few of them realized that these finds were important. They were concerned with animal pelts rather than geography, but most major features of the western mountains that we know today were noted by mountain men.

For many years this system was profitable for the Rocky Mountain Fur Company and others. Between five hundred and one thousand mountain men were probably in the field in the 1830s. They brought in $3,750,000 worth of furs in fifteen years. But the end eventually came. The demand for beaver hats and other garments declined. The number of beavers also diminished.

The success of the mountain men also helped bring about their own decline because they opened paths for others to follow. Newcomers changed the land as they built homes, planted crops, and raised families. The habitat of the beaver and the trapper was wilderness no more.

A few old mountain men became trail blazers and guides for missionaries and then for settlers. Others bought land and settled in the valleys. As their own lives changed, they helped change the West.

## Missionaries

After the fur traders came missionaries. Roman Catholics and many Protestants throughout the United States, including Methodists, Baptists, Congregationalists, and Presbyterians, believed that they had a duty to save souls and gain converts.

In the early 1800s, much of the United States experienced a religious revival. By the 1830s, several American denominations looked westward for new missionary opportunities.

Missionaries served three main functions. First, they sought to make converts, to bring the word of God and their religious beliefs to persons who did not share them. The Indians of the American West provided obvious opportunities.

Second, missionaries established Christian outposts in areas where there were none, such as the American frontier. Converts and pious settlers wanted instruction, sermons, and the sacraments of the church available to them. Church buildings, schools, and Bible classes could help fulfill such needs.

Third, missionaries frequently met needs other than spiritual ones. They offered medical care, reading and writing instruction, health and sanitation methods, agricultural and technical skills to their neighbors. For instance, Marcus Whitman was a medical doctor; his wife Narcissa and others were teachers. Other persons with special skills provided help while pursuing their religious duties.

Were missionaries wanted on the frontier?

Both Catholic and Protestant missionaries used "ladders" like this one to instruct Indians in religious doctrine.

training. One, Spokan Garry, returned and tried with little success to convert his people.

In 1831, four Nez Perce Indians appeared in Saint Louis asking questions about the Bible. They aroused great excitement in the city, but all four died before returning home, so no one knows what effect they might have had among their people. Many Indians who sought Christian instruction did not intend to abandon their traditional beliefs. They simply wanted to add the white man's powerful "medicine" to their own.

Indians were confused by missionaries because the missionaries spent so much energy competing with one another. Many Protestants, for instance, were strongly opposed to Catholicism. Dr. McLoughlin, who was helpful to missionaries, worried that the Indians were "perplexed beyond measure by the number and variety of their instructors."

Inspired by their religious convictions, American Protestants in the 1830s believed that they were wanted and needed on the frontier.

## JASON LEE AND THE METHODIST MISSION

The Methodist Church sent the first mission into the Pacific Northwest. Jason Lee, a layman and a recent convert, led it, assisted by his nephew, the Reverend Daniel Lee. Their task was "to throw themselves into" the Indian nation. "Live with them, learn their language, preach Christ to them, and, as the ways open, introduce schools, agriculture, and the arts of civilized life," the Lees were instructed.

The Lees came west in 1834 intending to settle among the Flathead tribes in the Rockies. But at Fort Vancouver, Dr. McLoughlin convinced them to stay in the Willamette Valley, where retired Hudson's Bay Company employees and a few Americans were starting homes. This valley of green rolling hills and rich bottomland outlined with oak and fir also reminded the Lees of their native Connecticut.

Sometimes—but in the beginning, just as often they were not. Few fur traders were practicing Christians; David Thompson and the Bible-carrying Jedediah Smith were exceptions. The Hudson's Bay Company sent two Indian youths to a Red River mission school to receive Christian

The emphasis of the Lee mission changed. Intended to serve Indians, it concentrated instead on whites. Mission buildings were established on a bend of the Willamette River thirteen miles north of present-day Salem, Oregon. This post included a mission station, an Indian school, a hospital, a store, and a farm.

Almost immediately Lee wrote home for reinforcements. Over the next few years several groups arrived, including married couples and single women, and the work expanded to five other locations. Jason Lee moved among them.

The Dalles mission up the Columbia River became the chief center for working among the many Indians who traded there. A briefly held post at Nisqually, near the Hudson's Bay Company fort on Puget Sound, penetrated the present state of Washington. Methodist operations peaked in 1840 when six mission stations included two mills, two stores, nine ministers, twelve laymen, and various hired helpers.

Methodist missionaries were not successful in converting Indians. They spent much time and effort meeting immediate needs and had little time for church duties and work with Indians. Instead, they attracted more settlers to the Northwest.

The mission created publicity about the Northwest. Enthusiastic about the fertile soil and mild climate, missionaries sent glowing letters back to their home congregations. They had a major effect on the Northwest even though it was not what had been intended, because the missionaries encouraged more Americans to come and live in the region.

## THE WHITMAN PARTY

The second group of missionaries in the Northwest was led by Marcus Whitman, whose murder was a momentous tragedy in Washington history.

The Whitman party was sent in 1836 by the American Board of Commissioners for Foreign Missions, which included Presbyterian, Congregationalist, and Dutch Reformed churches. This body sent people west in teams, with married couples preferred. The board even arranged marriages. Missions were intended to become permanent settlements.

Marcus and Narcissa Whitman were Presbyterians from New York state, but they had not met before the effort to form a missionary party. Marcus, a teacher trained as a medical doctor, decided he wanted to do missionary work. In 1835 he and Samuel Parker, a scholarly preacher curious about Indian ways, visited the annual mountain men's rendezvous to inquire about religious needs in the West. The fur traders' way of life disturbed Whitman's sense of right and wrong but did not dampen his enthusiasm.

Whitman returned east to prepare for the mission and to gather companions, including a wife. Narcissa Prentiss, in her late twenties, was a dedicated Christian when she heard about Marcus and this opportunity for service. Their cautious courtship turned to real love, and they were married the day before their departure.

The Whitman party also included Henry and Eliza Spalding. Eliza was well educated but frail and sickly. Henry, who had once been Narcissa's suitor, became intensely jealous of Whitman's leadership. A third couple started west, but the husband turned back after the wife died. Also along was William H. Gray, a bachelor; his quarrelsome personality and ambition to lead his own mission disrupted all their efforts. A black helper, John Hinds, was ill during most of the journey and died at Walla Walla. He was the first American to be buried on Washington soil.

Two features of the journey stand out amid the growing clash of personalities. Stopping at a fur-trader rendezvous, Narcissa Whitman first realized the crudeness of the world she was moving into, and Eliza Spalding began to develop compassion for Indians. The second feature was the Whitmans' determination to take wheeled vehicles as far west as possible. Four-wheeled wagons got no farther than Fort Laramie in the Rocky Mountain foothills, but a two-wheeled cart crossed on to Fort Boise, about forty miles west of present-day Boise.

The rest at Fort Vancouver was welcome. Dr. McLoughlin discouraged Whitman from establishing the mission among the Cayuse Indians near Walla Walla, but Whitman went ahead. He was impressed with that valley near the route west and close to the Hudson's Bay Company fort. Whitman selected a pastoral site on a small, winding creek at Waiilatpu, "the place of rye grass." Low and sheltered by trees, it had good soil surrounded by grassy hills.

The Spaldings moved east to Nez Perce land in what is now Idaho, where the Lapwai Creek joined the Clearwater River. Two years later Mary and Elkanah Walker and others established a mission among the Spokane Indians at Tshimakain, about twenty-five miles northeast of present-day Spokane.

These were three separate missions, not a chain under a single command. Differences and jealousies developed. Whitman believed that their first purpose was to save souls, to convert Indians by providing religious instruction and baptisms. Spalding and Walker felt that the Indians should first be taught to give up their nomadic ways for the settled life of farmers.

Despite disagreements, daily life was productive. Houses, workshops, storerooms, and schools were busy; crops were planted and harvested; grist mills provided flour; religious services were held. Lapwai and Tshimakain were somewhat isolated, but Waiilatpu became a stopping place along the trail to Fort Vancouver. In time a community developed around that mission. It included settlers, some Cayuse Indians, and several children whom the Whitmans cared for.

The whites soon learned that they could not force Indians to work for them; Indians would not be slaves. The Spaldings and Walkers got along well with the Indians, because of their own attitudes and because they settled among friendly chiefs and tribes. Spalding farmed successfully with the Nez Perce.

A missionary translated the Book of Matthew into the Nez Perce language, and it was printed on a press sent from a Hawaiian mission. This

Left to right: Narcissa Whitman (no known contemporary portrait of Marcus Whitman exists), Elkanah Walker, and Mary Walker

was the first book printed in the Northwest. Missionary women taught Indian children English and helped with handwork.

The women were especially troubled by Indians who lied or stole from them, who wandered unannounced through houses, who disturbed private moments, or who had an un-Christian moral code. Narcissa was puzzled by the Indians' curiosity about her baby's approaching birth.

Alice Clarissa Whitman was born on March 14, 1837. The parents adored their beautiful daughter. Then, one day soon after her second birthday, she toddled off to the Walla Walla River and drowned. Her parents never recovered from their grief. Narcissa became especially moody. Having no more children of their own, the Whitmans took care of those whose parents, like mountain man Jim Bridger, were often away, or the Sager children, whose parents had died. The Walkers, in contrast, had five children born in the Northwest.

## From a Missionary's Diary

*Mary Richardson Walker kept a diary of her trip west. These passages describe some of her first days as a missionary at Waiilatpu. Here the Walkers spent several months with Marcus and Narcissa Whitman and others before establishing their own mission at Tshimakain.*

"Sunday, [September] 2. Waiilatpu. We all united with the little church formed which now consists of sixteen members. Mr. Walker preached from the text... [Henry Spalding] closed by explaining to the Indians what we had been doing. We had an interesting, and I think, a happy season, notwithstanding all the hardness that has existed among us. We feel that we have great cause of gratitude, and much encouragement to go forward in the work.

"Thursday, Sept. 6. Waiilatpu. Assisted Mrs. Whitman, a little in washing. Sewed a little. Put up seeds &c. Mr. W.[alker] and Mr. Rogers returned. Mr. Eells and wife took a wrong road, and we know not what has become of them.

"Friday, 7. Waiilatpu. This morning rainy, Mr. & Mrs. Eells found their way back without getting much wet. Worked some in the kitchen; finished making Mr. W's pantaloons. Ironed.

"Saturday, 8. Waiilatpu. Repaired a pair of pantaloons &c. Mr. Eells commented lesson in musick on the blackboard. Had an interesting group of 20 or 30 Indians. They appear much interested. I feel anxious to be able to teach them myself, I think there is every encouragement to labor for their good.

"Sunday, Sept. 9. Waiilatpu. Prayer meeting in the morning. Then instruction to natives. Then sermon by Mr. Eells.

"Monday, Sept. 10. Waiilatpu. Rose early; worked hard as I could till Mr. Walker got ready to start [on a trip doing mission work] which was at three P.M. After crying a little picked up and found myself somewhat tired. Oh! dear how I would like to be at home about this time, and see brothers, hear from all the good folks! I wish I could have a letter from some of them."

[Three months later, on December 7, 1838, Mary Walker gave birth to her first child, Cyrus Walker, at Waiilatpu.]

*From Historical Reprints: The Diary of Mary Richardson Walker, ed. Rufus A. Coleman (Missoula: State University of Montana, c. 1931)*

The Whitman mission at Waiilatpu; this painting was based on survivors' descriptions.

None of the missionaries converted many Indians, but they kept trying. When the American Board ordered the Waiilatpu and Lapwai missions closed, Dr. Whitman traveled east to appeal the decision. He was persuasive and successful. The trip made him something of a celebrity, and the work of Northwest missions became widely known among church congregations. So did the fertility of Northwest soil.

Returning west in 1843, Whitman helped guide the largest wagon train yet to take the trail. This time he was the seasoned, experienced leader, and he fulfilled his dream of bringing a four-wheeled wagon through the mountains. Knowledge that wheels could cross the Rockies assured a large future migration. This increased the likelihood that Americans would ultimately settle and possess the Northwest.

### The "Massacre"

Whitman returned to find conditions at the mission worse than before. Narcissa was morose and disheartened. Her husband's success in the East seemed to assure that they would remain at Waiilatpu among unfriendly Indians and constant reminders of Alice Clarissa's death.

But circumstances were even worse than the Whitmans imagined. The Cayuse had lost respect for the white couple. Narcissa acted superior and cold toward them, and many Indians made fun of the Whitmans behind their backs. They also noticed the increasing numbers of settlers, and they understood that their traditional way of life could not continue if whites kept pouring in.

After Dr. Whitman put poisons and laxatives around his garden to ward off wild animals, several Indians who took some of the vegetables became sick. That, combined with unfamiliar diseases brought by the newcomers, convinced some Cayuse that they were being poisoned to make room for settlers. A measles epidemic in 1847 seemed to confirm such suspicions. Without natural immunity to the disease, nearly half the

Cayuse died, while whites recovered. Grieving survivors blamed Dr. Whitman, who could cure his own people but not theirs. And Cayuse traditions held that curers might be put to death if their patients died. Well-informed men at Fort Walla Walla urged the missionaries to take precautions, but they either underestimated the danger or felt helpless.

The mission was strangely silent on the morning of November 29, 1847. The Whitmans rested, discouraged and tired from their unsuccessful efforts to care for the ill. Several Indians quietly appeared. They were burying another measles victim, the son of Tilaukait who was well known at the mission.

After lunch, the seventy-four people about the mission went on with their normal activities. Children played, an elderly woman rested in her room, and Dr. Whitman relaxed and read. Tilaukait and Tomahas, two young Cayuse warriors, appeared and asked for the doctor. Narcissa called him and ushered several children to another room. Soon the men were talking loudly and then a shot sounded.

Realizing that her husband had been attacked, Narcissa and the older children tried to hide and calm the younger ones. Angry Indians stormed the house. Narcissa found a calm courage as she tried to save her dying husband and help others, but to no avail. She was shot when she turned toward a window to seek help. Terrified, many in the household hid, and a few escaped, but by the time the rampage ended, the Whitmans and twelve others were dead. Indians destroyed buildings and orchards. Forty-seven people captured by the Indians were later ransomed by the Hudson's Bay Company.

One escapee made his way to Fort Walla Walla with the news. When men from the fort reached Waiilatpu, they found smoldering ruins and scattered bodies. The remains were buried in a shallow grave. Twice in later years, the bones were

Tomahas, the Cayuse Indian who killed Marcus Whitman

removed, finally to a common grave on a mound above the mission site.

Rumors of danger spread to other missionaries. Henry Spalding, on his way to a meeting with Whitman, encountered a Catholic missionary who gave him the news. The Walker children were playing in their yard at Tshimakain when a messenger rode in with a note for their father. His face turned white as he read it. Soon afterwards, the Walkers visited the grisly scene at Waiilatpu. Mary Walker spotted something on the ground and stooped to pick up a lock of Narcissa's hair. Their own association with the Spokane Indians was warm and friendly, but the Walkers reluctantly closed their mission and moved to Forest Grove, Oregon. Here they helped establish a school that became Pacific University. When Mary died in 1897, she was eighty-six years old and the last survivor of the Whitman group of missionaries. Meanwhile, Spalding returned to work among the Nez Perces; he died at Lapwai in 1874.

*The Cayuse War*

News of the killings alarmed the Americans who lived in the Willamette Valley. It also gave many settlers the excuse they had been waiting for to fight the Indians. A militia of 500 citizens was organized to go after the murderers. They set up headquarters at The Dalles, and 130 men started in search of the fleeing Cayuse tribe. Additional enlistees followed later. The campaign to find the Cayuse continued for several months. There was little real fighting and casualties were few.

In April 1850, the accused killers of the Whitmans and three other Cayuse gave themselves up. Tried in American courts, they were convicted of murder and hanged. Meanwhile an army force occupied the mission area in order to maintain safety for travelers. The Cayuse wars ended, but within a few years, larger wars raged through eastern Washington and threatened the Puget Sound area.

In death Marcus and Narcissa Whitman became the most famous of the early pioneers. A statue of Marcus in Washington, D.C., occupies one of two spots in the Capitol Building allotted each state for its most important figures. A legend arose that his trip east in 1843 had "saved" the region for the United States against English threats. Responsible historians disagree, convinced that his purpose was to keep the missions open, but his importance in publicizing the Northwest should not be underestimated. By bringing wagons across the Rockies, he proved that people and supplies could successfully travel west in large numbers. Thus the Whitmans played a significant role in the settlement of Washington despite their lack of success as missionaries.

The effect of the murders extended beyond the Cayuse wars as the hanging of the killers incited further Indian retaliation. The pressure of increasing white settlement caused widespread wars and threats, and treaties were drawn up that affect Indian-white relations in the state today.

## ROMAN CATHOLIC MISSIONARIES

The Whitmans distrusted Catholics, but they occasionally hosted Roman Catholic missionaries. These "Black Robes" were first invited to Oregon by Dr. John McLoughlin, a Catholic convert, to serve his many French-Canadian employees and Indian converts. First to come was Father François Norbert Blanchet, who made his headquarters in the Willamette Valley. His assistant, Father Modeste DeMers, worked north of the Columbia from headquarters in the Cowlitz Valley. Members of the Jesuit order of the Catholic Church were led by Father John Peter DeSmet. Working out of Saint Louis, DeSmet established missions in present-day northern Idaho and ranged the vast area between the Cascades and the Rockies.

Catholic missionaries possessed certain advantages over the Protestants. They were trained, ordained priests, not merely well-meaning laymen, as many Protestants were. They were freer to travel about than family men, to live among both Indians and white settlers. They posed no threat of permanent settlements and growing families. Lacking personal ambitions to farm or build upon the land, the priests could devote most of their time to religious obligations. Catholic nuns built much-needed schools, hospitals, and orphanages.

The Catholics seemed more forgiving toward Indians and less demanding than Protestants. They were less shocked by Indian attitudes and by practices that people like Narcissa Whitman viewed as horrid vices. Priests accepted conversions freely, too freely, the Whitmans thought, without requiring continued instructions. They did not deliver moralistic sermons.

Catholics used objects that could be seen and handled: shrines, cups, beads. Such symbols easily lent themselves to Indian cultures in which

A Catholic priest (right) and his Indian pupils dressed up for a photographer at Tulalip, about 1865.

symbolic objects were already familiar. Father Blanchet devised the Catholic ladder, which could be held in the hand, and demonstrated how each step on the ladder moved an individual upward in Christian life to heaven. This graphic display worked so well that even the Whitmans and Spaldings adopted the idea.

In the middle 1840s there were fourteen Catholic missionaries in the Northwest. But most of the American settlers who came were Protestants, so the call for Catholic priests lessened. Catholics began to concentrate more on the Indian population, building schools that taught vocational skills along with religious doctrine.

## EFFECTS OF THE MISSIONARIES

The work of the missionaries is an important element in Northwest history. Their role was eventually filled by priests and ministers of many denominations and by community churches. Efforts to convert Indians were not successful, although Catholics fared better than Protestants.

In nine years at Tshimakain and despite friendly relations with nearby Indians, the Walkers made not a single convert. Furthermore, the bitterness between the Cayuse and the Whitmans introduced more than a decade of war between the races.

The accomplishments of the missionaries lay in other directions. They started the first religious centers on the frontier, some of which became permanent churches. Jason Lee opened what would become the first four-year college in the Northwest, Willamette University in Salem. Whitman College in Walla Walla, the oldest college in Washington, was established as a seminary in 1859 to honor Marcus and Narcissa Whitman's pioneer efforts at schooling.

Most important, letters to home congregations and to church newspapers conveyed the enthusiasm missionaries held for the region and encouraged other Americans to head west.

Fur traders, then missionaries, then settlers: the rush to the Northwest was underway.

## Chapter 4 Review

**I.** Identify the following people. Tell why each is important to Washington State.

*Fur trade*

John McLoughlin
George Simpson
John Jacob Astor
Washington Irving
John Colter
Jedediah Smith

*Missionaries*

Jason Lee
Daniel Lee
Marcus Whitman
Narcissa Prentiss Whitman
Henry H. Spalding
Eliza Hart Spalding
Elkanah Walker
Mary Richardson Walker
Father François Norbert Blanchet
Father Modeste DeMers
Father John Peter DeSmet

**II.** Define the following words and terms. Relate each one to Washington State.

*Fur trade*

North West Company
Hudson's Bay Company
Merger
Chief factor
Kanakans
The *Beaver*
American Fur Company
Rocky Mountain Fur Company
Mountain men
Rendezvous

*Missions*

| | |
|---|---|
| Missionary | Catholic |
| Convert | "Black Robes" |
| Protestant | |

**III.** Locate each of these places on a map. Tell why each is important in the history of the Pacific Northwest.

*Fur trade*

Fort Okanogan
Spokane House
Fort Thompson
Kootenai House
Fort Alexander
Fort Nez Perce
Fort Vancouver
Fort Astoria (Fort George)
Fort Spokane
Fort Nisqually
Fort Victoria

*Missions*

| | |
|---|---|
| Salem | Tshimakain |
| The Dalles | Lapwai |
| Waiilatpu | |

**IV.** Each question below should call your attention to factual information in the chapter. Try to answer each one. Then look back in the reading to check your answers, correct your understanding, and find any answers you do not know.

1. Which two countries took part in the inland fur trade in the Pacific Northwest?

2. What particular kind of wearing apparel became fashionable in Europe and aided the growth of the fur trade? What animal was the main object of the inland fur trade?

3. What was the first fur company to come into the Pacific Northwest?

4. Many trappers had a Canadian background. Explain who they were.

5. What happened to Fort Astoria during the War of 1812? What happened to that fort and the surrounding land after the war ended?

6. What did the North West Company and the Hudson's Bay Company do in 1821?

7. What was different about the way that fur traders and settlers wanted to use the land?

8. What major change did the Hudson's Bay Company make in the early 1840s?

9. What happened to the American Fur Company after the War of 1812?

10. What was different about the way the Rocky Mountain Fur Company handled its trapping?

11. How did many former mountain men assist missionaries and settlers after the fur trade ended?

12. What Protestant congregation sent the first missionaries into the Pacific Northwest?

13. How did the emphasis of the Lee mission change?

14. Which Protestant congregations combined their efforts to send the Whitman party into the Pacific Northwest? In what ways did this group differ from the Methodists in the kinds of persons they chose to send as missionaries?

15. What did Marcus Whitman decide to do when he approached the Rocky Mountains?

16. How closely did the Waiilatpu, Lapwai, and Tshimakain missions cooperate in their work?

17. Why did Marcus Whitman return East? What did he bring with him on his return trip?

18. How many persons were killed in the Whitman massacre? How many escaped and what happened to them?

19. What happened to the killers of the Whitmans?

20. Tell three ways that the Catholic priests conducted their missionary work differently from Protestant missionaries.

V. Think about, discuss, and answer these questions.

1. List ten personal characteristics that a fur trader should have. Make a similar list for a missionary. What things appear on both lists? Compare your lists with other students in the class. Find additional information about two of the persons mentioned in this chapter. Rate them on a scale of 1 (low) to 10 (high) as to how well they display the characteristics on your lists.

Think about your own friends and acquaintances who have the qualities and characteristics to be an effective fur trader or missionary.

2. Describe the geographical characteristics of places most likely to be chosen for fur-trading posts.

3. Describe in some detail at least five different activities that took place at Fort Vancouver.

4. List the trade items that were traditionally stocked in the early trading posts. Discuss the importance and use of some of these.

5. What qualities did Marcus and Narcissa Whitman have that were helpful to them in their work? What qualities were less helpful? List several reasons why the Indians might have wanted to kill the Whitmans. Explain which reason you think was most responsible for the murders.

6. What is a "massacre"? Does the word have an emotional tone that goes beyond its definition? Is "massacre" an appropriate word to describe the killing of the Whitman group? Explain your thinking.

## Chapter 5 Settlers and Settlements

In his old age, Ezra Meeker retraced the Oregon Trail.

McNeil Island, Washington Territory. A morning in July 1853. Ezra and Eliza Jane Meeker look out across Puget Sound from the piece of land they have claimed on McNeil Island. Towering above lesser peaks, Mount Rainier seems to fill the horizon. Below it, three miles away, the village of Steilacoom looks like a city with its collection of tiny buildings climbing the slope from the beach.

In 1853 Steilacoom is the busiest port on Puget Sound and the largest community in the territory. Lafayette Balch put up a precut New England house there just three years ago and opened a store and a hotel. There is a grist mill up the beach. A barrel factory, a brewery, a salmon-packing plant, and a shipyard are planned. The Meekers can see a ship in the harbor, taking on lumber for California. The quiet of their own island contrasts with that bustling village in the distance.

A baby sleeps in the Meekers' tent. More than a year old now, he is strong and healthy after the 2,000-mile journey that began when he was only a month old. The tent has been "home" in many different surroundings.

This morning crows dip to the beach for clams, carry them high in the air, and crash the shells against the rocks below to release the meat. The sound of Indian songs floats across the water from canoes bobbing in the waves. But Ezra is watching something else. Someone is paddling rapidly toward the island. It is his brother, Oliver, who had joined him on the long trip from their home in Indiana to the Pacific Northwest.

The brothers greet each other happily. Several days ago they had parted company while Ezra returned to the Columbia River to pick up Eliza Jane and the baby, whom he had left in camp while he looked for land on which to settle. In the meantime, Oliver has found work loading lumber at Steilacoom. He flashes his pay: California gold.

Now the brothers can start to build. Their home will be a small log cabin like the one Ezra was born in twenty-three years ago. It will have a stone fireplace with a clay and cattail chimney, a wood floor, a window with real glass, and furniture made from the trees nearby.

Soon Ezra will break ground for the farm he has always wanted. Ever since he and Eliza Jane were married, their dream has been to farm, just as their parents farmed.

Here on the island, the Meekers have reached the end of a trail begun fifteen months earlier when they packed their few belongings for the move west. Their party was never more than five wagons, but they became part of a stream of small wagon parties along the trail that seemed to blend into a continuous caravan.

They averaged fifteen to twenty miles a day and endured weeks of dust and boredom. During those long days of weary travel, they crossed the Missouri River in a rickety flat-bottom boat (a scow). They escaped the cholera epidemic that swept through the caravan, causing new graves to appear beside the trail each day. They encountered Indians, though they were never threatened, and they felt the dust from a stampeding buffalo herd. When they finally got to the Snake River, they had to caulk their wagons in order to float them across.

Now safely on McNeil Island, the dangers of the trip are behind them, although the memories are not.

Ahead are nine years on this island. Later will come homes at La Conner, Whidbey Island, and finally Puyallup. Ezra Meeker will make and lose several fortunes. In his sixties, he will head for the Klondike gold fields. He will start a new Northwest industry by growing hops for beer.

At age seventy-six he will head east from Puyallup with cart and two yoked oxen, hailed by crowds in many towns and cities, driving his team down Broadway in New York and then on to Washington, D.C., into the White House grounds to meet President Theodore Roosevelt. In 1915 he will drive over the Oregon Trail by automobile. In his nineties, he will fly the length of the trail in an open-cockpit airplane.

This young man on the McNeil Island beach in 1853 will become the extraordinary old pioneer, a white-bearded reminder of those years when he and his nation were young, when people traveled west on the Oregon Trail by ox team and covered wagon.

# The Nation in the Years of the Move West

**B**y the mid-1830s the United States had grown into a stable young nation. It had been more than half a century since the American Revolution. Most adult Americans had been born since independence, and immigrants were arriving all the time.

Every ten years the population had increased by a third. There were over 17 million people in the United States in 1840; a quarter of a million new residents made New York the largest American city.

East of the Mississippi River, most of the country was divided into states, and there were three states west of the river. Oceangoing ships regularly served Atlantic and Gulf Coast ports, and steamboats churned along the inland rivers. Exuberant Americans felt strong and confident about their young nation's future. Reformers called for improvements, but no one doubted that the nation could solve its problems. Although the ugly issue of slavery aroused concern, feeling had not yet reached the point of splitting the nation in civil war.

In the years before 1846, Mexican rule had replaced Spanish in the Southwest. North of the 42nd parallel, the Oregon Country (as the Pacific Northwest was called) was jointly occupied by England and the United States. Both nations assumed that the southern portion around the Willamette Valley would become American. But many Americans expected the entire Oregon Country to be settled by their own people.

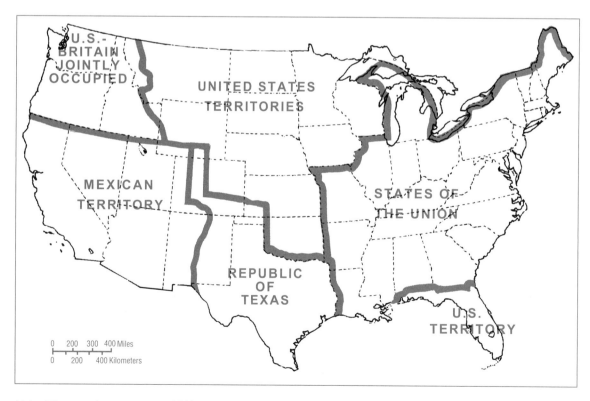

United States and possessions in 1840

A New York editor coined the phrase "Manifest Destiny" to predict that the West would inevitably and rightfully belong to the United States. This became the slogan of the movement west.

By 1848 that destiny was coming true. The United States possessed California, the Southwest, and Oregon. The Pacific coastline was American between the present-day borders with Mexico and Canada. Settlers were pouring into Oregon, first only a few and then up to ten thousand a year. Some traveled by boat around South America. Others came by wagon, crossing plains and mountains along a route called the Oregon Trail. These overlanders added a new dimension to the history of the Northwest.

## Why Move to the Oregon Country?

Between 1840 and 1860, nearly 300,000 Americans migrated west. About two-thirds of these were lured to California by gold; another 50,000 went to Mormon settlements in Utah; and some 53,000 headed for the Oregon Country.

The trail west was especially crowded in certain years. Only 875 people crossed into Oregon in 1843, but that year became known as the Great Migration because there were six times as many travelers as in the previous year.

Before 1848 five emigrants came to Oregon for every one who turned south to California. Then gold was discovered near Sacramento and the proportion was reversed. In 1852, 10,000 emigrants arrived in Oregon; the next year there were 7,500.

We can only guess what motivated people to move across the country. Missionaries, travelers, newspaper editors, and congressmen debating Oregon issues contributed to an impression that this was an Eden where soil and climate were good, where land was inexpensive, and where crops grew easily. Like Ezra Meeker, many early emigrants expected to farm, even though they often later turned to logging, fishing, shipping,

## Two Views of the Oregon Donation Land Act

*During the debate in the 31st Congress (1850), Senator Thomas Hart Benton of Missouri argued that each family should receive the full 640-acre section of land:*

*"Well, sir, six hundred and forty acres is but a small donation to a family so far off in the wilderness as these people are. . . . [The United States gets] in return for it settlers who will improve and defend the country, and who in all time to come will furnish defenders, not only for their own State, but for the service of the country, and who by their productions are promoting commerce and navigation, and bringing money into the United States from customs. They are paying a great price in the service which they render to the country, and . . . in the privations and hardships which they themselves endure.*

*". . . I shall vote for the largest amount [of land] that any gentleman will vote for."*

*In a nation of immigrants, Senator William Crosby Dawson of Georgia took the position that foreigners should be excluded from the provisions of the Land Act:*

*"Foreigners will throw themselves into your country. . . . Before the three years expire the whole of your immense lands will be gone. They will turn loose their whole population, and especissly [sic] their pauper population. Look at the inducements. Three hundred and sixty acres of land! For what? What service have they rendered to the country? Have they paid a dollar of taxation? Where do the millions come from that you expend in the purchase of these lands? They come from your citizens who have been here from the foundation of your Government up. And when the land is brought in, scarcely a dollar is returned to the Treasury, but it is given away to those who come from foreign countries. . . ."*

An artist depicted the spirit of Manifest Destiny moving along the Oregon Trail with the travelers.

or providing services for growing communities.

Federal laws helped people acquire public lands. The Oregon Donation Land Act of 1850 allowed a single person to acquire 320 acres and a married couple 640 acres if they lived on it for four years. In 1854 a similar law covered Washington Territory. These amounts were later reduced and the laws abused, yet such measures created an impression that fertile, free land was available.

Perhaps some people felt they were being squeezed out by growing populations in older settled areas. The Northwest provided tremendous opportunities for persons like Lafayette Balch, who founded Steilacoom, to organize and build communities. Surely many made the

trek west bursting for adventure and hoping to start a good new life. Evidence suggests that the Northwest attracted people who intended to stay and build. Bolder speculators often headed to the California gold fields.

The possible spread of slavery affected how some new territories grew. Several regions became battlegrounds between supporters and opponents of slavery. Much of the Northwest was settled by anti-slavery proponents from the Northeast, but there were pockets of southern sympathizers who disregarded the rights of blacks. Yet, many opponents of slavery believed that one way to keep slavery out was to keep blacks out. Laws excluded blacks from the Oregon Country after

Conestoga wagon

1844 as did the later constitution of Oregon Territory. The Donation Land Act also excluded blacks, and special laws had to be passed to protect claims of certain individual blacks.

The migrating population received plentiful advice. Some of it was accurate, some questionable, and some outrageously wrong. Hall J. Kelley, fresh from a fur-trading party, became Oregon's leading publicist, writing pamphlets telling settlers what to expect. A New England church group briefly published the *Oregonian, and Indians' Advocate*, a newspaper that described the region and its opportunities. Similar articles appeared in regular East Coast papers, although some argued that taking the trail was foolhardy. Maps were available, and guidebooks that resemble the road guides published today described what to expect along the way.

Reports by persons who had been west carried assurance of firsthand reliability. Along the trail, west-bound travelers often met east-bound returnees who described what lay ahead. Every source provided opportunities for rumors and exaggeration. Some pictured an easy trip to a fertile paradise; others, a disaster-plagued journey to the end of the earth.

## Getting Started

The journey to Oregon differed from year to year and from party to party. The first step was usually easy: reaching one of the towns on the Missouri River that served as a taking-off point. Both Independence and Saint Joseph, Missouri, rapidly grew to about two thousand residents, with stores, churches, and hotels.

Campgrounds were set up on the outskirts. People heading west usually spent about fifteen days at such towns, for there was much to do, to purchase, and to learn. For his book *The Plains Across*, historian John Unruh read hundreds of diaries and journals kept by pioneers. He sums up their activity:

"Most overlanders filled their days and nights with frenzied activity: seeking out bargains at street auctions, organizing traveling companies, drawing up constitutions, electing officers, writing letters home, warding off criminals and confidence men, visiting the many taverns and grogshops, and getting too little sleep as they pondered whether the motivations impelling them westward were worth braving all that the rumormongers claimed lay ahead. Greenhorn travelers also experimented—humorously and

The interior of a wagon at the beginning of the trip west; heavy items, such as the chair and the silverware, would probably have to be discarded along the way to make the wagon easier to pull up steep slopes.

sometimes painfully—with yoking oxen, packing mules, and cooking over campfires. The art of driving a prairie schooner was not easily learned—wagons overturned easily and wagon tongues were fragile. The combination of inexperienced drivers and untrained animals produced resounding collisions with trees and other novice teamsters" (pp. 115–71).

Even small groups organized with rules and leaders. Some leaders of wagon trains remained prominent in the new lands; others lost authority along the trail when situations called for skills they lacked. Guides were often hired, such as former fur traders Joe Meek and Kit Carson. Later, as the trails became more familiar and some emigrants had traveled them several times, guides were less essential.

Most wagons were small versions of the Conestogas that had long transported people and goods in eastern states. Some were simple farm wagons with canvas hooped high above. Parts of the wagon were made of hardwoods. Wheels usually had oak or hickory spokes. Tires were strips of iron riveted onto the spokes.

Wagons generally lacked standing room except in the middle. The covering of canvas or other heavy material, sometimes brightly colored, was oiled to shed rain. In front sat the driver. Animals to pull the wagon could be purchased in the outfitting towns. Mules and yoked oxen were hardy and sure-footed and required little special attention. Horses were rarely used.

Not everyone could sleep in the small wagons each night, so many carried tents. Travelers brought blanket rolls and quilts, and their woolen or buckskin clothing was warm and durable. Revolvers and ammunition were essential, as was a large cask of water. A small camp stove and Dutch ovens or iron pans were used for campfire cooking.

Only a limited amount of food could be taken by each family, and that was supplemented along the way. Flour and sugar in tight bags or tins, some bacon or pork, and salt to flavor and preserve food were necessities. Cattle followed alongside to provide dairy products and eventually to be butchered for beef. Emigrants hunted buffalo, deer, small game, and birds, and learned—as had the Indians long before—to gather seeds, roots, and plants.

Many families left comfortable homes in the East and started their journey carrying impractical items they couldn't bear to leave behind. Typically, emigrants began with too many supplies but not enough food. They soon learned to sell or drop non-essentials. Many a dejected pioneer was forced to dump along the trail a piano, a fine chest, a chair, or other dearly loved object that had become a burden. The trail became littered with discarded possessions. A rule of the road allowed people to pick up whatever they could use. Abandoned wagons or parts might well turn up at the crucial moment when a passing party needed repairs. One person's loss might be another's salvation.

## Along the Trail

Usually the journey began in the spring, late enough that forage could be found along the trail, but early enough that the mountains could be crossed before autumn snows. After the first years the difficult journey became almost routine. Traffic was heavy enough for constant contacts among travelers.

The several routes differed slightly and starting points ranged from Missouri to Iowa. Most parties crossed to the North Platte River to journey through the prairies. A "highway" forty feet wide became hardened under the pressure of hundreds of wagon trains.

Their different religious and social views and competition for forage often caused Mormon and non-Mormon travelers to take opposite sides of the river, the Mormons usually taking the north

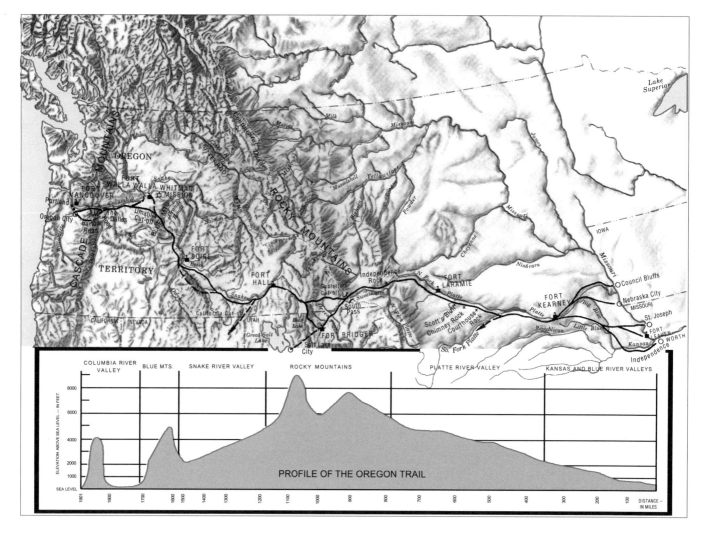

Oregon Trail

bank. Across hot, dry, and dusty plains that had been known as the Great American Desert, the rising elevation was almost unnoticed until the Sweetwater River. Then the climb steepened as the trail approached the Rocky Mountains. Certain landmarks stood out on the horizon miles before they were reached: Chimney Rock, Independence Rock, Scotts Bluff, Devil's Gate, and others. Travelers often inscribed names or left messages at such places.

During the slow climb into the mountains, pine trees and other vegetation began to thicken and fresh water became available. The gateway through the Rockies was South Pass in southwestern Wyoming, a valley so wide and grassy that many pioneers failed to recognize it as a pass. Just beyond were turnoffs to Salt Lake City and to California.

Legend has it that the road to California was marked by a gleaming pile of gold-laced quartz, while the northern fork had a sign that said "To Oregon." In those early days Northwesterners boasted that, clearly, people who could read headed for the Oregon Country!

The descent wound through desert valleys and beside rock cliffs above the Snake River. Before reaching the mouth of the Snake, pioneers set off across the piney Blue Mountains toward the Columbia River. Rapids in the Columbia Gorge were the last real obstacle. By the late 1840s, the early stopping places of the Whitman Mission and Fort Vancouver were replaced by such Willamette Valley villages as Portland and Oregon City. There people began to scatter from the trail to search out locations for their new homes.

The trip might last anywhere from fifteen to twenty-eight weeks, depending upon weather, flooding, disease, personalities within the parties, and other less predictable things. However costly, the journey was less expensive and shorter than boat passage around South America or across the isthmus at Panama.

Many wagons carried slogans or had distinctive colors. Some travelers inscribed their names on rocks so frequently that those following often felt they knew them long before they actually met. Nightly stops provided opportunities to visit, sing, square-dance, tell stories, and compare notes.

Mail was deposited along the way, and messages were posted; in this way news spread in 1850 that President Zachary Taylor had died suddenly. A few trading posts along the route broke the monotony and provided guidance and help. Thus, the sight of Fort Laramie, Fort Hall, and Fort Boise was greeted eagerly.

In later generations, legends, dime novels, movies, and television exaggerated the Indian menace. Few travelers ever saw an Indian. Especially in the early years, Indians were an important source of help, advice, food, and information. Only 400 of the more than 10,000 deaths in twenty years of western travel, or 4 percent, resulted from Indian encounters. A few Indians stole goods, harassed wagon trains, or robbed new graves, but even those who were hostile were more a nuisance than a danger. Ezra Meeker met

## Diary of an Overland Traveler

*Amelia Stewart Knight, traveling west on the Oregon Trail in 1853 with her husband and seven children, kept a record of the journey in her diary.*

*"Friday, August 12th . . . Lost some of our oxen. We were traveling along slowly, when he dropped dead in the yoke. We unyoked and turned out the odd ox, and drove around the dead one, and so it is all along the road, we are continually driving around the dead cattle, and shame on the man who has no pity for the poor dumb brutes that have to travel and toil month after month on this desolate road. (I could hardly help shedding tears, when we drove round this poor ox who had helped us along thus far, and has given us his very last step.) We have camped on a branch of Burnt River. . . .*

*"Wednesday, August 17th   Crossed the Grand Ronde Valley, which is 8 miles across and have camped close to the foot of the mountains. Good water and feed plenty. There 50 or more wagons camped around us. (Lucy and Myra have their feet and legs poisoned, which gives me a good deal of trouble. Bought some fresh salmon of the Indians this evening, which is quite a treat to us.) . . .*

*"Friday, August 19th   Traveled 13 miles over very bad roads without water. After looking in vain for water, we were about to give up as it was near night, when husband came across a company of friendly Cayuse Indians about to camp, who showed him where to find water. The men and boys have driven the cattle down to water and I am waiting for water to get supper. This forenoon we bought a few potatoes from an Indian, which will be a treat for our supper."*

*From Lillian Schlissel,*
*Women's Diaries of the Westward Journey*
*(New York: Schocken Books, 1982)*

Contemporary artist William Henry Jackson painted wagon trains rolling through the broad, grassy valley that was South Pass.

LEAVENWORTH TO SALT LAKE CITY.    269

Miles.
17. North Platte.—Road sandy in places; no wood; good grass and water; some buffalo-chips.
16½. North Platte.—Road good; no wood; good grass and water; cattle-chips in places.
18¾. North Platte.—No wood.  Camp opposite "Chimney Rock," which is a very peculiar formation on the south of the road, and resembles a chimney.  Grass good.  Road muddy after rains.

CHIMNEY ROCK.

17½. North Platte.—No wood; grass and water good.
16. "Horse Creek," branch of the North Platte.—In seven miles the road passes through Scott's Bluffs, where there is generally water in the first ravine about 200 yards below the road.  The road then descends the mountain, at the foot of which is the Platte and a mail station.  A little wood can be obtained at Scott's Bluffs; there is none on Horse Creek.

A page from the *Prairie Traveler* (1859), one of the numerous guidebooks that advised pioneers on their trek westward.

only three Indians in his journey, one of whom was demanding payment at a river crossing.

Disease was a more common threat. Cholera, an intestinal infection that brought vomiting, diarrhea, dehydration, and often death, was epidemic in some wagon trains. Travel conditions—crowded quarters, bad food and water, and little chance to wash—increased the likelihood of sickness. Yet, no Americans in that time understood the dangers of germs, of poor water supplies, or

of inadequate diet. Ailments flourished in established eastern towns as well as on the trail.

Drownings in unfamiliar rivers and other accidents were also the cause of deaths. With many travelers inexperienced in using firearms, accidental shootings were a major hazard. (The first person accidentally shot and killed on the way to Oregon was appropriately named Shotwell; he lifted his rifle from his pack, failing to notice that it was pointed at him.)

Doctors, such as Marcus Whitman and David Maynard, were particularly valuable train members. Doctors often moved from wagon to wagon, taking on greater burdens than most members of the party. Deaths in strange, isolated spots far from home, burials in hurriedly dug, shallow graves that might soon be ravaged by wolves, and families separated amid unfamiliar surroundings made the journey west tragic for many travelers. One diarist counted 401 new graves along the route, and she estimated that was only a third of the total.

Compassion was shown to persons who suffered. However little the pioneers had known one another, they were bound by common experiences and necessities. Often they went out of their way to care for widows, orphans, or others in need.

In some ways the people traveling together formed communities on the move, much like the ones they had known back home. Leaders emerged; some people campaigned for jobs, which were awarded by vote; others had specialized chores; and most took turns standing watch or caring for the animals. Friendships that developed along the trail often lasted a lifetime. Many young people met their future wives and husbands on the trip.

## Reaching the Northwest

Arrival in the Northwest gave little time to relax. Indeed, the task had just begun. Most of the early pioneers settled south of the Columbia River in the Willamette Valley. But in 1846 the boundary line between American and British possessions was set at the 49th parallel, the present boundary with Canada. Soon more arrivals were settling north of the Columbia.

Those who moved north followed valleys and trade routes. They scouted for sites where rivers joined, where soil was fertile, or where a harbor was deep. After finding a desirable spot, the newcomer could secure a claim at the nearest government agency and then try to live on the land long enough to "prove up" ownership and secure clear possession.

Few pioneers expected to live isolated and alone. Many had left eastern towns expecting to build similar towns on the western frontier. The Northwest needed such towns to supply products and services for the new settlers. Stores, warehouses, offices, banks, schools, churches, and other institutions had to be started. Most settlers hoped to become part of prosperous new communities.

## The Growth of Communities

Let us look at a few Washington communities that were started soon after travelers began arriving in the Oregon Country. Seattle, Oysterville, Centralia, Port Townsend, and Walla Walla are among the earliest settlements in the state. All were started during the 1850s by persons who had come on overland migrations.

### SEATTLE

In its earliest years, Seattle was only one of many logging and milling villages on Puget Sound. Few clues suggested that it would become the leading city of the entire Northwest.

Its first white settlers—Luther Collins, Joseph and Samuel Maple, and Henry Van Asselt—built cabins and farmed beside the Duwamish River, about where a Boeing plant is located today. But they did little to start a city. In the fall of 1851,

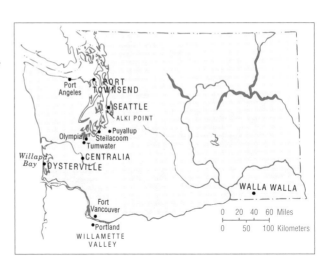

Early Washington communities

John Low and David Denny were scouting for a place to settle. These two young men had heard about Puget Sound during their wagon trip from Illinois. Attracted to a triangular point that juts into the water, they agreed that nineteen-year-old Denny would remain there along with a third man who stayed a short time. Low returned to Portland to secure a land claim and gather up the rest of their party.

On a rainy November day, the newcomers debarked at that point from the brig *Exact*, which was headed north to the Queen Charlotte Islands. The leader was David Denny's older brother Arthur. With him came Low and twenty other persons, several of whom were related to the Dennys. Twelve were children, the youngest two months old.

Their introduction to their new home was discouraging. While starting to build a small log cabin, David Denny had chopped his foot with an ax. Skunks had eaten his food. It was raining, and the cabin had no roof.

The pioneers finished four other houses before winter was over. They sold newly cut logs to ships bound for California, where the population (growing steadily since the gold rush) needed

Three founders of Seattle: (from left) Arthur Denny, Henry Yesler, and David "Doc" Maynard

more lumber than California forests could supply. Asked the name of their place, the Dennys answered, "New York," and then added "alki," the Chinook Jargon word for "by and by." The spot has remained Alki Point.

But the disadvantages of Alki soon became apparent. The location on a point meant frequent changes of wind, current, and tide that caused difficulties for ships trying to load or unload cargo. The flat area near the beach could be logged easily, but the cliff behind was too steep to bring timber from above. So Arthur Denny began looking elsewhere.

Using horseshoes tied on a fishing-line to locate the deepest water, he found a spot across Elliott Bay, near present Pioneer Square. In February 1852, Arthur Denny, his brother-in-law Carson Boren, and William Bell staked a claim and moved their families to the new site.

Shortly afterwards, Henry Yesler arrived from Ohio. He clearly understood the advantages of deep water at the base of a thickly wooded hillside, and he secured land and built a sawmill. As trees on the hill were cut, the logs were skid-ded down greased runners to the mill. This log run was called a "skid road," a term that has come to mean the run-down area of any city.

The leading industrialist, businessman, promoter, and first mayor of the town, Yesler was interested in building a city, as long as he could profit. His sawmill was the first industry of the budding town and the first mill on Puget Sound to use steam power. His log cookhouse served as a public building until he built another for meetings, dances, and public affairs.

Meanwhile, another important arrival had wandered in after a harried wagon train venture. Trained as a doctor, David Maynard continued his medical practice in the Northwest and opened the first hospital, but he had other interests. He started a fish-packing plant, the city's second industry, and he hired friendly Duwamish and Suquamish Indians to bring in salmon, which were sold in San Francisco.

"Doc" Maynard became well acquainted with a Suquamish leader named Sealth (also called Seattle). Through Maynard's efforts the new city was named after his friend.

Seattle in the 1870s; the territorial university building stands prominently on the hill at what is presently Fifth Avenue and University Street.

Arthur Denny also remained involved in almost every aspect of city building and civic affairs. He sold, bought, and traded property in a way that encouraged growth and development, and he became wealthy. As a member of the legislature, he had a part in making Olympia the territorial capital, Walla Walla the site of the penitentiary, and Seattle the home of the first university.

Henry Yesler, David Maynard, and Arthur Denny, working together but often in competition, were the strongest of the founders who steered Seattle through its earliest years. Denny was a steady and conservative (even stuffy) individual who generally kept himself in the background. Yesler was high-powered, domineering, and hated by some. Maynard was a friendly promoter who dabbled in many things but spent his profits before he could become rich. These three quite different men, each in his characteristic way, helped to create a city that grew.

Initially, Seattle's land claim was divided into lots for sale, a procedure called "platting." Denny and Maynard bought adjoining plats, which met at different angles along Yesler Street due to a curve in the shoreline. Workshops and businesses began to appear around the mill. Tide-flats circled the hillside to the south and east. Logged-off spots on the hill east of the village were soon occupied by houses. Those of Denny and Yesler might be considered mansions, but most were modest frame dwellings.

A white-columned university building dominated the hillside, even though it was little more than an elementary school with limited funds and few students. But the presence of the university was proof of stability, a sign that the village would continue to exist and attract newcomers.

When Seattle was just five years old, fear of neighboring Indians prompted citizens to build a small fort. Attackers were scared off by cannon fire from a warship that happened to be in the bay. Although it was a minor incident with no actual fighting, it was commemorated with a rhyming phrase, "the Battle of Seattle."

Seattle hoped to become the railroad terminus when track was built north from the Columbia River. Other communities had the same dream, and promoters from the rival mill town of Tacoma won. Seattle then ambitiously tried to build its own railroad. Having little money, volunteers undertook the project in May 1874, armed with picks and axes and muscle. The experience of working together in this heroic but doomed effort helped weld a sense of community for future endeavors. The railroad never reached much beyond Renton, about fifteen miles away and far short of Walla Walla, its goal. But even this proved fortunate: much-needed coal was discovered near Renton, and the train brought in carloads.

Seattle gradually spread from Yesler's mill along the shoreline. Events resembled those in many a growing city in the late nineteenth century, yet each city had unique experiences. In Seattle these included:

- riots against Chinese immigrants in the 1880s, which helped create a labor party

- a fire in 1889 that gave the thirty-eight-year-old city an opportunity to replace wooden buildings with stronger, more modern structures of stone and brick

- the arrival of the Great Northern Railroad and expansion of port facilities where trains and ships met

- the Klondike gold rush of the late 1890s, which brought Seattle national attention and ensured recovery from a recent depression

- the rapid growth of population and expansion into outlying areas in the early 1900s

- the expansion of the University of Washington at a new campus on the northeast edge of the city

- the tearing down of hills and the filling in of ravines and tide-flats to level the ground, straighten the shoreline, and make possible growth to the south and north

- the partial development of a system of boulevards and parks designed by the noted Olmsted Brothers landscape architecture firm

- the Alaska-Yukon-Pacific Exposition of 1909, a world's fair that advertised the Pacific Northwest to the nation and the world.

These crucial events helped change Seattle from a logging village into the preeminent city of the entire Pacific Northwest.

## CENTRALIA

The founder of Centralia was a typical western town-builder in most respects. He was intelligent, aggressive, visionary, hard working, and versatile. He had a clear idea of the kind of town Centralia should be, and he died an honored town father. Yet he had been born a slave in Virginia in 1817.

George Washington, founder of Centralia

He was named George Washington after his parents' owner, who may have been related to the first president. While a baby, George the slave was purchased and later adopted by James and Anna Cochran, a white couple who raised him as their son. They taught him to read, write, and do mathematics. They encouraged him to learn trades: brick making, logging, whiskey distilling, and tailoring.

When the Cochrans moved west to Missouri, George went with them. But when he set out on his own, he discovered greater racial prejudice than he thought existed. As a mill operator, he could not collect a bad debt because blacks were not allowed to sue. He started a distillery, but the legislature passed a law forbidding blacks and Indians to deal in liquor. When he moved to Illi-

nois, he learned that blacks must post a $5,000 bond simply to live there.

About this time, the Cochrans and their son determined to try life in Oregon. At Oregon City, George Washington discovered what others had learned before him: an 1846 law prohibited blacks from settling in Oregon Territory. And so the family moved north where laws were harder to enforce. In James Cochran's name they secured a claim to land where the Skookumchuck River flows into the Chehalis. Until Cochran's death, they ranched and operated an inn and ferry service at this valley location.

When Washington Territory was created in 1853, Oregon's laws against blacks no longer applied. George Washington was able to purchase land adjoining the original Cochran claim for $1.25 an acre, and soon he owned a sizable tract. At first he logged and farmed his land, certain that the location would prove to be excellent. He was right. The Northern Pacific Railroad built through in the early 1870s, and land values increased.

In 1875, he filed to plat a city, Centerville, which later became Centralia. Saving part of his property for himself and his family, he sold lots to people who would build on them. He donated land for streets, a park, a cemetery, and a church. By giving financial help, he encouraged businesses to start, and his little town flourished. Centralia remained an important shipping stop between the Columbia River and Puget Sound, and it became a farming, logging, and milling center.

Investments and land sales made George Washington wealthy. His character and relations with others earned him respect, despite occasional incidents of prejudice because of his color. During the depression of the early 1890s, he helped many persons in financial need and continued to work for worthwhile causes.

When he died in 1905, the town of five thousand people observed a day of mourning. They honored a man born into slavery who had become the founder and most honored citizen of Centralia.

## OYSTERVILLE

Robert Hamilton Espy came from Wisconsin logging country to Portland early in the 1850s and then headed northwest to Shoalwater Bay, the large coastal indentation now called Willapa Bay. He was successfully selecting and felling trees for dock pilings and waterfront buildings along the West Coast.

His travels brought him to Bruceport, a small settlement on the eastern shore of the bay. A group of Scottish fishermen, discouraged by their failure in the California gold fields, had brought a boat north. Inside this bay the boat—the *Bruce*—caught fire. The seven men came ashore, looked over the area, and decided to remain. They found that the small, succulent oysters along the beach could be sold at a profit to luxury hotels in San Francisco that catered to people who had grown rich mining gold or living off miners. The Scots were harvesting oysters when Espy arrived.

Soon Espy made new acquaintances: Isaac Clark, a New York tailor who had just come west, and Nahcati, chief of the Indians who lived along the bay. Nahcati told the newcomers that the oysters on the peninsula side of the bay were even more abundant and delicious. Espy and Clark discovered this was true. They built a cabin, secured a land claim, and Clark platted the town, appropriately named Oysterville. When the Bruceport men objected, a little war ensued until they realized the obvious: there were oysters enough for all.

Although Oysterville had only a dozen or so inhabitants, Clark and another man opened stores, a post office was secured, and town officials were elected.

When Indian wars seemed to threaten Wash-ington Territory in the 1850s, Oysterville citizens dutifully began to construct a fort, even getting help from local Indians. They stopped before it was finished, mutually amused by building a fort in a place where relations between whites and Indians were harmonious.

For thirty years, Oysterville thrived by selling seafood to distant cities. Several dozen houses were built. A walkway on pilings along the shore held a little business district with stores, bars, and two hotels, and townspeople walked paths made of oyster shells. The first public school in Pacific County was built by volunteers in 1863. A minister visited regularly after 1871, years before a church was built.

Boats sailing the coast stopped by, some to pick up oysters. Most seafood was transported to the Columbia River town of Ilwaco by a stagecoach each morning. In time a railroad was built to Nahcotta, a town south of Oysterville named for Chief Nahcati. Stagecoaches and trains kept irregular schedules affected by tides because boats could enter Ilwaco only on incoming flood tides.

In 1861, Oysterville became the county seat, starting a long rivalry with other settlements. A special election in 1892 transferred the county seat to South Bend, a lumber town above the eastern shore of Willapa Bay. County officials, led by several Oysterville residents, refused to turn over records. One evening a party of masked invaders rowed ashore, headed for the county building, injured a guard, ransacked file drawers, and made off across the bay with all the records they could carry. Oysterville gave up, accepting a court order to turn over all official papers to South Bend.

Oysterville's bustling prosperity was ending in the last years of the nineteenth century. Nearby resort towns along the Long Beach peninsula had been catering to wealthy Oregonians on weekends. These began losing business to new towns such as Seaside on the Oregon coast. Fewer

Wedding pictures of Robert H. and Julia Ann (Jefferson) Espy

people came to the peninsula. Cold weather, overharvesting, and disease took their toll on the oyster supply, and shipments fell off.

Oysterville was started with great hopes but never grew beyond a one-industry town, dependent on a seafood and tastes it could not control. Slowly, the community dwindled. Within a few years it became a near ghost town. It remains today a quiet, isolated spot brushed by the sea, where oysters once provided a thriving industry for one of Washington's earliest communities.

## PORT TOWNSEND

Port Townsend rests on a thin, hilly peninsula at the northeastern tip of the Olympic Peninsula. Geography is its chief asset, with high land, wide views, and a deep harbor where the Strait of Juan de Fuca meets Puget Sound. This location aided the growth and importance of Port Townsend in its earliest days but could not save it when times grew bad.

By the early 1850s, loggers had discovered seemingly endless stands of timber around Puget Sound. The growth of California cities, along with frequent fires in San Francisco and other towns, created a demand for Northwest lumber. Logging and milling towns, such as Seattle, Port Ludlow, Port Gamble, Port Orchard, Seabeck, and Utsalady, had major growth spurts. And every ship that sailed to or from any of these places had to pass by Port Townsend.

The federal government needed a port of entry with a customs house to inspect cargo and collect duties from ships coming from other countries.

An artist's sketch of Port Townsend, 1890s

The chosen town would have definite advantages over rivals. Olympia already had the customs house, but its south Sound location was impractical. And so, in 1853, the government moved the customs house to Port Townsend, a village with only about forty settlers.

The two-year-old community had started out much like other logging towns. Alfred A. Plummer and Charles Bachelder were the first arrivals. Plummer had joined the army to gain passage west toward California gold. From El Paso, Texas, he walked across Mexico and then took a steamship north to San Francisco where he ran a hotel instead of heading for the gold fields. A ship captain lured him to Puget Sound.

Plummer and his friend Bachelder stopped at Steilacoom and then headed on to start their own town. In April 1851, they staked claims at Port Townsend, became friendly with the Klallam Indians, built a two-room cabin, and planted a garden. Soon they were joined by Loren Hastings, who had crossed the plains by covered wagon, and by Francis Pettygrove, who had helped establish Portland, Oregon, naming it after his hometown in Maine. The newcomers platted 144 blocks with 63-foot-wide streets. They set up stores, and unsuccessfully tried to sell fish caught by the Klallams. Then they turned to logging and built a crude mill.

Port Townsend became a stopping place for ships after the customs house arrived. Prosperity seemed certain because all ships that entered and left the Sound had to stop there. Seamen spent time and money in Port Townsend stores and saloons.

When gold was discovered on the Fraser River, Port Townsend became an outfitting place for prospectors. The mix of loggers, gold seekers, sailors, and Indians made Port Townsend colorful and exciting. Like port towns the world over, it acquired a reputation for liquor, gambling, thievery, smuggling, prostitution, and violence. This reputation wounded the pride of the founding fathers. Even worse, several national newspapers ridiculed local backwardness, crudeness, and lawlessness. Townspeople and authors waged a bitter correspondence. But even bad publicity was making Port Townsend famous and aiding growth.

In 1861 Victor Smith arrived as customs collector. He quickly angered local citizens by recommending that the customs house be moved fifty miles west to a spot now known as Port Angeles. Smith had investments in the Port Angeles location. The customs house was moved. Port Townsend rallied to defend itself and battled Smith, who tried to seize records with a gunboat. He was indicted for embezzlement and other crimes but found not guilty. Fired by President Lincoln personally, he somehow got reinstated in a similar position in Port Angeles. Smith was being investigated for a missing three million dollars when he drowned in a shipwreck off northern California.

His death did not end the rivalry between Port Angeles and Port Townsend. But the investigation and a flood that destroyed the Port Angeles customs house, killing two officials, resulted in the transfer of the port of entry back to Port Townsend.

The next expectations of city leaders centered around railroads. The dream of becoming the western terminus of a transcontinental line created a boom in the early 1870s, which quickly burst when Tacoma was selected.

Later, in 1890, the erection of an iron smelter nearby and plans of the Oregon Improvement Company to build tracks north from Portland caused the greatest growth the town ever knew. Prosperity seemed assured. Population soared to seven thousand. Land prices skyrocketed. Brick business buildings lined downtown streets and Victorian mansions were built on the hill. Then the Oregon Improvement Company suddenly collapsed, destroying Port Townsend's hopes. The nationwide depression of 1893 sealed its defeat.

This time it was for good. The small lumber mills in the region were cutting back or disappearing. Sailing ships gave way to steamboats that did not need to stop on their way to Seattle or Tacoma. These towns overtook Port Townsend in prominence. In 1913 the customs house was moved to Seattle. Neither location, nor the customs house, nor the timber, nor the energy of its leaders was enough to save Port Townsend. It faded to become a gentle, well-preserved reminder of cities that dream of becoming a metropolis but fail.

## WALLA WALLA

Eastern Washington was settled later and more slowly than western Washington. Most emigrants who journeyed west were looking for green valleys and ample rainfall such as they had known in the places they left behind. Few knew how to use the treeless hills and deserts east of the Cascade Mountains.

The Indian wars after the Whitman killings virtually stopped white settlement in eastern

This early pioneer cabin at Walla Walla was the home of Ransom and Lettice Clark, 1855.

Washington. But most fighting ended as tribes were placed on reservations. On October 29, 1858, the United States Army officially declared that peace was restored and that lands were open to white settlement. An army fort had been established upriver from the old Walla Walla trading post and six miles east of the Whitman mission site. Soon cabins appeared near this fort and along the valley that led to it.

Since the Whitman deaths, a few whites had settled in the Walla Walla Valley. Several retired fur traders took claims under the Oregon Donation Land Act. So had Ransom and Lettice Clark. In 1855 they were building a cabin in the valley when the Indian-white conflict forced them back to the Willamette, where Ransom died. Lettice returned in 1859 to the original claim, and, with a new husband, Almos Reynolds, became one of the first permanent settlers in the valley.

The town of Walla Walla grew up in the center of the large valley. Most settlers intended to raise crops or livestock and were not concerned about creating a town. But a community clustered around the fort. Streets were laid out, and houses and stores were built. Walla Walla expanded to become the real center of valley activities with a surrounding area of dependent farms. It was also a major stopping point on a well-traveled route between the Columbia and Snake Rivers.

The town was platted and lots sold; a grist mill began operations; the post office was established; churches and schools opened; and, in 1861, the area's first newspaper began publishing. Stagecoach and freight lines developed. An army crew directed by Lieutenant John Mullan constructed a military road to connect Walla Walla with Fort Benton on the Missouri River; this new route ultimately brought more settlers across the mountains.

In 1859 Walla Walla was incorporated and became the seat of a large county embracing much of eastern Washington. The next year

A procession of carts pulled by a steam-powered tractor winds through downtown Walla Walla, about 1890.

close to 1,400 people were living in this valley, which only two years earlier had been almost empty of whites.

In the summer of 1860 gold discoveries on the Nez Perce Reservation created a rush to the nearby Idaho hills. A series of gold strikes forced Walla Walla to meet both the normal demands of a growing town and its new role outfitting prospectors heading to the gold fields. One visitor observed that "the dirty streets were crowded with freighting wagons and teams and pack animals and a considerable army of rough men."

The gold-field route became notorious for bands of criminals, epitomized by the Henry Plummer gang, who waylaid stagecoaches and robbed victims. Lawlessness and conflicts over land rights and property lines led citizens to create a vigilante force to protect themselves.

Walla Walla continued to develop as the regional center of transportation and service facilities connected to Portland, Oregon. A fire in 1865 destroyed much of the town, which was later rebuilt with sturdier buildings. A local promoter, Dr. Dorsey S. Baker, started a short-line steam railroad to connect the city with the bend in the Columbia River and other transportation routes. When he ran out of money, the city completed the line. Throughout the 1870s Walla Walla was the largest city in Washington.

An even more significant change was occurring on its outskirts. Farmers who believed that only green valleys could produce crops were discouraged by the long, harsh winters in the region. Stock raising brought little success. No one had yet learned how to use the treeless, rounded hills that stretched in all directions. Then, in the 1870s, farmers discovered that grains, particularly wheat, could thrive on dry hillsides. Overnight the nature of farming changed. Wheat, raised without irrigation and shipped by river and the new railroad to Portland, opened a new era of eastern Washington farming. The region and the city prospered with a crop that original settlers had not known they could raise.

There had been changes, setbacks, and then steady growth since Marcus Whitman had selected the valley for his mission. Forty years later, Walla Walla was the center of a large inland farming and transportation area.

## The Five Settlements

Seattle, Oysterville, Centralia, Port Townsend, and Walla Walla were neither the only nor the most important early settlements. Communities also developed at Fort Vancouver, Tumwater, Olympia, and Steilacoom, at various mill sites around Puget Sound, and elsewhere. Differences made each of the five featured here unique, but the communities also shared some characteristics that aided their growth.

Each location had clear advantages, although the Seattle pioneers quickly moved from their original site at Alki to a better one. Usually the location involved a good harbor or river landing that enabled successful water transportation. Each place had natural resources that were apparent or could be developed: timber, fish, oysters, wheat, or other crops.

Each town had individuals with the ability, energy, know-how, and foresight to spearhead development—to lay out streets, plat blocks, open businesses, construct buildings, and attract settlers. Each town established the necessities that would draw newcomers and serve a surrounding area. Thus, stores, schools, churches, newspapers, trading houses, piers, and government buildings seemed to appear overnight.

All five towns sought institutions that would ensure permanence, such as the county seat, the university, or the railroad terminus. Intense rivalries with neighboring communities were typical. Several towns bore disasters from fire, severe weather, or the loss of an expected source of income or an eagerly anticipated railroad stop. Often the townspeople recouped their losses and built a stronger community. Several pioneers took advantage of events and markets some distance away, such as the mining strikes in California, the Fraser Valley, the Idaho hills, and later the Yukon.

Of the five settlements, Seattle became the metropolis of the entire Northwest. Oysterville became a ghost town. The fate of the other three has been less dramatic, but all are well-established communities serving their surrounding areas.

## Chapter 5 Review

I. Identify the following people. Tell why each is important in the settlement of Washington State.

Ezra Meeker
David Denny
Arthur Denny
Henry Yesler
David ("Doc") Maynard
George Washington
Robert H. Espy
Nahcati
Alfred Plummer
Francis Pettygrove
Lettice Clark
Dorsey S. Baker

II. Define the following words and terms. Relate each one to Washington State.

Manifest Destiny
The Great Migration
Emigrants
Overlanders
Oregon Donation Land Act
*Oregonian, and Indians' Advocate*
Conestogas
Cholera

The *Exact*
Skid road
Platting
U.S. customs house
Transcontinental railroad
Metropolis

**III.** Each question below should call your attention to factual information in the chapter. Try to answer each one. Then look back in the reading to check your answers, correct your understanding, and find answers you do not know.

1. The introduction states that Ezra Meeker "will become the extraordinary old pioneer." What does this mean?

2. What were five major accomplishments of Ezra Meeker during his lifetime?

3. List four characteristics of the United States during the early 1840s. Why was this a time when expansion to the west might be expected to take place?

4. List five reasons why individuals might wish to move to the Oregon Country.

5. How did emigrants learn about how to travel west?

6. What did emigrants do in the towns that were the "taking off places" for Oregon?

7. What changes in geography, vegetation, and climate did travelers find along the Oregon Trail?

8. What dangers and irritations did the travelers find along the trail? What were some of the pleasures?

9. The chapter says that "people traveling together formed communities on the move." Explain what this means.

10. In what ways was Seattle similar to other small settlements in the early days of the Pacific Northwest? Why do you think Seattle grew to become the largest city in the region?

11. What characteristics made George Washington of Centralia a successful town father?

12. What caused Oysterville to grow and then to decline?

13. How did geography affect the growth of Port Townsend? Why did the city decline?

14. What slowed the early growth of Walla Walla? What circumstances helped it to grow?

**IV.** Do some of these suggested activities:

1. Draw a map of the Oregon Trail. Show, by sketches or symbols, the geography and landmarks along the way.

2. Sketch a wagon prepared for the journey along the Oregon Trail. Show some of the equipment and supplies that might be included.

3. Make a chart including the five communities discussed in this chapter. For each, answer the following questions:

a. What is the location of the community in the state of Washington? What are the special geographical features associated with it?

b. Who were the first settlers?

c. Why did the settlers select that particular site to build a town?

d. What major events affected or changed the community?

e. What became of this place in later years?

4. Study the picture on page 88. Make a list of all the items you see in that picture. Then divide the items into three lists: (1) those that were absolutely essential, (2) those that were quite necessary, and (3) those that the pioneers could do without.

**The scene at Olympia on November 18, 1889, as Elisha P. Ferry was inaugurated the first governor of the state of Washington**

# Chapter 6  From Tribal Lands to Statehood

Olympia, Washington Territory, November 11, 1889. Late in the afternoon, a telegram arrives at this tiny mill town on Puget Sound that serves as the capital of Washington Territory. The message is delivered to a small, white frame building where the territorial legislature is in session. It is read to the members: just a few hours ago in Washington, D.C., President Benjamin Harrison signed the bill creating the state of Washington.

Washington is now a full-fledged state of the Union!

A boisterous cheer rings through the assembly hall. As word spreads, ships in the harbor blow whistles and an evening torchlight parade winds through town. A cannon fires a forty-two-gun salute honoring Washington as the forty-second state. During the next few days, similar celebrations are held in other towns across the new state.

These events are the result of a long effort to achieve statehood. Months earlier Washington voters had sent delegates to a convention that proposed a state constitution outlining a plan of government. In a later election voters approved that constitution and chose Elisha P. Ferry, a former territorial governor, as the first state governor.

In Washington, D.C., Congress joined Washington's bid for statehood with those from Montana, North Dakota, and South Dakota, creating an "omnibus bill," which brought the four states into the Union together. The bill had passed both houses of Congress and was sent to President Harrison. He signed with a pen made of gold from Washington, making the action complete.

This day in 1889 symbolizes important changes that have taken place in this far western corner of the United States over many years. For centuries the region was the home of numerous communities of Native Americans who lived in the midst of abundant seafood, small game, berries, and trees. About one hundred years before statehood, Europeans and Americans arrived on the scene. First they explored the coastal waters and then the river valleys. Finally, they came to settle permanently on farms and to start small towns that are sprinkled about the new state.

In the century to follow, the growth will be almost overwhelming. The population will become fourteen times as large, great urban centers will develop, new products and industries will build a strong economy. One can but wonder what vision of the future passes through the minds of even the most farseeing participants in today's celebration of admission.

# The Road to Statehood

As more and more settlers moved into the Pacific Northwest, the informal government of the early days had to change. Within less than a hundred years different nations had occupied, claimed, quarreled over, and governed parts of the region. The Indian civilizations were first. Then came expanding European and North American nations, particularly Great Britain and the United States.

In 1848 Washington became part of Oregon Territory, five years later a territory in its own right, and, finally, a state. In turn, the nation sought agreements with the original occupants—the Indians.

## The Original Inhabitants

The Northwest Indians who occupied the region for centuries never formed a single, formally organized group. No confederation of tribes existed here as in some other areas. In fact, the term "tribe" does not accurately describe the groupings of Native Americans in the Northwest. Rather, there were numerous villages occupied by people who shared family ties. Clusters of language groups created cultural ties between communities, but there were no formal governments or political alliances.

The idea that nations owned territory was virtually unknown to the Indians. Kinship groups inherited rights to certain places like fishing spots and berry patches. Using these locations without permission was a serious offense, but land was not bought and sold. Neither did Indians know national borders. Even after a battle, the victors did not take the land of the losers. Raiding parties sometimes swooped down from the northern coast to vandalize villages, capture slaves, or carry off possessions, but the raiders did not keep the land.

Thus the Indians handled land quite differently than whites would. When immigrants from Europe arrived, disputes arose over who owned which piece of land, where boundaries should be drawn, and whose rules would govern the use of land.

## Four Nations, Take Away Two

By 1800 four nations were interested in the Pacific Northwest. Spain was moving north from its long-held colonies in Mexico and South America. Russia was looking south from fur-trading posts in Alaska. England was moving in from trading centers on the Pacific and around the world, and the United States was also interested in trade and a possible water route through North America. Each country established claims to the Pacific Northwest based upon exploration, trade, military occupation, settlement, and formal decree.

The claim that one nation makes upon unoccupied territories may appear to others to be unfounded or it may carry much weight. A claim may be a simple statement by a nation's explorers or leaders that their country has determined to take the land. It might appear in official documents or on maps. It might be expressed in formal agreements or in treaties between nations.

Claims are often based on the earliest discovery or the most significant exploration. Was the claim of Robert Gray, the American who discovered the Columbia River but did little to explore it, stronger or weaker than that of William Broughton of England, who sailed farther upriver and charted the river? Certain locations are especially advantageous in establishing claims. A claim at the mouth of a river usually covers all territories that drain into it, but selecting a point or headland along the coast gives only limited or vague claims to the region.

Occupation or settlement of an area usually provides a strong claim because it represents a possession that other nations must recognize. The large number of Americans living in the Willamette Valley by the 1840s probably assured that the United States would possess the region south of the Columbia River, despite early, strong claims by England.

How strongly a nation pursues its claim to an area depends upon a number of things: how that country intends to use it; political attitudes in the home country toward expansion; the willingness to enter war or seek peace; the concerns that country has in other parts of the world.

Although disputes over territory may lead to war, many are settled by formal agreements or treaties negotiated by a nation's representatives and agreed to by government leaders. In many countries a strong ruler can make a decision by himself. The United States and England, on the other hand, have representative forms of government; their treaties must be ratified or approved by a legislative body, such as the U.S. Senate or the British Parliament.

The idea and the meaning of land claims should be kept in mind while we consider the actions of countries in the Pacific Northwest.

## THE EARLIEST DISPUTES

The first dispute between European nations affecting the Northwest Coast was the Nootka Sound controversy between Spain and England. Both nations wished to retain rights in the region, but they realized that sole possession was not worth a fight. They avoided controversies for several years after the Nootka agreement.

Spain had little interest in the northern fur trade and concentrated on its older possessions in the Southwest and California. There Spaniards built missions and permitted ranching, trading, and other activities in line with Spanish culture. In 1819, Spain gave up any claims to the Pacific Coast north of the 42nd parallel.

Meanwhile, Russia was interested in the Far North. In 1799, the Russian-American Company,

a fur-trading outfit, established headquarters at Sitka, Alaska. Several colonies were set up elsewhere, including Fort Ross in northern California. As American interests in the area increased, Secretary of State John Quincy Adams strongly protested Russia's growing involvement. In an 1824 treaty, Russia gave up all rights to lands south of the 54°40' parallel, the present southern boundary of the Alaska coastal strip.

Both Spain and Russia eventually sold or lost all their possessions in North America. When Mexico won independence from Spain in 1820, the area south of the 42nd parallel and west of the Rocky Mountains became Mexican. The United States acquired most of the present southwestern states in 1848 following the war with Mexico and by the Gadsden Purchase five years later. Russia left North America when it sold Alaska to the United States in 1867. In time all of these areas became states.

## JOINT OCCUPATION

After Spain and Russia left the Pacific Northwest, both the United States and England claimed the region known as the Oregon Country. The Pacific Ocean was on the west. The southern boundary was the 42nd parallel, which today divides Oregon and Idaho from California, Nevada, and western Utah. On the east was the crest of the Rocky Mountains, a border of the United States since the Louisiana Purchase in 1803. The northern boundary of the Oregon Country was the 54°40' parallel stretching from the Rockies to the coast.

Put another way, the Oregon Country was a large rectangle of about 450,000 square miles. It included the present states of Washington, Oregon, and Idaho, portions of present-day western Montana and Wyoming, and southern British Columbia.

The United States and England had become relatively friendly after the War of 1812. In

Oregon City, 1857, the first white settlement
on the Willamette River

1818 they agreed to occupy this expanse of land together in a peaceful, cooperative manner.

The two countries agreed that citizens of each could settle in the Oregon Country. Land and water routes would be "free and open . . . to the vessels, citizens and subjects of the two powers." The countries would share Oregon without giving up their claims, although they realized that a further division of the area was likely. This arrangement became known as joint occupation. Later they agreed that either nation could end it with one year's notice.

Joint occupation continued successfully for about thirty years. Occasional discussions about dividing Oregon did not become serious until the early 1840s.

During joint occupation, Dr. John McLoughlin of England's Hudson's Bay Company ran most governmental affairs from Fort Vancouver. At first Americans accepted his power, but the area gradually changed. British and American fur traders and American missionaries established posts. American settlements began to appear. National politicians such as Representative John Floyd of Virginia and Senators Thomas Hart Benton and Lewis Linn of Missouri urged the United States to assume authority over the area and its people. Exploring parties, including those led by U.S. Navy Lieutenant Charles Wilkes and by Senator Benton's son-in-law, John Charles Frémont, increased American interest in the entire West.

As the American people became familiar with the Oregon Country, many wanted it to become entirely American.

Fur trader Joe Meek, who became a prominent settler in Oregon

## Local Government

Except for John McLoughlin, there was no clear authority in Oregon. Left to themselves, people in such isolated areas frequently create informal governments to run their communities. In the Willamette Valley a small, growing American settlement had developed around the mission of Jason Lee.

There were no major problems until Ewing Young, a mountain man turned settler, died in 1841. Young had become wealthy, but he left no will and no heirs. There were no courts to deal with his estate. Forced to act, the settlers developed a system to handle the estate, to pay for local improvements, and to set up a court system to meet future problems.

Jason Lee hoped these efforts would lead to a complete local government, but other settlers did not agree. A year or so later, another effort at starting a government was made by Dr. Elijah White, a former settler who had become a Bureau of Indian Affairs agent. He failed to gain the con-fidence of other settlers, and his efforts were not successful.

Another problem that required the settlers to take action concerned the packs of wolves that damaged livestock and crops. At two "wolf meetings," settlers organized patrols and established a tax to provide bounties on the wolves. As such meetings became routine and more settlers trickled into the valley, the need for laws and a way to handle emergencies increased.

Thus, at the tiny settlement of Champoeg, on a fertile bend of the Willamette River, settlers met in 1843 to plan a government. Disagreements between Americans, former Hudson's Bay Company employees, and French Canadians almost destroyed the effort. Then, according to a legend that may have some truth in it, the old fur trader Joe Meek stepped forward. He drew a line on the ground and called upon each person to cross over it with him and support the government. Enough joined Meek to ensure that a government would be established.

Following a big Fourth of July celebration in 1843, delegates assembled to create the first real government in the Oregon Country. They set up a lawmaking body and a system of courts. Nevertheless, funds to support the new government's needs were only given voluntarily.

This government affected only American settlers; those loyal to England did not originally fall under its provisions. Few Americans lived north of the Columbia River, so it essentially covered only the Willamette Valley. The establishing of government in the Pacific Northwest demonstrates how people supply rules and order where none exist. Here, as in other developing regions, settlers came first and government followed.

The new government was provisional. That is, it was to last only until a permanent government could be set up. By the middle 1840s, conditions in Oregon and in the United States as a whole were changing so as to ensure that this time would soon come.

## The Oregon Treaty

The year 1844 was a presidential election year in the United States. Many Americans wanted the country to acquire more land, and that became a major election issue.

James Knox Polk was one of several Democratic candidates. Born in North Carolina, he had moved west to Tennessee and in 1825 represented that state in Congress, becoming Speaker of the House of Representatives. Hoping to gain support from the extreme expansionists in his party, Polk promised to try to acquire Texas, the Southwest, and Oregon, if elected. Texas, recently separated from Mexico, was then independent, and Mexico still controlled everything west of it to the ocean. As for Oregon, Polk wanted to end joint occupation with England. He believed that the United States should acquire all of the Oregon Country north to the Russian border of 54°40'. The slogan "Fifty-four forty or fight!" became the cry.

Polk was elected, assuring that the United States would seek to acquire these western regions.

Congress brought Texas into the United States in 1845, and a war with Mexico helped secure the Southwest by 1848. Negotiations with England over Oregon got underway, but the 54°40' boundary threat was ignored. The northern portion of the territory seemed likely to become English and the southern part American. The British wanted to divide along the Columbia River, while Americans argued for the 49th parallel. A Columbia River boundary would have made present-day western Washington British property.

The Hudson's Bay Company was moving its headquarters from Fort Vancouver to Fort Victoria on the southern tip of Vancouver Island. Although well north of American settlements in the Willamette Valley, this was south of the 49th parallel. Despite war threats and objections from the Hudson's Bay Company, the problem was settled by negotiators in 1846. They set the boundary along the 49th parallel from the Rocky Mountains to the center of the main channel that separated Vancouver Island from the mainland. Then it curved south and through the Strait of Juan de Fuca to the Pacific. The Hudson's Bay Company could continue to use the Columbia River and other natural transportation routes. They eventually received payment for the properties they lost.

### THE PIG WAR

But what was the main channel between Vancouver Island and the mainland? Was it Haro Strait or Rosario Strait? Confusion lingered for a quarter of a century. Both American and British troops established posts on San Juan Island, which lay between the disputed waterways. Normally the opposing soldiers got along well with one another.

Then one day in 1859 a pig owned by a British soldier wandered onto the farm of Lyman Cutler, an American settler. Cutler shot and killed the pig. A minor dispute arose over how much he should pay for killing the animal. Both nations claimed the island, citing the border settlement. Each fortified military bases a few miles apart on San Juan Island. The dispute between England and the United States continued for thirteen years, until the German emperor arbitrated a settlement in 1872 that favored the Americans.

Haro Strait to the west of the San Juan Islands became the dividing channel and the island group was recognized as American. The Hudson's Bay Company received payment for its property in the islands. The "Pig War" settlement completed the boundary between American and British or Canadian territories all across the continent. With no military fortifications, this border has remained remarkably free of disputes for well over a century.

## Oregon Territory

A more permanent government became necessary for the American portion of the Oregon Country. Sixty years earlier, soon after the American Revolution, Congress had set up the Northwest Ordinances to handle thinly populated possessions. The laws established a "territory" in which the federal government and local residents shared governing.

"Territory" has a specific meaning, just like "state" or "county." In a territory, laws were passed by a legislature elected by resident citizens. Laws had to be approved by a governor who was appointed by the president of the United States. Judges were appointed by the president. Local governments, such as counties and cities, chose their own officials. The territory sent a delegate to the national Congress who could speak on issues but not vote. After more settlers filled in a territory, it could apply to enter the union as a full state.

On April 14, 1848, President Polk signed a bill

creating Oregon Territory. A year later Joseph Lane arrived as the first territorial governor. The job had first been offered to an Illinois lawyer named Abraham Lincoln, but he declined. The sparsely settled area north and west of the Columbia River and south of the 49th parallel was divided into two counties, Lewis and Clark (mistakenly spelled Clarke). Clackamas County to the east included today's eastern Washington and other nearby regions.

## Washington Territory

When the United States acquired Oregon, almost all Americans there lived in the Willamette Valley south of the Columbia. The Hudson's Bay Company had discouraged Americans from moving north where many former company employees were scattered. In 1844 a few Americans lived on the north bank of the Columbia near the present town of Washougal. The next year two groups headed north toward Puget Sound. Joseph R. Jackson remained in the Cowlitz Valley, while the Kentuckian Michael T. Simmons and the mulatto George Bush led several families to start the town of Tumwater near the Sound.

More Americans moved north in the next few years. Yet, territorial marshal Joe Meek counted only 304 people above the river in 1849. The official census of 1850 set the number at 1,049.

In the early 1850s population climbed and new communities were established. These settlers soon complained that they lacked full participation in Oregon government. Several meetings, one of them in Jackson's home, led to a convention at the tiny settlement of Monticello, where Longview is located today. Most towns in the area sent delegates.

The Monticello convention met on November 25, 1852. Delegates listed and discussed reasons why they desired their own territory separate from Oregon. They argued that Oregon Territory was too large for a future state, and that the long

Michael T. Simmons, Indian agent and pioneer settler on Puget Sound

former governor Joseph Lane, who had become the delegate to Congress. A bill was introduced to create a new territory. Its boundary would follow the Columbia River from the ocean to its bend and then the 46th parallel to the Rockies; this included part of present-day Idaho.

The name proposed for the territory was Columbia. This was changed to Washington because, oddly enough, some Congressmen feared it would be confused with the District of Columbia.

The bill easily passed Congress and was signed by President Millard Fillmore on March 2, 1853. Washington was a territory for thirty-six years until it became a state in 1889.

During these years, boundary lines in the eastern part were juggled several times. One effort would have placed the Walla Walla Valley in Oregon because most transportation routes through the valley headed toward Portland. Another proposal was to make much of eastern Washington a separate territory or state. When Oregon became a state in 1859, its eastern border was fixed along the Snake River and the 117th west meridian. Washington Territory became a wide, upside down L that included present-day Idaho and part of Montana. Disagreements about the eastern portion continued, especially after mining rushes attracted prospectors into Idaho.

In 1863 Idaho Territory was created, briefly including part of present-day Montana. When Montana Territory was formed the next year, Oregon, Washington, Idaho, and Montana acquired much the same locations and shapes that they have today.

### ISAAC INGALLS STEVENS

Isaac Ingalls Stevens, the first territorial governor of Washington, held that position for four years. As a child, he worked on a farm and in New England mills, but Stevens had a quick, mathematical mind and great ambition. He graduated

coastline should be divided. They complained that slow travel conditions prevented northerners from taking a real part in the territorial government and that Willamette Valley settlers received more than their share of federal money and other advantages.

A memorandum to Congress in Washington, D.C., expressed these views. It was supported by

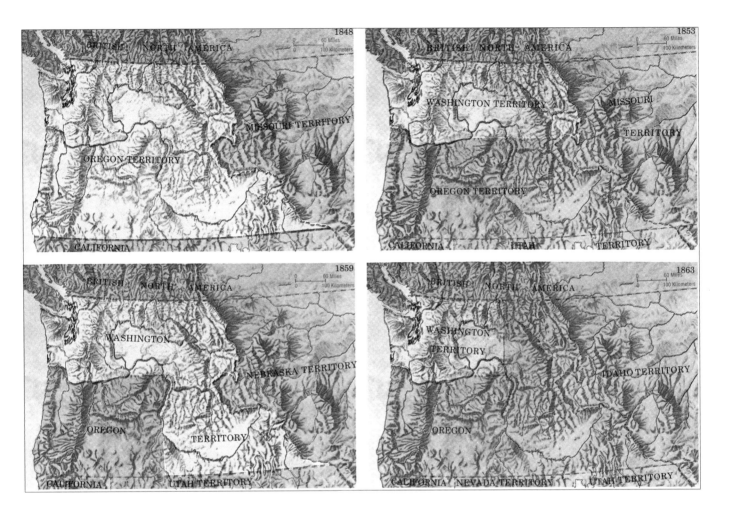

The evolution of Washington Territory. The 1863 territorial boundaries became the boundaries of the state in 1889. (From the *Historical Atlas of Washington*, by James W. Scott and Roland L. DeLorme, 1986.)

from the U.S. military academy at West Point first in his class and became a talented engineer. After serving in the Mexican War of 1846–48, he helped with the 1852 presidential campaign of an old classmate, Franklin Pierce. President Pierce rewarded him with the appointment as governor of Washington Territory.

Besides being governor, Stevens was assigned other duties. One was to survey a possible railroad route from the Great Lakes through the Cascade Mountains to Puget Sound. He did this on his journey west. Stevens arrived, rain soaked

and hungry, a day early in Olympia, the village that was the territorial capital. As the story goes, the townspeople were so busy preparing for the arrival of the governor that they ignored the bedraggled newcomer. He entered the most desirable eating place in town and drank a cup of soup in the kitchen. When he learned the reasons for so much activity, he surprised his hosts by telling them that he was the person they were awaiting.

Stevens quickly became known. Just as the first person in any new job sets standards and methods for doing things, he established the role of governor. He had loyal supporters among white newcomers anxious to develop the land. But he also made strong enemies among pioneer settlers and military leaders.

Bearing a large head on a small frame and saddled with the effects of a miserable childhood, Stevens developed a drive to overcome personal problems. He appeared arrogant, unswerving, and hungry for publicity. Great problems arose from another of his assignments; he was to negotiate treaties with Indians of the territory, calm them, and place them on reservations.

## Indian Treaties

Over these years, the American government had paid little attention to those people who actually lived on the land, the Indians. American policies toward Indians had never been consistent. At times they were regarded as primitive people to be wiped out; at times they were treated as foreign nations; at times American policy threatened to remove them to distant regions that white settlers found unattractive.

When Washington became a territory, government policy was to negotiate treaties that would place Indians on reservations, promising them certain rights and help if they gave up their land. Stevens was instructed to make such treaties with the Indians. Oregon governor Joel Palmer had a similar task, and the two men sometimes worked together negotiating treaties between 1854 and 1856.

They would meet with representatives from all tribes in an area, offer gifts and promise protection, and assign land where the Indians could live as they wished but under United States guidance. Stevens chose reservation sites with access to salmon fishing but did not include the prime farmland the settlers wanted. Negotiators hoped that tribal representatives would be satisfied and willingly sacrifice their lands. Ameri-cans assumed that the treaties could be translated fairly in writing into Indian languages. They also assumed that leaders (many of whom were selected by Stevens rather than by the Indians) could speak for all native groups and that the Indians would accept reservations away from their traditional lands.

Such assumptions proved false. Treaty terms were not always clear. They required awkward, cumbersome translations into various native tongues that had no written form. Indian leaders could not make commitments for their people the way an American official could. And few Indians were content to give up lands where generations of their people had lived.

With high hopes, a flair for publicity, and a desire to prove his abilities, Stevens traveled about the territory. The meetings with Indian groups grew similar to one another. The governor's party included his Indian agent, an interpreter, and several local whites, usually persons already trusted by local Indians. Sometimes Stevens wore a pipe in his hatband as a symbol of peace. Indian representatives would camp at a selected spot for several days. One member from each tribal group was designated as chief, and the negotiations began.

Stevens came prepared with copies of a treaty. This stated that the Indians would give up certain lands in exchange for stated amounts of money and would agree to move to small, well-defined reservations. Here they would receive schooling and medical aid.

A clause prohibiting slavery was often included, because slavery was a long-standing practice among many tribes. Indians were not citizens and could not vote or serve on juries. Translations of treaties were oral, first into Chinook Jargon, and then into the language of each tribe. Despite many misunderstandings, one point was clear: the Indians would lose their lands.

## Chief Seattle's Speech

*When Governor Isaac Stevens arrived to make treaties with the Indians in the mid–Puget Sound area in 1854, his welcome was answered by a speech from an Indian chief named Sealth, or Seattle. Given in Duwamish, the speech was translated into English years later by a local white doctor. Parts of this version are given below.*

*"My words are like the stars that never set. What Seattle says[,] the Great White Chief at Washington can rely upon with as much certainty as our paleface brothers can rely upon the return of the seasons.*

*"The Great—and I presume—good White Chief sends us word that he wants to buy our lands but is willing to allow us to reserve enough to live on comfortably. This indeed appears generous, for the Red Man no longer has rights that he need respect, and the offer may be wise, also, for we are no longer in need of a great country.*

*"There was a time when our people covered the whole land as the waves of a wind-ruffled sea covers its shell-paved floor, but that time has long since passed away with the greatness of tribes now almost forgotten. I will not dwell on nor mourn over our untimely decay, nor reproach my paleface brothers with hastening it, for we, too, may have been somewhat to blame.*

*"Every part of this country is sacred to my people. Every hillside, every valley, every plain and grove has been hallowed by some fond memory or some sad experience of my tribe. Even the rocks, which seem to lie dumb as they swelter in the sun along the silent sea shore in solemn grandeur thrill with memories of past events connected with the lives of my people.*

*"The very dust under your feet responds more lovingly to our footsteps than to yours, because it is the ashes of our ancestors, and our bare feet are conscious of the sympathetic touch, for the soil is rich with the life of our kindred.*

*"The noble braves, fond mothers, glad, happy-hearted maidens, and even the little children, who lived and rejoiced here for a brief season, and whose very names are now forgotten, still love these somber solitudes....*

*"And when the last Red Man shall have perished from the earth and his memory among the white men shall have become a myth, these shores will swarm with the invisible dead of my tribe, and when your children's children shall think themselves alone in the fields, the store, the shop, upon the highway, or in the silence of the pathless woods, they will not be alone. In all the earth there is no place dedicated to solitude.*

*"At night, when the streets of your cities and villages will be silent and you think them deserted, they will throng with the returning hosts that once filled and still love this beautiful land.*

*"The white man will never be alone. Let him be just and deal kindly with my people, for the dead are not powerless."*

*From John M. Rich, Chief Seattle's Unanswered Challenge (Seattle, 1932). (In the early 1980s, a rewritten version of the speech, created for a television audience, was widely circulated in the United States and abroad. Although historically inaccurate, it presented in eloquent language a respect for the land that became popular among a generation of environmentalists.)*

*Left to right:* Isaac I. Stevens, first governor of Washington Territory and Indian treaty negotiator; Yakama chief Kamiakin, who opposed Governor Stevens's treaty proposals; Leschi, leader of the Nisqually Indians in their resistance to the white settlers

Indian spokesmen often responded with eloquent speeches about what losing ancient lands would mean to their people. Local whites tried to interpret the treaties to their Indian friends. Finally, the governor and the chiefs affixed signatures or marks.

Most treaty sessions lasted several days. Stevens first met with tribes from southern Puget Sound at Medicine Creek, near the delta of the Nisqually River. This treaty has become particularly significant in recent times because fishing rights granted to the tribes have led to controversies with non-Indian fishermen.

Treaties were also negotiated at Point Elliott in Mukilteo, at Point No Point, at Neah Bay, and at the Quinault River. Stevens negotiated similar treaties with various eastern Washington tribes at Walla Walla. The expanse of land and the wandering nature of these tribes made negotiations even more difficult. The southwestern and northeastern corners of the state were never covered by treaty.

Indians soon discovered that signing did not end the process of making treaties. The whites had to send each treaty to Washington, D.C., for approval by the president and the Senate. Indians could not understand the reasons for such delays. When they gave their word, they considered it final; when Hudson's Bay Company officials had given their word, it had been final. Americans operated in a different manner.

All of these Northwest treaties were later ratified by the United States Senate. Stevens boasted that 11,300 of the 15,000 Indians in his area were placed under treaties.

## Indian Wars

The treaties brought war instead of peace. Disgruntled, bitter Indian leaders knew that they had lost land and much of their way of life. They were never allowed to actually negotiate but were forced to accept conditions the whites laid upon them. Some conflict between natives and settlers was probably inevitable, but discoveries of gold in the Colville region assured war. Even as treaties were being negotiated, white mining parties started to cross land being promised to the Indians. Apparently agreements were meaningless if whites wanted land.

Members of several mining parties violated treaty provisions by crossing Yakama Indian lands on their way to the Colville diggings. Men were killed. An agent sent to investigate disappeared and was rumored to have been killed by the Yakamas. A militia of whites was formed to pursue the Indians, and eastern Washington tribes began to unite. The events grew into a real war waged at several points throughout the eastern region.

Near Puget Sound, Indians attacked several families living along the White River. They killed the adults and destroyed homes and fields. Several terrified children hid out, possibly aided by friendly Indians, and made their way to safety. The raiders disappeared into the forests and were never found.

In 1858 rumors spread that Seattle was about to be attacked. Townspeople fled to a hastily built blockhouse. Two whites were killed in a day of scattered fighting, which involved cannon fire from a U.S. destroyer. The next day the Indians were gone. Yet, fear haunted the people of Seattle, who never knew when danger threatened from the woods behind the city. Throughout most of eastern Washington and along Puget Sound, fears of possible raids and occasional militia marches were more common than actual encounters. Battles were few. On both sides this was a war in which non-combatants were the losers.

## POLITICAL DISPUTES AMONG WHITES

Governor Stevens declared martial law in Pierce County. Six settlers who stayed on their farms with their Indian wives instead of joining the war were arrested. Only military courts were allowed under martial law. When Territorial Supreme Court Justice Edward Lander opened his civilian courtroom for a hearing for the settlers, Stevens had him arrested at gunpoint. Later Lander held the governor in contempt of court. Lander eventually won the legal points, but Stevens gained popularity among white settlers.

Another conflict was Stevens's running dispute with General John Wool, head of the United States Army on the Pacific Coast. Wool accused the governor and settlers of complicating Indian problems that cooler heads could have prevented or solved. Wool believed that Indians should be contained on their reservations, while many settlers craved the natives' annihilation. He criticized citizens for rushing to form volunteer companies and fight. Stevens, who felt betrayed by the Indians who disliked his treaties, urged strong action and took military matters into his own hands. Thus, the two men, each backed by determined followers, waged a war of words, orders, and counter orders as intense as the fighting on any battlefront.

## THE BATTLEFRONT

There was also the case of Leschi, a Nisqually chief and an honored friend of many early white settlers. This strong, proud leader did not want trouble, but he refused to sign the Medicine Creek treaty. He left the meeting deeply upset and claimed that someone else had put the mark beside his name on the document. When the White River families were killed, Leschi was blamed, although he was probably a calming influence among his people. Suspected of leading the attack on Seattle, Leschi left his farm and became a hunted fugitive.

The search for Leschi was long and frustrating. He finally surrendered to Dr. William Tolmie of the Hudson's Bay Company post at Nisqually. Expecting consideration and leniency, he was sadly mistaken. A long trial ended in a hung jury

Okanogan women on the prairies of the Colville Reservation

when Ezra Meeker, a juror, denied that evidence was strong enough to convict.

At a second trial, Leschi was found guilty. Claiming innocence and unjust treatment, he went to the gallows exhibiting a pride that earned him respect. "I felt I was hanging an innocent man," the hangman said afterwards.

The obvious power of the whites and Leschi's death ended Indian wars on Puget Sound. In eastern Washington, action lasted longer and was more violent. Two major battles occurred. In 1858, a strong force of Spokane and Coeur d'Alene Indians defeated Colonel E. J. Steptoe in the Palouse country, although his troops retreated to safety. The United States then organized two punitive forces. One traveled from the Yakima Valley up the Okanogan River but saw little action. The other, under Colonel George Wright,

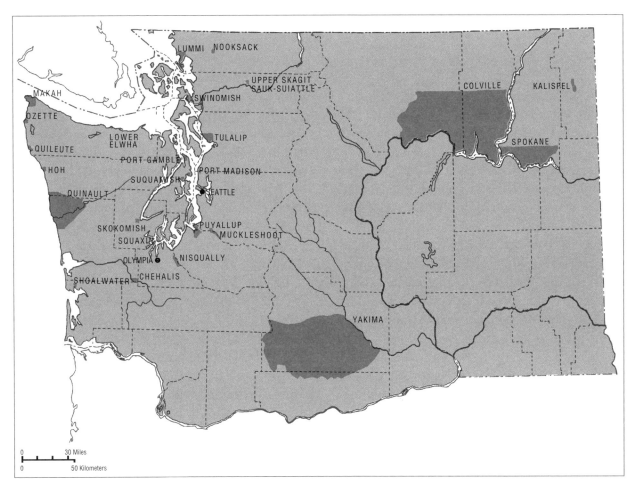

Indian reservations, 1980s

was large and well trained. They encountered several combined tribes on the plains outside Spokane.

Wright and his men won the skirmishes decisively. The troops turned east and cut a long swath through Indian lands, destroying homes and crops, killing horses, and hanging leaders captured along the route. It was a brutal and final ending to many months of war. As he reached his home post, Wright sent his superior a terse message: "The war is closed. Peace is restored to the Spokanes, Coeur d'Alenes, and Palouses."

The spirit of the Indians was broken. Most submitted to the inevitable and went off to reserva-

tions. Many had not even taken part in the wars. About 5,000 Indians around Puget Sound, who had been escorted to the Olympic Peninsula by Indian Agent Michael T. Simmons, remained out of the war. In the southeast, the large Nez Perce tribe stayed neutral until whites were allowed to settle on their land in violation of the treaty.

Disheartened, Nez Perce Chief Joseph led a band of his people on a dramatic retreat toward Canada. Captured just below the border, they were sent to Oklahoma, where many died; eventually they moved to the Colville Reservation in eastern Washington. As 1859 approached, the region that had belonged solely to native people seventy years earlier was clearly possessed by white Americans.

## Territorial Politics

After Isaac Stevens left the governor's office in 1857, he returned to the national capital as a territorial representative from Washington. In service as a general in the Civil War, he was killed leading a charge at Chantilly, Virginia, in 1862.

While Washington was a territory, its government was usually solidly run, secure, and conservative. Republican officials outnumbered Democrats. Political leaders were often businessmen or lawyers who wanted to help the state grow by expanding business. Legislators also worked to benefit their local communities.

Because the territorial governor was appointed by the president, the honor was often a political reward or a favor to a loyal supporter. Most of the early territorial governors came from eastern states and had little knowledge of or previous interest in Washington. One came mainly to escape an unhappy marriage; another never even showed up in Olympia. Later governors stayed on after serving their terms, and the last two were Washington residents when they were appointed.

## Washington Becomes a State

The process of creating a state involves several steps. Events begin when Congress passes an "enabling act." A state constitution needs to be drafted and approved by voters. Then Congress and the president accept the new state into the union. As the nineteenth century wound down, people in Washington desired statehood. They believed it would permit greater self-government and more local control of funds than were possible for a territory. The Washington legislature regularly asked Congress to grant statehood. In 1878 a convention proposed a state constitution,

which was approved by voters but failed to pass in Congress.

There were several reasons for the delays. Some people believed that the Walla Walla Valley should be separated from Washington and added to Oregon. Indeed, Walla Walla's transportation routes and products went down the Columbia River to Portland and the valley had closer ties with eastern Oregon than with western Washington. Another concern was whether the northern Idaho "panhandle" should remain with Idaho or join either Washington or Montana. Territorial boundaries could be adjusted easily, but once state borders are determined, they become fixed.

When Washington became a territory in 1853 there were 3,965 people. The population doubled several times but not until the 1880s did it reach 125,000. This was a figure considered desirable for statehood, although Oregon and other states had been admitted with fewer persons.

During most of this time Democrats had enough power in Congress to block actions that might be to their disadvantage. Because it seemed likely that Washington as a state would elect Republican officials and send Republicans to Congress, many Democrats opposed statehood. In 1888, however, Republicans won control of both Congress and the presidency. An "enabling" act permitted Washington, Montana, North Dakota, and South Dakota to hold conventions, draft state constitutions, and elect possible officials.

Things happened quickly in Washington. A convention met in Olympia with delegates coming from towns and counties throughout the territory. They approved a long, generally farsighted state constitution and decided Olympia should remain the capital instead of Ellensburg, Yakima, or other challengers. The voters approved this constitution at a special election and elected state officials.

These events received approval from Congress. When President Benjamin Harrison signed the proclamation admitting Washington as a state on November 11, 1889, thirty-six years of territorial government ended. Washington, with 173,181 people, was a state, the forty-second to enter the union. It was about to direct its own future.

For the first state governor, Washington voters chose between two former territorial governors, Democrat Eugene P. Semple and Republican Elisha P. Ferry. Ferry, a Seattle lawyer and banker who had served two terms as territorial governor in the 1870s, was elected. He was inaugurated on a gusty, rainy day a week after statehood was proclaimed.

The first state officials, including members of the legislature and those appointed by Governor Ferry, had to begin a state government where none had existed before. They passed laws to help the state operate. They established agencies to deal with fisheries, geology, and taxation.

Cities and counties made many proposals for "pork barrel" legislation, that is, laws to benefit their own localities.

Olympia retained the capital; Cheney and Ellensburg got teacher training schools that have become universities; Pullman, the agricultural college, which received federal funds; Chehalis, a reform school; Tacoma, the state museum; Medical Lake, a state hospital; and Walla Walla, the state penitentiary.

A century earlier, the area of Washington had been virtually unknown to most of the world. It was inhabited by Indians living in numerous villages and about to be claimed by several nations. The transition to statehood involved claims, proclamations, treaties, negotiations, wars, constitutions, and laws. Such activities demonstrate the way people direct events in changing conditions.

## Governor Ferry's Inaugural Address

On November 18, 1889, Elisha P. Ferry was sworn in as the first governor of Washington State, just days after the Territory had been admitted to the Union. A portion of his inaugural address follows:

"The substitution of a State Government for that of the Territory imposes upon the citizens of Washington more solemn duties and graver responsibilities than those to which they have been accustomed. Hitherto the powers of our Legislature to enact laws have been limited and restricted by the organic act and the amendments thereto, and by the various laws that have been passed by Congress relating to the territories. Further than this, Congress reserved the right to annul any law passed by the Territorial Legislature which seemed to be unwise or injudicious. We had no voice in selecting our Executive and Judicial officers and none in directing the course of the National Government. Hereafter all will be changed. The powers of our Legislature will be limited only by the Constitution of the United States and that of the State of Washington. Our citizens will be on an equality with those of any other State of the Union, and their wishes will have due weight in determining the policy of the National Government. We should, therefore, exercise a conscientious endeavor to bear well these new responsibilities and discharge faithfully the new duties which are ours, and prove ourselves worthy of the rights which we have secured. Let greater wisdom accompany the greater power that we now possess. Let us discharge the additional duties devolving upon us in a manner that will redound to our credit; advance the welfare and prosperity of our State and add importance and strength to the National Union."

From Readings in Pacific Northwest History: Washington, 1790–1895, Charles Gates, ed. (Seattle, 1941)

## Chapter 6 Review

**I.** Identify the following people. Tell why each is important to Washington State.

Elisha P. Ferry
Thomas Hart Benton
John McLoughlin
Elijah White
James Knox Polk
Joseph Lane
Joseph R. Jackson
Michael T. Simmons

George Bush
Isaac Ingalls Stevens
John Wool
Chief Leschi
E. J. Steptoe
George Wright
Chief Joseph

**II.** Define the following words and terms. Relate each one to Washington State.

Treaty
Joint occupation
Parallel
Oregon Country
Wolf meetings
Provisional government
"Fifty-four forty or fight!"
Pig War
Territory
Negotiators
Militia
Martial law
Enabling act
Pork barrel legislation

**III.** Locate these places on a map and tell why each is important in the history of the Pacific Northwest.

Champoeg
Colville
San Juan Island
White River
Haro Strait

Spokane
Monticello
Olympia
Medicine Creek

**IV.** Each question below should call your attention to factual information in the chapter. Try to answer each one. Then look back in the reading to check your answers, correct your understanding, and find answers you do not know.

1. How did Indians generally feel about boundaries and the ownership of land?

2. What four nations had strong claims to parts of the Pacific Northwest?

3. What part of the West was of most interest to Spain?

4. Which parallel became the northern boundary of Spanish possessions? Locate it on a map.

5. What area did Russia give up in the 1824 treaty with the United States?

6. Name the southern, eastern, northern, and western borders of the Oregon Country.

7. How did the death of Ewing Young cause people to take steps toward creating a local government?

8. Where did England want the dividing line to be between English possessions and the United States? Where did the United States want the dividing line to be?

9. What became the border in 1848? What part of the border was settled in the Pig War agreement?

10. Where did the first Americans who moved north of the Columbia River settle?

11. What occurred at Monticello on November 25, 1852?

12. What three duties did Isaac Stevens have when he came to Washington?

13. List three different attitudes that white Americans have held toward Indians.

14. What were the Indians required to do by the terms of the treaties negotiated by Governor Stevens?

15. What parts of Washington were never covered by an Indian treaty?

16. What event caused war to break out between Indians and whites in the 1850s?

17. What criticism did General John Wool make of citizens and of the governor?

18. Name the two major battles fought between Indians and whites in eastern Washington. Which was a victory for the Indians? Which was a victory for the whites?

19. What message did Colonel George Wright send out after his trip through eastern Washington?

20. Which political party tended to dominate Washington politics during the territorial years?

21. What boundary settlements had to be decided before Washington became a state?

22. When did Washington become a state?

23. List several important actions taken by the first state officials.

V. Think about, discuss, and answer the questions below.

1. Suppose that Spain or Russia or England had acquired the whole Pacific Northwest including what is now Washington. What are some ways that your life might be different today?

2. List the reasons why Spain, Russia, England, and the United States had claims to the Pacific Northwest. Then place a star alongside those claims that seem to be particularly strong. Place a minus sign alongside those that seem to be particularly weak. Discuss your reasons for marking these as you did.

3. Isaac Stevens was a very complex person whom you may wish to learn more about. What personal characteristics affected the way he felt about himself and the way he did his job? Discuss his methods of negotiating with the various Indian tribes. What things did he do well and what things poorly? How well did he understand the people he was dealing with? How well did they understand what he was doing?

4. Washington is the only state named for a president of the United States. What are the sources of names of other states? Was Washington an appropriate choice for the name of the state? What other names might you suggest? Explain the reasons for your suggestions.

5. The boundaries of Washington and Idaho changed several times because some settlers felt they were far away from the center of government. They felt they were being left out of important decisions. Can you think of similar situations that exist today? Was such a situation likely to be more or less important in the past than it is today? Why?

An amusement at the Alaska-Yukon-Pacific Exposition. Prince Albert, "the educated horse," was a popular attraction for young visitors.

Alaska-Yukon-Pacific Exposition grounds, Seattle, June 1, 1909. The skies are clear except for a slight June mist. Such weather can only brighten the excitement of the 80,000 people who will visit Seattle today. A military parade has wound through well-scrubbed and gaily decorated downtown streets. By noon, attention has moved here to the northeast edge of the city.

Sitting on a flag-draped platform in a grove of fir trees, a small group of dignitaries prepares to open the Alaska-Yukon-Pacific Exposition (AYP). Two stand out: J. E. Chilberg is president of the exposition and a onetime Alaska trader turned banker. He symbolizes the self-made leaders who have grown with this city of nearly a quarter million people. And James J. Hill, known as the "Empire Builder," is head of the Great Northern Railroad. This stocky and gruff capitalist is both loved and damned throughout the Northwest, where he wields great power.

Three thousand miles away, in the East Room of the White House, President William Howard Taft pushes a nugget of Alaska gold to send a telegraphic impulse across the continent and open the fair. A gong sounds. A huge American flag starts up a 240-foot pole of Douglas fir and drops a thousand tiny flags to the crowd below. Whistles and horns toot and blow. Bells ring all over town. The fair is open.

The fair will continue until mid-October. President Taft will come, as will three-time presidential candidate William Jennings Bryan, New York governor Charles Evans Hughes, and members of the imperial family of Japan. Auto manufacturer Henry Ford will greet winners of a cross-country auto race ending here. And over 3,700,000 lesser-known citizens will visit.

Fair goers will arrive in trolley cars, prowl exhibits, gamble on the Pay Streak, and marvel at the beauty of these fairgrounds in a forest. On clear days, Mount Rainier will loom behind artificial waterfalls and the Geyser Basin with its fountain spraying high in the air.

Visitors will stroll through the Forestry Building, a huge log cabin built of Northwest timber. They will view a scale model of a Newcastle coal mine, tour the Canadian building, and look at exhibits from Japan. They will watch Indi-

ans weave baskets and carve ivory, and meet Eskimos in fur parkas as well as native Filipinos. They will be fascinated by a reenactment of the battle between the Monitor and the Merrimac.

They will celebrate Seattle Day, Women Suffrage Day, Spokane Day, Canada Day, Minstrel Show Day, Brooklyn Day, Scandinavian Day, Portland Day, Elks Day, Minnesota Day, and a hundred other special days honoring groups and causes.

The AYP grew out of a simple plan to celebrate the tenth anniversary of the Yukon gold rush of 1896–97. In the minds of a newspaper editor and several businessmen, it mushroomed into a world's fair to publicize the continuing ties between Washington and the Far North. When planners added the theme of Seattle's trade with Pacific Rim countries, it became the Alaska-Yukon-Pacific Exposition.

Historian Edmund S. Meany suggested that the fair take place on the University of Washington campus. Ten years earlier, the school had moved from downtown Seattle to this barely touched woodland above Lake Washington. Holding a fair in a remote, forested area reached only by trolley cars seemed absurd to many, but the idea took root. No spot could offer greater natural beauty or more room. Furthermore, the fair's landscaped grounds and new buildings could later house a permanent, growing university.

Then came a delay. Norfolk, Virginia, was preparing a 1907 fair to honor the 300th anniversary of the founding of Jamestown, the first permanent British settlement in North America. Seattle agreed to wait. The extra two years assured more planning time and aroused greater enthusiasm. Thus small plans grew into a celebration of the role the Pacific Northwest played in the world. All aspects of the region's development went on display: the gold rush, trans-Pacific trade, the lumber industry, mining, railroads, the various groups of people who make up the Northwest.

The fair opening today shows how this city, this state, and the whole Northwest have grown in the past half century. This summer Seattle is saying to the world: "Look at us! This is what we are. And this is what we have done!"

## Years of Change

The Alaska-Yukon-Pacific Exposition climaxed four decades of exciting change in Washington. Growth was rapid and solid between 1870 and 1910. At the halfway point Washington changed from territory to state. Towns, industries, and patterns of settlement became well established. Older towns grew and new ones started. Growth continued after 1910 but at a slower pace.

In 1870 the population of Washington Territory, which had the same boundaries as the future state, was only 23,955; by 1910 it had jumped forty-seven times to 1,141,990. Put another way, 1,118,000 people arrived or were born there during these forty years. During the decade just before statehood, population increased over 375 percent, climbing from 75,116 to 357,232.

In 1870 Walla Walla, with 1,394 people, was the largest city, followed by Olympia with 1,203 and Seattle with 1,107. Tacoma's first spurt of growth was yet to occur, and Spokane had not even been founded! In the next forty years, Seattle moved ahead of other cities (237,194 people in 1910), Spokane became the second largest city (104,402), and Tacoma was third (83,743).

A map showing areas where people lived in 1910 would be shaped like a large U, thick from Puget Sound to the Columbia River, with an offshoot toward Grays Harbor, and then moving in a thin line along the Columbia River to Walla Walla and Spokane Counties. Central Washington had few people except for small centers near Wenatchee, Ellensburg, and Yakima.

By 1910 Washington was no longer predominantly rural. Over 53 percent of the people lived

The Court of Honor on the AYP grounds. The fountain remains a focal point of the University of Washington campus today.

in areas officially considered urban, that is, with 2,500 or more people. Despite farm areas and great expanses of forest and desert, Washington became urban before the nation as a whole; not until 1920 did over half of all Americans live in urban areas.

Between 1870 and 1910, the economic nature of Washington became fixed. The leading industries remained what they had long been: logging and lumbering, fishing, and mining. These are mainly extractive industries that take resources from the environment rather than manufacturing new products. As Washington grew, these industries changed from small, independent, locally owned mines and mills to involve large operations, heavy machinery, and big investments. Funds and leaders often came from outside the region.

Shipping continued to be important on Puget Sound, with most of eastern Washington using Columbia River routes to Portland. Wheat and other grains thrived in the Palouse hills and around Spokane; flour milling was important. Livestock—first cattle and then sheep—added to the rural economy. Some eastern Washington valleys became filled with fruit orchards after irrigation projects began in the early 1900s.

The 1910 residents of Washington were more diverse than earlier groups. In the 1870s a few wagon trains still came west, although railroads quickly replaced them. Railroad promotions and the need for unskilled workers attracted a broader group of Americans and many immigrants. Scandinavians and Finns arrived as did Eastern Europeans. Chinese who had been brought to do hard labor (such as railroad construction) stayed in Washington and became targets of racial violence.

Ethnic or national backgrounds were not the only differences. Long before 1910, clear differences divided several classes of people: workers and employers, farmers and industrialists, urban and rural residents. These differences became

## East Views West

When East Coast reporter Charles Nordhoff toured the West in 1873, he was not always enthusiastic about what he saw and heard:

"When, at Kalama, you enter Washington Territory, your ears begin to be assailed by the most barbarous names imaginable. On your way to Olympia by rail you cross a river called the Skookum-Chuck; your train stops at places named Newaukum, Tumwater, and Toutle; and if you seek further, you will hear of whole counties labeled Wahkiakum, or Snohomish, or Kitsar [Kitsap], or Klickitat; and Cowlitz, Hookium, and Nenolelops greet and offend you. They complain in Olympia that Washington Territory gets but little immigration; but what wonder? What man, having the whole American continent to choose from, would willingly date his letters from the county of Snohomish, or bring up his children in the city of Nenolelops? The village of Tumwater is, as I am ready to bear witness, very pretty indeed; but surely an emigrant would think twice before he established himself either there or at Toutle. Seattle is sufficiently barbarous; Steilacoom is no better; and I suspect that the Northern Pacific Railroad terminus has been fixed at Tacoma because it is one of the few places on Puget Sound whose name does not inspire horror and disgust."

From Nordhoff, "The Columbia River and Puget Sound," in Harper's New Monthly Magazine (vol. 48)

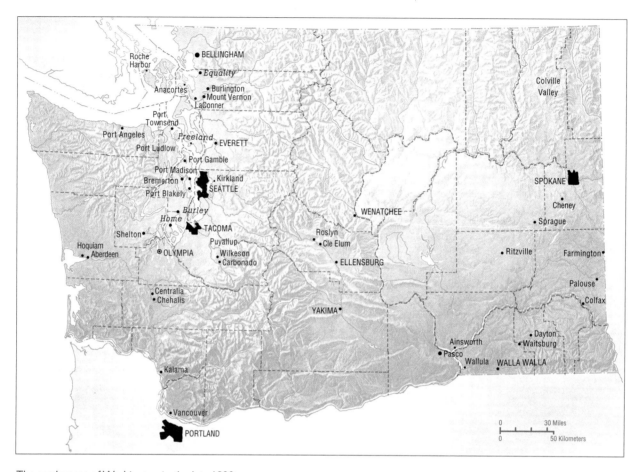

The settlement of Washington in the late 1800s

apparent in protest movements, reform efforts, and outbursts of violence. Yet for most people these seemed to be years of success and optimism, sometimes punctured by disappointment but then renewed with confidence in the future.

Much growth between 1870 and 1910 was due to the railroads that crept west and the men who directed them.

## The Railroads

It is difficult to imagine today the excitement that the railroad aroused over a century ago, before cars, trucks, and airplanes. First in eastern states and later in the broad expanses of the West,

people expected the arrival of railroad tracks to transform sleepy communities into thriving boomtowns and to assure permanent growth. So it was in Washington during the 1870s and 1880s. Many towns expected a railroad line to pass through or hoped to be made the terminus.

In the 1850s Congress authorized four surveys to determine the best routes for railroad construction across the continent. The most northern survey was made by Isaac I. Stevens as he traveled to his job as governor of Washington Territory in 1854. But northern capitalists and southern officials disagreed about the best locations as disagreements between northern and

A Northern Pacific Railroad crew with Chinese workman in the Green River Mountains, about 1885

southern states were leading toward the Civil War.

During that war, three railroad companies received charters to build. All received government help, including a 200-foot right-of-way and grants of public lands along the route. These could be used or sold to obtain funds for construction. The Union Pacific and the Central Pacific together created the first transcontinental track in 1869, connecting Sacramento and Omaha. The Northern Pacific faced a more uncertain future in the Northwest.

The earliest railroad line in the Northwest grew out of the Oregon Steam Navigation Company (OSNC). A group of Portland businessmen started the OSNC in 1860 by combining several competing steamboat lines on the Columbia River. The company soon controlled both the river route and its overland links. When the OSNC decided to add railroads, New York financier Jay Cooke became interested.

Cooke acquired the charter of the Northern Pacific and immediately included the OSNC railway route. He persuaded Congress to enlarge the land grant to sixty miles on each side of the right-of-way. He changed the proposed Northern Pacific route from one going up the Yakima Valley and across the Cascades to one following the Columbia River to Portland. From Portland he planned to build north to Puget Sound. The first leg used boats along the lower Columbia between Portland and a point named Kalama. From Kalama rails were started north.

## COMPETITION FOR THE RAIL TERMINUS

On Puget Sound great interest centered around which town would be selected for the rail terminus. Seattle and Tacoma particularly vied for the benefits the chosen town would receive.

Tacoma was started about the same time as Seattle when a Swedish immigrant, Nicholas Delin, settled on Commencement Bay in 1852. Job Carr followed in 1864. But the real developer of Tacoma was Morton McCarver, who had already lost investments in Linnton, Oregon, and Sacramento, California. He arrived on Puget Sound in 1868 and began to plan a city. McCarver's enthusiastic promotion attracted other settlers. When Northern Pacific officials began to show interest, Tacoma numbered about six hundred people. Seattle citizens were horrified when the railroad company selected Tacoma as terminus in 1873. Even in Tacoma, however, joy was dampened because the spot selected was a low, level point on the bay several miles southeast of McCarver's village. Nevertheless, citizens of "Old Tacoma" joined with those arriving at "New Tacoma" to build wharves, warehouses, streets, hotels, and businesses. The town acquired new importance on Puget Sound.

The railroad connected Tacoma and Puget Sound with Portland. Confident it would become the leading city in the Northwest, Tacoma expected connections with transcontinental lines to soon follow. Then, suddenly, in 1873, the Jay

Cooke Company collapsed, helping cause a national depression. Crews building the final stretch of road were left unpaid. Further Northern Pacific expansion halted, embittering many in the region. Even Portland still lacked eastern connections.

The Northern Pacific came no farther west than Bismarck, in Dakota Territory, and efforts to connect Portland with California transcontinental lines failed.

In 1873 Henry Villard, a journalist who had become a financier, arrived to investigate railroads for possible German investors. He first acquired controlling interest in several small Oregon lines, including the Oregon Steam Navigation Company, which he continued east to Wallula. Then, Villard set out to secure the Northern Pacific. Using what became known as the "Blind Pool," he raised eight million dollars from eastern investors without telling them what it was for. Villard soon won control of the company.

Reorganizing his companies, Villard continued to build east from the Columbia River. He also pushed west from Bismarck until the two lines met near Helena, Montana, in 1883. Washington finally had a transcontinental rail link from Puget Sound through Portland to Spokane, Saint Paul, and the eastern United States.

Meanwhile, Seattle citizens made two unsuccessful efforts to connect with larger lines. The short lines later became parts of major railroads. A Northern Pacific extension through the Cascade Mountains at Stampede Pass connected the Yakima Valley with Puget Sound in 1887.

By this time another railroad magnate was eyeing Puget Sound. In 1886 James J. Hill, a Canadian who had built profitable railroads around Minnesota, started building west to Everett, Seattle, and Vancouver, B.C. This became the Great Northern Railway.

Hill did not receive federal money or land, although he acquired land grants from another

Railroad magnate James J. Hill addresses the opening day crowd of the AYP exposition.

ers to handle this trade. Like Villard and others, Hill dickered with towns he might pass through, seeking land and buildings without revealing his real plans. He helped bring the Weyerhaeuser lumber interests into the Northwest.

In one sense, Hill truly built the Northwest by bringing tracks and settlers. In the process he gained tremendous personal power over towns, industries, local capitalists, and ordinary people. Eventually the federal government sued to break up such monopolies that so completely controlled transportation.

Tunneling through the Cascade Mountain pass named for its surveyor, John Stevens, Hill seemed about to make the mill town of Everett his terminus on Puget Sound. But the railroad and the larger benefits eventually went to Seattle. Everett and Tacoma did not die. They survived and grew through ups and downs. But by the turn of the century, Seattle's leadership as the major metropolis on Puget Sound was secure.

The importance of railroads in Washington over the next seventy years cannot be overestimated. As tracks were laid, new towns sprang up. These towns instantly became marketing places and exchange points for produce and goods being moved in and out of their surrounding areas.

Railroads brought new people, new businesses, new construction, and a bustling, quickened activity. Areas that had been bypassed earlier were settled. Several established communities, including Tacoma and Yakima, actually moved business districts several miles to sites near the railroad stations. And when railroad companies failed, as they often did, the impact was great enough to cause national economic depressions.

Railroad companies worked to attract newcomers. The Northern Pacific had experts survey and map their landholdings and evaluate the potential for agriculture, logging, mining, and other uses. Advertisements and publicity praised the

railroad. He secured timberlands and developed markets and customers along the route. He brought Americans and immigrants west at special excursion fares. Thus he actively encouraged potential farmers and settlers to purchase land in areas the trains passed through.

Hill also started shipping with Asia. He built piers at Smith Cove in Seattle and two ocean lin-

Downtown Yakima, 1908

richness of newly opened lands. Guidebooks and special low fares aided emigrants from the eastern United States and Europe.

The land grants that the railroads received from the federal government also helped determine growth. The alternate sections of land on each side of the track often passed from the railroad companies to other owners. Timber companies secured much of this land, and such cheap timberland helped entice the Weyerhaeuser Company into Washington. Eastern Washington ranchers were able to purchase railroad grant land at low cost and thus enlarge their privately held range land for livestock.

Along with big railroad companies, branch lines connected towns and routes with the main lines. Sometimes local communities helped to finance these, certain that a railroad connection assured growth and permanence. Short-line logging railroads made logging possible higher in the hills than in the past. By 1917 Washington had 1,810 miles of logging railroads.

## Eastern Washington

The harbors and bays of western Washington filled up quickly, but settling the expanses of eastern Washington was slow. The earliest settlers moved into river valleys, canyons, and scablands arching north around Walla Walla. Some raised livestock; others planted wheat and other crops;

Horse-drawn plows work a farm in Walla Walla County in the early 1900s.

some simply tried out the land for settlement or whatever use they could make of it. A few choice spots along the Mullan Road or on the route to the Colville Valley became stopping points for travelers.

Surrounded by parched land, sagebrush, and bunchgrass, many isolated settlers found life lonely and depressing. Winter was cold and harsh, and summer droughts could be disastrous. Yet, a store, a grist mill, and a crude hotel located in a valley bottom in the 1870s or 1880s suggested that a community was underway. If a railroad line passed through, so much the better. Many such towns were copies of their neighbors, but a few had particular distinctions.

Wallula, located where the Walla Walla River empties into the Columbia, was an early stop; railroad lines increased its importance. Ainsworth began as a headquarters for railroad construction near the Columbia. When Pasco was built as a railroad center for the lower Columbia Basin, local boosters dreamed that a flour mill, sawmill, foundry, meat-packing plant, and other industries would soon follow.

Cheney experienced name changes honoring various Northern Pacific officials, and it was the leading town in the north before Spokane rose to rival it. Farming and milling, sometimes lumbering and mining, centered around towns such as Waitsburg, Dayton, Colfax, Palouse City, Farmington, Ritzville, and Sprague, each with its own valley to support it.

## SPOKANE

The falls on the Spokane River marked one of the most beautiful spots in this dry land. In a broad piney valley below the plateaus, water cascaded gracefully over rocks and around three small islands. Early visitors admired the falls, but settlers preferred other locations.

The Hudson's Bay Company established Fort Spokane west of the falls at the mouth of the Spokane River, and Fort Colville was several miles north. Elkanah and Mary Walker ran a mission at Tshimakain, twenty-five miles northwest of the falls. The Mullan Road crossed the Spokane River upstream and angled southwest to Walla Walla, and routes to the Colville area skirted west.

In 1870 three families were trying to eke out a living by the falls. A small sawmill cut nearby pines. When James Glover arrived from Portland and inquired about buying the mill, its owners were ready to sell. One, a suspected horse thief, was especially eager after he learned that pursuers were close on his trail. Glover soon owned 320 acres straddling the falls and an inadequate sawmill, but he was enthusiastic about building a town. He opened a store alongside the mill, selling goods to whomever might stop by. But mostly he worked at persuading anyone who would listen that Spokane Falls had a future.

Expecting the Northern Pacific to build through Spokane Falls, and offering pieces of his own landholdings, Glover talked others into joining him. One such man was Frederic Post, a miller from Idaho. Glover promised Post forty acres if he would set up a grist mill at the falls, and the Spokane flour industry was born.

During Indian troubles, Glover persuaded the army to erect a temporary fort on one of the islands, making the settlement a haven for out-lying settlers. He also convinced a hotel proprietor, a minister wanting to start an academy, and a newspaper publisher to take a chance on his town. In time he sold his store and devoted himself full time to promoting the town and handling real estate. When Spokane County was created, Glover led the battle against Cheney to secure the county seat.

Spokane Falls was ten years old when the tracks and then the engines of the Northern Pacific arrived in June 1881. There were riotous celebrations. Although the Northern Pacific soon fell into a slump, short-line railroads fanned out from town and it remained a transportation center.

Soon gold was discovered in mountain streams above Lake Coeur d'Alene, and Spokane Falls flourished by outfitting miners. Then the gold fever was surpassed by silver and lead discoveries. The Bunker Hill and Sullivan mines in Idaho were the earliest and the largest. Daniel C. Corbin built a small railroad from Spokane Falls to the mines, ensuring that men and supplies traveling to or from them would have to pass through his town. Mills, hotels, stores, banks, and private homes multiplied, and Spokane Falls spread beyond both river banks. The population grew faster there than in any other large city in the state, faster than most in the nation. "Falls" was dropped and the name became simply Spokane.

During the late 1880s, Spokane experimented with a new use for the falls: flowing water could generate electrical power. A dynamo placed alongside was connected to a saw that cut cordwood for a local hotel. It worked. The promoters reasoned that electricity from the falls could perform other tasks around town. Why not try using it for other machines . . . other industries . . . street lighting . . . trolley lines . . . even home lighting?

Power from Spokane eventually extended to suburban areas and Idaho mining camps. In 1899 one of the first hydroelectric companies in the nation, the Washington Water Power Company (now Arista Corporation), was established. Hydroelectric power soon became the major source of energy in Washington.

Like Seattle and other cities, Spokane learned to benefit from disaster. Late on a summer Sunday in 1889, a small roof fire started. It should have been put out easily. But hydrants failed to work and flames leaped to nearby buildings and on to others. Wooden structures fueled the fire until much of downtown Spokane was ablaze. Astonished onlookers watched red-hot cinders

jump the river and ignite a lumber yard on the opposite bank.

Citizens tried to protect or salvage what they could. Help arrived from as far away as Walla Walla, but the fire burned until a block of buildings was dynamited and the wind changed direction. Thirty-two blocks of downtown Spokane were in ashes, although most residential areas remained untouched.

As in Seattle two months earlier, this destruction helped create a new spirit of hope and determination. Businesses reopened quickly

Local farmers sell their produce at an open air market in early-day Spokane.

in temporary locations or tents. Cooperation increased among the citizens. Generous bank loans were granted. The city rebuilt, not with wood, but with brick and stone. A more modern Spokane emerged.

During the 1890s, a nationwide depression slowed but did not stop growth based on the riches of Idaho mines and nearby forests. Farming and livestock raising in surrounding areas aided Spokane's prosperity. Fine residential neighborhoods were built, some with elegant homes. Hotels, parks, schools, a college, churches, an opera house, and an auditorium encouraged a new cultural life. In thirty years Spokane grew dramatically—from 350 people in 1880 to 20,000 in 1890 and over 100,000 by 1910. Rapid growth is often difficult for a town to handle, but in Spokane it was sound and solid.

Spokane began to boast it was the capital of a great diversified Inland Empire that embraced parts of Washington, Idaho, and Montana. Walla Walla, the dominant town in earlier times, settled back to lead a smaller region in the southeast corner of the state.

## Western Washington Industries

Near the slopes of the Cascades, in river and lake valleys around Puget Sound, at bays along the ocean, western Washington attracted more and more people between 1870 and 1910. The economy still relied on the extractive industries that had interested early white settlers: lumber, fishing, and mining. There was also some farming. But methods of developing these industries had changed, manufacturing started, and the area began to acquire urban services.

By the 1890s the lumber industry bore little similarity to the individual mills started by Henry Yesler, Lafayette Balch, and other pioneers. Large lumber companies were financed with eastern money and run by imported managers. Buildings, machinery, mill ponds, and docks sprawled along

bay shores. Company towns housed and served employees. They cut timber from surrounding hills, dotting them with numerous short-lived logging camps, and they shipped products to Japan, Australia, and South America. Port Gamble, Port Blakely, Port Ludlow, and Port Madison were among the earliest of these lumber towns.

In 1900 the Weyerhaeuser Timber Company, well on its way to becoming the biggest of all, moved into the Northwest and purchased 900,000 acres of timberland from the Northern Pacific Railroad for six dollars an acre. Soon it transferred its headquarters from Minnesota to Tacoma. It acquired or built mills at Tacoma, Everett, along the White River, at Grays Harbor, and finally on the lower Columbia River.

The vast timber resources of southwestern Washington were tapped when the Simpson Company built at Shelton and several firms erected plants at Grays Harbor. Related industries followed, such as shake and shingle milling, door and sash manufacturing, shipbuilding, and the manufacture of mill equipment.

In the late 1800s coal was found in the Cascades. Suddenly, mining towns developed near the upper Cowlitz River, along branches of the Puyallup, and in the hills southeast of Seattle at Carbonado, Wilkeson, Black Diamond, and Newcastle. Across the Cascades, coal was mined at Roslyn. Coal fields were found east of Bellingham, but they never produced to expectations.

At Roche Harbor in the San Juan Islands, John S. McMillan operated lime quarries and a processing plant. Other mineral discoveries fostered hopes for industries. Port Townsend's dreams of prosperity included refining iron at nearby Irondale, but the plant barely got underway. And an English industrialist named Peter Kirk excited Seattle investors with proposals for a steel mill on the eastern shore of Lake Washington. Kirkland was founded on great hopes, but the mill never was built.

The economy of Hoquiam was based on the lumber industry.

In 1890 William R. Rust organized the Tacoma Smelting and Refining Company, which bought out a small smelter and gave the Tacoma area a second major industry. That fall, a shipment of processed silver, gold, and lead headed south to San Francisco. Eventually Rust sold his smelter to the American Smelter and Refining Company (ASARCO), which used the plant for refining copper.

The Seattle area had shipbuilding firms by the 1880s. Moran Brothers Shipyard switched from making wooden to steel vessels early in the new century, with the construction of the battleship *Nebraska*. Fish- and food-processing plants and canneries were built in several towns.

Farming developed differently in western Washington than east of the Cascades. Instead of wide open spaces and extremes of climate, the region west of the mountains had fertile valleys and lowlands, a moderate climate, and a long growing season. Non-farming industries dominated the region, and newcomers settled in towns and growing communities. They created a demand for a variety of crops raised close at hand, including vegetables, fruits, and dairy and meat products.

In earlier days, food products were shipped north from the Willamette Valley, but the Puget Sound area soon began to supply its own needs. Around lowlands such as La Conner at the mouth of the Skagit River, diking provided flat cropland that was often remarkably rich.

Certain localities proved ideal for specialized, intensively grown crops. Fruits, especially berries, could be raised easily. Hops were an important early crop. Vegetable seeds and flower bulbs became important in some valleys, and dairying was widespread.

## THE TOWNS OF WESTERN WASHINGTON

Urbanization, the transformation of rural land into cities, was taking place around Puget Sound. Along with Seattle and Tacoma, lesser towns were growing rapidly. Below the Canadian border, three small communities along Bellingham Bay merged in 1904 to create Bellingham, a major port and mill town. Mount Vernon and Burlington grew as centers for farmers in the Skagit Valley, and nearby Anacortes had fish canneries. Everett alternated between hope and disappointment as railroad lines, lumber companies, and mining corporations held out promises to town builders which were not always kept.

Olympia, secure as headquarters for state government, was also supported by fishing and lumbering. In the valley to the south, lumbering and mining aided Centralia and Chehalis, which also served a large farming area. Vancouver continued to dominate the area just across the Columbia River from Portland. On Grays Harbor, Aberdeen and Hoquiam, somewhat isolated from the rest of the state, developed with lumbering and related industries as well as fishing. Port Angeles, begun as a rival to Port Townsend, in the mid-1800s attracted a colony of socialists who aroused a sense of community. Then, Port Angeles grew with lumbering and fishing. Bremerton acquired a naval shipyard in 1891. Smaller communities were interspersed in the valleys and along shorelines throughout the area. Small lumber mills and shake mills appeared almost everywhere.

Towns and villages around the Sound were connected by a few railroad lines, some crude roads, and small boats so numerous they were called the "mosquito fleet." The little launches criss-crossed the waters, carrying passengers, mail, and freight. Their arrivals and departures, the whistle that announced their approach, and occasional races between the faster ones marked a unique transportation era.

Growth itself created industries and jobs as buildings, roads, bridges, and homes were constructed. Businesses were needed to support the industries and people. The first stores in a new town were general stores that carried all sorts of goods. These were followed by shops that specialized in such things as food, dry goods, clothing, or hardware. Towns needed the professional services of doctors, lawyers, bankers, newspaper editors, surveyors, and dentists. Schools and churches were established early; several towns had small private academies.

As towns grew, their populations tended to become more diverse and more socially divided. Hillsides often held the mansions of the local elite, while rows and rows of look-alike, clapboard houses on the flats below housed workers. Swedes might congregate in one neighborhood, Chinese in another, and blacks in yet another. Many Scandinavians worked in fishing or lumbering, and some southwestern towns (including Aberdeen and Woodland) had large populations of Finns.

Chinese people were driven out of several towns during a period of racial violence. White Americans feared that the new immigrants were taking jobs away from the established labor force.

Immigrants tended to settle together, like the Norwegians of Poulsbo, the Germans of Odessa, and the Dutch of Lynden. Several communities, including Hoquiam and Tacoma, had large communities from Eastern Europe. During a labor dispute in 1888, several hundred blacks were brought into Roslyn to work in coal mines. Most left after a few years, but in 1900 only Seattle and Spokane had more African American residents than Roslyn had.

The first serious racial conflicts after the Indian wars were white hostilities directed against Chinese in the middle 1880s. The Chinese had been brought to work on railroad construction, in mines, and in canneries. Thousands of Chinese laborers helped build Northern Pacific Railroad lines. When that work ended, many moved into cities searching for work.

White workers who feared that the Chinese would undercut their wages used threats, house burnings, and killings to frighten them out of communities around the Sound. Near present-day Issaquah, three Chinese hops workers were murdered. A few miles away, masked men set fire to Chinese bunkhouses at the Newcastle coal mines. The residents escaped, but they left the area. Soon after, white laborers of Seattle and Tacoma organized strong movements that lasted over many turbulent weeks. Talk turned toward violence as citizens rounded up the Chinese from their shanties. Chinese of both cities were hustled aboard ships and forced out.

Towns quickly developed a sense of community loyalty, pride, and competition. Rivalries were apparent in slogans and mottoes. Disputes erupted over the location of county seats and other facilities, and ribald jokes about neighboring towns became common. At its best, local pride appeared in baseball rivalries and other athletic competition, in town bands, and in special celebrations. At its worst, the battle was waged with vicious newspaper campaigns and dirty tricks. When Seattle burned in 1889, gleeful Tacoma school children chanted, "Seattle,

Seattle, death rattle, death rattle." Orators debated whether the greatest mountain should be named Rainier as Seattle residents maintained, or Tacoma as that city wished. The argument raged long and finally led to a federal government decision in favor of Rainier.

Most towns developed a real sense of identity during the years between 1870 and 1910, including the city that was to become the largest of them all.

### Turn-of-the-Century Seattle

With the same spirit that helped Spokane rebuild, Seattle recovered from the June 6, 1889, fire that wiped out its business section. Business continued and new streets were laid out. New construction of brick and stone could withstand future disaster. A year later one could scarcely tell where the fire had raged except that new buildings several stories high rose along the waterfront. Reconstruction and a determination to survive strengthened the economy. In 1890 Seattle, not yet forty years old, had 42,837 residents spread along the hillside above Elliott Bay.

Seattle suffered from the national depression known as the Panic of 1893. Lumber markets declined, businesses went bankrupt, and population growth slowed. Then on July 17, 1897, the S.S. *Portland* arrived from Alaska carrying more than a ton of gold. The rush to the north was on, and Seattle made the most of it.

Rival cities also had good harbors, ships, and stores to provide the clothing, tools, and other goods that gold prospectors would need. But Seattle also had Erastus Brainerd, an out-of-work newspaper editor, and a group of energetic promoters. Brainerd valued publicity. He spread the "ton of gold" story, along with news of the Yukon gold fields. Brainerd advertised Seattle as the best taking-off place for southern Alaska and the Yukon. Prospectors heading north passed through Seattle, and many who returned, wealthy

or poor, remained there. Stores, banks, and steamship lines thrived. Seattle's lasting association with Alaska has helped the city grow.

But the forested hills that had helped start Seattle were becoming a drawback. Hills that had been ideal for skidding logs down to waterfront mills now blocked expansion. South and east of a peninsula that jutted into the bay, a muddy tide-flat circled around the base of Beacon Hill to the Duwamish River a mile or so south. At high tide this area was under water. At low tide it was mud. At all times it was useless.

Imaginative engineers suggested taking earth from the steep hills to fill in the tide-flats and level off the shoreline. They planned to dredge and straighten the rambling Duwamish River so that ships could enter, and to create a new island at its mouth. Work got underway with donkey engines and shovels to move the dirt, and horse-drawn wagons to cart it away. The project succeeded. As Seattle grew west across hills that now had reasonable grades, business and commercial sections appeared where mud flats had been.

Earth moving at the other end of town was even more dramatic. North of Pike Street engineers used giant water hoses to wash or sluice away the steep Denny Hill. Earth from the hill filled in ravines and created a secure waterfront area. A decade later, heavier and more modern equipment with conveyor belts finished building the new commercial area, which became known as the Denny Regrade.

Other cities have changed their geography, but the facelift in Seattle was spectacular and wide-ranging. A business district hemmed in on all sides by hills and water could achieve only a moderate size. These earth-moving operations gave Seattle room to become a modern metropolis.

In 1916 the Lake Washington Ship Canal was completed, connecting Lake Washington with

Yesler Way in Seattle before and after the fire of 1889

The outfitting business boomed in Seattle during the Alaska gold rush.

Lake Union and Puget Sound. Differences in water level required locks and fish ladders near the entrance to the canal at Ballard. The water level in Lake Washington dropped eight feet when the canal was completed. At the time these were the largest such locks in the world. Seattle expected the waterway would open its lakes to industrial development and to water routes on the entire Sound.

Seattle also annexed large districts north and south of the city limits. In the 1890s city boundaries leaped northeast beyond the new University of Washington grounds and Green Lake. In the first decade of the twentieth century, the city took in the suburban towns of Ballard, with 18,000 residents, West Seattle, Rainier Beach, Dunlap, and Georgetown. With these annexations and natural growth the area and population of Seattle more than doubled between 1900 and 1910.

Under farsighted engineers like Reginald H. Thomson and James D. Ross, and with wide-spread popular support, Seattle extended street-car lines and utilities. In 1908 Seattle built a small hydroelectric plant on the Cedar River southeast of town. Almost immediately engineers foresaw a need for more power and turned to the upper Skagit Valley a hundred miles north. In the 1920s Diablo Dam was built, and later Gorge and Ross

Horse-drawn wagons and early steam shovels cut through the hills of downtown Seattle to build new streets.

dams, along with hydroelectric plants and a community for workers at Newhalem.

Tacoma made a similar development at Lake Cushman on the Skokomish River on the southern Olympic Peninsula. Thus, early in the twentieth century, the three largest cities of Washington all took strides to provide abundant and low-cost electricity.

By 1909 when the Alaska-Yukon-Pacific Exposition was held, Seattle could celebrate real achievements in developing its economy and providing for a constantly growing population. Because it was the largest city in the Northwest, the achievements in Seattle seem large and dramatic. Yet, similar changes, developments, and annexations were occurring on a smaller scale in many other towns around the state.

## Reform Movements

Throughout the United States great industries were growing during the years after the Civil War. In Washington as elsewhere, businessmen and politicians worked together closely. Companies grew rich and powerful as profits increased. Smaller businesses could not keep up. Sometimes the boards of directors of a few companies became so large and intertwined that it became difficult to know who was actually running a company.

Factory workers and other laborers had to accept wages, hours, and working conditions they had no control over. Protesters were easily fired and replaced. There was no unemployment insurance, Social Security, or welfare for people out of work.

During the 1800s some workers began to organize labor unions to try to change these conditions. One of the earliest national unions, the Knights of Labor, had organized in 1869. Workers in all industries were recruited. In Washington, Knights locals started in several towns and were especially strong in the mining and smelting

20  *DIRECTORY OF THE CITY OF SEATTLE.*

# AMERICAN HOUSE,

GEO. W. WALSH, Proprietor.

MILL STREET, - - - SEATTLE, W. T

Board per day $1, Board per Week, $5, $6 & $7 according to room. Meals, 25 cts. Beds 25 to 50 cts.

Baggage conveyed to and from the house free of chagre.

### NO CHINAMEN EMPLOYED.

# WA CHONG & CO.,

# China Tea Store,

Brick Store, Corner of Washington and Third Sts., Seattle.

DEALERS IN

## RICE, OPIUM AND ALL KINDS OF CHINESE GOODS,

Chinese Landscape Pictures, Oil Paintings, also for Sale

Contractors, Mill Owners and others requiring Chinese help will be furnished at short notice.

THE HIGHEST PRICE PAID FOR LIVE HOGS.

Anti-Chinese sentiment and the use of Chinese labor were both evident in advertisements.

industries. One major goal was to see that jobs went to white workers. Knights in Seattle helped drive out the Chinese in 1886. The Knights of Labor died out after a few years, but it influenced later labor and political movements. Other labor organizations grew slowly.

Farmers had become discouraged because railroad companies controlled storage and shipping costs while prices of their products remained low. Bankers seemed to keep land prices and interest rates high. Farmers began to organize themselves as early as the 1870s, first with the Patrons of Husbandry, or Grange, and then with the Farmers' Alliances. Both were national organizations that moved into Washington from other rural regions.

The Washington Grange started among wheat farmers in southeastern Washington and spread to agricultural areas on both sides of the Cascades. It sought laws to regulate railroads and to lower shipping rates and became a noteworthy social organization in many rural communities. Many farmers in the southeastern corner joined the Alliances, which also took a strong stand against the railroads.

## THE POPULISTS

By 1892 such groups decided that they needed to elect representatives to the government. They organized a new political party to challenge Republicans and Democrats. In Washington, as in other states, a People's or Populist Party was formed, with its own platform and candidates. In 1892 this new party elected members to the Washington State Legislature and to local offices. Four years later, the Populists cooperated with Democrats who shared similar views and elected John R. Rogers governor, along with other state officials and legislators. Only Washington, Kansas, and Colorado ever elected Populist governors.

Rogers, who had been a newspaper man in Kansas, lived in Puyallup and had written books and articles expressing his views on many issues. In a novel called *Looking Forward, the Story of an American Farm*, Rogers described how good life would be if big businesses, railroads, and banks did not dominate the lives of ordinary people. As a state representative in 1895, he had sponsored the Barefoot Schoolboy Law, which assured every Washington child the right to a free education. This law established the state public school system. School children later contributed pennies to erect a statue of Rogers, which stands in Olympia.

The Populists wanted to reduce railroad and

Governor John R. Rogers in his Olympia office

utility rates, lower the salaries of public officials, prohibit the issuing of free railroad passes to officials, stop the courts from foreclosing debts, and start a state income tax. They wanted silver as well as gold to be the basis of the money system. This proposal would put more money in circulation and was popular in silver mining areas.

But little of the Populist program became law during those years. Opposition was strong. Populists and Democrats did not stay united, and alone the Populists lacked enough strength to put their proposals into law. The Democratic Party swallowed up many Populist ideas and promoted them at the next election. Rogers was reelected governor in 1900, but as a Democrat. He died soon after. By then, the Populist Party was also dead, although other groups and parties advanced many of their ideas.

## RADICALS

Some citizens of Washington wanted to bring about more extreme changes. Socialists wanted the government to own and run major industries instead of merely regulating them. In 1897 about a hundred socialists from Maine, the Midwest, and other parts of the United States established a small colony in Skagit County. They named it Equality. They farmed in rich soil, planted an orchard, and established a sawmill that cut timber from the hills behind them. Members lived communally in large, barracks-like apartments, and dined and carried on social activities as if they were one huge family. Colonists shared work responsibilities, property, and profits. All adult men and women shared in making decisions. Equality worked well for several years and then slowly died in disagreements among members. As times grew prosperous in the early 1900s, life outside the colony became more alluring.

Equality had planned to encourage similar colonies and bring enough socialists into Washington to convert the state government to socialism. These intentions never survived the difficulty of keeping even one colony going. Some disgruntled Equality colonists separated to settle on Whidbey Island at a place they named Freeland. Here they shared property and activities in a less structured manner than in the older community. Meanwhile other socialists with similar goals started a community at Burley in southern Kitsap County.

Socialists and the other radical groups never gained power in state politics. A strong state Socialist Party existed for many years, dominated by Hermon Titus, a Seattle physician turned editor, and later by other individuals. Its high point came in 1912 when the Socialist candidate for president secured 12 percent of the total Washington vote, a larger percentage than in any other state except Oklahoma.

Settlers at Equality Colony. *Industrial Freedom* was the colony newspaper.

On an inlet in southern Puget Sound, a lively and interesting community called Home attracted atheists, free thinkers, anarchists, and advocates of free love. These people discussed and explored a variety of ideas about politics, economics, and how to live the best life. Famous radicals from throughout the United States came to live and visit at Home. The community was looked on with suspicion and was frequently under attack or criticism from conservative neighbors. One editor was jailed for strongly criticizing the government; on another occasion a raiding party from Tacoma threatened to wipe out the community.

Of all the groups that advocated changes in Washington state, the most famous was the Industrial Workers of the World (IWW), whose members were called Wobblies. This labor union held radical views, and provoked extreme and sometimes violent reactions. The IWW sought benefits for workers who were not easy to organize. It appealed to workers in difficult, hazardous, and transient jobs such as logging and mining. Many Washington workers either joined or followed this union, and the Pacific Northwest became one of its strongholds.

## PROGRESSIVE MOVEMENT

Although many ideas of the radicals did not take hold, they did have an influence. In the early 1900s Democrats and Republicans in Washington and in other states passed many liberal, progressive laws. Basically, the people who advocated these changes believed in progress. They believed that the world could be made better, and they sought to bring about improvements. Thus, their efforts were called the Progressive Movement.

Washington State Progressives sought to bring the state government and its laws into closer touch with the people and to improve the quality of life. Commissions and boards of citizens were established early in the 1900s to super-

## In Praise of Home Colony

*Home Colony was established at Von Geldern Cove on southern Puget Sound in 1896. Here people of varying viewpoints assembled and generally got along well with one another. An enthusiastic visitor wrote:*

*"As an indication of the men (and women) to be found at Home I will simply tell of a few of the things I did not find there and some of those I did find.*

*"I found no church,*
*No saloon,*
*No gambling den,*
*No butcher shop,*
*No house of prostitution,*
*No one with a billy [club],*
*No society for the dissemination [spreading] of scandals or other gossip,*
*No one with a penchant for putting people on the black list because they might differ from them,*
*No goody-goody, smilee smirkee prisms and prunish people,*
*No extreme poverty or almshouse [poorhouse],*
*No prison or lock-up,*
*No bitter criticism of their fellow mortals—not being so very good themselves, the contrast is not so great as to arouse contempt for the coarser clay of the other fellow. . . .*

*"I found perfect freedom of thought and action, and as a consequence a high degree of naturalness. I saw no affected ribbon-proud females, or gentleman dudes. Plain common sense people seem to predominate.*

*"There are no rich and no poor, nor does the dollar appear to be the main motive for activity. They seem to love their books, and music and social intercourse more than the chase for the lucre [money]."*

*From Soundview, March 1903*

An IWW political poster makes fun of the capitalist system.

vise certain industries and other public activities. The *initiative* and the *referendum* allowed voters to pass laws without going through the legislature or the governor. The *recall* enabled voters to remove public officials who they believed had not honestly carried out their responsibilities. Some dramatic recall elections took place; two brought down mayors in Tacoma and Seattle.

Washington was the fifth state to allow women to vote. Actually, women had had the vote from 1883 to 1887, when Washington was still a territory, until a court decision ruled it out. The state constitution restricted the vote to men. Washington suffrage leaders included Emma Smith DeVoe of Tacoma and May Arkwright Hutton of Spokane, along with Abigail Scott Duniway from neighboring Oregon.

Many men campaigned to help women secure the vote. They succeeded in 1910, well before most states, and the national constitutional amendment of 1919 gave women the vote. In 1912, the first women—Frances Axtell from Whatcom County and Nena Croake from Pierce County—were elected to the state legislature. Yet several years passed before many women held high political office in Washington.

During these years Washington sent to the U.S. Senate a progressive who became more prominent in national politics than any Washingtonian before him. Miles Poindexter, a Walla Walla and Spokane lawyer, was a senator between 1911 and 1923. An admirer of former president Theodore Roosevelt, he joined a small group of Republicans who consistently opposed party leaders and worked to enact progressive laws.

Leaving his party, Poindexter helped form a short-lived Progressive Party that sought to reelect Roosevelt in 1912. He became the only member of that party in the Senate. During these years he balanced Progressive idealism with the needs of the small businessmen and farmers of eastern Washington.

Poindexter worked for such measures as the election of United States senators by voters instead of by state legislatures, woman suffrage, workers' compensation, low duties on imported goods, anti-trust laws, a graduated income tax, and the establishment of the Federal Trade Commission. Some of his ideas, such as an "industrial army" to create jobs for the unemployed, were ahead of their time but were later enacted. As World War I came, Poindexter returned to the Republican party and became increasingly conservative in his political views.

The early years of the twentieth century were a time of optimism. Even if few persons were wealthy and many were not living well, the expanding businesses, growing towns, and prospering industries seemed to offer success for all who worked hard. A historian describing the early years of the twentieth century in the United States called them the "Good Years" and explained his reasons. They were good years not because people were wealthy or because prices were low, not because there was peace in the world or in the nation; many people were so poor that low prices meant little, and widespread suffering existed. "These years were good," the author wrote, "because, whatever the trouble, people were sure they could fix it."

Nowhere was that feeling more true than in the young state of Washington.

## Chapter 7 Review

**I.** Identify the following people. Tell why each is important to Washington State.

Isaac Stevens
Jay Cooke
Morton McCarver
Henry Villard
James J. Hill
James Glover

Daniel C. Corbin
William R. Rust
Erastus Brainerd
John R. Rogers
Miles Poindexter

**II.** Define the following words and terms. Relate each to Washington State.

Alaska-Yukon-
    Pacific Exposition
Denny Regrade
Reform movements
Knights of Labor
Populist Party
Barefoot Schoolboy
    Law
Socialists
Radicals
Industrial Workers
    of the World
    (Wobblies)
Weyerhaeuser Timber
    Company
Referendum

Mosquito fleet
Extractive industries
Railroad surveys
Union Pacific
Central Pacific
Terminus
Oregon Steam Navi-
    gation Company
Northern Pacific
Great Northern
Washington Water
    Power Company
Progressives
Initiative
Urbanization

**III.** Locate each of these places on a map. Why is each important in Northwest history?

Kalama
Seattle
Equality Colony

Tacoma
Wallula
Home Colony

Everett
Spokane

**IV.** Each question below should call your attention to factual information in the chapter. Try to answer each one. Then look back in the reading to check your answer, correct your understanding, and find answers you do not know.

1. By 1910 over half the people in Washington lived in _____ areas.

2. How did industries change between 1870 and 1910?

3. What historic event delayed the building of a transcontinental railroad?

4. How did the federal government help the transcontinental railroads?

5. When Tacoma was chosen as the terminus of the Northern Pacific Railroad, how did the company leaders change the location?

6. Why did the Northern Pacific stop building in 1873?

7. What was Henry Villard's "Blind Pool"?

8. How did James J. Hill finance the Great Northern Railroad?

9. Which city eventually gained the most from the Great Northern Railroad?

10. What often happened to the land given to the railroads?

11. What kinds of locations attracted the first settlements in eastern Washington?

12. What discoveries in Idaho helped Spokane to grow?

13. How were the Spokane falls used?

14. What began to replace the small individual lumber mills of western Washington?

15. What important mineral was found in the Cascade Mountains in the late 1800s?

16. What important new industry came to Tacoma in 1890?

17. Which western Washington city was formed when three small communities merged?

18. Which part of the state developed quickly with lumber-related industries and fishing?

19. Which city acquired a naval shipyard?

20. As towns grew, their shops became more specialized. Explain what this means.

21. How did the character of their populations change as the towns grew?

22. Name three towns that were settled mainly by people of a single ethnic or national group.

23. List several towns that experienced racial disturbances in the mid-1880s. What racial group was involved?

24. What happened in July 1897 that helped bring Seattle and much of Washington out of a depression?

25. How did Seattle change its geography and its shoreline?

26. Where did Seattle construct plants to obtain electric power? Where did Tacoma build similar plants?

27. Give the name of the first national labor union to appear in Washington.

28. What were the goals of the Populists?

29. What was the goal of the members of Equality Colony?

30. What kinds of people settled the community they called Home?

31. In a few words, describe what the Progressives believed.

32. List five Progressive measures that Senator Miles Poindexter favored.

**V.** Think about, discuss, and answer the following questions.

1. Railroads played an extremely important part in developing the West. What were some specific ways that railroad construction affected growing areas such as Washington? What industries today also have a wide effect on other kinds of growth much as railroads did in the late 1800s? Explain and discuss.

2. James Glover of Spokane was typical of many persons who came west hoping to start new towns. Why do such people try to build new towns? What steps must they take? What problems are they likely to encounter? What successes are they likely to experience? Try to find out more about the individuals who settled the town you live in.

If you were starting to build a town today, what kind of a location might you seek? How would you try to attract settlers? What kinds of people would you especially try to attract? If you know about some towns that have been established recently, try to learn more about how they got started.

3. Seattle, Spokane, and Tacoma have been discussed in some detail in this book. What are some events in the growth of each that are similar? What did all of these young cities have in common? What were some unique features of each?

4. List all of the problems that reformers and reform groups mentioned in this chapter tried to solve or deal with. List the various kinds of tactics they used. Which tactics seem to you to be most effective and permanent?

What are some present-day reform movements? Who are the leaders? What tactics do they use? What tactics to bring about change are generally approved of by most people? What tactics are not widely approved of?

President Franklin D. Roosevelt's visit to the Grand Coulee Dam construction site, October 2, 1937

# Chapter 8  From War to War

rand Coulee Dam, October 2, 1937. A yellow Lincoln convertible inches through a crowd of several thousand construction workers, farmers, and families. It stops on the rim above the site where massive construction is changing the Columbia River. Smiling and waving, a familiar figure emerges from the car; Franklin Delano Roosevelt, president of the United States, has come to inspect the work on Grand Coulee Dam.

A gigantic concrete wall, 500 feet thick, stretches almost a mile across the river canyon. In places it rises as high as a fourteen-story building. This is only the foundation of a giant dam that will fill the wide coulee and hold back the river. When completed, it will contain more than 10 million cubic yards of concrete and rise 550 feet above bedrock. Water will pour dramatically over a spillway 1,650 feet wide. Local residents boast that this is the biggest thing ever built by man.

A wealthy New Yorker like Franklin D. Roosevelt might not be expected to understand the need of western farmers to irrigate desert lands or the craze for harnessing rapidly flowing rivers. Yet, in many respects, this is his dam. For a quarter century people in the Inland Empire have argued the necessity for a dam on the upper Columbia River. Wenatchee World publisher Rufus Woods, Ephrata attorney Billy Clapp, Jim O'Sullivan, who organized support for the dam, U.S. Senator Clarence C. Dill, and others have lobbied for the dam. But not until Roosevelt became president in 1933 did their hopes become reality.

As the new president pushed for the dam, government funds and know-how were made available. The project and its potential expanded beyond earlier dreams. The dam on the Columbia joined many other New Deal programs designed to create jobs and permanently change America.

Three years ago, in 1934, Roosevelt had visited here when work was just getting underway. A vast desert and a few hundred workers greeted him at that time. Today is different. The president and the first lady have already toured western Washington. Traveling along the Oregon side of the Columbia, they viewed the nearly completed Bonneville Dam. They relaxed at their daughter's home in Seattle. Then they went to picturesque Victoria, British Columbia, returning by destroyer to Port Angeles. Circling the Olympic Peninsula, Roosevelt praised a bill to make a national park in that rugged cluster of mountains. He lunched at the rambling Lake Quinault Lodge, stopped in Grays Harbor lumber towns, and visited Governor Clarence D. Martin in Olympia.

Finally he reached this remote but busy desert location. Over 25,000 spectators lined the sixty miles of highway between the Ephrata railroad depot and the dam site. They were anxious to glimpse the president who seems like a personal friend. For these are depression times. Many in the crowds feel that Roosevelt understands and cares personally about their needs. Many owe their livelihood to his public works programs. Sixteen thousand people have moved to this area in the past three years. A dozen small construction towns have been built. Some neighborhoods look permanent with paved streets, neatly painted homes, green lawns and gardens, shopping areas, schools, and churches. A few will endure to serve the new area after the dam is finished.

President Roosevelt addresses the crowd at the Grand Coulee Dam construction site.

*President Roosevelt eats a picnic lunch and delivers a brief greeting. Above the sound of conveyor belts carrying and dumping concrete, his familiar voice rings with confident enthusiasm:*

*"We look forward not only to the great good that this [dam] will do in the development of power, but also in the development of thousands of homes, the bringing in of thousands of acres of new land for future Americans. . . . You young people are going to see the day when thousands and thousands of people will use this great lake [created behind the dam] not only for transportation purposes and power purposes, but for pleasure purposes—small boats, motor boats and shipping lines—running from the northernmost boundaries of the United States into Canada. It is a great prospect, something that appeals to the imagination of the whole country."*

*Work on the dam will go on after the president departs. One day, power plants will generate hydroelectric power and broad irrigation canals will carry water to create rich new farmlands. The 155-mile-long lake behind the dam, named for Roosevelt, will provide boating, fishing, camping, and other recreation for unborn generations.*

*In four years, the Second World War will increase the demand for electricity that Grand Coulee Dam can provide. But on this sunny autumn day, nobody imagines that power from their dam will make possible a great secret development of World War II. A hundred miles south at Hanford, atomic energy will be harnessed for wartime and then peacetime uses.*

*This is a memorable day in the little towns around the dam, the day the president of the United States visited. But other memorable days lie ahead. The hills and canyons of the Columbia River Basin can never again be the untouched deserts they were for centuries past.*

## Thirty Eventful Years

By age thirty, an American born in 1915 had lived through a prosperous decade, a major depression, and two world wars. These thirty years brought upheavals and new concerns to the United States. The nation assumed a responsibility for world leadership greater than anyone might have imagined a few years earlier.

During these years Washington became less isolated and more connected to the rest of the country. No longer was the Northwest a frontier region concerned mostly with problems of settlement and early growth. Railroads and highways, seagoing traffic, radio, airlines, and films helped link Washington with the rest of the nation. Business ties, nationwide merchandising, increased migration, and common interests completed the link. National and worldwide events affected people's lives.

The Northwest's resources were called upon when the United States entered world wars in 1917 and 1941. New industries resulted and the labor force grew, and there were varied concerns on the home front.

The general prosperity of the 1920s and the Great Depression of the 1930s also affected Washington. Yet these years were also a leveling off time. Population growth slowed. Settled areas remained much as they had been and no new urban centers emerged. Lumber and farming remained the backbone of the economy.

### World War I

World War I started in Europe in 1914 with Germany leading the Central Powers and Britain and France leading the Allies. In 1917, Russia, one of the Allies, experienced a revolution against its czarist government that brought Bolsheviks, or Communists, to power. Russia then stopped fighting.

Between 1914 and 1917, the war in Europe

dragged on with no conclusion. Although the United States was officially neutral, sympathies favored Britain and the Allies. In April 1917, after Germany threatened American ships in the Atlantic war zone, the United States entered the war. Its manpower and ability to produce military goods helped bring about the surrender of Germany on November 11, 1918. World War I, which many hoped would be "the war to end all wars," was over.

American industry supplied many of the materials of war. Washington State had fewer industries than other regions of the country, but it still was affected by the emphasis on war manufacturing. Shipbuilding was most important.

Puget Sound yards had been making wooden hulled ships for many years, with the Hall Brothers Shipyard at Port Blakely the largest. That yard, along with others in Seattle, Tacoma, and Grays Harbor towns, early in the war sold ships to several Allied countries for transporting goods. But this war required ships with steel hulls.

The federal government created the Emergency Fleet Corporation to encourage and supervise shipbuilding. With federal funds, Seattle, Tacoma, Vancouver, and several Oregon cities acquired new, well-equipped shipyards. Largest was the Skinner and Eddy facility in Seattle. By June 1919, 41 Northwest shipyards had turned out 297 vessels at a cost of $458 million. Other industries essential for shipbuilding, such as metal fabrication, also expanded. Workers came from all across the United States. After the war, shipbuilding slowed but did not cease. Washington—with a new major industry and a larger work force— became the scene of serious labor problems.

World War I affected daily life all across the country. The drafting of men into the armed forces disrupted families. Civilians observed meatless and heatless days to conserve food and energy. Ordinary American citizens bought Liberty bonds to raise money for the war, and

The sale of U.S. "Liberty Bonds" encouraged ordinary people to help pay the costs of World War I.

Schoolboys learn to knit and girls and boys sort sphagnum moss to aid the war effort. Sphagnum moss was used to dress wounds.

they joined rallies and parades to build enthusiasm. Military installations, such as Fort Lewis near Tacoma, were built or enlarged. Citizens of German background or with ideas critical of the United States were pressured to prove their patriotism. They were forced to participate in the war effort and purchase Liberty bonds.

The wartime governor of Washington was Ernest Lister, an English-born foundry owner from Tacoma. He had entered politics when John R. Rogers was governor, and he shared some of Rogers's populist attitudes. Elected as a Democrat in 1912, Governor Lister understood the problems of workers and farmers. Despite his industrial background, he wanted Washington to remain basically agricultural. He sought laws to help farming and protect natural resources. He told the legislature that "you gentlemen are sent here by your constituents to get your share of the pie. I am sent here by all the people to see that not too much of it is disturbed."

Nevertheless, Lister had to deal with problems of industry and of working groups, and to make sure that they cooperated with the war effort. The Washington State Council of Defense was established to supervise war-related industries and to make sure that businesses did not profit too much from the war. The head of this board was the dynamic president of the University of Washington, Henry Suzzallo.

Lister died while governor in 1919. During seven years he had faced serious labor and industrial problems, especially in the lumber industry.

## LUMBER AND THE WAR

The lumber industry of Washington had grown rapidly and was powerful. It attracted varied workers. A few trained lumbermen made careers and acquired wealth in the industry. But in places like the Cowlitz Valley, "stump ranchers" logged part-time while trying to turn logged-off acres into productive farmlands. Thousands of other workers were migratory, wandering men, some highly skilled, who moved from company to company and from camp to camp wherever work was available.

Logging camps were scattered throughout the evergreen forests of western Washington and the pine hills east of the Cascades. Most were temporary communities of men isolated in the woods miles from the nearest town. Many were crude, uncomfortable places. Bunkhouses were often crowded and filthy. Vermin shared mattresses with the men. There was little privacy. On payday, men headed for town to spend earnings on drink, women, and gambling. Then they went back to more long hours of hazardous work. Some loggers had families in distant homes; many viewed logging as a temporary pastime before starting permanent careers. But many had no families, few roots, and little training for other work.

In this world of swinging axes, mighty saws, and falling trees there were few safety precautions. A worker who was injured was on his own. Employers felt little responsibility, reasoning that the worker who took a dangerous job accepted its hazards. Benefits were few for the injured logger who was laid off and might never be able to work again. The future was never certain.

In nearby towns, mills cut lumber or made shakes and shingles. Some mill workers were permanent residents with homes and families. Conditions were better in mills than in the camps, but only slightly. Fast-whirring saws could easily slice a finger, hand, or arm and permanently disable a worker. Shingle mill workers, who cut and packaged shingles so fast and skillfully that their flashing hands wove patterns in the air, came to be called "shingle weavers." They formed a union in 1903 to try to obtain better and safer working conditions, higher wages, and an eight-hour work day. But several strikes proved unsuccessful.

A loggers' bunkhouse shows the crowded conditions in which they lived.

## THE INDUSTRIAL WORKERS OF THE WORLD

By the 1910s, several labor unions existed in the lumber industry. Fastest growing, most feared, and best known was the Industrial Workers of the World (IWW), or Wobblies. Started in Chicago in 1905 by workers, socialists, and other radicals, the Wobblies wanted to unite all American workers into one big union instead of separating them by trades. They used strikes, propaganda, and sabotage. Leaders claimed that this meant slowing down or being inefficient on the job—"a poor day's work for a poor day's pay" was one slogan —rather than destroying property. Wobblies were accused of more than they were actually responsible for, including strikes, bombings, killings, and even the murder of a former Idaho governor. Employers and many citizens viewed Wobblies as irresponsible and dangerous anarchists.

Mill owners tried to prevent the IWW from recruiting their employees. They did not want any unions, but they particularly did not want the IWW. They locked out workers and circulated blacklists of suspected Wobblies. They fired

**Industrial Workers of the World**

ONE UNION     ONE ENEMY     ONE LABEL

AN INJURY TO ONE AN INJURY TO ALL

IWW poster

members and organizers and sometimes ran Wobblies out of town forcibly. Business leaders, town officials, and newspapers usually supported such efforts. The first Northwest lumber strike by the Wobblies occurred in Portland, Oregon, in 1907, and was easily put down by hiring non-union workers. But the union grew to become especially active throughout Washington.

## The Spokane Free-Speech Fight

One popular Wobbly tactic was the free-speech fight, largely patterned after a year-long incident in Spokane. By 1909 Spokane was a stable, respectable, middle-class city of citizens concerned about keeping up homes, lawns, and appearances. It was also a hiring center for migratory workers needed in the nearby pine forests, agricultural fields, and mines.

In the spring of 1909, IWW organizers set up boxes near the hiring halls in downtown Spokane and began to make speeches, sing labor songs, and harangue passersby. Angry city officials outlawed such street speaking, although religious groups were allowed to speak in similar spots. Wobblies who spoke were arrested. But when one speaker was jailed, another would rise to take his place, and then another and another. They claimed that their constitutional right to free speech was being violated.

Wobblies and sympathizers from all over the West came to Spokane to join the free-speech fight. After about 1,200 had been arrested, the jails were packed and prisoners were placed in an abandoned schoolhouse. They complained about the cold, about crowded cells, about beatings by guards, about cold showers, water hosings, and general filth. Still they kept singing their Wobbly songs. The IWW publicized these goings-on in "barbarous Spokane" across the nation.

The Spokane fight brought into the limelight a nineteen-year-old pregnant Irish girl, Elizabeth Gurley Flynn. Small and feminine, in contrast to the burly loggers around her, she spurred on the men and taunted officials with fine oratory, fiery wit, and great energy. Gurley, as she was called,

Elizabeth Gurley Flynn speaks to a rally about workers' rights and free speech.

became one of the most famous IWW leaders and remained a prominent radical until she died in 1964. She lived to see the free-speech tactic used by other radicals in later generations.

Eventually the Wobblies in Spokane gained the speaking privileges they sought. They moved on to similar efforts in other towns including Aberdeen in 1911 and Everett in 1916. Few succeeded.

## The Everett Massacre

Everett was started in 1888 when three enterprising town builders formed a land company. Hoping for wealth from the silver, gold, and lead mines in hills to the east at Monte Cristo, they persuaded oil magnate John D. Rockefeller to help build an industrial city on Port Gardner Bay. It would have a lumber mill, smelter, shipyard, nail factory, and other industries. Rockefeller's investment encouraged others. Many people moved there, and Everett seemed sure to become a thriving economic and cultural center. When James J. Hill talked of making Everett the Puget Sound terminus for his Great Northern Railroad, a rich future seemed certain.

But during the 1893 depression, Rockefeller pulled his money out, Hill turned toward Seattle, and Everett fell on bad times. Then Weyerhaeuser and other lumber manufacturers arrived from the Midwest and the town expected prosperity again. Other ups and downs followed. By 1916 Everett was dependent upon several large lumber mills. A few wealthy "lumber barons" generally controlled the economy and dominated politics.

In 1916 the Wobblies joined a mill workers' strike in Everett and used the Spokane street-speaking tactic. Outsiders began to arrive. The city outlawed street speaking. Citizen vigilantes, including business and professional men led by an aggressive sheriff, formed a volunteer army to keep the Wobblies out.

Minor clashes fed on one another as violence and fear mounted. Several arrested Wobblies were taken to woods outside town, beaten with sticks of the plant called devil's club, and whipped. When Wobblies tried to reenter Everett for a rally, the stage was set for the "Everett Massacre." As some 250 Wobblies and sympathizers arrived at the city dock aboard the small ship *Verona* on November 5, 1916, they were met by several hundred members of the citizen army. A shot was fired. Whether that first shot came from the dock or the boat remains uncertain, but the Everett waterfront became the scene of terrorizing gun-fire. Within minutes five Wobblies and two townspeople were dead, and an unknown number drowned. Fifty others on both ship and shore were wounded, including the sheriff.

No charges were filed against townspeople, but seventy-five Wobblies were promptly arrested for murder. After much conflicting testimony, the first defendant was acquitted and charges against the others were dropped. The incident demonstrated how terror could arise in such disputes. Bitterness remained in Everett for years. Despite their courtroom victory, the events reinforced the IWW's violent reputation. The emotions aroused by World War I and the Russian Revolution heightened feeling against Wobblies and other radicals.

## The War and Strikes

When the United States entered World War I in 1917, some labor unions saw a chance to have employers meet their demands. The timber industry had been suffering from oversupply and low prices, but now wood was essential to the war effort. Spruce that grew along the southwest coast was needed for wooden airplane construction.

War also led to a shortage of workers in mills and logging camps. Efforts to reduce the work day from ten to eight hours and to improve working and living conditions resulted in a statewide strike. The unions sought to raise wages to $3 a day in mills and $3.50 in camps. Despite support from prominent leaders, most employers refused to agree.

The strike spread. By summer, over 85 percent of the logging camps west of the Cascades were closed. Without logs, mills could not operate. Although Governor Lister and many members of Congress supported the eight-hour work day, the mill owners held firm, lumping the IWW, the American Federation of Labor, and all unions together as enemies.

Meanwhile, government officials raided various IWW headquarters in the United States and arrested leaders for interfering with the war effort. These arrests helped break the Northwest lumber strike. Many timber workers returned to work but slowed down and produced less, doing only eight hours work for ten hours on the job. Government troops patrolled forests and farm regions in Washington and the Idaho mining country to keep peace.

To ensure production the army created another union, run by soldiers under military discipline. This was the Loyal Legion of Lumbermen and Loggers, or the Four-L, and it was headed by Colonel Bryce P. Disque. Disque followed the employers' bidding closely. In return for a stable labor force, employers accepted an eight-hour day. The Four-L helped to weaken the IWW and the American Federation of Labor in the lumber industry.

Wartime patriotism heightened fear and hatred toward anyone suspected of being disloyal. Army officials questioned many persons in the Seattle area about their activities and beliefs. The recall of Mayor Hiram Gill because of his connections with racketeers and prostitution increased the image of Seattle and the Northwest as both corrupt and radical. Seattle was declared off-limits to soldiers stationed at Fort Lewis.

Vigilante citizen groups took more and more violent action. A mob destroyed the plant that published Seattle's IWW newspaper. At Cle Elum,

Pasco, and Vancouver, men suspected of IWW connections or of unpatriotic acts were hustled off railroad cars as they came into town and jailed. Persons thought to have foreign backgrounds or sympathy for Germany were shunned, harassed, or arrested. A hundred IWW leaders around the country were arrested for opposing the war. Aliens were rounded up and deported.

## THE SEATTLE GENERAL STRIKE

During the winter after World War I ended, Seattle's reputation as a radical city grew to unexpected extremes. Shipyards and other businesses began to convert from wartime needs to peacetime production. Workers whose wages had remained the same during the war sought increases to $8 a day for skilled workers, $5.50 for unskilled. Complaining that the government board which still supervised shipbuilding was stalling, shipyard workers went on strike. Other unions voted to join in sympathy, creating a general strike that involved all the union workers in Seattle.

The idea of a general strike was frightening. No American city had experienced one before. A city could be paralyzed if no one worked. Products would not be manufactured; goods would not be sold or delivered; services would not be available. Businesses might close. The effects would be overwhelming.

At 10 A.M. on February 6, 1919, 65,000 strikers left their jobs. Another 40,000 workers stayed home. Workplaces, shops, stores, and restaurants closed. Streetcars did not run; some schools closed; and many frightened citizens stayed off the streets. In the words of Mayor Ole Hanson, "The life stream of a great city stopped." Yet, strike leaders promised to meet emergency needs. Ambulances ran and hospitals stayed open. Milk was distributed for small children; electric power was maintained; newspapers published shortened editions.

## U. S. OFFICERS TO DISCUSS STRIKE
—SEE PAGE 2

**The Seattle Star**

FULL Leased Wire of the United Press Association.
COMPLETE Service of the News paper Enterprise Association.

FINAL EDITION
TWO CENTS IN SEATTLE

THE GREATEST DAILY CIRCULATION OF ANY PAPER IN THE PACIFIC NORTHWEST

VOLUME 21. NO. 290          SEATTLE, WASH., TUESDAY, FEBRUARY 4, 1919          Weather Forecast:

# STOP BEFORE IT'S TOO LATE

This is plain talk to the common-sense union men of Seattle.

You are being rushed pell-mell into a general strike. You are being urged to use a dangerous weapon—the general strike, which you have never used before—which, in fact, has never been used anywhere in the United States.

It isn't too late to avert the tragic results that are sure to come from its use. You men know better than any one else that public sentiment in Seattle—that is, the sentiment of the ninety per cent of the people who are not directly involved in the wage dispute of the shipworkers—*is against a general strike.* You know that the general public doesn't think the situation demands the use of that drastic, disaster-breeding move. *You know, too, that you cannot club public sentiment into line, and you know, too, that no strike has ever been won without the moral support of the public.*

The people know that there is a decent solution of the issue at stake. And the issue at stake is merely a better wage to the average unskilled worker in the shipyards. To a large extent public opinion is with these unskilled workers now, but public opinion will turn against them if their wage issue brings chaos and disaster upon the whole community unnecessarily. Seattle today is awake to the fact that she is on the brink of a disaster, *and Seattle is getting fighting mad.* The people are beginning to visualize the horrors that a general tie-up will bring. They see the suffering that is bound to come and *they don't propose to be silent sufferers.*

Today Seattle resents this whole miserable mess. Seattle resents the insolent attitude of the shipyard owners; Seattle resents the verbosity of Director General Piez, whose explanation does not explain, and just as emphatically resents the high-handed "rule or ruin" tactics of the labor leaders who propose to lay the whole city prostrate in a vain attempt to show their power. Let us not mince words. A general strike cannot win unless one of two things happens. Either the ship owners and Piez must yield or else the workers must be able to control the situation by *force.* The latter method no doubt would be welcomed by the agitators and the babblers of Bolshevikism. But the latter method is bound to be squelched without much ado, and you decent union men of Seattle will be the sufferers then. *A revolt—and some of your leaders are talking of a revolution—*to be successful must have a country-wide application. There isn't a chance to spread it east of the mountains. There isn't a chance to spread it south of Tacoma *and today fifty per cent of the unions of Tacoma have turned down the proposition for a general strike.*

Confined to Seattle or even confined to the whole Pacific coast, the use of force by Bolsheviks would be, and should be, quickly dealt with by the army of the United States. These false Bolshevik leaders haven't a chance on earth to win anything for you in this country, *because this country is America—not Russia.*

A newspaper urges workers to "stop" before rushing to join the general strike.

Even though the strike was conducted in a remarkably orderly way without violence, it aroused fear. A few months earlier, the Bolsheviks had taken power in Russia, vowing that workers would take over the economy and destroy the upper classes. The Seattle events led some Americans to fear that a similar revolution was beginning in the United States. Mayor Hanson aggravated those suspicions and quickly became nationally famous as he promised to end the strike.

After three days, the strike died of its own weight and the inability to maintain enthusiastic support. The unions had never really settled on a goal and did not know what to do with their victory while they had it. Hanson claimed credit.

Resigning as mayor, he traveled the nation denouncing communism and boasting that he had prevented a revolution. He offered himself for the presidency in 1920, but could not win a place on the ballot.

The Seattle General Strike failed to improve working conditions and wages. It was not the beginning of a communist revolution, but it was a serious effort to secure gains for workers. Local excitement leveled off, but a confrontation in a small town to the south would soon make more national headlines.

## The Centralia Massacre

November 11, 1919, was a special holiday throughout the United States. It was Armistice Day, the first anniversary of the end of World War I. (It was also the thirtieth anniversary of statehood for Washington.) Community festivities celebrated the victory and honored the return home of local boys who had fought.

The American Legion, a new and powerful organization of war veterans, sponsored many celebrations, including one in Centralia. This logging and farming town south of Olympia started by the black pioneer George Washington had grown to 7,500 people. A large crowd lined gaily decorated Centralia streets for the parade. A strong labor town, Centralia nevertheless feared the IWW. Wobblies had recently been run out of town but several had returned to open headquarters in the Roderick Hotel. Rumors circulated that this office might be raided. Armed Wobblies positioned themselves on building tops near the hotel and on a hill above town.

Townspeople cheered as local war hero Warren O. Grimm led uniformed veterans down the street. The parade passed IWW headquarters, circled a block, and marched back toward the Roderick Hotel where Grimm ordered a halt. At that moment a shot was fired. Witnesses never agreed whether the shot came from the hall or the marchers, but gunfire soon erupted from several directions.

Within minutes, Grimm and three other Legionnaires were dead; another later died of wounds. Nine Wobblies and a sympathetic lawyer were promptly charged with murder. Their office was raided and materials destroyed. Late that evening, masked citizens captured Wesley Everest, one of the accused, from his jail cell. They took Everest to the Skookumchuck River, killed him, and hung his mutilated body from a bridge.

Heartache and terror overwhelmed the small town. Newspapers across the country labeled these events the "Centralia Massacre" and denounced the Wobblies. At their trial, the defendants claimed that they had only meant to defend their hall. Seven were found guilty and sentenced to long prison terms. Three others, including the lawyer, were freed. No one was charged with killing Everest, nor was there a full investigation of his death.

The IWW was on the decline in Washington. In time, many of its goals would be achieved: the eight-hour day, better working conditions and wages, and the right of all workers to organize into unions. But the IWW itself was broken by public fear, suspicion, and the arrest of its leaders. Most historians today doubt that the Wobblies were attempting to overthrow the government, and consider them no more violent than their opponents.

## The Red Scare

Washington was in the forefront of events in 1919 and 1920 that became known as the Red Scare. Wartime patriotism and the Russian Revolution were the background to such incidents as the Seattle General Strike and the Centralia Massacre. Politicians traded on fears of radicals and dissidents. In 1920 the U.S. attorney general had alien radicals arrested throughout the country, seeking

Anna Louise Strong, political activist

to imprison or deport them. Fear of violence seemed real when several national leaders, including Seattle's Mayor Hanson, received bombs in the mail.

Anna Louise Strong was a young woman who became a famous radical. Holding a doctorate in social work, Strong was intellectual and energetic. She moved to Seattle where her father, a prominent minister, and her brother were living. A welcome addition to women's groups and liberal causes, she was the first woman elected to the Seattle School Board. But boredom with contracts and funding issues led her to pursue other concerns. Soon she became known as sympathetic toward such groups as the Wobblies and individuals she believed were being mistreated. Like many citizens, she opposed the United States entering World War I.

As criticism of her mounted, opponents petitioned to recall her from the school board. The recall device was intended to remove dishonest or incompetent officials. This time it was used, successfully, to remove an honest but controversial figure from a nonpaying job because of her political beliefs and activities.

Discouraged that the Seattle General Strike had collapsed, Strong left Seattle for a career in journalism. She lived in and defended the policies of the Soviet Union and the People's Republic of China, while keeping ties to her onetime Seattle home. She died in Peking (now Beijing) in 1970.

Another Washingtonian prominent in the period was Congressman Albert Johnson. As a Hoquiam newspaper publisher, Johnson had strongly opposed the IWW since its earliest days. He distrusted aliens and radicals generally. Elected to the House of Representatives in 1912, he later became chairman of the powerful House Immigration Committee. He steered through Congress important revisions to immigration laws, which set quotas on the number of aliens allowed to enter the United States each year from any given country. Japanese were excluded altogether.

After twenty years in Congress, Johnson was defeated during the Democratic landslide in 1932. He dropped out of public life and died at American Lake in 1957.

## The 1920s

Between the end of World War I in 1918 and the stock market crash in 1929, prosperity seemed widespread and life good in the United States: the decade is sometimes called the Golden Twenties. Many things that are commonplace today first appeared during these years. Over half the American people lived in cities; small farms were disappearing. Automobiles allowed people to move easily and frequently over great distances. In Seattle a man set up tanks of gasoline specifically in order to pump gas into cars, and thus began the first gas station.

Radio enabled persons thousands of miles apart to hear the same news, sports, or entertainment at the same moment. In 1922 KJR, one of the earliest radio stations in the country, began to broadcast from Seattle. Motion picture theaters became common in towns, and silent films were replaced by "talkies." Refrigerators, electric ovens, vacuum cleaners, washing machines, and other appliances helped daily chores move faster.

Changes occurred in attitudes and moral standards. The old ties that held families closely together were weakening. Women, who had just received the vote nationally, secured greater social freedom and became more politically active. Bertha Landes was elected mayor of Seattle, the first woman mayor of any major American city. Prohibition made alcohol illegal and unintentionally caused disrespect for laws and authority.

The 1920s began with a slight depression as the country adjusted to the change from a wartime economy, but by 1923 all seemed to be going well nationally. Most people had jobs. Many had extra funds to invest in real estate or in the stock market. Prosperity seemed widespread among white, urban Americans, but large groups, including farmers and racial minorities, did not share in the good times.

This national pattern was followed in the Pacific Northwest. But the growth slowed. Between 1920 and 1930, Washington's population increased only 15 percent, and the three largest cities remained about the same size.

The early 1920s were a time of depression in Washington. Industries that had grown during the war received few contracts. Shipbuilding slowed; lumber retrenched; agricultural production was not good and prices were low.

Slowly but steadily, more money became available. New industries helped to diversify the economy, although most were related to the old standbys. Pulp and paper industries grew, as did printing, publishing, building construction, furniture making, clothing manufacture, and food processing. Almost half of the manufacturing plants were small, however, with most located in the three large cities.

## POLITICS IN THE 1920s

Washington politics in the 1920s centered around two men, Mark Reed and Roland Hartley. Both were Republicans from the lumber industry, but they had different attitudes toward government and the people.

### Mark Reed

Mark Reed, a Shelton lumberman, was the most influential state political leader during the 1920s. As a young man Reed worked in the woods, got an education, and failed in his first logging venture during the Panic of 1893. But unusual business ability and sound judgment helped him climb rapidly in the Simpson Logging Company. He also married the owner's daughter, and after his father-in-law's death in 1906, Reed became head of the company. Soon he was a powerful and highly respected businessman.

The Simpson Company dominated the logging industry in southwest Washington. Adding expansive tracts of logging land, Simpson grew to control more timber interests in western Washington than any company except the giant Weyerhaeuser Company. Simpson then expanded to making shakes, milling hemlock, and encouraging related industries around Shelton and nearby McCleary.

Shelton was not technically a company town, but the logging company clearly dominated it. The Simpson and Reed families helped make it a pleasant, healthy town for employees. The families personally built or promoted a town hall, parks, a library, and schools along with attractive streets and homes. For many years Mark Reed was mayor. His loyalty to employees extended to help during the 1930s depression when the company had to lay off workers. He improved working conditions in his logging camps and mills.

Elected to the state legislature in 1914, Reed quickly became a respected leader and was repeatedly reelected. In 1919, Louis Hart, a Ferry County lawyer, became governor. But he quietly remained in the background as Reed, now Speaker of the House of Representatives, emerged as the most powerful official in state government.

Reed viewed his control of vast areas of timber as a stewardship. He felt a strong responsibility to the public and to his employees, yet he was also the practical businessman seeking support for industry and his district. He helped shift tax laws to favor the lumber industry but also encouraged conservation in timberlands long before this need was generally recognized. He worked to deny raises to state employees. He pushed laws to restrict Asians from owning farmland, which caused many Japanese farmers to leave Washington. He thought private companies should control hydroelectric resources and opposed the public power movement. He favored a sales tax and a tax on utilities. After favoring a poll tax, Reed became convinced that it discouraged poor people from voting and was unfair, and he worked to repeal it.

Reed favored increased funds for schools, colleges, and the highways that automobiles suddenly made necessary. He encouraged laws for workers' compensation—that is, relief for a worker laid off or injured in an industrial accident. Many people expected Reed to become governor, but he declined to run. In 1924, voters elected another lumberman governor while Reed remained in the legislature.

### Roland H. Hartley

The new governor was Roland H. Hartley, a Republican, who served between 1925 and 1933. An Everett mill owner and former mayor, he was a leading opponent of the Wobblies during the Everett Massacre in 1916. Like Reed, Hartley demonstrated strong business drive and ability, and he married the daughter of the owner of his company. He convinced voters that he would

Mark Reed, about 1920, and Roland Hartley, governor from 1925 to 1933

fight big bosses, big interests, and big spenders, and that he would look out for the common people.

As governor, Hartley proved to be shrewd, heavy-handed, and conservative. He tried to bring state government more directly under his personal control and cut programs he considered expensive. He believed that government aid interfered with an individual's incentive to work hard. He opposed large appropriations for schools, reclamation projects, parks, and libraries. He argued that labor unions were trying to destroy business and he fought them. He disapproved of child labor laws and called their supporters "bolshevists" and "pusillanimous blatherskites."

Many groups and prominent individuals began to oppose Hartley. He was threatened with recall, the first and only such move against a Washington governor. This came after big cuts in University of Washington appropriations and the firing of U.W. president Henry Suzzallo. The recall effort failed and Hartley was reelected.

In the next session of the legislature, Hartley was milder toward his opponents and willing to compromise. He even increased funds for highways and the university. Soon after his

reelection, however, the nationwide depression began. Again, the governor and the lawmakers began to quarrel, this time over how to fight the depression. Defeated in the Republican primary election of 1932, Hartley retired to his home above the Everett waterfront. He sought reelection in 1936, but was unsuccessful and stayed out of politics for his remaining years.

## Prohibition

The Eighteenth Amendment to the Constitution brought prohibition to the United States. Manufacturing, selling, possessing, and consuming alcoholic beverages became illegal. Washington started statewide prohibition in 1916, three years before the national amendment was ratified. It was poorly enforced at first, but after the federal government passed the Volstead Act to enforce prohibition, federal agents and the Coast Guard were brought in.

Border states such as Washington offered opportunities for widespread smuggling of liquor, or rum-running. All along the Washington-Canada boundary, liquor could be cached away easily and then sneaked across a border that was long, often isolated, and difficult to patrol. Many people in border communities took part in this illegal traffic. Canadian officials did little to stop it and United States forces were small.

Smuggling was particularly common along the waters, coves, and islands north of Puget Sound. Rumrunners with high-powered boats eluded Coast Guard cutters. Low fogs frequently aided getaways. Rumrunners about to be apprehended could easily dump overboard a hundred or more cases of illegal cargo before agents had time to get on board. The resulting lack of evidence hindered arrests.

Some smugglers skillfully hid liquor aboard their ships or in caves along the beaches. Eventually the government used fast, high-powered boats with long-range guns. Increased violence brought deaths and injuries. Yet the pursuit remained a cat-and-mouse game with advantages to the culprit who was well prepared to deliver illegal liquor at much profit to powerful and otherwise law-abiding citizens.

"King of the Rumrunners" was Roy Olmstead, a Seattle police lieutenant who found it more profitable to be a criminal than to catch them. His smuggling operation was a big business and he was able to undersell his competitors. Well financed, Olmstead had over eighty employees, fast boats, and secure customers. It was rumored that his wife broadcast coded instructions to his boats through a children's radio program. His knowledge of police tactics helped frustrate pursuers—but not forever. Over ninety-six cases of Canadian whiskey, the largest cache of illegal liquor ever found, were uncovered from an Olmstead boat on a beach north of Edmonds. Authorities who searched Olmstead's home found enough evidence to convict him. A long prison term ended his role as the biggest rum-runner in the state.

In 1933 the Twenty-first Amendment ended the Prohibition experiment, and Washington along with other states passed laws to control the sale and use of liquor.

## The Great Depression

On October 29, 1929, the New York Stock Exchange recorded more stock sales than on any day in history as prices dipped lower and lower. Sellers tried to unload stocks and few buyers wanted to purchase. That stock market crash represented the start of the ten-year Great Depression. Throughout the United States, store sales declined, businesses failed, banks closed, wealthy and poor individuals found themselves equally broke, and millions were out of work and unable to find jobs. Marriages and families broke up; suicides increased. The confidence and pride of once secure individuals were shattered.

Because the depression was worldwide, Americans could sell few products abroad. Even weather played a part. Dust storms drove thousands of people from homes and farms in the Midwest. Many headed farther west with the few possessions they could load into cars and trucks.

The depression began during the presidency of Herbert Hoover, whose response to it did not satisfy most Americans. In 1932 Governor Franklin D. Roosevelt of New York was elected president. His many New Deal programs experimented with ways to improve the economy. They inspired many states, including Washington, to create smaller "new deals." Yet this economic disaster continued until World War II erupted in Europe in 1939. Then wartime production ensured economic growth.

Washington suffered along with the rest of the country. Reliance on a few major industries hurt an economy that was not varied and well balanced. Extractive industries and farming suffered because American and foreign markets could not buy goods. The lumber industry endured another long strike as labor unions battled for control.

Economic statistics for the years between 1929 and 1933 are shocking. Wholesale trade—the selling of goods to stores—dropped by almost half in Washington. Total incomes of individuals were only 55 percent of what they had been in 1929. Businesses and banks failed, and only half as many people were working in 1933 as in 1926. Many people lost mortgaged homes.

The population of Washington grew, but slowly. It increased by about 11 percent between 1930 and 1940. Many came from the dustbowl states and other unproductive areas. The West still held a lure as a place of opportunity.

Ordinary life became tense. Occasionally violence erupted between groups, especially among unemployed workers and "scabs" brought in to work during strikes. Some communities tried

Seattle Mayor John Dore addresses a crowd of unemployed workers at the height of the 1930s depression.

These girls on skates support strikers with the message "Don't Be a Scab."

was pre-TV. And we ate lots of potatoes and stew, when there was a good buy on stew meat. We were waiting for our 'ship to come in.' And there was always somebody to crack, 'I think my ship has gone on the rocks.'"

On the fringes of many large cities there appeared makeshift communities called Hoovervilles, ridiculing the president. Homeless men and a few women built shacks out of crates and tarpaper and obtained food any way they could. The name originated in Seattle, where one of the largest was located on nine acres between railroad tracks and the waterfront, near where football and baseball stadiums now stand. This area had been tide-flats a few years before. Smaller Hoovervilles were located elsewhere in Seattle and on edges of other large towns around the state.

Seattle's largest Hooverville was remarkably well-run with its own "mayor," "council," and "police chief." Politicians and journalists visited; nearby businessmen came to respect it; but some civic officials, including the health department, considered it a menace. Several times it was burned down, only to rise again. Finally, in the spring of 1941 as the depression ended, officials again set the torch to the shacks and Hooverville passed out of existence.

## Clarence D. Martin and Washington's New Deal

Republicans had held most state offices over the years until the worsening depression drove them out. Led by President Roosevelt, 1932 was a year of Democratic election victories. In 1931 only eight Democrats were in the state House of Representatives and only one in the Senate. After the 1932 election there were seventy Democrats in the House and twenty-five in the Senate. Most of the twenty-one Republican senators were still completing four-year terms held since 1930.

to provide temporary jobs, such as roadwork, for their own unemployed, but city and county funds were low. Several times, groups of the unemployed —once as many as 1,500 of them—marched to Olympia seeking a special session of the legislature to provide help. Governor Hartley met with them but would not act.

Yet life wasn't entirely grim. Those with money found prices low. Radio and movies brought cheap entertainment. A boy growing up in Seattle later recalled these days:

"Did we despair? Well, yes and no. Parents hung on and did the best they could for their children. The family unit was tempered in adversity. We even laughed. At Will Rogers jokes about bureaucracy. And we sang, 'Brother, Can You Spare a Dime?' We found a few nickels here and there to finance a baseball game, or a Saturday matinee. We tuned in on the radio, because this

During the Great Depression, homeless men scavenged for food and built shacks out of crates, old lumber, and tarpaper. Communities of such makeshift dwellings, such as this one in Seattle, were called Hoovervilles.

Democrats won all partisan statewide offices in 1932 and Clarence D. Martin became the new governor. The state's first Washington-born governor, Martin was a wealthy wheat farmer and flour mill owner from Cheney.

In his inaugural address, Martin declared that the greatest needs of the state were not political but economic, and he sought to cooperate with Republicans. Martin and the legislature immediately enacted programs for relief. Some were clearly patterned after programs coming out of President Roosevelt's New Deal. For instance, the state Emergency Relief Act tried to help the unemployed. This was the beginning of welfare

plans in Washington State. Pensions for the elderly were approved although adequate money was not supplied.

Most Americans had traditionally expected help for the needy to be provided by families and private individuals or by churches and other local organizations. In their opinion, the job of government was to govern, not to administer welfare. The depression changed that attitude as federal and state governments took on more responsibilities.

Washington State also tried to regulate prices and wages. Agencies were established to help business and agriculture. The costs of those efforts

Men eating supper in a Works Project Administration (WPA) workcamp. "There are over 300 men in camp and they are fed in two groups.... The food is plentiful and usually consists of two meat dishes, three different vegetables, and always, pie, pudding, and cake and cookies for dessert."

were great. The legislature put a lid on the amount of money that could be raised from taxes on property, and added an income tax, which the courts quickly declared unconstitutional. Governor Martin then steered through the legislature the state sales tax that has remained since 1935. It began as a 2 percent tax on every item sold except for a few foods. Taxes on purchases less than a dollar were paid with newly designed aluminum tax tokens, jokingly called "Martin money."

Taxes are always unpopular. Martin suffered from his association with a sales tax that seemed to take money from people when they needed it

the most. Yet his loudest critics complained that he and other Democrats did not go far enough. Centered in the Seattle-Tacoma area, new voices proposed even more radical changes. They echoed a variety of views being expressed throughout the United States. Some remaining Wobblies and other labor radicals made proposals. Technocrats offered a scheme to conduct government along scientific principles.

In California, author Upton Sinclair moved into politics with a work program he called End Poverty In California, or EPIC. His program had counterparts in Washington and other states. Another Californian, Dr. Francis

Townsend, gained perhaps 150,000 supporters in Washington by proposing to give each elderly person two hundred dollars a month that had to be spent within the month. Thus the individual would be helped while more money was put in circulation. Pension unions, made up of persons on welfare, were organized in several cities.

Early in the depression, an Unemployed Citizens League (UCL) was formed among people out of work in the Puget Sound area. It established "self help" programs in which unemployed people could trade for services. Tailors made clothes in exchange for haircuts. Loggers traded firewood for medical treatment. The UCL advocated spending government funds to provide jobs. This sounded like socialism to some, but it sounded like survival to many others.

By the middle 1930s several radical groups had joined to create the Washington Commonwealth Federation (WCF). The Federation proposed government ownership of banks, utilities, and natural resources to deal with the depression. The UCL and the WCF gained enough influence to help elect and defeat candidates. But by the late 1930s disagreements arose within both groups, and a growing distrust of increasing radicalism weakened their influence.

When Governor Martin sought reelection in 1936, opponents arose within his own party. However, a newly established "blanket primary" enabled voters to cross over party lines in a primary election. In other words, it was possible to vote for a Democrat for one office and a Republican for another. Many Republicans thus voted for Martin in the primary election and helped defeat a more radical opponent. After that victory, Martin easily defeated the Republican challenger, former governor Roland Hartley.

During Martin's second term, federal funds aided the state and put additional money into circulation. Led by the construction of Grand Coulee Dam, the federal government built dams,

## "Roll on, Columbia"

*The federal government sent folksinger Woody Guthrie to write songs about the construction of Grand Coulee Dam. The most famous, "Roll on, Columbia," celebrated the changes on that river.*

Green Douglas fir where the waters cut through,
Down her wild mountains and canyons she flew,
Canadian Northwest to the ocean so blue,
Roll on, Columbia, roll on.

> *Roll on, Columbia, roll on,*
> *Roll on, Columbia, roll on,*
> *Your power is turning our darkness to dawn.*
> *Roll on, Columbia, roll on.*

Other big rivers add power to you,
Yakima, Snake, and the Klickitat, too,
Sandy, Willamette, and the Hood River, too.
Roll on, Columbia, roll on.

At Bonneville now there are ships in the locks,
The water has risen and covered the rocks,
Shiploads a-plenty are soon past the docks,
Roll on, Columbia, roll on.

And on up the river is the Grand Coulee Dam,
The biggest thing built by the hand of a man,
To run the great fact'ries and to water the land,
Roll on, Columbia, roll on.

*Copyright Ludlow Music 1957*

parks, bridges, highways, and public buildings throughout Washington. Martin took pride in some of these accomplishments, while his own policies moved toward less state spending for welfare and relief. Despite these efforts, the depression did not truly end. Additional hardships resulted from a long strike in the lumber industry. Furthermore, many persons from other states came to Washington seeking jobs that did not exist. Instead, they created more need for relief.

Once again dissatisfaction grew. In 1940, liberal Democrats helped nominate Clarence C. Dill, former U.S. senator from Spokane, for governor. Dill was defeated by the young mayor of Seattle, Arthur B. Langlie.

*Other Political Careers*

The depression years brought many new figures into state politics. Some were conventional, some radical, some colorful. Victor A. Meyers, a dance band leader from Seattle, campaigned for mayor in 1930 as a publicity stunt. He dressed in a sheet and led a goat, mimicking the Indian leader Mohandas K. Gandhi. No one took his campaign seriously, except possibly Meyers. Two years later he ran for lieutenant governor in a more serious vein and promised to follow the Democratic leadership. He was elected and began a long, successful career in government. He earned a reputation as a reliable, conscientious, yet colorful official. He was repeatedly elected lieutenant governor and then secretary of state until an upset defeat in 1972, forty years later.

Homer T. Bone, at various times a Socialist, a Republican, and a member of several minor parties, was a Tacoma lawyer who advocated public power; that is, he believed that power companies should be owned by government rather than by private investors. As a young member of the House of Representatives in the early 1920s,

Bone introduced a power bill that came to be called the Bone Bill. The plan would allow city-owned power companies to provide power outside the city limits. Heatedly opposed by private companies, it was turned down several times by legislators and voters.

Finally, early in the Great Depression, Washington voters approved a similar bill as a referendum in 1930. Its passage allowed public power companies to compete with private companies. Taking effect just when several great public projects, like the Grand Coulee Dam, were getting started, it enabled public power companies to prepare to use the vast amount of power that would soon be available. Bone was elected to the U.S. Senate in 1932 and remained a liberal supporter of the New Deal until he was appointed a federal judge.

The other two U.S. senators from Washington during the 1930s were Clarence C. Dill of Spokane and his successor Lewis Schwellenbach of Tacoma. Bone, Dill, and Schwellenbach backed most New Deal measures and especially worked to secure Grand Coulee Dam and other power projects.

Mayor of Seattle for four years was John Dore, nicknamed "Revolving Dore" after he switched his position on several major issues. He was a jovial, light-hearted man who bluffed his way through numerous antics and accusations. Seattle voters also elected Marion Zioncheck to Congress. A brilliant young man who had worked his way up from poverty, Zioncheck held a serious commitment to the needs of the common people. But his drinking problems and mental illness resulted in several highly publicized arrests. One August day in 1936, while running for his third term, he leaped to his death from a Seattle office building.

This potpourri of officials and organizations helped give Washington in the 1930s a reputation for colorful public officials and radical ideas.

## World War II

World War II began in Europe when German troops invaded Poland on September 1, 1939. Even though the United States did not enter the war for over two years, it had an immediate effect on American life and the American economy. American sympathy and support were with the Allied countries, Britain, France, China, and later the Soviet Union. The Pacific Northwest began to produce war materials for the Allies.

On December 7, 1941, Japanese planes bombed naval and military installations at Pearl Harbor, Hawaii. Congress quickly declared war on Japan, and then on Germany and other Axis nations. The Pacific Northwest experienced those home-front conditions common throughout America: the enlistment and drafting of young men into the services and the enlistment of many young women; the establishment or enlarging of military and naval bases, including small posts in many Washington communities; increased production of war goods and the arrival of people to take jobs; shortages and the rationing of food, gasoline, and other necessities; bond and stamp rallies that helped raise money for the war; the return home of wounded veterans, of bodies of those killed, and, finally, of victorious troops.

Washington, with ports and production facilities facing the Pacific, was directly affected. Shipyards and shipbuilding increased in numbers and size. The Boeing Airplane Company converted to producing warplanes. Thousands of men and women bound for or returning from the South Pacific and Asia passed through Seattle and other port cities.

The abundant hydroelectric power from recently built dams aided new industries such as aluminum production. Dramatic and highly secret was the establishment of the Hanford atomic energy plant in the Tri-Cities area.

Americans all along the Pacific Coast feared

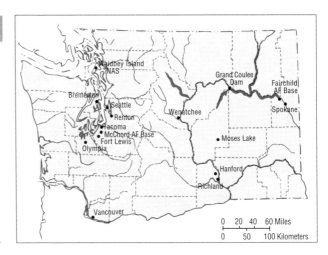

Sites of importance in World War II

attack. The surprise bombing of Pearl Harbor, some minor shelling off the coast, an air raid against Dutch Harbor, Alaska, and the capture of several islands in the Aleutian chain heightened these fears. The government ordered blackouts and brownouts in major cities, camouflaged defense plants and war installations so they could not be recognized from above, and placed mines in inland and coastal waters. Civilians prepared for possible air raids. People of Japanese descent along the Pacific Coast were evicted from their homes and farms and moved inland. Yet, no direct attacks were made on Washington.

The military presence became commonplace in Washington. Between Olympia and Tacoma, Fort Lewis expanded to become the second largest army post in the nation and a major training base. McChord Air Force Base was built nearby, along with other air bases on Whidbey Island, at Moses Lake, and near Spokane.

The Puget Sound Naval Shipyard at Bremerton became one of the largest repair bases for ships in the United States. Defenses were stepped up along the coast, on Puget Sound, and at the mouth of the Columbia River. A submarine net guarded the entrance to the Strait of Juan de Fuca.

Boeing's B-17, the "Flying Fortress" of World War II. Nearly 13,000 of these planes were built for the war.

## WARTIME PRODUCTION

Before the war, manufacturing was a minor part of the Washington economy. Shipbuilding had increased during World War I, but it grew to mammoth proportions during World War II. At least eighty-eight shipyards employed 150,000 workers, 80 percent of whom had never been inside a shipyard before. Tiny yards that had built small craft for years underwent remarkable growth. An Olympia builder of barges and tugs had employed only ten workers before the war; suddenly, it had two hundred workers. Todd Shipyards in Seattle was an older giant. Henry Kaiser built new yards at Vancouver, which grew large with government contracts for the rapidly produced Liberty Ships.

Vocational school students and prisoners also produced ships for the war. Altogether, Western Washington shipyards produced destroyers, escort aircraft carriers, landing craft, patrol boats, mine sweepers, troop ships, airplane tenders, seaplane tenders, tugs, barges, lighters, torpedo mother ships, floating dry docks, and other vessels.

Air power had been new and only slightly used in World War I, but it became a mainstay of World War II. Boeing Airplane Company was already manufacturing passenger, commercial, and military planes.

As war threatened in Europe, Boeing developed the B-17, the "Flying Fortress." Using several sizes of guns mounted on turrets, it flew high, for great distances, and at high speeds. Because it was durable, Air Force General Henry ("Hap") Arnold called it "a tank in the sky." Boeing sold bombers to England and France before the United States entered the war. In time, massive air raids by Flying Fortresses over German cities and industrial plants marked an important phase of the European war.

Meanwhile Boeing engineers designed the B-29, a superfortress that could carry large bomb loads, fly higher, faster, and farther than any plane known, and still fight off pursuit planes. Skeptics doubted that such a plane could be built. Wind tunnels and other research units were specially built for experiments, and Boeing reshaped the wings and body structure many times.

Disaster struck in February 1943, when a B-29 heading toward Boeing Field caught fire and crashed into a meat-packing plant. Test pilot Eddie Allen, eleven crew members, and nineteen plant employees were killed. Despite this tragedy, testing continued.

By the end of 1944, sixty-eight superfortresses were sent to China and to Pacific bases where special landing fields had been constructed. From these came the massive air raids that crippled much of Japan. B-29s carried the atomic bombs dropped on Hiroshima and Nagasaki that forced Japan to surrender in August 1945.

During the war, the threat of possible air raids led Boeing to camouflage its Seattle factories with a huge covering of wire mesh laced with fake plants, trees, bushes, houses, and streets. From the air the plant appeared to be a residential neighborhood. The success of the deceit can

This quiet "neighborhood" was actually a net of camouflage attempting to hide the Boeing plant from possible air attack.

New factories were built to turn out B-29s.

Women stepped in to fill traditionally male-held jobs when men were called into the armed services during World War II.

from out of state and many who had not worked before. Women and retired persons took factory jobs. A popular wartime song, "Rosie the Riveter," could have described thousands of women who assumed jobs traditionally done by men. In fields and orchards, women, teenagers, and younger children planted and harvested crops. Many schools closed briefly so that students could work in the fields.

Workers were spurred on with symbols and rewards. "E" for "Excellent" flags flew above many plants. Employees were cautioned not to discuss work that might be secret: "A slip of the lip may sink a ship" warned one poster. Rallies whipped up enthusiasm to work hard and buy war bonds and stamps. Celebrities, including movie stars, band leaders, and war heroes, were paraded into parks and auditoriums and onto makeshift stages inside factories to sell bonds and encourage greater production.

A block in downtown Seattle was closed off and renamed Victory Square. War bond rallies were held there each noon beneath replicas of the Jefferson and Washington monuments. More than any other war in our history, World War II was a total effort.

## THE JAPANESE RELOCATION

Not everyone was present to take part in the wartime activity, however. Approximately 12,000 persons of Japanese descent lived in Washington in 1941. Many were American citizens. The Japanese had already suffered some persecution and segregation. Exclusion laws prohibited newcomers from becoming citizens and those who weren't citizens could not own land; many communities allowed them to live only in certain areas.

About 9,000 Japanese and Japanese Americans lived in the Seattle area. Tacoma and other sizable towns also had Japanese populations. Hundreds farmed near Puget Sound and in the Yakima

never be known, for attack planes never reached the region.

Other industries started during the war. Iron and steel production increased. Abundant cheap hydroelectric power enabled aluminum rolling mills to be built at Spokane, Wenatchee, and Vancouver, and that industry continued after the war. Older industries were converted to meet wartime needs. A Seattle fireworks company produced explosives and smoke bombs. Wood and pulp mills produced for the war. Food production and packing increased with new government contracts.

The expanding labor force included newcomers

A Japanese American family arrives at Camp Harmony, Puyallup, with belongings strapped to their car.

Valley. Immediately after Pearl Harbor was bombed, rumors spread questioning their loyalty. Stridently patriotic Americans suspected that Japanese Americans would feel stronger loyalty to Japan than to the United States. Fears mounted that they would use shortwave radios or other methods to help guide bombing raids or landing parties.

The Federal Bureau of Investigation promptly questioned several hundred people of Japanese ancestry. Many were taken to jails or internment camps without trial or a chance to defend themselves. No similar steps were taken to round up Americans of German or Italian origin, even though we were also at war with those countries.

On February 19, 1942, President Roosevelt signed Executive Order 9066. This permitted the War Department to restrict or remove from certain areas persons who might be considered a danger to the war effort. Removal was encouraged by California politicians and supported by most political leaders and residents in Washington. On March 2, General John L. DeWitt, commander of all armed forces on the West Coast, ordered the internment of all persons of Japanese ancestry in the western part of the coastal states and southern Arizona. In a few days they had to dispose of all but a few personal belongings and report for "relocation." By bus and train, Japanese Americans of every age were moved.

Many from western Washington were taken to the fairgrounds at Puyallup, which was named "Camp Harmony." Here they were held in makeshift housing, much of it hastily converted from animal stalls. Conditions were crowded, food was poor, sanitation lacking, and constitutional rights ignored. After several weeks, many were moved away from the coast to camps at Tule Lake, California, and Minidoka, Idaho. Some went to other parts of the Mountain States or the Midwest.

Many lost their possessions and money they had saved or invested. Bank accounts were impounded. Businesses were closed, with stock and equipment left behind. Fields were soon overgrown, or other persons harvested crops that the Japanese Americans had planted. Here and there some church groups, other organizations, or individual friends aided them or cared for belongings left behind. But these actions were the exception rather than the rule.

A few protested, some less quietly than others. University of Washington student Gordon Hirabayashi refused to sign a statement consenting to be moved. To attempt to remain behind was a criminal act. Arrested, Hirabayashi appealed his conviction all the way to the U.S. Supreme Court, which upheld the evacuation. Hirabayashi remained in prison for most of the war. After the war, he returned to the university to earn graduate degrees in sociology, specializing in the plight of the Japanese and other similarly treated minorities. In 1986, more than forty years later, a federal judge reversed Hirabayashi's conviction. He ruled that the government had imprisoned Japanese Americans illegally.

Most white leaders supported evacuation. Governor Earl Warren of California, later a well-known defender of individual rights while chief justice of the United States, and Governor Arthur B. Langlie of Washington encouraged the evacuation. So did Seattle Mayor Earl Millikin and U.S. Supreme Court Justice William O. Douglas. One

Japanese Americans were housed in temporary quarters at Camp Harmony.

of the few prominent individuals to speak against the action was the mayor of Tacoma and future United States senator, Harry P. Cain.

Gradually individual Japanese internees were allowed to swear their loyalty to the United States and were released. Almost legendary is the 442nd combat team of the United States Army, which consisted entirely of Japanese Americans. Many were volunteers recruited from the camps. Serving in Italy, the 442nd became the most decorated unit in the army.

In December 1944, Executive Order 9066 was revoked, but many Japanese Americans who returned to their former homes were greeted with hostility. Signs denounced them; storekeepers told them to stay out. They found their homes or farms destroyed, run down, or taken

## The Internment of Japanese Americans

*A Japanese American university student describes his family's relocation to Camp Harmony just after the bombing of Pearl Harbor:*

*"We could take only what we could carry, and most of us were carrying two suitcases or duffel bags. The rest of our stuff that we couldn't sell was stored in the Buddhist church my mother belonged to. When we came back, thieves had broken in and stolen almost everything of value from the church. . . .*

*"They took all of us down to the Puyallup fairgrounds, Camp Harmony, and everything had been thrown together in haste. They had converted some of the display and exhibit areas into rooms and had put up some barracks on the parking lot. The walls in our barracks were about eight feet high with open space above and with big knotholes in the boards of the partitions. Our family was large, so we had two rooms.*

*"They had also built barbed-wire fences around the camp with a tower on each corner with military personnel and machine guns, rifles, and searchlights. It was terrifying because we didn't know what was going to happen to us. We didn't know where we were going and we were just doing what we were told. No questions were asked. If you get an order, you go ahead and do it. . . .*

*"We had no duties in the sense that we were required to work, but you can't expect a camp to manage itself. They had jobs open in the kitchen and stock room, and eventually they opened a school where I helped teach a little. I wasn't a qualified teacher, and I got about $13 a month. We weren't given an allowance while we were in Camp Harmony waiting for the camp at Minidoka [Idaho] to be finished, so it was pretty tight for some families.*

*"From Camp Harmony on, the family structure was broken down. Children ran everywhere they wanted to in the camp, and parents lost their authority. We could eat in any mess hall we wanted, and kids began ignoring their parents and wandering wherever they pleased.*

*"Eventually they boarded us on army trucks and took us to trains to be transported to the camps inland. We had been in Camp Harmony from May until September. There was a shortage of transportation at that time and they brought out these old, rusty cars with gaslight fixtures. As soon as we got aboard we pulled the shades down so people couldn't stare at us. The cars were all coaches and we had to sit all the way to camp, which was difficult for some of the older people and the invalids. We made makeshift beds out of the seats for them, and did the best we could."*

*Quoted in Satterfield, The Home Front:
An Oral History of the War Years in America: 1941–1945
(Playboy Press, 1981)*

over; belongings they had stored or left with friends were often missing or destroyed. Many never did return to the Northwest but made new lives in the areas where they had been forced to live during the war.

For many years after the war, this harsh treatment was little noted outside of the Japanese American community. Families kept memories to themselves. Then, books, memoirs, and other reminders fueled efforts to redress these wrongs. Congress in 1988 voted to give payments, or reparations, to all Japanese Americans still living who had been interned. Payments of about $20,000 for each individual began several years later, a long-overdue admission that the government had acted unconstitutionally toward Japanese Americans during the war. They had been treated unjustly solely because of their race.

## THE HANFORD ATOMIC ENERGY PLANT

During the war years, a dramatic and secret development was taking place in the deserts of eastern Washington. Throughout years of feverish competition, both American and German scientists had sought to develop a new source of power by splitting the atom. Atomic or nuclear power had many potential uses, but the wartime objective was to create a bomb, which turned out to be more destructive than even scientists close to the project could have imagined.

Dr. Albert Einstein, who had fled Hitler's Germany a few years before, pointed out to President Roosevelt the possibilities of atomic energy. A nuclear reactor was built at the University of Chicago, where scientists created a small amount of plutonium. Plutonium was structured so that it could be split, releasing a tremendous amount of energy.

But usable atomic energy required far larger amounts of plutonium than the small Chicago efforts could produce. A vast, isolated area was needed to produce the element because no one was sure how much damage its radiation might do. Abundant power for plutonium production and water to cool the heat that built up were also needed.

Attention turned to a barren corner of Benton County east of the Cascades. About 1,500 people ranched and farmed around the tiny towns of White Bluffs and Hanford. The land was desert but the climate was fairly mild. The Columbia River flowed through it, and Grand Coulee Dam was producing hydroelectric power nearby.

In January 1943, U.S. Army engineers selected the site for their project, and started to acquire 560 square miles of land. Occupants were told only that their land was needed and they must move. They were given only fifteen to thirty days to leave homes and farms. Grumbling, they wondered why the seeming wasteland was suddenly so valuable.

Rumors spread that the soil contained a mineral that was the source of aluminum. At a mass meeting residents were assured that there was not enough of that substance to make a six-cup coffee pot. The general in charge dodged questions about the real reasons for the land purchases. Unsatisfied, the owners reluctantly moved.

Construction crews moved in, recruited from all across the nation. Crew members were given security clearances and put to work. Dormitories were erected along with eating halls and recreation centers. A booming construction town of over 50,000 people suddenly sprawled in the desert—briefly the fifth largest city in the state.

None of the newcomers knew why they were there, what the plant was producing, or even exactly where they were. All swore to remain silent about what they saw and their specific tasks. Military Intelligence opened mail and listened in on phone conversations. Some—unhappy with living conditions, secrecy, dust, and wind—moved on, but others came to replace them. About 140,000 workers passed through in two years.

Construction moved rapidly. Once the workers' town was built, monstrous new buildings—atomic piles—were constructed several miles to the north. Overall plans were seen by practically no one, but each new feature was added on schedule.

Rumors continued. Because the Dupont Company, which made dynamite, was involved, many persons suspected that a new explosive was being manufactured. Another rumor of poison gas production aroused fears of leaks. The danger that really did exist was from radiation. Several accidents that injured individuals were kept secret for many years.

Secrecy was complete. Even when an atomic bomb using Hanford plutonium was tested successfully in New Mexico on July 16, 1945, the Hanford workers knew nothing of that or of the part they had played. By that summer Germany had surrendered, and American efforts concentrated on defeating Japan.

On August 6, the first atomic bomb used in war was dropped over Hiroshima, Japan, unloosing power equal to at least 20,000 tons of TNT. Four square miles of the city were devastated. The blast killed or injured 160,000 persons, and thousands more suffered from radiation injuries and illnesses.

Three days later a second bomb was dropped on Nagasaki.

On August 14, the stunned Japanese government, leading a nation weaker than had been suspected, requested an end to the fighting. The war was over.

President Harry S. Truman announced that the devastating new weapon was the result of secret projects in Tennessee, New Mexico, and Hanford, Washington. Only then did the residents of the area learn what they had been producing.

This end to the war opened a new era of hopes and concerns. Atomic energy was frightening, but many hoped that it could aid mankind. The world would never be the same. Neither would the onetime desert around Hanford. The site of this remarkable new industry would become vastly different from the scattered ranches of a few years before.

In the autumn of 1945, Hanford and the rest of Washington joined the nation to look ahead toward what all hoped would be a new era of peace and development. The world was tired of war and depression.

## Chapter 8 Review

I. Identify the following people. Tell why each is important to Washington State.

Franklin D. Roosevelt
Ernest Lister
Elizabeth Gurley Flynn
John D. Rockefeller
Ole Hanson
Anna Louise Strong
Albert Johnson
Mark Reed
Roland H. Hartley
Roy Olmstead
Clarence D. Martin
Clarence C. Dill
Victor A. Meyers
Homer T. Bone
Gordon Hirabayashi
Harry P. Cain

II. Define the following words and terms. Relate each one to Washington State.

World War I
Skinner and Eddy Shipyards
Shingle weavers
Labor unions
Free-speech fight
Everett Massacre
Loyal Legion of Lumbermen
   and Loggers (Four-L)
Aliens
Russian Revolution
Seattle General Strike
Centralia Massacre
Immigration
Golden Twenties
Prohibition
Rumrunners
Great Depression
New Deal

Hooverville
Emergency Relief Act
Sales tax
Unemployed Citizens League
Washington Commonwealth Federation
Bone Bill
Pearl Harbor attack
B-17
B-29
Flying Fortress
Executive Order 9066
Camp Harmony
Plutonium
Hiroshima bombing

III. Locate these places on a map and tell why each is important in the history of the Pacific Northwest.

Grand Coulee Dam
Spokane
Everett
Centralia
Hanford
Puyallup
Bremerton
McChord Air Force Base
Fort Lewis

IV. Each question below should call your attention to factual information in the chapter. Try to answer each one. Then look back in the reading to check your answer, correct your understanding, and find answers you do not know.

1. What important industry in Washington expanded during World War I?

2. What was the purpose of the Washington State Council of Defense?

3. List several problems in logging camps.

4. What was the goal of the free-speech fight in Spokane?

5. How did the Everett Massacre affect attitudes toward the IWW?

6. Why was spruce lumber especially needed during World War I?

7. How did the government maintain lumber production during the 1917 strike?

8. Why were many people in Washington and the rest of the United States frightened by the Seattle General Strike?

9. What event was being celebrated in Centralia on the day of the Centralia Massacre?

10. By what method was Anna Louise Strong removed from the Seattle School Board?

11. What did the laws sponsored by Congressman Albert Johnson do?

12. List three ways that life in American homes changed during the 1920s.

13. Describe the positions that Mark Reed held on three public issues.

14. What was Governor Roland Hartley's attitude toward spending?

15. How did the Great Depression affect population growth in Washington?

16. Which political party took most offices in the 1932 election?

17. List three ways the Great Depression affected life in Washington.

18. What is the idea behind a self-help program?

19. How did voters in Washington "cross over" in a primary election? How did this practice apparently help reelect Governor Clarence D. Martin?

20. List several ways that the federal government helped put more money into circulation in Washington during the New Deal years.

21. Give three examples of ways that World War II affected the lives of people in Washington.

22. Tell three things that people in Washington did to prepare themselves for a possible enemy attack during World War II.

23. Why was Washington an attractive site for producing aluminum?

24. Name two groups of people that entered the work force to work in war industries.

25. Why were Japanese Americans who lived in western Washington removed from their homes during World War II?

26. How were many Japanese Americans received when they returned home after the war ended?

27. What new industry and new weapon were developed in a desert area of eastern Washington?

**V.** Think about, discuss, and answer the questions below.

1. Sometimes events in very distant places affect local happenings. In 1917, the Bolshevik Revolution in Russia brought the communists into power. What were some ways that this affected events and attitudes in Washington State?

What are some important world events that are happening now? In what ways do these events directly affect Washington and your community?

2. List and discuss some of the ways that Grand Coulee Dam has affected eastern Washington. How has the dam changed the way people live?

3. List and discuss several ways that World Wars I and II affected Washington. Which changes were temporary? Which were permanent? Perhaps your family members or the family of someone you know moved to Washington during World War II. Talk to some of these people. Ask them why they moved here and what they found when they arrived.

4. Because of its location and geography, the Puget Sound region and other places in Washington were extremely active during Prohibition. Discuss reasons for this. Try to learn more about law breaking and law enforcement during these years.

5. In recent years, Japanese Americans have received some compensation for jobs, possessions, and money they lost when they were removed from the Pacific Coast during World War II. What are some arguments for and against providing this compensation from local and national governments? What other groups that have been badly treated might also be entitled to help or compensation?

Chapter 9  **The Maturing State**

Steam and ash billow from Mount St. Helens during its violent eruption on May 18, 1980.

Mount St. Helens, May 18, 1980. At dawn on this clear spring Sunday, Mount St. Helens stands elegantly above forests and rivers. At 9,677 feet, this is the most symmetrical of the five Washington volcanoes, a picture of peace and beauty. Streams from its snowcap become rivers flowing into the Cowlitz and then the Columbia River, some forty miles away. The mountain cone is reflected in the deep blue of Spirit Lake, framed by fir-covered hills. Farther below, the villages of Toutle and Cougar quietly serve loggers and vacationers as they have for a century. A Weyerhaeuser Company yard at Baker Camp holds logs and heavy machinery.

This will be the last dawn to break upon that scene.

For two months, geologists and a curious public have noted seismic activity within the mountain and beneath the earth's crust. In March recurring earthquakes and bursts of steam warned that the mountain was changing. A few days ago, a huge bulge formed on its northwest face. Of all North American volcanoes, this is the one considered most likely to erupt. But when?

It happens at 8:32 this morning.

The rumble of shaking earth is heard as far away as Canada. Suddenly a white cloud gusts from the north side of the mountain a thousand feet below the summit. Seconds later the rising cloud turns gray and darkens as steam and ash and bits of mountain rock shoot forth. Billowing higher, the cloud blackens the sky. It will rise 60,000 feet—over eleven miles and more than six times higher than the mountain itself.

As the eruption continues, winds carry this giant cloud northeast. Observers have seen nothing like it before, a black mass churning across a clear blue sky. Daytime becomes darker and more forbidding than night. The cloud is so large and powerful that it creates thunder and lightning.

Some people assume that a great rainstorm is approaching. Only after they feel the drops do they realize that the rain is dry—not water but ash and dust. Coarse particles of pumice fall upon Morton, Randle, and Packwood, the small lumber towns that are first in the path of the cloud. Soon they will be inches deep in pebbles and fine ash.

In the great agricultural valley of the Yakima River and on ranches around Ellensburg, falling ash halts normal activities. Wheat fields and ranges of the Columbia Plateau are covered. Moses Lake and Ritzville, more than a hundred miles from the mountain, are among the towns hardest hit as winds swirl powdery ash into unsettled drifts a foot deep.

By afternoon, Spokane, second largest city in the state, is covered with a choking rain of ash. The cloud widens as it moves across the Rocky Mountains through Montana and much of the eastern United States. Slowly dissipating, it will pass over the eastern coastline within three days and proceed around the world. A comic bumper sticker will show a volcano with the slogan: "Don't come to Washington; it's coming to you."

There is little humor close to the mountain. Thirteen hundred feet of its top are gone, and a giant crater gapes on the north side. There is no lava, but melted snow, mud, and ash flow out to desolate thousands of acres. Spirit Lake becomes ghostlike, colorless, deepened, but held in place by a huge new dam of mud. No green tree or living thing remains. Cabins and lodges are buried several feet deep. Heavy lumber equipment is pushed about, and thousands of logs tumble like toothpicks down the raging Toutle River.

Flowing mud scours through valleys, wiping out homes and farms. It knocks down bridges, destroys roads, and interrupts traffic on Interstate 5; threatens the towns of Castle Rock, Longview, and Kelso; and stops ship movements on the Columbia River.

*The number of dead and missing persons approaches one hundred: campers and hikers, geologists studying the volcano, loggers, a photographer covering the activity for the Vancouver Columbian and National Geographic magazine, and eighty-three-year-old Harry Truman, owner of the Spirit Lake Lodge. In recent weeks, Truman had become a legend by vowing never to leave the mountain. Only two days ago he talked with Oregon schoolchildren and then returned home. His lodge is buried and his body will never be found. The bodies that are recovered become grisly reminders of sudden, unexpected horror.*

*Ash and dust, swirling in the slightest breeze, will halt traffic and work for many days in much of the Northwest. Travelers will be stranded when state highways are closed. The effect upon wheat and other crops, on livestock, wildlife, and fish runs may not be known for years. Estimates of total damage will reach several billion dollars.*

*After flying over the region, President Jimmy Carter will declare it a disaster area. This will permit government aid for some who have lost their homes, farms, and investments. But much can never be replaced.*

*A week later, a second eruption will send ash toward Olympia and ocean beaches. A June eruption will affect Vancouver and Portland. Only the heavily populated Puget Sound area will remain untouched as small eruptions occur throughout the summer.*

*The eruption of Mount St. Helens was not a total surprise. Much fertile Washington soil consists of old volcanic deposits. The mountain had a major eruption in 1842 and intermittent smaller ones for the next fifteen years. But its past ferocity was forgotten as the mountain quieted and the population grew. Today, a new generation learns that a rich, productive society can be brought to a standstill by a natural force. Nature affects rich and poor, young and old, healthy and unhealthy with relentless equality. From this day in May, residents of Washington know they must live with a volcano in their midst.*

# At War's End

**M**ajor wars bring great changes even to regions untouched by actual fighting. World War II permanently altered the Pacific Northwest. The war created new industries, helped older ones grow, and brought tens of thousands of new residents into the state. Many were black and Hispanic.

The traditional lumber and fishing industries remained, but much about them changed. They were joined by such new giants as transportation and aircraft manufacturing, aluminum production, atomic energy, and tourism. Trade increased.

Transition from a wartime to a peacetime economy was not easy. On the same day in 1945 that William Allen became president of the Boeing Airplane Company, the government canceled wartime contracts. In a year, Boeing employment dropped from 50,000 to 11,000 workers. Sales of airplanes fell from $600 million per year to $14 million.

Shipyards closed down or drastically reduced production. Manufacturers had to convert to making new products using new methods; this cost time and money and resulted in the loss of jobs. When construction at the Hanford atomic energy plant ended, the government had to determine whether and how this new, unfamiliar energy source would be used.

War often brings economic gains, and much of Washington's economy depended upon the military. The growing conflict between the United States and the Soviet Union became known as the Cold War. Actual fighting broke out in Korea between 1950 and 1953. Both wars aided the state's economy. Defense production continued, even though at a slower pace than before. Boeing began to build new bombers and to develop jet engines and aerospace projects. The nearness of Asian Russia and mainland China, which became

Communist in 1949, added to Cold War fears in the Pacific Northwest.

Additional construction was needed to house the thousands of newcomers and to replace buildings that had deteriorated during depression and war. Major highways were built north and south and east and west across the state.

Many city dwellers moved beyond old city limits to new homes and communities in suburbs. The population around Seattle quickly spread north and south, and then east across Lake Washington and west to islands in Puget Sound. Farmlands surrounding Vancouver attracted city workers who commuted across the Columbia River to Portland, Oregon.

Spokanites spread north and into the valley east of town. Tacoma stretched south to fill in the Lakes area and east toward the valley communities of Puyallup and Sumner. Small towns grew big, and new ones appeared where there had been none. In eastern Washington, Richland, Pasco, Moses Lake, and Ephrata became sizable new urban centers.

By the mid-1950s, the area including Everett, Seattle, and Tacoma had become a megalopolis that fused the three cities almost into one. Old towns like Edmonds, Richmond Beach, Burien, and Des Moines merged with new areas called Lynnwood, Shoreline, Highline, and Federal Way. The eastern shore of Puget Sound acquired the appearance of one long city. Some people called this "Pugetopolis." Streets and houses, shopping centers, office buildings, and then warehouses and manufacturing plants replaced dairy farms and berry fields.

Two Washington cities dramatize the growth that took place. Before World War II, Bellevue was a quiet, rural, lakeside town even though it was only a few miles across Lake Washington from downtown Seattle. Richland was a desert community of two hundred persons. A few years after the war ended, these were among the largest and most important cities in the state.

## BELLEVUE

Bellevue is Washington's fifth largest city. Its history began in 1869. Seattle was only a few years old when William Meydenbauer, a Seattle baker, acquired property on the eastern shore of the lake. On weekends, he rowed across to improve his property and marveled at its beauty and quiet atmosphere. Other Seattle residents and several eastern investors bought acreage on sloping hillsides. A few miles north, plans for a steel mill at Kirkland in the 1880s hastened property purchases along the whole east shore.

Slowly a community called Bellevue emerged as timber was logged and more residents came to make homes. Yet, by the 1930s, it remained a tiny town in the midst of rolling hills, truck farms, berry patches, and vineyards. Along a two-block Main Street merchants operated stores and shops. A small fleet of whaling boats spent winters in Meydenbauer Bay. Each June a weekend strawberry festival attracted several thousand visitors.

Many residents worked in Seattle and a few wealthy families built stately lakefront homes. Commuters spent almost two hours each day traveling to and from Seattle aboard ferry boats, small passenger launches, buses, streetcars, cable cars and in private automobiles.

Some hoped to replace the ferry runs with a bridge that would connect Seattle with the eastside of Lake Washington. But a conventional bridge over the deep lake was not practical. Engineers and state Highway Department director Lacey V. Murrow envisioned a bridge made of hollow concrete pontoons that would float. Skeptics doubted such an idea would work, but the promoters finally won out and construction began.

Cars and walkers line up for their first crossing of the Mercer Island floating bridge on opening day in June 1940.

In the summer of 1940, the first major floating bridge in America connected Seattle with Mercer Island, neighboring towns, and the highway through the Cascade Mountains. No community benefited more directly than Bellevue.

World War II delayed the expected suburban boom, but by 1950 it was well underway. New neighborhoods grew up with hillside views of Lake Washington, Seattle, and the Olympic Mountains. The Bellevue Shopping Square included branches of downtown Seattle stores and other shops. Many newcomers were young adults starting families and building professional careers. The fast-growing suburban area developed a strong sense of community spirit and pride. New residents formed social and service clubs, opened golf courses and a yacht club, consolidated a school system, and began an annual arts and crafts fair and a theater group. It was not an inexpensive place to live; many new homes were costly.

Incorporated as a city in 1953, Bellevue kept growing toward the east and south. New shopping centers and commercial buildings were needed. A second floating bridge was built a few miles north of the original and later a third one alongside the first. Then, on the stormy Thanksgiving weekend of 1990, thousands of Bellevue television viewers watched that first floating bridge sink into Lake Washington as its pontoons filled with water. The bridge that had helped create one of the state's strongest cities was gone.

Meanwhile, Seattle businesses moved offices into sleek new buildings in eastside suburbs. Warehouses and manufacturing plants appeared. High-tech industries transformed the east side and brought affluent newcomers. Apartment and condominium complexes began to compete with single-family houses for space. Downtown Bellevue acquired an expanding skyline of glass and steel high-rises. It had its own cluster of residential suburbs and a sturdy cultural life not dependent upon Seattle. Likewise, a whole set of urban problems developed, including traffic jams, crime, and pockets of poverty.

But Bellevue thrived. By 2002 it had grown from a quiet rural village to a complex urban center with 117,000 residents.

Aerial view of a reactor at the Hanford Atomic Energy plant on the Columbia River

## RICHLAND

Richland was a small, isolated farming village. Then, during World War II, atomic energy development converted it into a sizable city. Its rise was surprising and dramatic.

Nelson Rich was a pioneer who suspected that eastern Washington soil could produce varied crops if enough water were added. He acquired desert acreage near the southeastern loop of the Columbia River and in 1892 constructed an irrigation canal from the Yakima River. The region soon was producing vegetables and fruits, becoming well known for grapes. In 1905 a town was founded bearing the pioneer's name.

Five years later Richland had three churches, three general stores, a bank, hardware store, drugstore, barber shop, meat market, restaurant, three hotels, a livery stable, and lumber yards. After a spurt of growth the population declined. For many years Richland remained a small, dusty, isolated community in a fruit-raising area.

No one could have anticipated that atomic energy would be produced a few miles away. When construction on the Hanford plant was started during World War II, Richland housed the earliest workers. Thousands of employees and their families lived in government-owned trailers, barracks, and hastily built prefabricated homes. The population reached 50,000, then declined as construction ended.

The end of World War II aroused concern about what would happen to the Hanford area and 15,000 remaining Richland residents. Soon the General Electric Company took over the atomic energy plant and assumed responsibility for Richland. The company and the federal Atomic Energy Commission agreed to expand operations. New reactors and plant facilities were built and additional construction started. Two thousand new residences went up, many of them north of the original town site. In the late 1940s company expansion created a housing shortage and the neighboring towns of Kennewick and Pasco started to grow.

Richland began to acquire the pleasant appearance of a permanent community. By 1950 it had 22,000 people and looked like any small city with trees and parks, wide streets, shopping centers, recreational facilities, churches, and schools. But it was not really like other towns. Few residents actually owned their homes. Six thousand housing units were owned and managed by the United States government and General Electric rather than by their occupants. Only Hanford workers lived there. Businesses and local affairs were regulated by the federal government and the company.

Slowly the town began to open up. In 1955 Congress permitted the sale of land and buildings. Individuals began to buy the houses that they had lived in for many years. By the end of 1958 most had been purchased. Richland became an incorporated town of homeowners governed by elected officials rather than by a government agency and its contracted company.

The Richland area continued to prosper. Surrounded by farming, the hub of the community remains a sophisticated industry that has drawn highly educated and technically trained individuals. They not only produce nuclear energy but engage in related fields of scientific research and production. The Richland High School logo is a mushroom cloud, a reminder of the town's growth and its leading industry.

In time, Kennewick outgrew its more dramatic neighbor to reach a population of more than 55,000. There are 40,000 people living in Richland and 34,000 in Pasco. The Tri-Cities area of the Columbia is an important urban center in a once isolated setting.

## Recession and Recovery

The economy of Washington has been unsteady since World War II. During the 1950s, Washington shared in the general prosperity of the nation. This was symbolized in 1962 by the Seattle world's fair, called Century 21. The fair publicized the Pacific Northwest and dramatized an optimistic future based on space-age technology. But the outstanding example of the space age, the Boeing Company, fell on hard times in the late 1960s with harsh effects on the region.

Even while the company led in developing commercial jet carriers, Boeing depended heavily on government contracts. Competition from other manufacturers grew, and the number of new aircraft purchases was unpredictable. During the 1950s and 1960s, Boeing occasionally had to reduce the number of its employees.

Every change at Boeing affected other businesses around Puget Sound. It was estimated that about three persons in other fields benefited from the paycheck of each Boeing employee as that salary was spent and circulated. In the late 1960s and early 1970s, Boeing shut down many Seattle operations. About half of its employees were dismissed.

Meanwhile, problems in the lumber and forest products industries appeared to be permanent. Wood was being replaced in many of its traditional uses by plastics and other materials. Housing construction that depended upon lumber was declining.

Competition from the growing lumber industries in the southeastern United States and Canada hurt the Northwest. When large mills closed in such centers as Everett, Raymond, and Grays Harbor, the economic effects snowballed. By the 1980s, most experts agreed that the lumber industry of the Northwest could never again be the giant that it had been since the earliest days of white settlement.

Nevertheless, some of these economic problems were offset by changes and advancements. Many men and women laid off by Boeing had unusual skills and abilities. They used their talents and energy to begin new companies and services. Boeing itself began to regroup and to branch into such new activities as making hydrofoil boats and computerized people movers.

Spokane publicized the opportunities of the Inland Empire with a world's fair in 1974.

The tourist industry sought to expand. Government and business leaders made specific efforts to attract new companies and increase trade.

The state emerged from its slump with a stronger, more diversified, and more sophisticated economy. Yet a recession hit during the 1980s when the aircraft and lumber industries slumped and federal money became scarce. Much of the state prospered during the 1990s with increased trade and the newer high-tech and software industries.

## Politics

The popularity of President Franklin D. Roosevelt throughout the depression and World War II helped Democrats remain the leading political party in most states. Washington, where Republicans had long dominated, shared in this trend but only to a degree. Washington citizens often divided votes between Democrats and Republicans instead of staying loyal to one particular party.

This independence from party control has created some unusual situations and prompted cooperation between political rivals. A governor from one party frequently must work closely with other officials or a majority of legislature members from the opposite party. Republican governors and Democratic legislators, for instance, have cooperated several times to conduct the state's business. Yet it can lead to stalemates and squabbling.

All of Washington's governors in the last half of the twentieth century came from the Seattle-Tacoma-Everett area. All had considerable experience in politics and government, locally, statewide, or nationally. Several had previously served in the state legislature, two in Congress, one headed a major federal agency, and four had been city mayors or county executives. Several were attorneys. Dixy Lee Ray (1977–1981) was a well-known biologist and television personality

and still the only woman to have been elected governor. Mon C. Wallgren was the only person to have served in the three positions of U.S. representative, U.S. senator, and governor. Arthur B. Langlie (1941–1945 and 1949–1957) and Daniel J. Evans (1965–1977) were the only governors elected to three four-year terms.

All of these governors dealt with issues involving a rapidly growing and changing state that was affected more and more by national and world affairs. They concerned themselves with developing trade and the economy, with funding and taxation matters, with such institutions as schools and prisons, with transportation, with energy and conservation issues, and with improving state government.

A notable example of Washington's governors is Republican Daniel J. Evans, who was first elected in 1964. An interesting trend continued that year: elsewhere in the nation, Democratic candidates were generally being elected, while Washington chose several Republican officials. A Seattle civil engineer, Dan Evans campaigned with professional terminology, outlining a "Blueprint for Progress" to develop Washington.

Although he surely had opponents, Evans gained a reputation as a forthright and honest politician. He enjoyed high standing among liberals of his party and was occasionally mentioned for a national office. A prominent historian later proclaimed him one of the ten most effective governors ever to serve any state. After leaving office in 1977, Evans became president of The Evergreen State College, which he had helped establish just outside Olympia. He became a U.S. senator after the death of Democratic senator Henry M. Jackson in 1983. He did not run for reelection in 1986, but he remained active in political and civic activities.

When Gary Locke first took office in January 1997, the former legislator and King County Executive was familiar with the issues that the state faced. A Democrat, he often had to work with a legislature led by Republican opponents. His principal concerns included long-standing issues of education, medical care, transportation, taxation, and trade. Locke kept a relatively quiet profile as governor. He was decisively reelected in 2000, defeating a well-known conservative radio-talk-show host. In his second term, he had to deal with a poor economy.

For many years after World War II, Washington's two United States senators were Democrats, Warren G. Magnuson of Seattle and Henry M. Jackson of Everett. Both had entered the U.S. House of Representatives as supporters of Franklin Roosevelt. Magnuson moved to the Senate in 1945 and Jackson in 1953. Their long time in office (seniority), their close attention to local needs, and their association with important national issues made both of them powerful Senate figures by the 1960s.

By 1979 Magnuson had served longer than any other senator had. He chaired or served on powerful committees that dealt with business, trade, and government funding. He showed particular concern in matters dealing with health, medicine, and consumers' rights. At each election Magnuson seemed unbeatable, until his surprise defeat in 1980 by Washington attorney general Slade Gorton.

Henry Jackson chaired the Senate Energy Committee and was a major advocate of a strong military defense. A leading contender for the Democratic presidential nomination in 1976, Jackson remained a force in the Senate until his sudden death at his Everett home in September 1983. Led by Magnuson and Jackson, Washington in the late 1970s reputedly had the most powerful congressional delegation of any state.

Slade Gorton, a quiet and learned man, served three Senate terms. He became a prominent leader in budget matters (especially as they concerned the West), salmon recovery, aviation, and Indian

Senator Warren G. Magnuson    Senator Henry M. Jackson

issues. He was narrowly defeated for reelection in 2000 by former congresswoman Maria Cantwell, who had become a wealthy executive in the high-tech industry.

That election placed two Washington women in the Senate. In 1992 voters had chosen Democrat Patty Murray, who was reelected in 1998. This former school board member and state senator from a Seattle suburb portrayed herself as "a mom in tennis shoes": an ordinary person who understood and would serve ordinary people. Murray took a particular interest in education, health care, and aiding the growing technology industry.

The number of seats a state has in the U.S. House of Representatives depends on its population. As Washington grew, it moved from seven seats to eight in 1981 and nine in 1992. Both of the new districts were in the rapidly growing Puget Sound area. Most of Washington's representatives in the early twenty-first century were Democrats, but party members generally cooperate on issues affecting the state.

Tom Foley grew up in Spokane and was first elected to the House of Representatives in 1964. Like Magnuson and Jackson, he paid attention to local needs while developing a national reputation in Congress. In 1989 he was elected Speaker

Senator Patty Murray          Senator Maria Cantwell

of the House of Representatives, its presiding officer and the most powerful person in the House. This was the highest position ever held by a representative from Washington. Defeated for reelection in 1994, he later became ambassador to Japan.

But two Washingtonians prominent on the national scene after World War II were not elected officials. One was labor leader Dave Beck; the other was U.S. Supreme Court Justice William O. Douglas.

## DAVE BECK

According to the "American dream," anyone, even the poorest, can make it to the top. Energy, hard work, and ambition lead to wealth and power, usually in business or industry. Such a "rags to riches" story is that of Dave Beck, except that he took the unusual route of labor leader.

Beck came to Seattle in 1898 as a child of four. The city was in its robust, growing years following the Alaska gold rush. But the Becks were poor and Dave Beck quit high school to take a job as a laundry truck driver. After serving in World War I, he became active in his local Teamsters union. In 1925 the national union hired him as a full-time organizer.

In dealing with both employers and workers,

Beck started with persuasion but didn't hesitate to use force. His organizing tactics included threats and beatings and window smashing. But despite his violent reputation, he was no radical trying to bring about a takeover by workers. Rather, he insisted that workers and employers could work together for the benefit of both. He called his method "organizing the bosses," persuading employers to pay higher wages in return for a stable and reliable work force.

His control of truck drivers who delivered goods to and from businesses made Beck powerful. He secured good wages, hours, and working conditions for his union members, and he did favors for businessmen who supported him.

During the 1930s, Beck's Teamsters battled the longshoremen's union for control of Seattle waterfront workers. Beck strengthened his position during a successful 1936 strike against the *Seattle Post-Intelligencer*. As a result of these efforts, many Seattle workers were able to live better, to own their own homes, and to show other signs of the good life. The most powerful person in Seattle labor, Beck influenced business and politics as well.

Far more than most union leaders, Beck became a respected community leader, a role usually held by people in business and professions. He served on civic and state committees and boards and was honored as Seattle's "first citizen." Although he had never graduated from high school, Beck served on the Board of Regents, which supervises the University of Washington. He became wealthy through real estate and other investments.

Meanwhile Beck rose within the International Brotherhood of Teamsters. He controlled the union along the Pacific Coast, and he became international president in 1952. Under his leadership, the Teamsters was the largest and one of the most powerful labor unions in the world.

Beck's tight control of the union prompted investigations by the federal government. Beck had received generous loans from union funds and other benefits including a spacious waterfront home. He had not paid income taxes for several years. Convicted of tax evasion, he served thirty months in prison. Nevertheless, he remained a prominent figure in Seattle, taking pride in a city he had done much to build. Beck died there late in 1993 at the age of ninety-nine. Quite likely, no other local individual had such a wide effect on the national economy and politics.

## WILLIAM O. DOUGLAS

While young Dave Beck was learning city ways, William O. Douglas was growing up in the farm town of Yakima and coming to know the vast expanses of eastern Washington. Douglas was six when his minister father died. His mother raised her family in severe poverty and with strict discipline. The three Douglas children worked at odd jobs to raise money for family necessities and schooling.

Slightly crippled from polio, Bill Douglas began to hike and climb to strengthen his legs and body. He fished, hunted, camped alone for days at a time, and explored the coulees, hills, and mountains near his home. Valedictorian of his Yakima High School class, he received a scholarship to Whitman College in Walla Walla.

After graduation, he returned to Yakima to teach high school, but he was developing an interest in law. Douglas rode the rails to New York City, where he entered Columbia University Law School. Studying under some of the best legal minds of the time, he built an outstanding academic record, briefly joined a New York law firm, and taught at Columbia and Yale Universities. Then President Franklin D. Roosevelt appointed Douglas to the Securities and Exchange Commission (SEC), an agency created during the Great Depression to supervise financial institutions. Douglas became its chairman and a major force within the New Deal.

In 1939 Roosevelt appointed Douglas to the U.S. Supreme Court, a position he held until the effects of a stroke forced his retirement in 1975. His thirty-six years on the court were more than any other justice has served. He spoke and voted for liberal views, for the protection of civil and individual rights, for "getting the government off the backs of the people." Many of his opinions were controversial and frequently not shared by other court members, but they were firmly held and clearly expressed.

Douglas was convinced that all Americans must share the freedoms expressed in the Bill of Rights. He believed that unpopular opinions had a right to be spoken and published along with those generally held, that all defendants must be guaranteed their constitutional rights, that the privacy of every person should be protected. He played a significant part in making the civil rights decisions that opened opportunities for minority groups during the 1950s and 1960s.

Although most Supreme Court justices take little part in political matters, Douglas was an exception. Presidents Roosevelt and Truman both sought him as a vice-presidential candidate. He expressed strong views on public issues, includ-

Supreme Court Justice William O. Douglas in the relaxed mood of an outdoorsman

ing the conservation of natural resources, opening relations with China, and opposition to the war in Vietnam. Frank and outspoken, he was often controversial. His personal life, which included four marriages, was widely publicized. At least three efforts to impeach him were started.

Many Americans knew Douglas best as an outdoorsman and author. He wrote over twenty books about politics, the outdoors, world travel, and finally his own life. He maintained a cabin home at Goose Prairie in the mountains above Yakima and continued to hike the Cascades. Some hikes were public demonstrations for preserving land, scenic spots, parks, and trails. He was a naturalist who could write as eloquently about elk or a quiet pond as he could argue a legal point.

Douglas's life and views were formed in Washington's workplaces, classrooms, and outdoors. He remained personally and emotionally close to the state until his death in 1980.

Doubtless no other person from Washington did so much to shape the ideas, attitudes, and conscience of twentieth-century Americans as Douglas. He was one of the most influential Americans of his time.

## Issues and Controversies

The World War II alliance between the United States and the Soviet Union evaporated as Communism spread across eastern Europe. The rivalry between the two great powers became known as the Cold War, and many people feared that Communism might spread throughout the United States. Senator Joseph McCarthy of Wisconsin led a national campaign to expose suspected Communists. But he recklessly moved beyond that to denounce all liberals and others who merely challenged government policies or his own efforts. His anti-Communist campaign spawned similar efforts in various states, including Washington.

With a reputation as a radical stronghold,

Washington was a fertile field for such denunciations. Several prominent politicians, including U.S. Representative Hugh DeLacy of Seattle, came under attack. The state legislature appointed a committee to investigate local "un-American" activities. Its chairman, Albert Canwell of Spokane, patterned his techniques after McCarthy's. A major target of the investigation was the Washington Pension Union, which included elderly persons living on pensions but was headed by several longtime radicals.

Six University of Washington professors were accused of past Communist activities and of promoting Communist ideas in classrooms and a campus theater. Three faculty members were fired and many more feared expressing opinions freely. Philosophy professor Melvin Rader dramatically proved the falseness of accusations made against him, but others lost jobs and found their reputations ruined.

The state superintendent of public instruction and a politically active Okanogan County ranch couple were similarly accused by political opponents, but they cleared their reputations through lawsuits.

## VIETNAM

Washington was affected by issues and problems that have been felt across the entire United States since 1960.

An example is the Vietnam War. After 1964, the United States took on a major role in the war between non-Communist South Vietnam and Communist North Vietnam. U.S. involvement in this small country on the other side of the world came to overshadow most other concerns. Involvement of American troops, money, and material increased steadily. Once again, Pacific Coast states were directly affected by a war in Asia.

In the early 1960s, the economy of western Washington boomed and the population grew.

In May 1970, this rally was held at the University of Washington to protest the Vietnam War and to mourn the deaths of four students shot by the National Guard at Kent State University.

Government defense contracts generated by the war played a part, although many companies were producing mainly for commercial, civilian markets rather than for military needs. Boeing, for instance, filled most of its orders for military aircraft at its plant in Wichita, Kansas, while Washington plants turned out commercial jets.

Lumber companies benefited from orders headed for Southeast Asia. The shipping of goods by water and by transport planes increased greatly during the Vietnam War. For a while, more shipping left Seattle than at any time since World War II. Some argued, however, that other reduced government spending hurt the Northwest more than wartime contracts benefited it.

Almost from the beginning many people disagreed about American participation in the Vietnam War. Supporters, including Senator Henry M. Jackson, believed that American military support was necessary to fulfill U.S. obligations to South Vietnam and to stop the spread of Communism. Others viewed the conflict as a civil war in a distant land not vital to American interests. Increasing numbers simply believed that this war was morally wrong.

Discontent with the war grew in Washington State. Leaders of the anti-war movement included college students, several church groups, and some long-standing activists. Among the most vocal were Alice Franklin Bryant, who had been interned in a Japanese prison camp during World War II, and Giovanni Costigan, a popular and eloquent history professor.

By 1968 the anti-war movement was becoming linked with other causes, such as the civil rights movement and a variety of protests against what came to be called "the Establishment." The term included the government, universities, large corporations, and other powerful and entrenched groups.

Protesters published bulletins, held mass demonstrations, threatened violence, and caused a rash of firebombings between 1968 and 1970. One small group of radicals, soon known as the Seattle Seven, served prison terms for vandalizing the federal courthouse in downtown Seattle.

The University of Washington campus was the scene of emotional confrontations. The university was criticized for releasing student records to recruiters and doing research for firms that made war materials. Blacks, Indians, Asians, and Hispanics complained that the university discriminated against minority students and faculty. Many students also opposed athletic agreements with colleges that practiced racism.

In the spring of 1970, President Nixon sent American troops into Cambodia, a neutral neighbor of South Vietnam. Demonstrations immediately erupted throughout the country. Young people were killed by National Guard troops at Kent State University in Ohio and by police at Jackson State College in Mississippi.

At the University of Washington mass rallies denounced the war, the Kent State and Jackson State killings, the government, and university officials and policies in general. This spurred on local activities.

One day 10,000 marchers headed across the freeway bridge for downtown Seattle, blocking traffic for hours. The university was forced to close for a day. One demonstration broke up when two hives of bees escaped from a small pickup truck and swarmed through the crowd of demonstrators, police, and onlookers.

Racial conflict also led to violence in Tacoma, Pasco, and Seattle. But the turmoil in Washington was on a smaller scale than that in many American cities as opposition to the war mounted and the civil rights movement grew.

Before the war dragged to its conclusion, Americans of all backgrounds were questioning its purpose and the failure of the United States to win decisively. American combat troops were withdrawn from Southeast Asia in 1973, and Vietnam later came under Communist rule. As in earlier wars, returning troops passed through Puget Sound ports and airports. Soon, refugees from Southeast Asia were also arriving, adding another population element in Washington State.

## INDIAN FISHING AND THE BOLDT DECISION

In 1855 Governor Isaac Stevens traveled Washington Territory making treaties with groups of Indians. Most tribes gave up their land and were placed on reservations. In return the treaties gave the tribes who signed them the right to fish on reservations in their usual locations and to take fish for their own use and for ceremonies.

The treaties stated that Indians and non-Indians should share "in common" the salmon caught off reservations. A small matter to the few whites then in the territory, this was vastly important to Indians who saw fishing as a mainstay of their life and culture.

During the next century, salmon runs on Puget Sound and all over western Washington were fished out by Indians and non-Indians, by commercial and sport fishers. Indians caught the smallest percentage of fish, but their traditional methods of setting nets in the spawning rivers put them last in line for returning salmon. Purse seiners, trollers, and gill netters took fish at sea. State officials said that Washington State should control conservation practices by both Indian and white fishermen. This would limit the Indians' catch. The Indians argued that they were being punished because others overfished.

When a state court ordered the small Puyallup tribe to stop fishing in the Puyallup River, the Indians acted. They reexamined the old Medicine Creek Treaty of 1854, which guaranteed their right to fish in their accustomed places. Encouraged by other civil rights efforts of the 1960s, the Puyallups challenged the state. Tribal members, sometimes joined by Hollywood celebrities, openly violated state fishing laws and were arrested, often in front of television cameras.

Ultimately, twenty-seven tribes joined to sue in federal court. They argued that their treaty rights were being violated. The case was heard in the chambers of Judge George Boldt in Tacoma.

Boldt, a white-haired conservative, had been a federal judge in western Washington since 1953, and had presided in many prominent cases, including the Dave Beck and Seattle Seven trials. He listened carefully while attorneys for the Indians presented their case and while the state, encouraged by non-Indian fishermen, presented the opposing view. He reviewed early decisions on Indian cases and researched the meaning of the term "in common" as it was understood when the treaties were written.

On February 12, 1974, Judge Boldt issued one of the most significant and controversial decisions to come out of a court in Washington.

The judge agreed that the treaties did not limit Indian fishing on reservations or for fish used for their own food or ceremonies; there was little disagreement with this. The heart of his decision was that "in common" meant 50 percent. The treaties guaranteed Indians half of the salmon caught off reservations, and non-Indians, who had been accustomed to more than 90 percent, could

receive the other half. Indians were overjoyed. Whites were angry and many became defiant. They saw their livelihood being destroyed. Commercial fishermen feared they would lose investments in equipment and be driven out of work. They joined with sport fishermen in great outcries against the ruling and against Judge Boldt.

After the U.S. Circuit Court of Appeals in San Francisco upheld Judge Boldt's decision, the case went to the Supreme Court of the United States. In the spring of 1979, the Supreme Court agreed six to three that Judge Boldt had been correct. The state and white fishermen were forced to accept the fact that treaties were supreme over other laws. The Boldt decision would endure.

The years of controversy were frustrating for all involved. Indians rejoiced that white judges had agreed with their understanding of old treaties. They became more determined to assert their fishing rights and to handle other affairs on their reservations, such as selling tobacco, liquor, and fireworks, without regard for state laws and taxes. State and federal officials quarreled as to which had authority over fishing in Washington waters. White fishermen grew bitter because their means of making a living was hampered while the few Indians could get 50 percent of all fish caught. Many non-Indians openly disobeyed the rulings, facing arrest, confiscation of their fish, and jail terms.

On several spring evenings in 1979, conflicts broke out on lower Puget Sound between several hundred fishermen and federal wardens. One fisherman was shot and paralyzed by a state officer.

The Supreme Court decision and a renewed effort by the state Fisheries Department to reduce friction cooled much of the controversy. Most whites agreed that any future changes would have to come from Congress or by the Indians allowing adjustments to the treaties. In 1984, voters passed an initiative which attempted to bring fishing back under state control. But it had little real effect. The earlier court ruling held.

## A CONCERN FOR THE ENVIRONMENT

Fish were not the only natural resource being depleted. By the late 1960s, many Americans were deeply concerned about the environment and the nation's natural resources. Washingtonians, surrounded by mountains, open plains, and many miles of shoreline and riverbank, had expected clean air, clean water, open land, and natural beauty to remain forever. Some warning signals, however, suggested that this would not be.

Air pollution became evident above cities. All over Washington more industries were sending more wastes into the air, some visible, some unseen. In lumber towns along the coast, great plumes of sulfur fumes rose from the stacks of mills and turned the skies gray and the air smelly. The 562-foot tall stack of the American Smelter and Refining Company (ASARCO) copper smelting plant at tiny Ruston, a town surrounded by Tacoma, was visible for miles around the Sound. When it was demolished early in 1993, the sight was spectacular.

But industry was not the greatest offender. Two-thirds of the pollutants in the air came from the increasing number of automobiles and trucks using an expanded highway system. Industrial and automotive fumes mingled over populated areas. In eastern Washington agricultural areas, pollution from the burning of grass seeds and grain stubble hovered over some areas for months. Winds and offshore breezes had once carried away such smog. But a smelly, irritating, brownish haze seemed constant over many cities and towns.

In 1970 Congress established the Environmental Protection Agency, which set limits on the acceptable amount of pollutants in the air. In Washington, the Department of Ecology was created along with regional pollution control agencies. These agencies publicized the causes and effects of air pollutants. They could also levy fines.

If pollution became so great that health was endangered, these agencies had the power to limit public activities including work and travel. Some manufacturers protested having to install expensive emission control devices at their plants, but others complied. Efforts to reduce pollution received much public support.

Similarly, waterfronts, harbors, and rivers near cities were being polluted by sewage, industrial waste, and agricultural chemicals that flowed into them. The ground around the old ASARCO mill was contaminated with lead and arsenic and had to be cleaned up. The greatest cleanup in the state centered on the Hanford atomic energy site.

The effort to reduce water pollution was highlighted by the cleanup of Lake Washington, which is circled by Seattle and densely populated suburbs. Their residents use the lake for water

Disappointed swimmers survey a closed Lake Washington.

and for recreation. Two bridges carried thousands of commuters across the lake each day. By the 1960s, studies indicated that Lake Washington was dying. Sewage and water runoff from the million people living near its shoreline polluted the lake so heavily that it could no longer support marine life. The lake was closed to swimming and other water activities.

A group of Seattle and Bellevue civic leaders proposed a master plan to clean up Lake Washington. They wanted to create a new government unit, the Municipality of Metropolitan Seattle (METRO), that would include those communities directly affected by the lake. Governed by representatives from King County and Seattle governments, METRO would build sewage lines and treatment facilities. METRO also intended to include a rapid transit system and an office for future area-wide planning. But a bond issue to finance the project was defeated by the voters. Trimmed to just the sewage treatment proposal, reduced in area to just the cities around the lake, and effectively advertised, the issue carried on the second try.

METRO went into operation. New sewage lines and treatment plants were built and fewer pollutants entered the lake. Within a few years Lake Washington was nearly as clean and clear as ever, an object lesson to other cities of how community cooperation could bring about a major cleanup. Swimming, boating, water-skiing, and fishing could again be enjoyed on a lake that remained a place of beauty in the Seattle–King County metropolis. Later, METRO developed a county-wide transit system, and in 1993 METRO was merged with the King County government.

A similar cleanup took place on the heavily polluted Spokane River. Carrying chemicals and other waste from mines and milling operations miles above the city, the Spokane River collects additional pollutants as it flows through the thickly populated urban area. The cleanup effort was one of the major features of Spokane's Expo '74. Environment was the theme of that world's fair, and a chief demonstration was Spokane's successful effort to clean up its river.

In 1972 state voters approved the Shorelines Management Act. This law required strong safeguards and environmental impact statements before any construction or development could take place along the bodies of water and rivers throughout the state.

Environmentalists became concerned about how increasing population and industry would affect the land itself. Occasionally they thwarted proposed industrial developments in scenic recreation areas, such as the North Cascades and Guemes Island. Elsewhere they demanded that industrial growth should injure the environment as little as possible.

The media publicized issues affecting nature and the environment. Thus conservation groups, an aroused public, and an increased sensitivity among officials and business groups became a new force in the politics and economy of Washington. They sought to ensure that future developments would include a high regard for environmental needs.

In 1990 the state legislature passed the Growth Management Act. This required counties and local communities to plan and coordinate where jobs, housing, and open spaces would be located in the future. In the past, changes and expansion had often occurred case by case in a generally haphazard manner. Now, new developments would be phased into the existing infrastructure: transportation routes, sewer systems, power lines, and the like. Specific plans were to be put in place. The act marked the beginning of consistent efforts toward preparing for future population growth. Yet it was an unpopular law because many felt it took away the right to use or develop private property.

Meanwhile additional areas of land were set

Opening day celebrations at Spokane's Expo '74

aside for varied public uses and for preservation. Groups with contrasting interests studied and debated how they could best balance the needs for wilderness preservation, recreation, and the use of resources. The Olympic National Park, created during controversies over timber cutting in the 1930s, was enlarged during the 1960s to include a long strip of magnificent ocean coast.

In 1968 a third national park joined those at Mount Rainier and on the Olympic Peninsula. The North Cascades National Park included the rugged mountains between the Skagit River and Lake Chelan that had not been accessible to the general public. Its establishment involved many

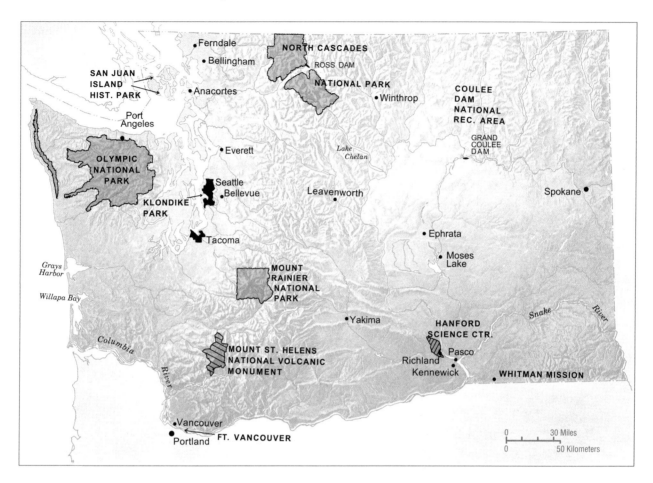

National Parks and Monuments

groups. Seattle City Light had power plants on the upper Skagit River and had long promoted the scenic and recreational attractions of the area. A state highway across the mountains opened in 1968 and allowed travelers to visit areas that only backpackers had known.

Interested groups had differing ideas about what the park should include. Several corporations wanted to take minerals, timber, and other resources from proposed park lands. Some environmentalists wanted the park open to various kinds of recreation, while others insisted that true wilderness areas should be accessible only

by foot or horseback. A compromise was reached. Irregular park boundaries enclosed areas that were set aside for special uses.

Another series of compromises led Congress to pass the Washington Wilderness Act in 1984. Part of a national preservation program, this bill designated over a million acres of Washington State as wilderness.

Logging, roads, dam construction, and motorized vehicles were banned from these wilderness areas. Much of this land was in the high Cascade and Olympic mountain ranges. They included a strip along the North Cascades Highway and huge areas in the Cougar Lakes region east of Mount Rainier and bordering Lake Chelan. Over seven thousand acres of juniper and sand dunes near Richland were also set aside. Two large mountain areas were named to honor the recently deceased Senator Henry M. Jackson and Supreme Court Justice William O. Douglas.

Cooperation between Washington and Oregon and the federal government led Congress to create the Columbia River Gorge National Scenic Area in 1986. Steep, forested mountainsides line a long stretch of the wide river east of Portland-Vancouver. The majestic waterway is also rich in history. The law seeks to preserve the beauty of the gorge, but it limits landowners from using their property as they wish. The act is an example of protecting a land area for its scenic beauty rather than for recreational or environmental purposes.

New state parks were created in varied settings and providing for a range of activities. In urban areas, some remaining open lands and parks were saved against the rush of population. Seattle created new parks out of an abandoned gas plant, a freeway covering, and many acres given up by the federal government—Fort Lawton and part of the Sand Point Naval Air Station. After Expo '74, Spokane had a new park on the river and two islands in the center of town.

A recession in the early 1990s posed a challenge for people concerned about the environment. Increasing numbers of persons believed that protecting the environment caused too many lost jobs and deprived property owners of the value of their land. A hot political issue in the new century concerned whether the government should breech or destroy dams on the Snake River so as to enhance declining salmon runs. Washingtonians constantly struggled to find a balance between environmental concerns and economic needs. When the World Trade Organization met in

Seattle in November of 1999, protesters from around the country gathered to voice their concerns about the impact of global trade practices on workers and the environment.

## ENERGY CONCERNS

It also seemed that supplies of energy might lag behind expected demands. Since the early 1900s, abundant electricity had been produced as snow-packs melted into streams and rivers that flowed throughout the state. The three largest cities and many small ones built plants to generate electricity from the flowing water. Public utility districts, local power companies, and the federal government built more plants. Hydroelectric power was cheap and people thought it would always be available.

This was not to last. Occasional power shortages were hinted at in years when snowfall declined and an increasing population and new industries required more and more electricity. Conservationists expressed alarm that dammed rivers blocked fish runs, destroyed salmon spawning grounds, damaged forest growth, and eroded land.

When Seattle City Light proposed raising the height of Ross Dam on the Skagit River to increase power for the city, objections thundered out of neighboring British Columbia. The lake behind the dam would flood a river valley in Canada.

Furthermore, the large network of power plants coordinated by the federal government's Bonneville Power Administration faced demands from other parts of the West. Surplus power from the Northwest increasingly went to California and the Southwest. By the 1980s Washington citizens were cutting their use of electricity and paying higher rates. Despite some success with conservation, major power shortages loomed in the early 2000s.

The two Satsop nuclear power plants of the Washington Public Power Supply System as they appeared in May 1985. They have since been shut down.

### Nuclear Power

Nuclear power presented a different set of problems. Dixy Lee Ray, Washington's governor from 1977 to 1981, was a scientist who had recently headed the federal Atomic Energy Commission. She saw nuclear power as a significant energy resource. Nuclear power was renewable because the radioactive fuel could be recycled. It was also believed to be comparatively inexpensive to generate once production plants were constructed. Dangers from radiation required that safeguards be taken.

Opponents of nuclear power feared nuclear energy had harmful effects that were not fully known or realized. They felt the disposal of radioactive waste should not be left for future generations to handle. Waste escaping into streams and rivers could endanger fish and other wildlife and disrupt the whole life cycle. A malfunction at the Three Mile Island nuclear plant in Pennsylvania in 1979 reinforced these worries.

Nevertheless, by the late 1970s, over seventy-five nuclear power plants were producing energy across the nation and more were under construction. One in Oregon loomed just across the Columbia River from Kelso. Nuclear power opponents blocked construction of plants on several small islands in Puget Sound and another near Sedro-Woolley. There, fears about the effects on farmlands and the growing population increased when geologists discovered two earthquake faults nearby. After voters overwhelmingly opposed the plant, the power company quietly shelved its plans. No new nuclear plants have been planned since, although the George W. Bush administration began investigating such programs in 2001.

### Washington Public Power Supply System

Meanwhile the Washington Public Power Supply System (WPPSS) had entered the state's energy picture. Created by seventeen public utility districts in 1957, WPPSS eventually reached eighty-eight members. Together they could build dams and power plants that none could afford individually.

In the 1960s, WPPSS built its first dam to produce hydroelectric power at Packwood Lake, just south of Mount Rainier. WPPSS officials also looked toward producing nuclear power. In 1968 they decided to build five nuclear generators, three on the Hanford Atomic Reservation and two near Grays Harbor.

Work began smoothly, but difficulties soon surfaced. Work delays, protests, accidents, poor workmanship, labor disputes and strikes, quarrels with contractors, and numerous other problems slowed construction. The estimated cost of building the five plants quadrupled from under $6 billion to almost $24 billion. It became the most expensive construction project in American history.

Groups of "Irate Ratepayers" feared higher electric rates and organized extensive opposition. In 1981 voters approved an initiative limiting the amount of money public utilities could raise without a public vote. (The courts later overturned the initiative.)

The leak of radioactive water and gases at Three Mile Island in 1979 aroused increased opposition to nuclear power plants in Washington. In 1981 WPPSS decided to stop work on two plants and to "mothball," or postpone, construction on two others. Only a single plant at Hanford was completed. It began to produce power in 1984.

The failure of WPPSS to pay off on the bonds it had sold angered investors. This made it hard for WPPSS and other Washington agencies to obtain financing for additional projects. Nuclear energy no longer seemed a desirable energy source in Washington.

Hanford also became the site of a controversy over the disposal of nuclear waste. Unusual safeguards were essential. Because radioactivity declines slowly, plans had to consider a future as distant as 100,000 years. If Washington was to become a dumping ground for nuclear waste, then Washington and the federal government should cooperate in establishing protection.

There had been problems for years. In 1990 the federal government admitted that radioactive waste had occasionally leaked from storage tanks and other sources at the Hanford reservation ever since World War II. Soil was contaminated and milk supplies were affected. Persons living "downwind" from the Hanford plant worried about the effects on their health. How to safely dismantle the old plants became another serious problem.

Yet even environmentalists found some advantages. Much of the 560-square-mile site had remained in its natural state while surrounding areas were developed or farmed. Elements of the region's past were preserved. The last non-tidal free-flowing portion of the Columbia River in Washington formed much of the reservation's border. Native plant and animal life flourished in their desert environment. In June 2000, President Bill Clinton set aside 195,000 acres along the river as the Hanford Reach National Monument, preserving it for future generations.

## Additional Energy Sources

No commercial quantities of oil have been found in the Pacific Northwest despite drilling efforts along the coast and in eastern Washington. Yet petroleum refining became an important industry in the 1950s when plants were built near Ferndale and Anacortes. Both were located so that oil could be transported by tankers or pipelines.

However, people feared that large tankers might spill oil in the often narrow and tricky waters of Puget Sound. Senator Warren Magnuson secured legislation to keep tankers west of Port Angeles. From this point, oil would have to be piped farther inland, and several companies sought to build pipelines.

Disagreements centered on whether Port Angeles should become a major tanker port and whether or where pipelines should cross Puget Sound and the Cascade Mountains. Oil also came by pipeline from Alaska. In 1999 a pipeline explosion in Bellingham killed three young people and devastated a large area. This alerted people to the potential dangers surrounding oil and its transport.

Energy production in Washington State

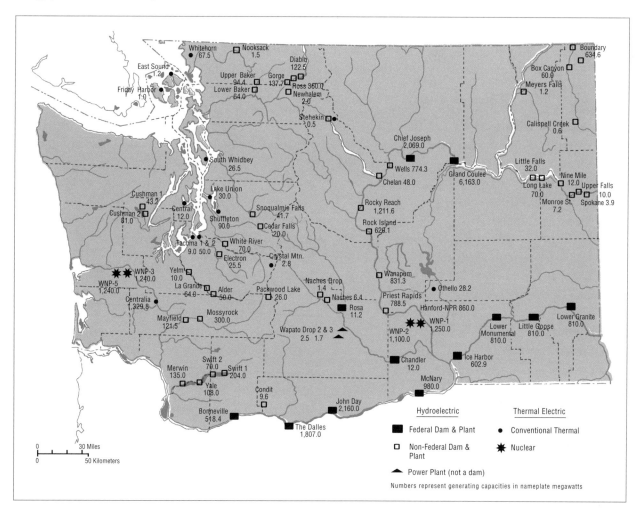

Other sources of energy were being explored. Even in the Puget Sound area with its frequent gray skies, more and more houses and buildings were taking advantage of solar energy. In the Columbia River Gorge near Goldendale, at Moses Lake, at Ellensburg, and near Walla Walla, gigantic windmills were constructed to use the winds that constantly whipped through. Perhaps sun and wind would join flowing water as an important source of power in Washington.

Increasing concerns about sources and shortages of energy led Congress to pass the Pacific Northwest Electric Power Planning and Conservation Act in 1980. Commonly called the Northwest Power Bill, this law emphasized that power problems cross state borders. It set up a council with eight members representing Washington, Oregon, Idaho, and Montana. This council is responsible for maintaining a long-range plan to meet energy needs. They are required to pay attention to conservation of resources, including Columbia River fish runs, and to consider renewable sources of power along with conventional ones. Costs, both for home consumers and for large industrial users, are to be maintained fairly.

## THE SPOTTED OWL AND LOGGING

It is a small and gentle creature, the northern spotted owl. With mottled brown feathers and weighing less than two pounds, it blends into its forest surroundings and is rarely seen by humans. The spotted owl seems an unlikely object of hatred and violence. Yet in the late 1980s its image was being crudely displayed on posters, T-shirts, bumper stickers, and cartoons. The mutilated bodies of several birds were displayed in prominent places.

The northern spotted owl became the innocent symbol of a bitter argument over the environment versus the economy. Pairs of the birds customarily live among giant fir, cedar, and spruce trees that are a hundred or more years old, underlaid with logs, shrubs, mosses, and ferns. Barely a century ago such old-growth forests were widespread. But decades of logging removed everything from ancient trees to undergrowth. New trees had little chance to become old. The region's magnificent forests seemed likely to disappear forever.

A newspaper reader wrote: "Old forests don't just host owls and produce lumber and beauty. When allowed to mature and continue, they serve as custodians over our air, streams, drinking water, fish, wildlife, soil, crops, weather, climate and numerous nutritional and medicinal resources."

Environmentalists discovered that the national Endangered Species Act could protect habitats of wildlife likely to become extinct. If the spotted owl was declared to be threatened, the forests it inhabited might be saved. With only about 2,000 pairs of the owls in Pacific Northwest forests, the owl was listed as endangered. Logging could be halted in the federal forests where the birds lived, although not in national parks and wilderness areas or on private land.

The possible end of logging ancient Douglas firs and Sitka spruce aroused fears and protests. Logging companies might fold. Loggers whose families had worked in the woods for several generations found their livelihood threatened. Some feared that as many as 40,000 jobs might be lost and whole towns could die. Following a 1990 federal study, Judge William Dwyer ordered that logging stop on almost four million acres until a firm plan was put in place.

Loggers and foresters, their families, and whole communities organized protests; caravans of logging trucks paraded to the state capital. Government officials and politicians scrambled to defend their differing points of view and to propose solutions and compromises. Particular attention centered on the Olympic Peninsula.

*Forks: The Evolution of a Logging Town*

Greatly affected by this dispute was Forks, a small town located on the Olympic Peninsula fifteen miles inland from the coast. Surrounded by timbered foothills and mountains, Forks is one of the state's most isolated but scenic communities. The Olympic Loop Highway that circles the peninsula gives Forks its only land contact with the rest of Washington.

On the prairie land near present-day Forks, the coastal Quileute once burned ferns and low brush to provide forage for the deer and elk they hunted. The first whites in the area settled near the coast or upriver. Like pioneer John Huelsdonk —the "Iron Man of the Hoh"—they lived off the land. They hauled supplies long distances from boat landings. One legend describes Huelsdonk carrying a cast-iron stove—loaded with household supplies!—on his back to his Hoh River homestead.

In 1878 Luther and Esther Ford and their two daughters acquired acreage and built a log cabin on the Forks prairie. They hunted, farmed, and raised livestock. Supplies and mail were brought in from Neah Bay, often by Quileute neighbors. Life was hard but comparatively successful. When a post office was established, the town's name became Forks.

A creamery, a search for oil, and a promised logging railroad failed to bring prosperity. For decades the area was connected with neighboring settlements and larger towns only by trails from the ocean beach or along the peninsula.

Finally in 1931 the Olympic Loop Highway cut through rugged land and linked Forks with the outside world. An early traveler on the highway was President Franklin D. Roosevelt. Forks would prosper for the next half century due to the logging of thickly forested hills and mountains.

By the 1950s, Forks had 1,100 people. It was described as "lively and growing. The fleet of logging trucks based there (the largest in the state)

roars through the streets. Loggers in tin helmets (to keep off 'widowmakers'—falling branches) stride about, striking sparks from the pavement with their caulked boots. . . . It is a lusty place, with a real logging-town flavor, and its citizens scorn the effete qualities of [Port] 'Angeles' some sixty miles down the highway."

Forks was the ultimate timber town, proud of its place in the state's prime industry. It became a stopping point for vacationers and outdoor enthusiasts. A dozen miles west, Quileutes at their reservation village of La Push fished traditionally along a magnificent coast.

But the logging crises of the late 1980s threatened all that. There were complex reasons why forestry declined. Older mills had not changed their equipment to cut smaller logs even though automation eliminated some manual labor. Other states and Canada competed against Northwest timber. Housing construction was lagging. But the closing of richly timbered acres so as to protect the spotted owl gave focus to many diverse problems.

Men and women who had been in the timber industry all their working lives were suddenly out of work, unable to find jobs and untrained for other careers. They were reluctant to leave the community where they had grown up and now owned homes. Timber families had always been affected by economic trends, changing prices, and uncertain weather. Now their livelihood was being altered by government decisions and pressure groups that seemed out of touch with their real needs.

In 1989, local loggers cut a third less timber than they had the previous year, and the outlook suggested that conditions would only worsen. Why? They blamed the spotted owl.

A reporter in 1992 found a town vastly different from that of forty years earlier. While "the nation is struggling to decide how far to go to save plants and animals, and at what cost to human beings . . . Forks, a soggy little place of 2500 [*sic*] people where it rains 12 feet a year, is living that struggle now. Unemployment is 20% and counting—up from about 10% in 1990 and 7% in 1989. Main Street is a forlorn strip dotted with bare storefronts, such as that of Birdwell Ford, whose manager one morning last summer put up a handwritten sign saying 'Closed. Moved to Port Angeles.'. . . . The sign still dangles in the empty auto showroom, next to an earlier placard: 'This Business Supported by Timber Dollars.'. . . . With fewer trees and fewer paychecks being cut in Forks, local businesses are wilting. Receipts from city sales and property taxes are way off. In addition to the car dealership, the pet store, the main clothing retailer, the movie theater and a half a dozen other businesses have closed in recent months. . . . Social problems are erupting too."

Forks and similar communities looked to lawmakers and to their own initiative to improve conditions. Some citizens wanted to save the ancient ecology by protecting the spotted owl, but others were hurt by the loss of both jobs and the industry that supported them. In May 1992, a federal panel allowed logging on 1,700 acres in Oregon that had previously been closed. This clearly indicated that the Endangered Species Act would be weakened in Washington as well. Neither environmentalists nor loggers were satisfied by this compromise that seemed to delay a real solution. The people of the Northwest, and especially those in communities like Forks, remained engaged in a controversy that appeared to pit the environment against the economy.

Forks survived. Forestry remained its central industry despite less logging and fewer mills. There was greater emphasis on research and improved forest management. A new industrial park was built around a dry kiln where milled lumber could be dried locally before it was shipped out. Shipping facilities, high-tech businesses, and increases in tourism and recreation

helped. Local amenities included a forestry museum, an arts complex, and a regional hospital. Once again storefronts along Forks Avenue were occupied. Despite its difficulties, the town grew to 3,100 residents, many of them less tied to the traditional industry. Forks had begun as a pioneering village on the edge of the continent; that pioneering spirit helped it meet new challenges as it entered the twenty-first century.

## THE ENDANGERED SALMON

A similar controversy developed around some of the region's most notable species, wild salmon.

The salmon's life cycle is distinctive and heroic. Spawned in streams of the region, wild salmon have for centuries made their way down the Columbia and other rivers and out to sea. After several seasons they return upriver, struggling to reach the stream they came from, spawn new eggs, and die. The young salmon then repeat the cycle.

During the twentieth century, man-made obstructions and natural changes threatened the cycle of the salmon. Along with irrigation ditches, culverts, and other problems along the route, the great hydroelectric dams of the Columbia, Snake, and their tributaries made the journey of the wild salmon increasingly difficult. Engineers who built the dams sometimes added fish ladders to assist the salmon, largely for the swim upstream. Efforts were also made to increase the number of salmon by breeding them in hatcheries and releasing them into the sea. But such aids were not enough. The number of wild (non-hatchery) salmon returning to spawning grounds each year declined. Fish also had difficulty traveling downriver through reservoirs and past dams.

Concern for the wild salmon and their journeys spread to local groups and government agencies, including Indian tribes, local power districts, the Army Corps of Engineers, commercial and sport fishing groups, fisheries departments of Northwest states, and private corporations that used electricity from the dams. In 1991 the National Marine Fisheries Service started plans under the Endangered Species Act to protect some Columbia River salmon runs. Only four sockeye salmon returned to Idaho spawning grounds on the Snake River that year; there had been none in 1990.

To protect the salmon and their habitat and migration routes, great changes may have to be made concerning the dams and other obstructions along the rivers. Much hydroelectric power and irrigation water could be lost, and other effects would be immense. In time, every user of electricity in the West could be affected. At the turn of the century there were arguments over breaching, or cutting through, dams on the Snake River so as to restore salmon runs. The controversy is likely to endure for years to come.

## The Livable State

Several years ago, people from all parts of Washington were asked to judge their community's livability. About nine out of every ten persons felt that their town was either a "pretty good" or an "excellent" place to live. Only 2 percent considered their community a poor place to live. Positive feelings were highest in rural areas and small towns in eastern Washington and lowest in Seattle. But even there, three-fourths of the residents participating in the study were positive; only 4 percent rated Seattle as "poor."

"Livability" means how pleasant or convenient a place is for the people who live in it. Frequently there are national studies to try to measure how "livable" a place is. These are usually based on such things as climate, jobs, arts, recreation, and the cost of living. The Greater Seattle area almost always rates high marks, and other communities often fare well also.

Whether the studies of livability prove anything significant or are merely interesting conversation pieces is a matter of opinion. Yet, they do suggest that residents and visitors alike consider Washington State desirable. Air and water have generally been clean; there is space and privacy even in congested urban areas; varied recreational opportunities are close at hand and available to people of all economic brackets; people have become increasingly attuned to cultural advantages; natural beauty abounds. On the other hand, urban areas have major traffic problems, crime rates have been high, and visitors and critics sometimes complain that people are overly smug about this supposed "livability."

### The Seattle World's Fair

Much pride and optimism was sparked in 1962 when Seattle put on a world's fair to advertise the Northwest and enhance the downtown area. Called Century 21, it seemed a brash adventure for a middle-sized city located in a remote corner of the nation. But the fair attracted almost 10 million visitors during its six-month run and was the first world's fair to be a financial success.

More important, the fair left behind a new enthusiasm and a new center of community interest near downtown Seattle: the Seattle Center, as the old fair site was renamed. Features include the Space Needle (which quickly became a recognized symbol of Seattle), the Pacific Science Center, an indoor arena, a grouping of theaters and exhibition buildings, a small outdoor stadium, an amusement park, a monorail to downtown, and a cluster of eating places and import shops.

Before long the Seattle SuperSonics were playing basketball there, the first major professional sports team in the Northwest. An opera company and a repertory theater joined the older symphony orchestra to use the Opera House and adjacent theaters. From this nucleus, Seattle developed into an important cultural center as art galleries,

By 2002, the skyline of Seattle had grown to a complex of office, retail, and residential buildings.

theater groups, music and dance companies, and major-league sports teams arrived.

By the end of the century, the Seattle Center remained a focus of many activities. Several world's fair buildings were renovated or rebuilt as new ones appeared. Elsewhere around town, an aquarium was established on the revitalized waterfront, the Kingdome stadium was built near Pioneer Square, and a convention center straddled the downtown freeway.

Yet, for a time the central downtown core seemed to be losing business and its traditional appeal. Then steps were undertaken to reinvigorate downtown. A bus tunnel improved transportation, and new office high-rises, stores, and restaurants appeared.

By the end of the twentieth century, the Seattle Art Museum had moved downtown into an elegant structure marked by a tall moving sculpture called "Hammering Man." A concert hall was built nearby, and a library was under construction. New buildings and upscale shops clustered around the flagship store of the national Nordstrom chain. Modern baseball and football stadiums replaced the Kingdome, and a flight museum was located at Boeing Field. The world's fair had helped to usher Seattle into the "big time," with effects that continued decades after the fair closed.

*Spokane and Tacoma*

World's fairs are not the only means to enhance a community, but within a few years Spokane tried a similar endeavor with marked success. Expo '74 was designed as an environmental fair, and the site dramatized that theme. Downtown Spokane had grown around a spot where the Spokane River cascades over a series of waterfalls and around three rocky islands. On the south side of the river, aging buildings and skid road shacks combined to overshadow the former natural beauty. Railroad and automobile bridges crossed the river at irregular angles. The river itself was heavily polluted.

For the fair, pollution was cleaned up. The worst of the old buildings were torn down and others were renovated. Railroad tracks were ripped out. New buildings included a cone-shaped amphitheater and a wedge-shaped opera house. The old area of town became a vital new center that remained after the fair closed. The waterfalls and the park were a glittering setting of natural beauty in the state's second largest city.

But increasing population and the construction of suburban developments and malls drew activity away from downtown Spokane as in other cities nationwide. Continued growth forced citizens to recognize that highways were inadequate and that the water supply was in danger of overuse and contamination. By the end of the century, the older downtown area was being enhanced while keeping its long-standing atmo-

Spokane's environmental-themed Expo '74 highlighted the cleanup of the Spokane River and surrounding areas.

sphere. Change centered around the Riverpark development of new stores and renovation of the landmark Davenport Hotel.

Downtown Tacoma also sought to revive activity lost to suburban malls. A large, domed stadium, appropriately constructed of wood, was erected alongside Interstate 5. A green strip with bike and walking paths and varied restaurants lined Commencement Bay. Palatial old movie theaters were renovated. The city's most notable structure, the copper-domed Union Station, dating from 1911, was renovated. It was flanked by a new federal courthouse and the arched Washington History Museum. Across Pacific Avenue the University of Washington erected its Tacoma campus around old buildings on a sloping hillside. A glass museum, an antique car museum, and waterfront refinements were opening along the water to the east.

## REGIONAL CITIES

Modern urban areas easily cross state lines. A good example is Clark County, Washington, which is located directly across the Columbia River from Portland, Oregon. For years Clark County has been growing out of its rural heritage and into the orbit of Portland. The area began to thrive with high-tech industries and light manufacturing. Some Oregonians were attracted by tax advantages north of the river and preferred to live in Washington but work in Oregon. Two freeway bridges aided commuting. During the 1990s, the population of Clark County surged from 238,000 to 345,000. The largest city, Vancouver, grew from 46,000 to 143,000, partly by annexing former farm and pasture lands now filling with houses. During the 1990s Vancouver became the fourth largest city in the state. Smaller Clark County towns also grew; Battle Ground and La Center more than doubled their populations. In some ways, the people of Clark County are linked economically and socially to Portland

### Thirty-five Largest Cities in Washington, 2002*

| | City | Population |
|---|---|---|
| 1. | Seattle | 570,800 |
| 2. | Spokane | 195,500 |
| 3. | Tacoma | 194,900 |
| 4. | Vancouver | 148,800 |
| 5. | Bellevue | 117,000 |
| 6. | Everett | 96,070 |
| 7. | Kent | 84,275 |
| 8. | Federal Way | 83,850 |
| 9. | Yakima | 79,120 |
| 10. | Bellingham | 69,260 |
| 11. | Lakewood | 58,580 |
| 12. | Kennewick | 56,280 |
| 13. | Renton | 53,840 |
| 14. | Shoreline | 53,250 |
| 15. | Redmond | 46,040 |
| 16. | Kirkland | 45,790 |
| 17. | Auburn | 45,010 |
| 18. | Olympia | 42,690 |
| 19. | Richland | 40,150 |
| 20. | Edmonds | 39,460 |
| 21. | Bremerton | 37,530 |
| 22. | Longview | 35,310 |
| 23. | Puyallup | 34,920 |
| 24. | Sammamish | 34,660 |
| 25. | Pasco | 34,630 |
| 26. | Lynnwood | 33,990 |
| 27. | Lacey | 31,860 |
| 28. | Burien | 31,810 |
| 29. | Bothell | 30,820 |
| 30. | University Place | 30,350 |
| 31. | Walla Walla | 29,550 |
| 32. | Des Moines | 29,510 |
| 33. | Wenatchee | 28,270 |
| 34. | Marysville | 27,580 |
| 35. | Mount Vernon | 26,670 |

*The city of Spokane Valley, with approximately 80,400 residents, was approved for incorporation in 2002.

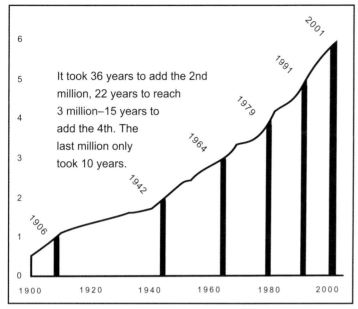

It took 36 years to add the 2nd million, 22 years to reach 3 million–15 years to add the 4th. The last million only took 10 years.

This graph shows how Washington's population has grown. Note how many years it took to reach the second million, compared with the single decade of the 1990s when a full million were added.

and Oregon more than to Washington.

Spokane, located just west of the Idaho border, has a similar situation although the Washington city dominates smaller Idaho towns nearby. Since its earliest days, Idaho minerals, ores, and forest products helped Spokane to grow. Today, Coeur d'Alene, Post Falls, and other towns fall into the suburban orbit of their larger Washington neighbor. Walla Walla is also closely linked with small towns across the border in Oregon. Clarkston, Washington, and Lewiston, Idaho, bridge the Snake River to constitute a small urban center. A graphic example of towns virtually merging across state lines occurs in the small communities of Newport, Washington, and Oldtown, Idaho. No clear division marks them. The towns' streets blend into one another with few clues to suggest that the two are different towns in two different states.

As the world, nations, and states become more interconnected, such border towns may become more unified and the borders that separate them may seem less important. The influences of a

neighboring state could be as important as what happens in the state to which a town belongs.

## A NEW SENSE OF DEVELOPMENT

In the late twentieth century, smaller localities also improved their towns and developed a sense of community. Many undertook comprehensive planning studies for the first time. New municipal parks, bicycle paths, and swimming pools were common, but some towns undertook more elaborate projects. In the North Cascades, Winthrop transformed itself into a community resembling an Old West frontier village, while Leavenworth imitated a picturesque Bavarian mountain town. Two of the earliest settlements on Puget Sound, La Conner and Steilacoom, refurbished historic areas to remind themselves and visitors of their past.

The past and the future are intertwined. When Seattle officials supported plans to eliminate the Pike Place Market, where farmers had been selling produce since 1907, a group of citizens rallied under the slogan "Save the Market." Led by architect Victor Steinbrueck, they were able to preserve the market's lively mixture of fresh food and crafts, now joined by modern specialty shops.

Across town, Pioneer Square, site of the original settlement that grew around Henry Yesler's mill, was revitalized into an old-new blend of weathered brick buildings and sophisticated shops and restaurants. The old town of Fairhaven, now part of Bellingham, underwent a similar renewal. Older buildings and neighborhoods in other towns were preserved and converted to new uses.

The national bicentennial celebration in 1976 and the state's one hundredth birthday in 1989 helped instill a sense of where people had been. Around the state, local groups reconsidered their own history. They interviewed pioneers, prepared videos and pageants, and compiled the past of their neighborhoods in books. There were festivi-

Merchants and shoppers at Seattle's popular Pike Place Market

and man-made phenomena. How might this affect timber resources, wheat and fruit crops, the supply of fish and other seafoods? The unusually warm ocean current called El Niño and the contrasting cold trend labeled La Niña have already shown the effects of climatic changes. They hint at what may come in the future.

Changing climate and weather patterns always affect geography and the way we live. They will in the future. Residents of the tourist and retirement town of Ocean Shores became increasingly aware of the power of wind and tides during the late 1990s. Built on a seven-mile-long sandspit, Ocean Shores marks the northern entrance to Grays Harbor. Constant dredging to create a deep harbor entrance, a jetty built into the surf, and construction on shore have combined with natural forces to create major erosion problems.

Just north of the harbor entrance a cluster of large condominiums and a few private homes rest picturesquely upon a bank above the surf. But strong winds and waves constantly eat away this bank, especially during winter storms. Two layers of huge stone bulkheads were built to protect them, but erosion continued. The buildings may well be undercut or surrounded by powerful ocean waters that could also permanently flood nearby flat areas. Local citizens and government officials work with professional experts to consider how to cope with erosion and set future policies. Possible procedures range from letting nature take its course to building giant seawalls. Many factors are involved, and concerned people disagree about the best solution. Around the same time, dozens of homes built above the Columbia River in Kelso were being destroyed by shifting earth caused by constant rain and water flow. How Ocean Shores and Kelso handle these erosion issues might well help set standards that other communities will follow in the future.

ties and community improvements throughout the state. It seemed as if the people of Washington State were entering their second century while looking both backward and forward.

But warnings about the future came from unexpected, powerful natural sources. Even as new growth appeared in the areas devastated by the massive eruptions of Mount St. Helens, thoughtful citizens recognized that humans, after all, are not in control. Scientists pondered the long-range results of the "greenhouse effect," the gradual warming of northern regions by natural

Washington has matured as a state in the more than five decades since World War II. Its economy is more diverse, less dependent on the resources of land, sea, and forest. Washingtonians have become national leaders in politics, business, and the arts, changing an old image of an isolated, provincial state. Even its food has become famous, with whole cookbooks devoted to "Northwest cuisine." Thousands of people from other regions have moved here, drawn by beautiful surroundings, friendly people, and a strong economy. Few states seem so fortunate.

The good fortune has brought problems. Rapid population growth, water and air pollution, diminishing resources, an uncertain economy, and increasing traffic and crime are all issues that must be tackled if Washington is to remain a truly livable place. Our lives are subject to forces that are constantly changing.

### September 11, 2001

That life would not remain the same forever was clearly brought home on the morning of September 11, 2001. Washingtonians awoke to news that a commercial airliner had crashed into one of the 110-story twin towers of the World Trade Center in New York City. Eighteen minutes later, a second plane hit the other. Both towers soon crumbled to the ground. Another jet plummeted into the Pentagon, headquarters of the Department of Defense, just outside Washington, D. C. A fourth crashed in western Pennsylvania. The four planes had been hijacked and used as weapons.

Although these events took place 3,000 miles from Washington State, they immediately affected Americans everywhere—indeed, people throughout the world. Even in the early hours, the attacks appeared to be the work of Muslim extremists led by Osama bin Laden. This wealthy former Saudi was hiding out in the arid, impoverished country of Afghanistan, where a sympathetic government protected him. By nightfall, President George W. Bush was mounting forces to fight a new kind of war against terrorism, a war that he promised to win even if it took months or years.

Some of Washington State's most prominent buildings, such as the Space Needle, closed briefly. So did many government offices. Military bases remained on high alert. For several days, no planes flew. Groups of citizens demonstrated to show patriotism; American flags were raised above homes and buildings. Travelers crossing the border from Canada found long waiting-lines and were closely examined. Some local Muslims and their mosques were viewed with suspicion and even faced acts of violence. Yet many Muslims found fellow Americans anxious to protect them and were treated with kindness and respect. The small band of religious extremists who committed the deadly acts were not representative of the Muslim faith.

In weeks that followed, private lives changed. Military personnel at places such as Oak Harbor and Fairchild Air Force Base were activated. The National Guard was called up. Security at commercial airports was tightened permanently. Many civilians cancelled flights or other travel plans, especially to foreign countries. Police, firefighters, and paramedics received new appreciation for the work they regularly do; several headed east to assist at the disaster sites.

Some Washingtonians were affected directly. Those who had family or friends in New York and the national capital rushed to learn what they could. A native of Edmonds was among the military personnel killed at the Pentagon. The planes had been built by Boeing. The twin towers themselves had been designed by Seattle-born architect Minoru Yamasaki, whose local structures include the Pacific Science Center. When the towers opened in 1972, he had envisioned them as symbols of peace.

## Chapter 9 Review

I. Identify the following people. Tell why each is important to Washington State.

Mon C. Wallgren
Daniel J. Evans
Dixy Lee Ray
Gary Locke
Warren G. Magnuson
Henry M. Jackson

Patty Murray
Maria Cantwell
Tom Foley
Dave Beck
William O. Douglas
George Boldt

II. Define the following words and terms. Relate each one to Washington State.

Transition
Cold War
Suburb, suburban, suburbia
Megalopolis
Pugetopolis
Recession
Recovery
International Brotherhood of Teamsters
Vietnam War
Civil rights movement
"The Establishment"
Boldt decision
Environmental Protection Agency (EPA)
Department of Ecology
Municipality of Metropolitan Seattle (METRO)
Shorelines Management Act
Environmentalist
Growth Management Act
Conservationist
Bonneville Power Administration (BPA)
Nuclear energy
Northwest Power Bill
Livability
Greenhouse effect
El Niño
Erosion

III. Locate each of these places on a map. Tell why each is important to Washington State.

Mount St. Helens
Bellevue
Richland
Ruston
Hanford
Skagit Valley
Ross Dam
Forks
Ocean Shores

IV. Each question below should call your attention to factual information in the chapter. Try to answer each one. Then look back in the reading to check your answer, correct your understanding, and find answers you do not know.

1. How did the end of World War II affect Washington's economy?

2. What new areas became attractive places to live after the war?

3. What new transportation routes helped change Bellevue and the east side of Lake Washington?

4. Describe the Richland area before World War II.

5. Who owned and regulated the city of Richland in the ten years before 1955?

6. What important contract did Boeing lose as the company was forced to shut down some operations and lay off workers?

7. How did Boeing try to improve its business during the 1970s?

8. What factors caused a decline in the lumber industry?

9. What has been the chief characteristic of politics in Washington since the 1940s?

10. Why were Warren G. Magnuson and Henry M. Jackson able to rise to powerful positions in the United States Senate?

11. What did Dave Beck mean by "organizing the bosses"?

12. How might one describe the views that William O. Douglas expressed while he was on the United States Supreme Court?

13. Tell some ways that the war in Vietnam affected the economy of Washington State.

14. What groups led the opposition to the Vietnam War?

15. What other protest group joined forces with those protesting the Vietnam War?

16. How did Judge George Boldt interpret the term "in common" in the Indian fishing cases?

17. Name three important sources of air pollution in the Puget Sound area.

18. What steps were taken to clean up Lake Washington?

19. What was the theme of the world's fair held in Spokane in 1974? How was this theme demonstrated?

20. Name the national park that was created in Washington in 1968.

21. What major worry about the use of nuclear power disturbed many people?

22. What happened to the five power plants that WPPSS started to build in the 1970s?

23. What city was established as the most eastern point where large oil tankers could dock when they entered Puget Sound?

24. What source of power is being experimented with near the towns of Goldendale and Ellensburg?

25. What is the natural habitat of the spotted owl?

26. What is the Endangered Species Act? How was it used in the spotted owl controversy?

27. List several turning points that have affected the town of Forks throughout its history.

28. What has caused the salmon to become endangered?

29. What has been built on the sites of Century 21 in Seattle and Spokane's world's fair?

30. How did bicentennial and centennial celebrations affect activities in the state?

31. List several ways that Washington State was directly affected by the events of September 11, 2001.

V. Think about, discuss, and answer the questions below.

1. Which different groups of people felt they were personally affected by Judge George Boldt's ruling concerning Indian treaties and fishing rights? What might each group see as the advantages and disadvantages of that ruling? What measures can people take to offset the effects of an unpopular decision by the courts? Should they try to do so? (Remember that court decisions usually provide the final word on a controversial issue.)

2. What is the traditional "American dream"? How do most people achieve or try to achieve that dream? How do Dave Beck and William O. Douglas represent that dream? How did they try to achieve it? What other persons do you know who are good representatives of the "American dream"?

3. Seek information about one of the recent governors, senators, or political leaders mentioned in this chapter. What in their backgrounds helped prepare them for that office? What particular problems or issues did Washington face during their years in office? How did these people

tackle the problems? How successful were they? What particular qualifications or characteristics do you believe a major officeholder should have?

4. In your own opinion, what makes a place a truly good place to live? What does your community or your particular neighborhood have that makes it desirable? What does it lack? Do you know of groups that are working to improve the livability of your community? What specific goals do they want to achieve? How are they going about securing these goals? Perhaps you could interview some of them.

Develop a scale of twenty items that might be used to measure "livability." Rate your community on those items on a scale of 1 (low) to 10 (high). Remember to include items that are necessary though not especially fun or of interest to you, such as hospitals, a sewage system, police protection, etc.

5. All around us we see symbols. These symbols are often simple objects or pictures that represent more complex things or ideas. Most countries, including the United States, have flags that are symbols of the nation. When we see that flag, we think not of a piece of cloth but of the country it stands for. The bald eagle is another symbol of the United States. Golden arches symbolize a popular fast-food chain.

This chapter describes how the spotted owl became a symbol of a major dispute in the Northwest timber industry. Some people saw that owl as a symbol of an environment that they wished to save and protect. Others saw it as a symbol of jobs or a livelihood and way of life that were disappearing. The owl became a very emotional symbol.

List at least five other objects that have become symbols of businesses, places, products, or controversies. Tell what each represents. What kind of emotion does each arouse in you? Does it cause you to feel pride or disgust or hunger or anger? Compare your list and feelings with at least one other person in your class. Do you have an emotional reaction when you see a picture of a spotted owl? If so, what is that emotion and why does a bird produce that emotion? If you live in a timber-producing area, ask the same questions of older relatives and friends.

6. Suppose you were asked to express your views about finding a solution to the problems in the Northwest timber industry.

Express the views that you might have if you were an out-of-work logger or family member . . . an environmentalist . . . a tourist from a distant state . . . a backpacker . . . a businessperson in Forks . . . a lawmaker who must find solutions to the problems of the industry.

Meet with others in your class who represent roles that are different from the one you have assumed. Hold your own forest conference. What solutions can you offer to solve the changing problems in the timber industry?

Perhaps you might try to do the same thing regarding the endangered salmon. What roles might you play in this case? What different attitudes might you express? What problems would you find and what solutions might you suggest?

7. Suppose you were living in a community that was being changed by natural causes such as major erosion, storms, earthquakes, or a volcanic event. What roles might different people have? What different attitudes might they express? What solutions might they—or you—suggest? How might people prepare themselves and their communities for such unknown and unpredictable possibilities?

# Chapter 10 The Economy

Wedding portrait of Joshua and Laura Green

**S**eattle, Friday, January 25, 1975. Virginia Mason Hospital hugs a Seattle hillside. Just below it a busy freeway canyon cuts through the city's high-rise business district. Beyond, Elliott Bay is alive with freighters, tugs, and ferries. On a day clearer than this winter Friday, one would be able to see the craggy Olympic Mountains on the western skyline.

All of these places have been important in the life of a man who is dying in this hospital tonight. He is Joshua Green, 105 years old. Until yesterday he had seemed as healthy and vital as a man a generation younger. As boat pilot, shipping man, banker, outdoorsman, and public citizen, Green's extraordinary life has touched upon almost every facet of the economic growth of this region.

Born to prominent parents in Mississippi, Joshua Green traveled to Seattle with his family by railroad and steamship when he was seventeen. When they arrived in May of 1886, the city was a bustling frontier town of 20,000 people. Its founders were still living. The great fire was three years in the future. Washington was not yet a state.

Green first worked on a crew surveying a railroad route along the waterfront and on toward Snoqualmie Pass. By winter he was a clerk for another railroad builder, carrying supplies along wooded trails over the hills to Lake Washington. Lured to the steamboats that scurried about the harbor, Green soon was hired as a purser aboard the Henry Bailey. The boat delivered supplies to many places around the Sound and up the Skagit River. Then he and three partners acquired their own boat, the 100-foot sternwheeler Fanny Lake. They carried passengers and produce between Seattle and the La Conner flats.

# of Washington

One boat led to more, and within a few years Green had founded the future Puget Sound Navigation Company. It became a major company on the Sound, carrying cargo and passengers in smooth, modern, and fast vessels. The growing Alaska trade helped the company prosper.

Competition was fierce in the shipping business, but Green's company often came out the winner and sometimes bought out weaker competitors. Green began to build ships as well, and he became a prominent and wealthy businessman.

By the 1920s, small boats swarmed Puget Sound so thickly that they were called the "mosquito fleet." But they faced competition from a different source. Increasing numbers of automobiles required more roads, and cars and trucks began to replace water carriers. Several Puget Sound Navigation Company boats were converted to carry cars; in time ferry boats designed for that purpose were added.

Meanwhile Joshua Green had left the company, and in 1926 he entered a different career, banking. At fifty-seven, an age when many people look toward retirement, he bought control of a struggling Seattle bank. Using skills built up in the shipping business, he made this bank profitable. Soon he acquired others. Thus began People's National Bank, later one of the largest in Washington.

As soon as a change in the law permitted it, People's opened branches in Seattle neighborhoods and other western Washington towns. During the Great Depression of the 1930s, when many banks failed and customers made "runs" upon them to draw out savings, Green personally calmed depositors and employees. He confidently promised that their money was safe. People's survived the depression, backed by mortgages taken on other properties Green owned.

People's helped to establish and finance many large businesses as the bank expanded around Puget Sound and throughout Washington. In the 1930s, Green and others foresaw the changes that irrigation and hydroelectric power would bring to eastern Washington. When he acquired a small bank in Ephrata, he began a continuing involvement with the growth of that region. He also built a downtown Seattle office building that bears his name.

Joshua Green's wife and faithful confidante during all these years was a childhood friend from Mississippi. She died only three weeks ago on New Year's Day. They had been married for seventy-three years, and their children and grandchildren had long been involved in family businesses and community affairs. Green was also an avid golfer and hunter, making an annual pheasant hunt only four days before his 100th birthday. An Alaska river and valley are named for him. Tonight, within view of the waterfront spot where he arrived almost ninety years ago, only a few blocks from the mansion where he lived, surrounded by the city and the region whose growth he served, Joshua Green has died.

Joshua Green's life has touched upon most facets of Washington's economic growth thus far. Neither he nor others could guess that in 1975, the year of his death, a new phase will begin. This same year, Bill Gates and Paul Allen will found a new kind of company linked to computers, and it will change many aspects of life. They will name their company Microsoft.

# Economics

Economics may be defined as the way people get the most from their limited resources of land, labor, and man-made materials. Every place has its unique combination of geography and natural resources that affect people and how they make a living. Much of the economy of Washington results from the state's physical environment.

Forest-covered hills and mountains, coastal and inland salt waters, rivers, lakes, and stream beds, valleys, plateaus and rolling plains, all provide resources that are the basis of Washington's economy. The mild, moderate climate of the western part and the extremes of cold and hot in the eastern part affect agriculture. Ores and metals beneath the surface of the ground and sea life in the waters have created industries. Yet, a controlling factor in how an economy develops must be the people who see and seize an opportunity or join a work force, and who use the natural resources.

As an area develops, its economy may progress through several stages. In the beginning, early settlers on a small, individual scale exploit the easily available natural resources through such activities as fishing, cutting timber, farming, and mining. This stage is frequently followed by entrepreneurs who begin companies and build industries, sometimes large ones, to engage in manufacturing and trade but rely on local workers and capital. These industries generally use local resources.

A third stage is often the arrival and then the dominance of giant companies. Often these come from outside the region and use outside capital and control to further develop local resources. Sometimes local companies become strong and wealthy enough to invest large amounts of money in their own growth.

Several other factors that contribute to the economic development of a region are constantly in the background. There must be sources of capital, that is, funds and materials that can be used to begin and develop production of goods. There must be a source of labor, people available and willing to work. There must be a market, an opportunity to sell what is produced. Consumers, ordinary people with everyday or special needs, compose much of this market, as do large businesses that obtain goods for their own development. The market may reach outside the region and thus require suitable transportation. There will also likely be a form of government with leaders who support economic growth.

Before looking at how the economy of Washington has developed, let us summarize how the essentials have been met.

## Natural Resources

The natural resources of Washington include many forests in the western section, the northeastern corner, and the far southeast. These forests provide Douglas fir, red cedar, western hemlock, Sitka spruce, pines, and other woods, generally softwoods. From the beginning to the present these have been the backbone of the economy in much of the state.

Other important natural resources are the fish and other seafood found off the coast, in inland salt waters, and in rivers, streams, and lakes. Minerals are not found in great abundance, although soft coal exists in the Cascades and various ores are found in the mountains of the northeast.

Western Washington valleys are fertile, as are the eastern dry lands after moisture is provided by irrigation. When harnessed by dams, flowing water provides electric power and water for crops. Harbors and navigable rivers enable trade to develop easily. Washington seems blessed with a broad combination of basic natural resources available for development.

## Capital

Essential for development is capital, the money and materials that are used to produce more goods. After the investments of the Hudson's Bay and North West Companies, the earliest capital to arrive in the Northwest was what the founding settlers brought with them, and that was very little. As tiny industries appeared and began to prosper, some settlers had money to invest in further development. Thus men like Henry Yesler and Arthur Denny in Seattle, Daniel C. Corbin in Spokane, or Russell Peabody and Henry Roeder in Bellingham began with little money but used available resources and acquired capital for further investments.

Another early source of capital was new wealth from northern California. In time, however, more distant outside investments began to come in. Railroad companies, using federal government funds and land grants, and such eastern and midwestern concerns as the Pope and Talbot Company, Weyerhaeuser in lumber, and Guggenheim in metals moved into the Northwest. Capital from outside sources was beyond the control of the local region. As the economy expanded, more large companies incorporated and raised funds by selling stock to thousands of investors.

## Labor

Money and resources depend upon people to perform work. Washington has never lacked a labor supply. In frontier days, some Indians found work with white employers; later Chinese, Filipinos, and Hawaiians were brought in; Indians and Mexican Americans have long worked in agricultural fields. But for the most part, the labor force has consisted of white Americans and immigrants eager to move into an uncrowded area in search of jobs and opportunity. Rarely have there been too few people to work in fields or factories or in construction.

During both world wars, people from out of state moved here to work in war industries and remained. Many blacks came from southern states. Scientists, engineers, and technicians came to the Tri-Cities area during World War II to work in nuclear energy. Companies may recruit workers from other states during times of expansion. The Boeing Company did this in the 1960s to build the 747, and Microsoft regularly recruits talent from around the world. New industries often create their own labor force as they grow.

Good wages, the reputation of the area as a desirable place to live, and the increasing variety of jobs available have helped ensure a steady supply of labor in the Pacific Northwest. At times, the large numbers have created unemployment problems. In the late 1990s, over three million workers made up Washington's labor force, a third of them in professions and technical work, a fourth in the growing service industries.

## Market

A market—the opportunity to sell products—is essential for economic growth. Good harbors and water transportation systems have always been an advantage to Washington. The local population, not always large enough to consume all that is produced, has been able to move goods to places where products are in demand. The first Puget Sound timber was cut during a time of spectacular growth in northern California when local supplies were insufficient or hard to ship. Thus California became the first major market for Washington's products. Seafood was also in demand in the San Francisco area.

Although a growing population creates its own market as newcomers buy houses, groceries, and other goods, Washington will always need to sell many of its products outside the region. Washingtonians cannot eat enough apples or buy enough airplanes to keep orchardists or Boeing workers in business. Apples, other fruits, and wheat are shipped across the country and to Asia and Russia. Wood pulp, newsprint, airplanes, trucks, and software have become other Washington exports to world markets. In the late 1990s, numerous "dot-com" companies created new markets using the Internet.

## Transportation

Getting goods to market requires an adequate transportation system. Washington's many excellent harbors have been an advantage in shipping, and its location is excellent for trade with Japan and China. Both private companies and government bodies have dredged waterways and constructed piers and warehouses.

The Port of Seattle became an early leader in container shipping, and Tacoma has also developed such facilities. Goods are packed only once in large containers that then serve as railroad boxcars, shipping compartments, or truck bodies. National markets are served by railroads and trucks, although high transportation costs from Washington to populous East Coast markets have sometimes put the state at a disadvantage in national trade.

## Organizers

Adequate economic development also requires leadership. Business leaders must be able to predict economic changes and organize effective ways to make and sell products. From John McLoughlin at Fort Vancouver to Bill Gates of Microsoft, Washington has had such leaders. Some have grown up in local industries. Others from outside the area have been crucial to local development. A few such individuals include Cyrus Walker of the Puget Mill Company; Frederick Weyerhaeuser and other officials of the Weyerhaeuser Company; Sol Simpson and Mark Reed of the Simpson Company; D. C. Corbin in railroading and mining; William E. Boeing, William Allen, and others in the aircraft and aerospace industry; the Pigott family in cars and trucks; Robert Moran and Henry Kaiser in vastly different shipbuilding eras; the MacGregor family and others in eastern Washington farming; James J. Hill and Henry Villard in rail transportation; Dorothy Stimson Bullitt in communications and television; and Jeff Bezos in Internet marketing. Numerous others no less important have led particular industries and communities.

## Industrial Growth and Government Support

Economic development can be supported by local, state, and federal government agencies and policies. Tax structures and benefits sometimes favor developing industries and economic growth. Governments can grant land and shipping privileges, among other benefits. Some people believe that Washington's political leaders should give greater support to industrial growth. Business executives and those who represent business have frequently held high and influential positions in Olympia and in Washington, D.C.

Federal land grants encouraged the spread of railroads, and the timber and mining industries found ways to acquire or use public lands. State and city governments have aided shipping with dredging operations and port facilities. Local voters often support bonds and taxes that permit such activities.

State and civic officials have sought trade arrangements and increased business with other states and regions of the world. Canada and other Pacific Rim nations, such as Japan, Korea, Australia, and China, are important. Government analysts study and survey conditions that encourage economic development and predict future needs.

Government also plays a role in balancing conflicting needs and desires within the economy. Sometimes, trade-offs must be made between choices that seem to be almost equally

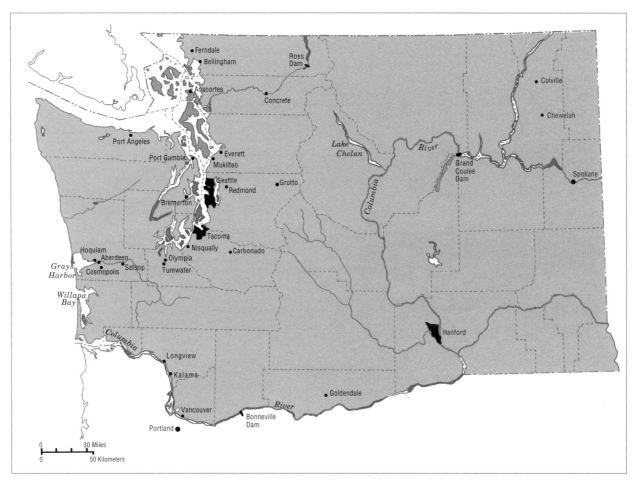

Locations of important industries in Washington

desirable and undesirable. In Washington, these questions have involved the need for industrial growth versus pollution control, logging versus fishing, tourism versus open pit mining, the development of land for present profit versus holding it for future uses, and the spread of urban conditions into farmlands. Government bodies affect the economy when they influence such decisions.

## THE FOREST PRODUCTS INDUSTRY

Logging and lumbering is the oldest industry in western Washington and still an important one. Indians used timber from along the shore

for their houses and boats and cedar fiber for baskets, hats, clothing, and other uses long before the whites appeared. In the late 1700s sailors from Spain and England shipped Northwest timber down the coast to California and across the Pacific to Hawaii and Asia.

The first mills in Washington were erected by the Hudson's Bay Company because of California's demand for Northwest lumber. Small mills seemed to sprout up all over the area. Port Gamble was a company town built to become a major lumbering center. Here Andrew J. Pope and William C. Talbot, two Easterners enthusiastic about the Northwest, formed the Puget Mill

Sailing ships at the Port Blakely lumber mill, 1900

Company and in 1853 started one of the largest lumber operations in Washington.

Over the next two decades, the successes and failures of mills all along the Pacific Coast were tied to the economy of San Francisco. But some Puget Sound lumbermen sought more trade with Hawaii, China, and Australia. Many small mills could neither keep pace with constant changes in the economy or the industry nor compete with large California money interests. New giants, usually supported by San Francisco financiers, dominated the local industry. The largest mills were at Port Gamble, Seabeck on Hood Canal, Port Madison and Port Blakely on Bainbridge Island, and Tacoma. Markets embraced the entire Pacific Rim, but the lumber was sent through San Francisco.

The southwestern corner of Washington entered the forestry industries more slowly. Logging took place south of the Columbia River long before it began on the Washington side. Portland quickly became a leading shipping center with direct contacts to China.

In the 1880s, shippers found that the dreaded bar blocking the entrance to Grays Harbor was less dangerous than they had believed. Thus another valuable forest area opened. Giant firs and hemlocks were cut in the Willapa Hills and lower Olympic Mountains along the Chehalis and Hoquiam Rivers and their tributaries. Aberdeen, Hoquiam, and Cosmopolis rapidly built large lumber mills and other facilities to handle the timber.

East of the Cascades, park-like forests of Ponderosa and Idaho white pine rim the Columbia River Basin. Sawmills appeared later here than in western Washington although many small ones were scattered throughout the region. Cutting pine was the earliest industry at Spokane Falls, for instance. But it was difficult to transport logs over the generally dry lands. Few streams flowed fast enough to float logs to mills. Water flumes solved this problem. These were narrow wooden troughs built on stilts and trestles above the ground. They wound down and around hillsides and held small streams of water that could float logs.

These flumes transported pine logs to sawmill towns like Dixie and Dayton, which prospered by supplying cut lumber for buildings, railroad ties, and bridges as well as fences and firewood. After railroads arrived in the region, transportation problems were eased. The lumber industry grew, but wood never became as common for construction as it was in western Washington.

### Logging at the Turn of the Century

By the 1890s the nature of Pacific Northwest logging and lumbering was changing. Transcontinental railroads had spurred the building of short lines into the timber country. Mill sites with rail connections often became more important than those directed toward seagoing trade. The first logging railroad was built near Tumwater. Such lines allowed loggers to move farther into the hills for timber, away from the rivers and deep harbors which had been needed to float out logs. Logging camps—often temporary, crowded, filthy, and entirely male communities—were built throughout the hills.

Some said that logging was the most dangerous industry in the world, equaled only by war.

Loggers pose with their crosscut saws around 1907.

In 1913, some 47,000 men worked in the woods of Washington. In that year, 268 of them were killed, an average of two deaths every three work days. Hundreds more were injured.

Double-edged axes swung in the woods to begin the hazardous process. Huge cables attached to tall "spar" trees lifted, swung, and lowered giant logs. They were swept high into the air and then to the ground below, crashing against trees and stumps. Then the logs were pulled or skidded to yards for loading. No one

## A Hazardous Trade

*Logging and lumbering accidents were frequent, dangerous, and often fatal. These accounts were published in industry newspapers:*

*"John Hilligar was killed by a falling tree at Leland Houghton's logging camp on Lake Sammamish. He was 21 years old and a young man of good habits."*

*"A. D. Davis, a Pomeroy, Wash., saw mill man, was killed recently by a tree falling on him. He was hauling logs with an ox team, and in drawing the logs by an old dead tree the chain caught on the roots of the tree and pulled it over striking him on the head and shoulders."*

*"The boiler in Charles F. Reed's saw mill . . . near Traverse City, Wash., exploded on June 9th, killing three men and injuring ten others."*

*"Grant Smith . . . was badly cut on a shingle saw . . . . the whole palm of his hand was severed."*

*"George H. Maxwell, an employee of the Chatteroy Lumber Co. of Spokane was caught by a revolving shaft, whipped over it, and his body was torn to pieces at the old saw mill in Spokane, August 19th. He was a handsome young man and one of the most popular employees of the company."*

*"William Whitney was killed on the Port Crescent logging road near East Clallam, Wash., June 29. He was firing up a donkey engine when the boiler exploded. He was blown fifteen feet against a tree, killing him instantly. He was only 18 years old and a good, industrious boy."*

*From Prouty, "More Deadly Than War: Pacific Coast Logging, 1827–1981" (Ph.D. dissertation, University of Washington)*

could predict where rolling logs might go as they were lifted onto cars or barges or into booms.

Chaining and lifting at the sawmill was also dangerous. Even experienced woodsmen were crushed or pinned beneath or between logs. Many were thrown from logs to drown in rivers or mill ponds. Boilers on donkey engines exploded without warning; railroad cars jumped from tracks, throwing men and timber.

At the mill, the threat of instant death or injury continued. Huge saw blades, planes, and edgers whirred rapidly. Clothes sometimes became caught in machinery or in moving belts.

Few of the injured received adequate medical care. Companies sometimes expressed regret but felt little responsibility toward their workers. A few of the injured received less hazardous jobs where their injuries would not hinder them. Rarely was compensation paid to injured persons or to widows or families. Often the companies blamed carelessness by the workers for the tragedies. To accept a job was to accept its hazards.

Inventions changed the industry but did not necessarily lessen its dangers. The ax gave way to the crosscut saw. Steam-powered donkey engines replaced older methods of pulling giant logs. Where railroads had not penetrated, splash dams were built to store the water until it was released in a giant flood that carried the logs downstream.

Such changes were costly. During the 1890s a nationwide depression and a local lumber surplus hurt many companies. They either slowed operations severely or went bankrupt. Only the biggest survived. And the biggest included newcomers that could dominate all phases of the industry.

In 1900 the Weyerhaeuser Company arrived from the Upper Midwest. The timber of that region was giving out, and company founder Frederick E. Weyerhaeuser began searching for new sources in the West and South.

Tree topping remains a dangerous part of logging in Washington.

est fires devastated much of western Washington and Oregon. This came to be known as the Yacolt Burn. On the famous Dark Day of September 12, smoke hung so thick that the sky was dark at noon and people in Tacoma carried lanterns in the streets. The direct loss from the Yacolt Burn near Mount St. Helens was estimated at $13 million, and thirty-eight people died. Additional damage came from soil erosion, loss of wildlife, and potential future growth. Weyerhaeuser took a strong interest in forest fire prevention. Many fires were started by lightning and could not be prevented. Others were the result of human carelessness. Private companies and governments worked together to help prevent and contain forest fires.

For fourteen years Weyerhaeuser owned timber but milled little of it. In 1902 the company bought its first mill in the Northwest, a small, old plant on the Everett waterfront. Then, just before World War I, the company took greater interest in milling and manufacturing. A second Everett mill was built. Electrically operated, it was called the most modern and efficient lumbering operation in the world.

In the following years, Weyerhaeuser built mills at Snoqualmie Falls; at Longview on the final bend of the Columbia River; at Enumclaw; and at Aberdeen and Raymond in the southwestern corner of the state. A third Everett mill cut hemlock. The Longview mill became the largest wood products plant in the world.

The company sought ways to use waste materials. Experiments led to the development of important products such as plywood, pulp, pressboard, kraft paper, and Presto-logs. The company took an interest in conservation, including planting tree farms. It expanded its public information campaign, which benefited both the company and the industry.

In 1972 Weyerhaeuser moved to the suburbs, opening a huge headquarters and research complex at Federal Way, north of Tacoma. By this time

## The Weyerhaeuser Company

Weyerhaeuser bought 900,000 acres of Washington timberland from the Northern Pacific Railroad at $6 an acre. This was an area larger than the state of Rhode Island. Headquarters were established in Tacoma and George S. Long was put in charge.

Long began to survey the amount and kinds of trees on the new holdings. He bought additional land in Washington, Idaho, and Oregon. The original purpose was to own land and to sell its timber to other companies.

Fire prevention soon became a concern. During the late, dry summer of 1902, over a hundred for-the Weyerhaeuser Company was a true business giant and the largest private landowner in Washington with over 1.5 million acres of timberland. Over 150 mills, plants, and service centers were located in the Northwest, other parts of the United States, and foreign countries. In the early twenty-first century it has 60,000 employees, including 8,400 in Washington. Sales totaled $14 billion in 2001.

Around Shelton, the interests of Sol G. Simpson expanded during these same years to include all phases of the industry from logging and milling to manufacturing shakes and finished products. The Simpson Company pioneered the practice of the "sustained yield." By this practice a company balances the rate at which it cuts timber and the rate of replanting to provide a steady supply.

Simpson timberlands and U.S. Forest Service lands were merged in 1946 and supervised to ensure continuing forest resources. In the 1920s the Long-Bell Company of Texas moved into the lower Columbia area, building mills and a model town at Longview.

Each large development attracted related businesses. Doctors, school teachers, store owners, food servers, and other workers in logging towns were dependent on the timber industry for their jobs even if they never set foot in a logging camp or mill.

### The Second Century of Logging and Lumbering

Although over half of Washington remains forested today, most of the virgin forests are gone. In the second century of logging and lumbering, smaller second-growth and third-growth trees were harvested. Many logs come from tree farms and the private landholdings of such companies as Weyerhaeuser, Simpson, Boise Cascade, Plum Creek, and Rayonier. National forests in the state still provide some timber, mostly to small logging companies under government contracts.

In 1986 the last true logging camp closed. During its final years, Camp Grisdale, thirty-four miles up the Wynoochee River from Montesano, was far different from camps of the past. This small community included wives and families, but a hundred or so loggers commuted each morning from homes in neighboring towns.

Many companies use clear-cut logging, a practice that cuts all of the timber in an area, regardless of type or maturity. Some environmentalists object that clear-cutting denudes a region in an unnatural manner. They say it prevents natural cycles of growth, destroys animal habitats, leaves ugly scars across the landscape, and promotes erosion and water pollution.

Logging companies defend the practice as being less expensive than selective logging. Reseeding clear-cuts creates a managed forest where all the trees are the same age and type. This allows for more efficient logging. Newer logging techniques include helicopters and even balloons to lift logs out of forests.

By the year 2000 there were far fewer sawmills than the state once had. Edmonds, where eleven mills once lined the beach, has none. Port Ludlow, Port Blakely, and Seabeck have converted to recreation and retirement communities. In Seattle, the last mill along the Duwamish River cut its final log in 1984, long since dwarfed by other industries. The Weyerhaeuser Company ended ninety years of milling in Everett, one of the great mill towns, when its last pulp mill there closed in 1992. The historic mill at Port Gamble closed in 1997.

Small mills can still be found in little towns and rural areas, but the dominant ones are owned by great companies. There, logs are moved on giant conveyor belts and stripped of bark. Computers help determine the most valuable parts and the most advantageous cuts. Huge circular saws swiftly slice logs crosswise and lengthwise.

Kiln-dried and shipped out, Washington logs are transformed into lumber, shakes, shingles, and wood by-products for shipment throughout the nation and the world. Plywood is made by peeling sheets from a circular core and then gluing them under heavy pressure. Presto-logs, particle board, and paper products come from what once would have been waste. Clearly, the term "forest products" describes the industry more accurately than the older terms "logging" and "lumber."

This industry has always known periods of boom and bust, but its future is uncertain in the twenty-first century. Plastics and other materials have replaced wood in many products. Environmental concerns have reduced the supply of available timber. Major companies have closed large mills, including some with outdated machinery, and they have slowed or halted logging operations.

Competition has increased from existing industries in British Columbia and from southeastern states where labor supplies are cheaper and softwoods are grown as crops. The shipment of logs to Japan and other nations that made pulp and resold it was for many years a common practice that threatened jobs and the Washington economy.

Since the 1970s, production has declined dramatically. One year in that decade the industry grossed $3.5 billion and employed some 55,000 workers in camps, mills, offices, and sales. In 2000 about 33,000 people were thus employed.

Many more thousands of jobs stem from this one industry. When the forest products industry declines, many communities and other parts of the state also suffer. Sales of goods and services are affected and markets are lost. If at the same time interest rates become high, there is likely to be less home and building construction. And when people do not buy houses, the lumber industry again is affected. One factor leads to another with a snowball effect. The years when the forests seemed endless and the profits seemed limitless are gone. Companies themselves, along with labor unions, government officials, and concerned citizens, are seeking ways to stabilize the industry's role in the economy of the state. The future of the forest products industry will likely undergo many changes in the generations to come.

## MINING

Washington has never been an important mining state. It has benefited from nearby mining rushes, however, and some ores have been profitably extracted. In its early years, Washington Territory experienced several exciting gold rushes. After the rush of forty-niners to California calmed, rumors about other gold finds circulated. The Colville region attracted hundreds of anxious prospectors to the northeast corner of Washington, many from California.

In 1858 gold strikes on the Fraser River, just across the Canadian border, also drew many hopeful miners. In little villages along Puget Sound and the coast, normal life was interrupted as gold seekers sought passage north. Rival towns competed to sell prospectors the tools, food, and clothing they needed. Often more money was made in outfitting miners than in prospecting.

In the 1860s mining strikes in Idaho, still part of Washington Territory, hastened the growth of such towns as Lewiston in Idaho, Walla Walla in Washington, and The Dalles in Oregon. Later Spokane became the chief outfitting center for persons going to the Coeur d'Alene mines. Starting in 1896 Seattle met similar needs for speculators heading for the Alaska-Yukon gold fields. Seattle and Spokane owe much of their early wealth and growth to mining rushes in other areas because they made themselves the chief supply and departure centers.

A few rushes for gold and silver occurred

Miners wearing accident rescue equipment around 1914

in Washington itself, particularly in the north-eastern mountains. Where valuable metals were discovered, placer or individual mining efforts quickly were replaced by hardrock or quartz mining. This required heavy equipment and railroad lines. Thus individual prospectors gave way to wealthy companies. Gold, the metal that prospectors dreamed of finding, never became important to the economy of Washington. Yet even today, people still look for gold, more as a hobby than a business.

Coal was more important than gold.

Coal was first discovered in the hills east of Bellingham in 1849, and mining began six years later. When Isaac Stevens surveyed for a cross-Cascades railroad route in the 1850s, he estimated there was enough coal of appropriate quality to fuel the railroads of the region. These predictions turned out to be somewhat true. Coal was found

in several parts of the Cascades. Soon the mining towns of Carbonado, Wilkeson, and Black Diamond were established on the western slopes, and Cle Elum and Roslyn on the eastern. These towns were typical mining camps. They attracted immigrants who formed close-knit communities with their own churches, social functions, and fraternal lodges.

Mining towns were small and isolated. Most houses and stores were owned by the company although individuals could sometimes lease or build their own. Residents in company-owned towns rarely had full control over their own lives.

Death or injury in the mines was a constant fear and a frequent reality. Underground explosions killed forty-five persons at Roslyn in 1892 and thirty-three at Carbonado in 1899. More common were separate, individual accidents that killed or maimed workers. For several years

239 THE ECONOMY OF WASHINGTON

Washington had more mining fatalities for the number of miners than any other state. Grieving families were often left with nowhere to turn.

Washington coal was of a soft grade. It was satisfactory for fueling railroads and steamboats but expensive and wasteful to extract. Commonly found in pockets in narrow ravines, much coal lay in crooked streams, making it difficult to mine and transport. By 1900 coal from the Rocky Mountain states was proving more valuable and practical.

When petroleum replaced coal as a major energy source, Washington's declining coal production slipped disastrously. For example, in 1900 one-fourth of Washington's production—700,000 tons—was shipped to San Francisco, an old, reliable customer. Seven years later, the San Francisco shipment was a mere 90,000 tons, and by 1919 it had disappeared. World War I needs led to 4.1 million tons being mined in Washington in 1918, but production soon declined again as the industry was beset by rapid technological changes, labor disputes, outside competition, and the increasing use of oil. By 1930 the Washington coal industry had almost ceased to exist.

As the nation considers seeking new fuel resources, Washington may again turn to its coal reserves. State geologists believe that there are six billion tons of coal reserves in the state, but much of it would be difficult or expensive to mine.

Other minerals found in Washington include magnesium near Chewelah and lead and zinc in the far northeast corner. For many years a copper mine operated at Holden in the mountains northwest of Lake Chelan. Others have been proposed in the North Cascades and near Spokane. There may be mineral deposits in the Olympic Mountains.

The most important and financially successful mineral products are less glamorous but essential items, such as Portland cement, sand and gravel, and stone. Widespread around the state, these products together make up about one third the dollar value of all the mineral production in Washington. The towns of Concrete and Grotto were important centers for cement, while stone and gravel pits are found in many locales, especially in the western part of the state.

## THE FISHING INDUSTRY

Native Americans have fished in Northwest waters for thousands of years. Indians traded fish to early explorers along the coast. The Nez Perce supplied the Lewis and Clark party with salmon when they arrived, near starvation, from the Rocky Mountains.

Indians continued to supply fish long after many whites had settled. Although white settlers took fish and shellfish for family use, Indians caught most of the fish for sale. Whites raised few objections to the treaties of the 1850s that allowed Indians to continue fishing in their usual places, with their customary methods, and to gather fish "in common" with the whites.

Before 1880 only a few commercial fishermen were scattered about the area and many of these were Indians. Most of the boats used for fishing were small canoes; fish were caught in nets and traps. During the next few years, production increased rapidly. Commercial fish canneries were located on the Columbia, the first in 1866, but most were on the Oregon side rather than in Washington. In 1877 the first cannery on Puget Sound opened at Mukilteo. Canneries required large supplies of fish and attracted more whites to commercial fishing. Many European immigrants came to the Pacific Northwest to fish: Greeks, Slavs from the coast of the Adriatic Sea, Scandinavians, and Finns. Large numbers of Chinese laborers worked in canneries cleaning and scraping fish, until a new fish-processing machine put many of them out of work in the early 1900s.

Changes in fishing and in canning came after

## The Fish and Shellfish Industries

Salmon is the most valuable fish resource in Washington. Spawned high upriver, salmon swim down to salt water and spend years at sea before returning to their birth places to mate and die. Sockeye salmon are found in both Puget Sound and the Columbia River; many caught in the Sound are from spawning grounds in the Fraser River. Chinook, or king, salmon appear off the Washington coast and in Puget Sound. The chum and the coho, or silver, salmon are in both the Sound and the Columbia; while most pink, or humpback, salmon come from the Sound and its rivers. Other important commercial fish are halibut and various forms of sole, rockfish, and cod, all of which are found along the Pacific Coast.

Oysters on Willapa Bay were among the state's earliest exports. Oysters from Japan have been planted on the Strait of Juan de Fuca, on Samish Island and other parts of the San Juans, and in southern portions of the Sound. Annual reseeding is required.

Clams and crabs are gathered commercially on parts of the Sound and on coastal beaches. Both industries have declined in recent years. In 1983 a little-known parasite reduced the number of razor clams, and the crab catch has been lowered by pollution and overfishing.

With some help from the state, the fishing industry is exploring new products such as geoducks, squid, mussels, sea cucumbers, octopus, and different shellfish. Bottom fishing off the coast has become more important. Experiments have been made with seaweed farming.

Bringing in a day's catch

1880. Purse seining, in which nets encircle a school of fish and are then pulled in, was successful in large bodies of water. Today this practice gathers about 80 percent of the catch. Gill netting —dragging long nets behind the boat with a mesh that traps fish as they try to escape—was introduced. Fish traps, fish wheels, and pound nets, since outlawed, were used, especially on the Columbia.

After statehood, the state Department of Fisheries regulated and assisted the industry. Hatcheries were started on rivers to offset the effects of dams, logging, and overfishing. The number of fish caught increased several times during those early years.

As with other natural resources, the supply of

fish once seemed inexhaustible. But as the industry grew and new equipment and techniques were perfected, the catch peaked and then declined. Changes created by people accounted for much of the decline. A massive slide caused by railroad construction on the Fraser River of British Columbia, a source of many of the sockeye salmon caught in Washington, closed much of the river to fish in 1913.

Pollution in places such as Grays Harbor and Puget Sound reduced the number of fish, and logging operations destroyed spawning grounds. The most significant impact was from the construction of dams on large rivers, which blocked the natural run of salmon returning to their spawning grounds. Fish ladders around the dams helped, but many dams were built without ladders.

Recent international rivalries involving fishing fleets from Canada, Japan, and Russia have created tension and reduced Washington's share of fish from mid-Pacific grounds. The 1974 decision by federal judge George Boldt, which guaranteed Indians half of the salmon supply in Washington waters, has reduced the number available to non-Indians. The seemingly inexhaustible supply of fish turned out to have limits.

During the 1980s large factory trawlers became a new aspect of the industry. Sixty or more boats, some of them longer than a football field, operate out of Puget Sound in North Pacific and Alaskan waters. They take about a million tons of fish annually. All aspects of the industry are conducted on board, from catching the fish to processing and freezing them. Along with cod and rockfish, many pollock are made into surimi, a fish paste. It is sold in the United States for imitation crab and in Japan for fish cakes.

Fish cannery workers near the end of the nineteenth century

Washington is regularly among the top four states in commercial fishing. There are about 2,500 commercial vessels. About 7,000 persons work in commercial fishing in Washington State, along with large numbers who are self-employed. Several thousand more are involved in processing, distributing, and handling fish products. In 1999 over 128 million pounds of fish products were brought in. About half of these were various marine fish (including cod, rockfish, and flatfish), a third were shellfish, and 5 percent were salmon. The remainder included halibut and non-salmon species such as sturgeon and smelt that also return to spawning grounds. The total value of fish processed in the state in 1999 was $135 million.

## TRADE AND COMMERCE

Washington was involved in trade from its earliest days. Indian trading was so extensive that the tribes developed the Chinook Jargon as a common language for bargaining. Explorers from Europe and New England, who came seeking trade routes and furs, found excellent natural harbors and navigable rivers.

Later, boats of the fur trading companies plied the coast and rivers to exchange goods. The Hudson's Bay Company brought in the *Beaver* in 1836, the first steamship along Washington waters. This 100-foot paddle wheeler was a familiar sight for almost four decades as it moved between fur posts and settlements along the coast, on the Columbia River, and throughout Puget Sound. Besides carrying supplies to company employees and other residents, it took out products from farms and stores, and it carried passengers.

As the lumber trade and other imports and exports increased, shipping became vital to the economy. Sawmills were located on deep harbors so that cargo ships could come and go easily. Small steamboats made regular runs on the Columbia and smaller rivers. The growing towns lining Puget Sound required ever more transportation. The "mosquito fleet" of small boats scurried from settlement to settlement with cargo and passengers until highway transportation put the boats out of business.

Today, no state depends upon trade more than does Washington. The state is especially well located for trade with countries across the Pacific and with Alaska and Canada. Trade and shipping are especially important in western Washington. Most of the waterborne commerce passes through the many ports on Puget Sound, 90 percent through Seattle and Tacoma alone.

Farther south, the Columbia River ports of Longview, Vancouver, and Kalama are sometimes linked with Portland, Oregon. On the coast, Aberdeen, Hoquiam, and Cosmopolis line Grays Harbor. The huge inland Columbia–Snake River system includes thirty-four different ports.

Although two-thirds of imports arrive by water, most exports go over land. Many goods are trucked into neighboring states and Canada. The use of double-stacked railroad cars has reduced the cost of trade with the East Coast. The amount of air cargo trade is on the rise, and polar routes have increased air traffic to Europe. At least one out of every three jobs in the state is related in some way to trade and commerce.

The amount of international trade passing through Washington ports has almost tripled since 1980. In 2000 Washington ports had $107 billion worth of two-way trade. Although exports tend to increase each year, the value of imports is much greater. This is generally considered an unfavorable balance of trade. Yet, many imports continue on to other states, so Washington itself enjoys an export trade surplus.

In 2000 over $40 billion worth of goods were exported from Washington each year. About half of this was in aircraft and aircraft parts; these are easily the leading exports in dollars. Another billion dollars worth of aircraft and spacecraft parts

A nineteenth-century advertisement dramatizes the size of Washington apples.

are exported; Boeing exports more than any other American company. The addition of trucks and auto parts makes all forms of transportation equipment the overall leading Washington export. Over $3 billion worth of various kinds of computer and electronic equipment and industrial machinery were exported in 1999. Software itself is considered a service rather than a product. The quantity exported is rising rapidly and amounted to about $3.5 billion that same year.

Agricultural crops and products are another leading export, totaling almost $2 billion. Wheat remains the major agricultural export produced within the state. In 2000 Washington shipped out $650 million worth of wheat. Much of that passes down the Columbia River through Portland rather than through Washington ports.

Major customers include Japan, India, Korea, and Egypt, where wheat is used for noodles and pastries. Corn and soybeans are other leading exports. Grain from elsewhere in the United States also leaves the country through the Pacific Northwest. This includes unmilled maize, or feed corn.

One traditional export is softwood of various kinds. In 2000 over a billion dollars worth of lumber and wood products were exported from Washington. Many logs went to Japan to build houses and produce pulp. Another major customer is Canada. Paper products are a related export.

Many of the goods that the state imports—about 80 percent—pass through to other states. This has increased tremendously since the mid-1980s. One outstanding example is passenger motor vehicles, the leading import amounting to $4 billion. The majority, coming from Japan and Italy, enter through Puget Sound ports, while German cars frequently pass through Columbia River ports.

It may seem odd that some of the products we export are very similar to those we import. Many parts for aircraft and spacecraft are imported. Sawn and chipped wood and data processing units are brought into the country. Crude oil and internal combustion piston engines are among the top ten kinds of imports into Washington.

The fact that we import toys and arcade and parlor games, many of which are electronic, illustrates the importance of leisure time activities in our society.

As suggested earlier, many exports and imports simply pass through the state. Washington is thus a "trade corridor" for automobiles, electronic equipment, and clothing that will be sold outside the Pacific Northwest. Some products are processed or assembled en route. Potatoes, apples, dried green peas, corn, oranges, and lentils are among the agricultural products from nearby states that pass through Washington. Such trade requires storage facilities and the means to handle goods.

During the 1960s, the Port of Seattle prepared to handle something new: container shipping. Previously, items being transferred to or from ships had to be unloaded and repacked, with the process repeated at the next destination. Thus a single shipment might be carried on trucks, trains, and boats, with many handlers removing the items at each transfer point. Constant packing and repacking took time and sometimes damaged goods.

Containers provided a new method. Huge boxes that look like railroad boxcars are packed at the point of origin. The loaded container is then placed aboard a flat railroad car, for instance, and moved to the dock where the container itself

Many demonstrators, including these on the University of Washington campus, protested against the World Trade Organization (WTO) when it met in Seattle in 1999.

is lifted aboard ship by gigantic cranes. When the ship docks, the container is lifted to truck or train for passage inland. Container shipping has proved to be less expensive, faster, and more efficient than previous shipping methods.

When Seattle adopted container shipping, it gained a great advantage over ports using older systems. Other ports soon followed. Vancouver, B.C., and Tacoma have built extensive container facilities and lured some business away from Seattle. Yet together, Seattle-Tacoma remains the second largest container-shipping center on the continent, behind Los Angeles–Long Beach.

Japan remains Washington's most important trading partner, accounting for 25 percent of all foreign trade. Canada is second with 22 percent. Not surprisingly, Asian nations such as China, South Korea, Taiwan, Hong Kong, Thailand, Singapore, and Malaysia are major trading partners. So are countries in the South Pacific including Australia, the Philippines, and Indonesia. But countries in western Europe receive airplanes, agricultural crops, fish, and forest products from the Pacific Northwest. The United Kingdom, for instance, is our sixth largest trading partner, Germany seventh, and the Netherlands tenth.

The important role of Washington in international trade was highlighted in late 1999, when Seattle hosted a major international conference of the World Trade Organization. Government and business leaders came from all over the world. Protesters also came. They denounced business practices and the power of major companies and nations. Several days of riots disrupted conference proceedings but also dramatized the fact that changes might be necessary.

## AIRCRAFT AND AEROSPACE INDUSTRIES

To many people in the Seattle area, the production of Boeing airplanes has long been at the center of economic life. Since World War II, the Boeing Company has been the largest corporate employer in Seattle and in the state. It produces 18 percent of the value of all products in Washington. Boeing brings in more money than any other single company and makes a product with which Seattle is closely identified around the world. It has been estimated that every job at Boeing creates 2.8 additional jobs in the area.

At first glance, Seattle does not seem a logical location for aircraft production. The principal materials for manufacturing are not present locally and have to be brought in. The Boeing Company was started in Seattle largely because its founder, William E. Boeing, lived there.

"The Red Barn" in 1917, where Boeing's early planes were built. The building is now part of the Museum of Flight in Seattle.

A wealthy young man who was fascinated by boats and early airplanes, William Boeing gathered a circle of skilled, enthusiastic workers about him in 1915. He learned to fly, purchased a Martin seaplane, and then financed the construction of two airplanes. In 1916 the company began in a small shipyard on the Duwamish River.

When World War I began, the company designed and built early training planes. For several years after the war, Boeing survived by making other products, including furniture and boats. During the 1920s, it constructed fighter planes for the United States Army and planes to carry mail for the post office. The Boeing Air Transport System, which later became part of United Airlines, was formed. Thus the small industry made its way through the 1930s. Meanwhile, William Boeing handed over direction of the company to others.

By World War II, Boeing was an important Seattle firm. War brought contracts for the B-17 and the B-29, which carried bomb loads over Europe and Asia. Two plants on the Duwamish River were supplemented by another at Renton. When the war ended and government contracts

Women workers sewing wings for early Boeing planes

were canceled, Boeing's future was uncertain. Efforts to convert warplane designs to commercial uses were not generally successful. But the beginning of the jet age opened new opportunities.

Under William Allen, a lawyer who became president of the Boeing Company at war's end, the company built the first practical jetliner. The 707 entered service at the end of 1958. The success of this plane led to a family of jets. To build the massive 747, the largest building in the world was constructed at Everett in the late 1960s.

By that time Boeing was the world's largest manufacturer of commercial airliners. But problems arose. Once airline companies had the planes they needed, they stopped buying. The federal government reduced purchases of military aircraft. Then, in 1971, a federal contract to build a supersonic transport plane, the SST, fell through as opposition to the plane mounted.

Boeing laid off thousands of workers. In 1968 the company had a high of almost 150,000 employees. Within two years there were less than half that many. This decline affected the whole Northwest, which depended heavily on Boeing and its planes. A recession hit the state. Business in general suffered. Thousands of unemployed workers, including highly educated engineers and technicians, took whatever work they could find.

Boeing's response to the crisis was to diversify and to seek additional commercial contracts. Company efforts turned to mass transportation systems, general construction, helicopters, hydrofoil boats, and military manufacturing.

Boeing also continued to seek contracts from airlines and nations around the world. Soon these efforts were paying off. A reputation for solid, safe construction with good backup systems and reliable service kept Boeing ahead of competing companies. It remained the world's leading supplier of commercial jets.

Billions of dollars worth of orders poured in. In the late 1970s, Boeing launched new jet aircraft, the 757 and the 767, that now lead in the number of trans-Atlantic flights. The latter plane has a medium capacity and long-range capability for secondary destinations. The first 777 was turned out in Everett in 1994. In 2001 the company had revenues of $58 billion. Airlines from all over the world purchase Boeing jets, with about 11,000 in service worldwide. Year after year, airplanes and parts are the leading export from Washington and frequently from the entire nation. Boeing also manufactures components for the nation's space program.

In 1997 Boeing merged with its chief United States rival, McDonnell Douglas, and became one of the world's largest manufacturing firms. This merger brought the company back into major production of military aircraft along with commercial jets. The previous year, Boeing had

acquired the defense and space units of Rockwell International. These events left Europe's Airbus as its only real competitor.

With approximately 175,000 total employees, a third of them in Washington, Boeing remains a dominant factor in the economy of the Northwest even when large layoffs occur. Boeing maintains plants in southern California, Kansas, Missouri, and locations in states and countries far from Washington. Its home base and center of operations remained in Seattle until 2001 when its headquarters were moved to Chicago. Perhaps other changes were to come. Nevertheless, to people around the world, Seattle has traditionally meant Boeing.

## BILL GATES AND MICROSOFT

A newer, very powerful industry has developed around electronics and computers. The Microsoft Corporation of Redmond is the world's leading manufacturer of computer software and its influence has changed the region. William H. Gates III was born in 1955 to prominent Seattle civic leaders. While a student at the Lakeside School in the city's north end, Bill Gates and his friend Paul Allen became excited about the school's new computer. They taught themselves how to program for it. At Harvard University, Gates continued this enthusiasm. But he dropped out during his junior year to devote himself full-time to Microsoft, the company he and Allen founded in 1975. From the beginning, they believed that this new industry would center around personal computers; they foresaw "a computer on every desk and in every home." And they intended that Microsoft would supply the essential software operating programs.

Under Gates's vision and hard-driving leadership, Microsoft emerged from backroom beginnings to become the country's and the world's leading maker of computer software. Its modern campus in Redmond sprawls above Lake Sam-

Aerial views of Redmond before and after the Microsoft headquarters were built show the growth that has taken place in the surrounding area. The Microsoft campus is visible near the center of the photograph below, to the right of the freeway.

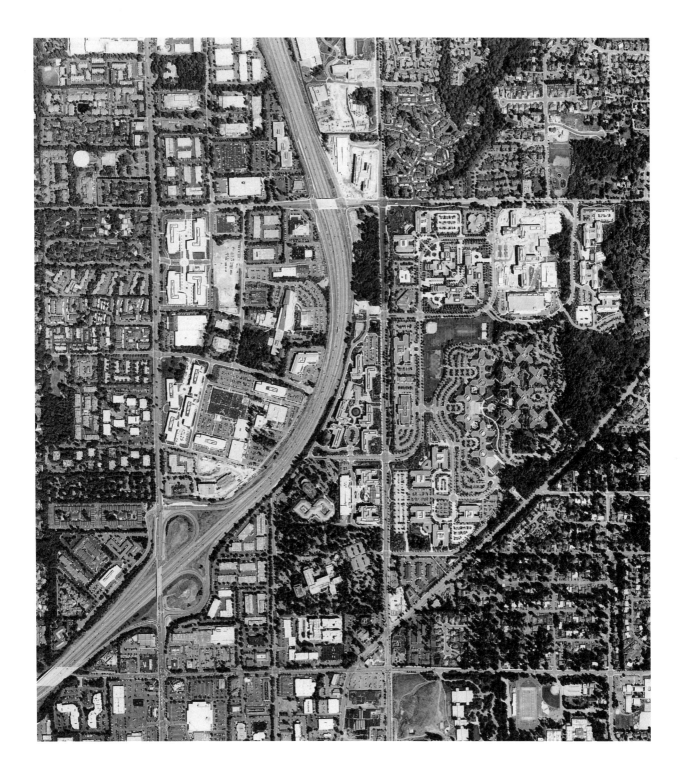

Bill Gates delivers a speech at the United Nations General Assembly Special Session on Children.

mamish. From those headquarters Microsoft sets trends and dominates a highly competitive market. Its many innovations are headed by the popular Windows operating system, which is used in most personal computers. Gates's company proved to be aggressive in marketing as well as in research and manufacturing. The company had a net revenue of over $25 billion in 2001, far more than any other Northwest company. Its products are translated into thirty languages and sold worldwide. Microsoft has revolutionized the way people around the world work and live.

But its success and aggressive practices led rival companies and federal authorities to charge that it was unfair to competitors. By the late 1990s Microsoft was embroiled in several lawsuits and court cases. A federal judge ordered the company to separate into two companies, but a higher court overturned that decision in 2001. Arguments on the issue and the decision seemed certain to continue for many years.

In its growth Microsoft became one of the region's dominant influences. Although the company has offices in the world's major countries, most of the manufacturing, marketing, and research takes place in Redmond. Over half of the company's 50,000 employees work in Washington State. Often a new or very large company attracts other, smaller companies that provide similar or supporting products and components. This happened in the area surrounding Redmond where a number of companies related to computers and electronics are located. Largely because of Gates and Microsoft, the Seattle suburbs have become a leading center of the electronics industry.

Gates is possibly the most instantly recognized citizen of the region. With a fortune hovering around $100 billion in the late 1990s, he was the richest person in the world. He engages in various philanthropic enterprises aimed at helping humankind. Gates and his wife have created the Bill and Melinda Gates Foundation, which donates billions of dollars toward solving world health problems and improving education and computer access in North America.

Allen left Microsoft early on, but he remains a commanding figure in the industry as well as in civic and sports affairs in the Northwest. Already owner of the Portland Trail Blazers, in 1997 he purchased the Seattle Seahawks. He has been involved in many development activities in the Puget Sound area including the Experience Music Project, an interactive museum devoted to rock and popular music. Other Microsoft millionaires have added a wealthy new class of leaders and philanthropists in the Seattle area.

Although the biggest by far, Microsoft was only one of 2,500 software companies in Washington as the twenty-first century began. Altogether they generated $20 billion in sales. A dozen years earlier, there were only eight hundred software companies. Many were small, and combined they employed as many workers as the giant.

New firms were increasingly located in eastern Washington and rural areas of the state.

## THE DOT-COMS

The widespread use of personal computers and the development of the Internet prompted some farsighted individuals to create a new kind of industry by the late 1990s. A driving figure was Jeff Bezos, who moved to Seattle with the idea of creating a business in which customers would purchase books over the Internet. He started his company in the summer of 1995 and named it Amazon.com. This new kind of business generally became known as a dot-com. As sales quickly expanded, Bezos began to offer other items: CDs, videos, electronics, and an increasing variety of other products.

*Time* magazine, which annually announces its "Man of the Year," selected Bezos for that honor in 1999, largely because of his influence in creating a new industry. Although Bezos's company was the largest and best known, a number of similar companies appeared selling a variety of goods and services: groceries, flowers, theater tickets, and even help with household chores. Dot-com companies were established elsewhere in the nation, but the Seattle area was home to many. Yet by the year 2001, the "bubble" was bursting. Many of the smaller companies were failing and others struggled to keep going.

## MANUFACTURING

The forest products, aerospace, and software industries are so prominent in Washington that they overshadow other manufacturing. But they are not the only industries in the state.

Other kinds of transportation besides aircraft are important. One early industry was shipbuilding. Wooden ships were built at several localities around Puget Sound by the late 1800s. The most famous was the Hall Brothers Shipyard, located first at Port Ludlow and later at Port Blakely and Winslow between 1874 and 1914. Fast and handsome, Hall Brothers vessels were known along the coast and in the western Pacific for many years. Lumber schooners were built at Aberdeen and Hoquiam by 1900, and shipbuilding continued to remain important on Grays Harbor.

By the early twentieth century, steel was replacing wood for shipbuilding, and the new Moran Brothers Shipyard was operating in Seattle. In October 1904, the Moran yards launched the largest ship yet built in the Northwest, the USS *Nebraska*. This 15,000-ton, 441-foot battleship was built after Seattle citizens raised $100,000 of the $3.7 million cost in an effort to reduce the shipyard's bid. Thus Seattle took double pride in the launching.

World War I contracts greatly aided modern, large-scale shipbuilding. New, enlarged, well-equipped yards flourished. Workers who came to find wartime jobs stayed on after the war ended. Although World War II also increased shipbuilding temporarily, the effects were not as long lasting.

Shipbuilding has remained important. Todd Shipyards is a large Seattle industry, and the Puget Sound Naval Shipyard in Bremerton handles heavy maintenance for the navy. Small boats and recreational craft have been increasingly important since 1945. But shipbuilding has been surpassed by aerospace and other industries.

After the first dams on the Columbia River were built during the 1930s, the inexpensive electric power they provided attracted an aluminum industry to Washington. The Aluminum Company of America (ALCOA) opened a plant in Vancouver in 1940, in time to produce aluminum needed during World War II. After the war the industry grew rapidly as other companies including Reynolds, Kaiser, and INTALCO entered the state. Plants at Ferndale, Vancouver, Tacoma, Longview, Goldendale, Wenatchee, and Spokane turn out aluminum ingots and rolled sheets for manufacture into finished products as well as cable and wire. Today, Washington produces about 40 percent of the nation's aluminum and ships large amounts overseas.

Early efforts to produce iron and steel near Port Townsend and at Kirkland were unsuccessful, but steel has been produced in Seattle. Ruston, near Tacoma, had a copper smelter until recent years. Early in the century, a smelter at Northport was a major industry in the far northeast corner of the state.

A newly emerging industry is biotechnology, which develops products by biological means. This includes the use of natural substances such as yeasts, bacteria, and enzymes from living organisms. Work is done in such fields as human therapy—including wound healing, hair growth, and anti-inflammatory medicines—and improving agricultural products. Seattle-based Immunex, started in 1981, researches, develops, and markets drugs to treat cancer and other diseases. In 2002 Immunex merged with Amgen, a California company.

The Kenworth Motor Company in Seattle and the Pacific Car and Foundry Company (PACCAR) in Renton manufacture and export trucks and railroad car bodies around the world. Food and fish processing plants are found along the waterfronts and in agricultural areas. Seattle also became the center of a flourishing market for coffee drinks; like Boeing, Starbucks is instantly identified with the city where it was founded. The production of clothing, skis and other recreational equipment, furniture, wine, and beer proves that Washington manufacturing is growing and diverse. Aerospace, forest products, and software dominate, but other kinds of manufacturing round out the industries of the state.

## The Tourist Industry

The role of tourism in the economy of Washington is easily overlooked. Although the state lacks the fame of Hawaii or eastern historical sites, tourism is among the top five industries in the state. Each year about 13 million tourists from both within and outside the state spend almost $10 billion in Washington. This aids the entire economy. Jobs are created, additional services must be provided, products are made and sold.

For many visitors, Washington is a stop on a circle around the West; others come for vacations and conventions. Out-of-state visitors are drawn by the state's scenic beauty and variety. The Olympic and Cascade Mountains, especially Mount Rainier, attract spectators and outdoor enthusiasts, and thousands have viewed Mount St. Helens since its May 1980 eruption. State parks and national forests draw large numbers of visitors from all areas. The San Juan Islands and the Columbia River Gorge offer remote, spectacular beauty.

Many visitors enjoy riding the state ferries and participating in water activities on Puget Sound. Grand Coulee Dam and Lake Chelan are leading attractions in eastern Washington. Coastal areas lure sport fishing enthusiasts, with Westport, Ilwaco, and Neah Bay important spots for ocean charter fishing. Ocean Shores and Long Beach are popular ocean-side resort towns.

Superior accommodations are necessary to draw tourists. Spokane, Seattle, Tacoma, and other cities have major hotels, as do some resort areas. The quality of restaurants, bars, and entertainment has improved. A downtown convention center built over the Seattle freeway hosts large gatherings of national importance. Smaller convention facilities are available at resorts along the ocean and Puget Sound, in the mountains, and in inland areas. Special events like the Skagit Valley Tulip Festival and the Hot Air Balloon Stampede at Walla Walla attract visitors. Some events draw worldwide visitors as have several All-Star games and the Goodwill Games of 1990.

State and local communities and business

groups combine their publicity with booklets, brochures, websites, and photographs to attract tourists. One popular ad campaign highlighted this as the "other" Washington, contrasting its attractions with those in the national capital.

## Agriculture

Commercial agriculture began in Washington with the Hudson's Bay Company. Touring the region in 1824–25, Sir George Simpson insisted that HBC forts become more self-sufficient and make use of the fertile land and mild climate. Company headquarters were moved from Fort George (Astoria) to Fort Vancouver where farming opportunities were greater. There, Chief Factor John McLoughlin shared the interest in farming. Meanwhile a new fort was built in the fertile Colville region east of the Cascades. Simpson knew the fur trade would not last forever, and he thought the HBC could make good profits from agriculture.

Soon HBC forts were raising grains, fruits, vegetables, livestock, and other products for their employees. A grist mill near Fort Vancouver ground grain into flour. New company sites were selected with an eye to farming possibilities.

Dr. McLoughlin established the Puget Sound Agricultural Company to raise crops and livestock. A large farm was started in the Cowlitz Valley midway between the Columbia River and Puget Sound, and Nisqually Indians were hired as cowboys. The company sold produce to British and Americans along the entire coast, to crews of passing ships, and to other travelers.

Missionaries who settled the Willamette Valley south of Vancouver praised the land, soil, and growing season so emphatically that farming helped bring Americans into the Northwest. In eastern Washington, the Whitmans and other missionaries settled where land was fertile, and they raised a variety of crops.

When Michael T. Simmons and George Bush led settlers to the Puget Sound area, farming possibilities influenced the choice of homesites. Even settlements that expected to depend upon logging or fishing needed to raise food. Homestead laws and the Donation Land Act allowed a person to secure 160 acres of farmland by living on it and developing it. Married couples were eligible for 320 acres. Farms were appearing west of the Cascades by the mid-1800s.

In time western Washington was sprinkled with family farms, some of which supplied towns that grew nearby. Most were small operations in which a family and maybe a few employees raised vegetables, fruits, dairy products, and livestock, but some specialized crops began to appear. The Puyallup Valley for several years was one of the nation's chief growers of hops. Bulbs and seeds were also grown there and in the Skagit Valley. Berry farms appeared along the western slope.

Early haying in Skagit County

## FARMING EAST OF THE CASCADES

Agricultural developments east of the Cascades followed different patterns. Dry land and extremes of climate seemed unsuitable for the kind of farming familiar to most early settlers. The parts of eastern Washington that appealed to farmers, therefore, were the several rich valleys.

Walla Walla attracted attention after the 1858 announcement that the Indian wars had ended. Walla Walla enjoyed a quick growth with small farms that produced a variety of crops, but it increasingly concentrated on grain. Similarly, Yakima Valley farming grew around the Ahtanum Valley and Fort Simcoe.

But in eastern Washington generally, ranching was the first major activity because cattle could take advantage of the native grasses on the plains. Most cattle were shipped or driven up from California, although many immigrants brought their own herds. Cattle for sale were driven downriver to Portland or across the Mullan Road to mining camps or farther east.

Eventually annual cattle drives were made to Puget Sound. Overgrazing became a problem as the number of cattle increased; about 10 percent of eastern Washington cattle died in the harsh winter of 1881. Along with cattle, the region raised hogs, sheep, horses, and mules.

Oats were an important early crop, but wheat rose in importance around Walla Walla and then in other valleys. Some farmers experimented with new ideas, crops, lands, and methods of planting and harvesting. By the 1880s wheat was spreading from valleys into higher areas. It became a major cash crop. Beautiful, prosperous wheat fields carpeted round hillsides each spring and fall. Farmers ventured to try other crops as well.

There was continued prosperity but no sudden boom. The sod, hard to break, required plows and harrows that were expensive and difficult to obtain. Competition with wheat from midwestern states remained strong. Yet north from

Walla Walla, around Dayton and Waitsburg and Colfax, new fields were broken by farmers willing to work hard. Wheat moved to higher and higher, hilly lands in the Palouse country.

By the 1890s, eastern Washington was attracting more and more settlers. Railroads aided this growth. Farms, ranches, and small towns sprinkled the whole area north from Walla Walla to Spokane. Bunchgrass provided prospective wheat farmers with a clue that the soil could grow crops.

Walla Walla turned also to fruits and vegetables. The valley filled with orchards and berry fields. Farms specialized in raising peas, sugar beets, sweet potatoes, and various grasses. Other eastern Washington areas followed.

Between the Cascades and the Columbia River lay Yakima. But that broad valley required irrigation. By the 1890s a few farmers were diverting river water into the sagebrush and finding rich soil. Grains and fruits flourished.

To the north, a rival town of Ellensburg was started in the Kittitas Valley where grain and cattle were raised. Early in the twentieth century, Wenatchee developed as soil and growing conditions in surrounding valleys proved right for fruits and other crops. The whole Columbia Basin seemed to have a rich agricultural future. It would be based on cattle and other livestock, wheat and other grains, and fruit.

But clearly much eastern Washington land required additional water. Small-scale irrigation had been practiced by Indians, missionaries, and early settlers. Some farmers who started to irrigate in the Yakima Valley sold water to neighboring farms. Soon large irrigation companies arose and squeezed out small competitors.

President Theodore Roosevelt urged that land and resources be conserved for future use. This philosophy encouraged demands for federal support and control of irrigation during the early 1900s. With a Washington congressman serving

A winding irrigation ditch provides water for patterned farms in eastern Washington flatlands.

on its planning commission, the Reclamation Service was created. This agency had to battle some of the large private companies, but it brought the distribution of water under federal control.

New reclamation projects appeared in the Yakima Valley and other areas. Soon such visionaries as Rufus Woods, publisher of the *Wenatchee World*, and Ephrata lawyer William Clapp began to promote an even larger scheme. These men wanted the Columbia River dammed to provide irriga-

tion throughout the entire dry region. They began the campaign that resulted in Grand Coulee Dam. First conceived as an irrigation project, it was converted into a multipurpose proposal that included hydroelectric power.

By the early twentieth century, the pattern of agriculture in Washington had been set. Small farms were located throughout the valleys west of the Cascades. The eastern portion of the state had expansive wheat fields and cattle and sheep ranches. In several eastern valley pockets, vegetables and fruits were raised, while the broad valleys below the eastern Cascade slopes were filled with orchards. Eastern Washington agriculture was on a large scale. Western farms were smaller and usually served local needs.

## FARMING AND RELATED INDUSTRIES AT THE CENTURY'S TURN

Today agriculture remains a big business in Washington, producing varied crops and livestock valued at about $5.3 billion each year. Related industries include processing, packaging, marketing, and transporting harvests and supplies. Taken together, these industries employ about 350,000 people. Washington products are consumed at home and shipped to many parts of the world. Some, including grains and apples, are among the leading exported products from Washington.

Some things have changed, however. Only one of every twenty-five persons in Washington is engaged in farming today. In 1935 there were about 85,000 farms in the state. Today there are fewer than 30,000. Over half are small, less than fifty acres in size and with sales less than $10,000. Many are part-time operations owned by people who have other jobs as well.

Individual farmers have become astute businesspeople. It is almost impossible for a newcomer to acquire land in the eastern Washington wheat country. Land is divided among individu-

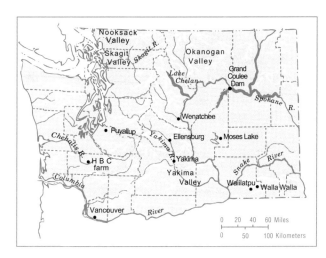

Agricultural areas in Washington State

als and families that have held it over many years. Big, expensive machinery is essential and must be maintained. Thus, it has become possible for a small number of people, perhaps an individual family with a few seasonal workers, to maintain thousands of acres of wheat from planting through harvesting and marketing.

Apples are the state's most valuable crop and one in which Washington leads all states. Centering in the Yakima, Wenatchee, Chelan, and Okanogan valleys, the state raises about four billion pounds or 125 to 130 million boxes each year. These four valleys produce about half of the entire fresh apple crop of the United States. The yearly sales value ranges around $850 million. Red Delicious apples have usually made up about 60 percent of the total crop, with Yellow Delicious and Granny Smith also popular. Yet the desire for Red Delicious apples has recently declined, causing a slowdown in apple sales in the late 1990s. This raises questions about the future of this important crop.

The second leading agricultural product of Washington is whole milk. Most of the 1,200 families that make their living on dairy farms live in western Washington and the Yakima Valley. There are 246,000 dairy cows, which in 1999 produced almost 429 million pounds of milk for a value of over $825 million. About half is processed into cheese, butter, ice cream, and other products. Some is exported as condensed, evaporated, or dried milk.

Potatoes are the second largest crop, valued at $476 million. Only Idaho produces more potatoes. Peas and sugar beets are other major crops raised mostly in eastern Washington.

Wheat is Washington's third most valuable agricultural crop. In 1990 farmers raised 125 million bushels on three million acres of prairies, hills, and valleys. Much but not all of this land is irrigated.

The value of Washington's wheat crop in 2000 was $459 million, an amount that has been declining in recent years. Most of it was shipped overseas. Washington is the only major wheat-producing state outside the Midwest. It ranks third among the states as a producer of wheat. The state produces both winter wheat, which is seeded in the early winter, and spring wheat. Washington scientists, most notably Orville Vogel of Washington State University, have been leaders in developing new strains, controlling diseases, and increasing yields. Hay, barley, corn, and other grains are also important crops.

Other fruits besides apples are important to the state's economy. Mostly grown in eastern Washington valleys, these include sweet cherries, pears, peaches, apricots, and various berries. Controlled-atmosphere storage enables apples and pears to be held for marketing year-round. Grapes and a rapidly growing wine industry are largely centered in the Yakima Valley.

Hops have been a major crop since early settlement, although the emphasis has shifted from western Washington valleys to the irrigated Yakima Valley. Washington produces three-fourths of the nation's hops. Almost half the crop is shipped to breweries in various foreign countries.

Flower bulbs and vegetable seeds are raised for export in several valleys in the western portion of the state, particularly the Skagit. Christmas trees are another important crop. Western Washington valleys provide vegetables for local consumption and some export. A somewhat unusual crop is grown in the southwestern corner of the state where cranberry bogs mark the landscape. Mint is a major crop in south central Washington, which produces three-fourths of the nation's spearmint oil and one-third of the peppermint oil.

Beef cattle and other livestock are raised on the plateaus east of the Cascades. The value of Washington's 1.2 million head of cattle in 2000 was over $560 million, making it the fourth most valuable agricultural commodity. Poultry farms remain important, some producing broiler chickens while others produce eggs. The many small farms have mostly been replaced by a few large ones.

In its many forms, agriculture continues as an important and varied part of Washington's economy.

## Power and Energy

Climate, snow fields, and fast-flowing rivers have given Washington abundant water power. In the nineteenth century water turned wheels for lumber mills and grist mills. Later, it generated millions of kilowatts of hydroelectric power. This abundance led to a confidence that Washington would always have plentiful, inexpensive power for homes, businesses, and factories, with more to spare. Washington's electricity flowed into California and other places where large populations demanded more power than local rivers could produce.

Washington still has more abundant and less expensive power than many states. But occasional low rainfall and snowfall years and threats of major power outages arouse concerns about future supplies of power.

Wood and flowing water provided power for early settlers. Abundant timber meant mills could be fueled by their own waste cuttings. In Spokane, flour mills were built alongside waterfalls. Throughout the state, small communities appeared beside similar falls and rapids. The growth of population coincided with improvements in technology that made electric power affordable and practical for personal, community, and industrial uses. Hydroelectric power is generated by forcing water to rush through large turbines where a magnetic field produces electricity.

Tacoma became the first large city to produce its own power when it acquired a local utility company in 1898. The city later built dams on the Nisqually River and the North Fork of the Skokomish River on the Olympic Peninsula, which created Lake Cushman. Tacoma City Light proudly boasted for years that it provided the cheapest electricity in the nation. Spokane and Seattle soon generated power from their own sources and several smaller cities followed suit.

Along with municipal power companies, private ones were established. The largest were Puget Sound Power and Light Company (now Puget Sound Energy) in the western part of the state, Washington Water Power Company (now Avista Corporation) in the east, and Pacific Power and Light in the southeast. These three controlled power transmission in much of the state.

In 1907 the state legislature allowed yet another form of power company to be established, the public utility district (PUD). These districts can be formed to provide power for areas that are growing or thinly populated. Many counties and parts of counties have since created PUDs. Thus the power situation became a collection of municipal agencies, private companies, and public utility districts.

In the 1930s under Franklin D. Roosevelt's New Deal the federal government entered the

Giant transmission towers cross eastern Washington hills, their cables carrying electricity to communities, farms, and homes throughout the region.

scene. Bonneville Dam, the first federally built dam on the Columbia River, was completed in 1938. Forty-five miles upstream from Portland, it straddles the river between Washington and Oregon. Bonneville generates 518,400 kilowatts as part of a project to provide power and flood control and aid navigation on the Columbia;

seven years earlier a private firm opened Rock Island Dam just south of Wenatchee.

By the time Bonneville was generating electricity, Grand Coulee Dam was under construction. Originally designed for irrigation, the dam's height was raised in the mid-1930s so it could produce electricity. Grand Coulee power was available for World War II production needs, and power from the dam overshadowed its irrigation aspects.

In the years since, the Columbia River has been converted into a chain of lakes behind dams in both Washington and British Columbia. Fourteen dams block the Columbia, leaving little free-flowing river.

Smaller dams were built on tributaries flowing into the Columbia in four states and Canada. During the lifetime of a single person, the river was permanently altered by the craving for electric power. One author has called the Columbia River "a colossal utility, a kind of man-made electric river."

In 1937 the Bonneville Power Administration (BPA) was created to oversee, handle, and sell power from these dams and to coordinate the use of power throughout the region. BPA can make sure that electricity is sent during peak load times to places where it is most needed. Electricity cannot be stored, but it can be transmitted easily wherever power lines go. In the 1960s, almost all the electricity in Washington was hydroelectric; today 62 percent is, with coal and nuclear energy producing most of the rest.

But dependence on hydroelectricity brings continuing problems. Many rivers have been damaged by extensive dam construction. We have been forced to choose between kilowatts and salmon, which have difficulty swimming upriver to spawn or downstream to the ocean. Canadians fought attempts by Seattle City Light to raise the height of Ross Dam on the Skagit River. This would produce additional power for Washington, but it would also flood a valley in British Columbia. The sides compromised in 1984. In return for not raising the dam, Seattle was promised power from Canada.

The abundance of cheap power attracted industries that use unusually large amounts, thus reducing the amount of power available for other users. The aluminum industry, for example, has been a heavy user.

Some observers suggest exploring alternative sources of power. Nuclear power, which once seemed attractive, has probably been ruled out. Coal reserves, until recently considered too expensive to mine, are attracting new attention.

Despite the many overcast days in western Washington, some people believe solar energy can heat homes and offices and serve other purposes. Geothermal energy, which is produced from heat inside the earth, is receiving attention. For many years there have been experiments using windmills to produce power in the Columbia River Gorge and southeast Washington. In 2001 plans got underway for the world's largest "wind farm" near the Columbia and Walla Walla: 450 wind turbines would be built in Washington and Oregon, enough to provide power for 70,000 homes.

Environmentalists feel that the first need is to conserve what we already have. Conservation was firmly encouraged in the Northwest Power Bill of 1980. Many people look to the future and argue that we can never again use electricity as freely as in the past. We must change life styles, build energy-efficient homes and offices, and use fewer appliances. Environmentalists argue that business and industry must cut down, as well as home consumers. On the other hand, prominent leaders believe that there must be increases in power production, including a search for new or abandoned sources.

The future of energy in the Pacific Northwest has become a critical problem. Perhaps there are even more dramatic changes ahead than those brought about by the building of great dams and the abundance of electricity familiar to past generations.

## Chapter 10 Review

**I.** Identify the following people. Tell why each is important to Washington State.

Joshua Green
Andrew J. Pope
William C. Talbot
Frederick E. Weyerhaeuser
George S. Long
William E. Boeing
William Allen
William H. Gates III
Jeff Bezos
John McLoughlin
Michael T. Simmons
Rufus Woods
William Clapp

**II.** Define the following words and terms. Relate each to Washington State.

Economics
Natural resources
Capital
Labor
Market
Transportation system
Organizers
Government support
Donkey engine
Splash dam
Sustained yield
Virgin forests
Natural cycles of growth
Factory trawlers
The *Beaver*
Mosquito fleet
Trade corridor
Container shipping
B-17   B-29   747   767   777
Supersonic Transport (SST)
Software
USS *Nebraska*

Puget Sound Agricultural Company
Hydroelectric power
Public utility district (PUD)
Bonneville Power Administration (BPA)
Solar energy
Geothermal energy

**III.** Be able to locate each of these places on a map. Tell why each is important to Washington State.

*Forest products industry*

| | |
|---|---|
| Fort Vancouver | Snoqualmie Falls |
| Cosmopolis | Port Blakely |
| Raymond | Longview |
| Port Gamble | Tacoma |
| Shelton | Federal Way |
| Seabeck | Aberdeen |
| Everett | Camp Grisdale |
| Port Madison | Hoquiam |

*Mining*

| | |
|---|---|
| Bellingham | Concrete |
| Carbonado | Cle Elum |
| Roslyn | Grotto |
| Black Diamond | Holden |
| Wilkeson | |

*Other industries*

| | |
|---|---|
| Willapa Bay | Longview |
| Tacoma | Renton |
| Fraser River | Kalama |
| Port Townsend | Wenatchee |
| Samish Island | Vancouver |
| Bremerton | Redmond |

*Agriculture*

| | |
|---|---|
| Walla Walla | Ellensburg |
| Waitsburg | Willamette Valley |
| Puyallup Valley | Kittitas Valley |
| Colfax | Cowlitz Valley |
| Skagit Valley | Yakima Valley |
| Spokane | Dayton |
| Vancouver | Grand Coulee Dam |

**IV.** Each question below should call your attention to factual information in the chapter. Try to answer each one. Then look back in the reading to check your answer, correct your understanding, and find answers you do not know.

1. List three stages of growth in the economy of a growing area.

2. Name at least three major natural resources found in Washington.

3. What source outside of Washington supplied much-needed capital in early days?

4. What has been the most common labor supply for Washington?

5. Where were the first lumber and fish products from Washington sold?

6. List three ways that government can help businesses in a region.

7. What company built the first lumber mill in Washington?

8. Which distant city greatly affected the early economy of Washington?

9. What trees grew in the southwest part of the state?

10. How did railroads affect the logging industry?

11. What was the usual attitude of companies toward injured workers?

12. What large lumber company moved into Washington in 1900? How did this company acquire large amounts of timberland?

13. What is the name given to the great forest fires of 1902?

14. About how much of Washington is still forested?

15. Name three mining rushes outside the state of Washington that affected Washington.

16. Describe the quality of Washington coal. Why was it difficult to bring out?

17. What are the most profitable mineral products found in Washington?

18. Where was the first fish cannery on Puget Sound located?

19. Give some reasons why the number of fish has declined.

20. Name Washington's top three exports in dollar value.

21. What is Washington's leading import in dollar value?

22. With what country does Washington carry on the most trade? Which country is second?

23. What company is the largest single employer in the state?

24. What government orders helped the Boeing Company survive during the 1920s?

25. What new type of airplane did the Boeing Company develop in the years after World War II?

26. What did the Boeing Company do to adjust to the economic problems of the late 1960s?

27. What was Bill Gates's vision for the future of the computer industry?

28. What was the most famous early shipbuilding company on Puget Sound?

29. Where did the Hudson's Bay Company locate a large farm?

30. What became the specialized crop in the Puyallup Valley? In the Skagit Valley?

31. Which was the earliest part of eastern Washington to develop farming? Tell several changes it passed through.

32. What became the most important economic activity in the Columbia Basin?

33. What grain spread rapidly throughout eastern Washington after the 1880s?

34. How were dry areas changed to improve possibilities for agriculture?

35. Tell several major changes that have taken place in agriculture in recent years.

36. Why did the people of Washington expect always to have inexpensive electricity?

37. How did the federal government help produce power?

38. In what way was the original plan for Grand Coulee Dam greatly changed?

39. About what percentage of the power produced in Washington is hydroelectric power?

40. What industry was attracted to Washington after World War II by inexpensive electric power?

41. What do many environmentalists believe to be the best solution to energy problems?

**V.** Think about, discuss, and answer the questions below.

1. Take the seven elements listed as being essential for economic growth and relate them to your own community. For instance: What natural resources affect the economy of your community? Where are these resources obtained? Where are the products of your community sold?

2. Why is "forest products industry" a more accurate term than simply "logging and lumbering"?

3. Find some information about the practice of clear-cut logging. What are some arguments for and against the practice?

4. What things tend to make a particular place attractive for manufacturing? What is likely to make it unattractive? Consider how attractive your own community is for manufacturing. You might want to discuss this with local business-people or a representative of the chamber of commerce.

5. What arguments exist between industrial groups and environmentalists? How would each use and develop lands and resources? Assuming that both industrial development and environmental quality are necessary, what things can be done to reach a reasonable balance between the two?

6. List five major tourist attractions in Washington State. What attractions does your own community have? What things do you show people who come to visit? What does your community do to attract tourists?

7. What factors are needed for the production of apples and soft fruits? What areas of the state are particularly suitable for fruit production? Why? Be specific.

# Chapter 11 Washingtonians and How They Live

Yakima, April 1, 2000. The Yakima River skirts the city of Yakima as it flows from Cascade snow fields to the Columbia River. The river unites and waters this broad agricultural valley.

Behind this city rise rounded hills and distant snow-capped peaks. There was lumbering in the early days, but Yakima prospered as the center of a rich agricultural region. Fruit storage and packing facilities line the railroad tracks. Apples, peaches, pears, cherries, grapes, hops, potatoes, alfalfa, asparagus, mint, and cattle built this town.

It is a sunny but breezy Saturday in the Yakima Valley with the temperature reaching 78 degrees. This last day before daylight saving time is also the beginning of spring break for many students. Washington Middle School students ended the term yesterday with a march recognizing Drug Awareness Week, and Davis High students presented Shakespeare's A Midsummer Night's Dream at the school auditorium. Spring sports are underway, with local baseball rivalries well in force and the Eisenhower boys and girls track teams capturing titles at statewide relay meets at Zaepful Stadium.

Their teachers are also making news. A Sunnyside fifth-grade teacher and trivia fan is keeping quiet about his success on a recently taped session of the television contest Who Wants to Be a Millionaire; it will be shown tomorrow evening. Terry Smith, principal of Wapato's alternative school, has just been honored as the Educator of the Year by the Washington Alternative Learning Association, and Eisenhower football coach Greg Gavin has resigned. Yakima has a new school superintendent, its first Hispanic leader. Born in Mexico, Ben Soria comes from Tacoma, where he promoted small class size and bilingual education.

Sports fans are celebrating Friday's surprise victory of the Yakima Sun Kings over the Rockford, Illinois,

A. C. Davis High School Homecoming Court, 2000

Lightning in the semifinal game of the Continental Basketball Association championships at the Sun Dome. The local team will meet the La Crosse, Wisconsin, Bobcats the next day at home. And in a Toppenish casino, two legendary world champion middleweights, Sugar Ray Leonard and Roberto Duran, are putting on an exhibition match.

Movies showing at local theaters include the Academy Award winner American Beauty, along with Julia Roberts in Erin Brokovich and Johnny Depp in Sleepy Hollow. Yakimans are hosting visitors from their sister city of Morelia, Mexico. A march through the Valley commemorates the birthday of the late Cesar Chavez, a labor leader who had frequently visited migrant farm workers in the area. Local groups are holding a quilt show and a barbershop chorus concert. And this weekend, a bottle with a message was discovered, dropped in the Yakima River sixteen years earlier by a ten-year-old boy. Of local concern was news that plans for a major water reservoir near Sunnyside seemed to be slipping away and that faulty pipes were delaying cleanup at the Hanford Atomic Reservation. And Governor Gary Locke has just signed the bill that will put the thirty-dollar license tab into effect.

Few residents realize something else is happening this day: they are being counted. Every ten years, the federal Census Bureau takes a population count throughout the nation. The primary purpose of the census is to decide how many representatives each state will have in Congress. It will also help determine the amount of funding that cities and counties will receive from other governments. These figures may also help local officials predict where to place new public utilities, schools, highways, and hospitals.

Almost 17,000 newcomers since 1990 have raised the city's population to 71,845. Smaller towns in the valley are also growing rapidly. Grandview rose from 7,169 to 8,377; Sunnyside, founded as a religious cooperative community, grew from 11,238 to 13,905. The far southeast corner of the county near the Hanford atomic energy plant has also gained substantial numbers. Valley towns—Toppenish, Selah, Wapato, Union Gap, Zillah—and rural areas contribute to the 222,581 people who live in Yakima County.

Yakima County is multiracial. More than 6,000 Yakama tribal members live on their million-acre reservation, farming, lumbering, and leasing out land. Whites settled after Indian conflicts in the 1850s ended. When they found that irrigation made the soil rich, the land blossomed. A visiting journalist in 1894 called this valley in the desert a miracle; he admired Yakima's lush gardens and tree-lined streets.

Many settlers arrived from eastern Europe. Later came Japanese and Filipinos. By World War II, a thousand Japanese lived in the valley, and their descendants remain. Today, 2,157 African Americans live in Yakima County, two-thirds of them in the city.

For many summers, Mexican Americans have come to pick crops, stopping on their annual pilgrimages in search of work. Now 79,905 Hispanics live permanently in the valley, one of every three residents. Some own land and homes, with firm roots in valley towns. When cherries ripen in a few weeks, more migrants will arrive to stay through the fall harvest.

The figures suggest issues this community must deal with. Many schoolchildren are from migrant families. For 12 percent of the city's children, English is a second language. There is poverty. The average income in Yakima is lower than in any other urban area in the state.

But this valley is rich in resources, and there is richness in the variety of its towns and people. Today they go about their usual activities. It is an ordinary Saturday—except that the people are being counted.

The Davis High cheerleading squad

# The Washingtonians

Along with geography, history, and the economy, people determine what a place will truly be like. Nations and regions with geographical advantages and varied natural resources have sometimes languished while places that appear to be poor develop thriving cultures. People's ideas and actions make a difference. The character and quality of a large body of people are difficult to measure, and broad generalizations may be inaccurate. Yet some things about the people of Washington may help one to understand the state better. Who are these people, where have they come from, what are they like, where do they live, what do they do and believe, and how have they helped to make the state the way it is?

In the year 2000, 5,908,684 persons were living in Washington, a 21.1 percent increase since 1990. Only nine states added more. The 1,027,429 additional people were far more than the combined populations of the three largest cities, Seattle, Spokane, and Tacoma. Soon the state would have well over six million people.

Washington's growth, however, slowed during the late 1990s. The growth was less than 1 percent a year. The 21.1 percent increase in Washington during the 1990s was similar to that in recent decades. But it was much less than that during the rapid growth just after World War II. Much earlier, during the pioneering decades of the 1870s and 1880s, the population increase was 213 percent and 375 percent respectively. The first ten years of the century saw a 120 percent increase. But these were growth years in a new and rapidly developing region with much available land and obvious natural attractions. The current stability of Washington, a national birth rate that is lower than it once was, and the increasing average life span help account for some differences between those early years and today. Many Americans are moving to "sun states" such as Florida and the Southwest.

Where do these people live? Most—nearly four out of five—live west of the Cascade Mountains, and two-thirds are in the Puget Sound Basin. A single county, King, which includes Seattle, has nearly one-third of the entire population of Washington. Rapid growth is taking place in the metropolitan areas around Puget Sound although the greatest percentage increases are in Clark, Jefferson, and Grant counties. Despite vast deserts and mountainous areas, Washington is an urban society. Generally speaking, a center with a population of 2,500 or more is considered to be urban. Over three-fourths of Washington's people live in urban areas.

About 40 percent of the growth is a "natural increase," due to more births than deaths. Sixty percent stems from the movement of people to Washington from somewhere else. About half of the residents were born in the state. Americans tend to move about, some moving out of and back to the state. In the past many migrants moved almost directly west from their former homes, so Washington drew from the northern Plains and Rocky Mountain states. Minnesota, Iowa, and the Dakotas account for large numbers. In recent decades, however, more people have come from or moved to heavily populated California than any other state.

In the past, immigrants from other countries usually came to Washington after living in states farther east. The more recent influx of persons from Asia and Mexico has altered this somewhat. About 7 percent of Washington's people were born in other countries, and the percentage in the Greater Seattle area is over twice that.

## Northwest Identity

*If there is a Northwest Identity—and a new poll suggests there is a strong one—it is linked inexorably with the region's mountains and forests and water.*

*. . .*

*We love the mountains, the trees, the greenery. And though we're not wild about all the rain, we really wouldn't want to live anywhere else. Not even if you paid us.*

*Life is good and getting better, we are making progress on most of our problems, and we like our jobs. We worry, however, about the traffic and high-priced housing in the Puget Sound area.*

*. . .*

*One of the most striking findings . . . is the strong sense of identity with the Pacific Northwest region. Four out of 10 people throughout the region, from Port Angeles to Boise, say the phrase "the Northwest is an important part of who I am" fits them exactly.*

*The land and the environment were the top answers when people were asked what makes the Northwest different from the rest of the country.*

*. . .*

*When asked what worried them most about their communities, one-third of those surveyed cite growth and traffic. One in five mention crime and almost the same number say nothing.*

*The issue of growth is particularly dominant in the larger cities surveyed. King County residents were the most likely group to say we're losing ground on affordable housing (70 percent vs. 50 percent for the whole region) and transportation (60 percent vs. 42 percent for the whole region).*

*King County residents are also likely to say they're losing their sense of community and quality of life and are the least likely to know their neighbors.*

*. . .*

*Asked what they would miss most about the Northwest if they were to move, the overwhelming response was the area's natural beauty.*

*What would they not miss, if they moved? No surprise: the weather.*

*. . .*

*King County residents are most likely to say their community is making progress in the economy and as a place of opportunity. But they are also more likely than residents of any other area to say they are losing ground on housing, transportation and overall quality of life.*

*Concern about growth peaks in King County and is lowest in eastern Washington. Those who moved to the region are most likely to say traffic is a mess, while natives are loudest in complaining about the lack of affordable housing.*

*The biggest cities have the lowest church attendance. Church attendance is highest in eastern Washington, lowest in King County. Protestants have lived here the longest and non-Christians say they fit in the least.*

*. . .*

*The longer someone has lived in the community, the less willing he is to move. People say smaller communities are friendlier than larger ones. Homeowners are more likely than renters to say they fit in; couples with no children say they fit in the best and are most likely to say they're getting ahead.*

*We are a generous region. An overwhelming majority, 86 percent, say they contributed to charity in the past year and 61 percent say they volunteered at a community organization, church or school.*

*Susan Gilmore, "Fertile Ground for Optimism, Part 1: Northwest Identity."*
*Copyright 2000, The Seattle Times Co.*

## The White Majority

The white population has long been the largest and most influential racial group in Washington. Emigrants from Western Europe were among the first white settlers. The British Hudson's Bay Company and the Canadian North West Company helped set traditions of culture and government. Some English- and French-Canadian fur traders became permanent settlers. American missionaries, particularly from northeastern states, reinforced white, Protestant influences.

Walla Walla and other early towns took on a New England appearance they retain today. When logging and lumbering firms built towns on Puget Sound inlets, they brought workers from New England states. Seabeck, Port Gamble, Port Ludlow, and Port Madison were established by New Englanders whose families had originated in Britain. Later lumber giants such as the Weyerhaeuser Company moved west from northern states and brought or hired workers of English, German, Scandinavian, and Finnish backgrounds. More workers of these nationalities migrated westward as forests ran out in other regions.

Scandinavians also fished and farmed. The landscape and climate around Puget Sound were similar to Norwegian fjords and Swedish inlets. Ballard, Poulsbo, and Gig Harbor acquired the complexion of Scandinavian communities. Early Swedish immigrants started the Nordstrom stores and Isaacson Steel Works.

Many Germans settled on the Sound. Bremerton and Bellingham were founded by Germans. Others headed for the interior to farm and helped build Ritzville, Odessa, Colton, and Uniontown. Dutch families, many of them dairy farmers, moved to Lynden and Oak Harbor. Immigrants often wrote home extolling the glories and advantages of their communities and this attracted relatives and friends.

Many town founders in Washington had trav-

An early view of Nordstrom's Shoe Store

eled west by wagon train from the Ohio River Valley, New York State, and New England. The communities they started often resembled the small, bustling towns they had known in the East. Newcomers who followed the founders had similar backgrounds, interests, and dreams.

The influence of other races has broadened since the early settlements, but whites dominate business, politics, and society. Almost 82 percent of the population is classified as white, including Spanish-speaking persons.

Political offices in Washington have traditionally been held by whites. For a long time, Scandinavian and Anglo-Saxon names seemed to be the key to political success in Washington. Office holders have had names such as Magnuson, Jackson, Gorton, Evans, Gardner, Foley, Adams, and Murray. Leading business executives have names of Wilson, Pigott, Weyerhaeuser, Nordstrom, Carlson, and Gates. White Anglo-Saxon Protestants (WASPs) predominated when settlement began, and the trend continues more than a century later.

## Native Americans

When white settlers began to arrive in the present state of Washington, an estimated 80,000 Indians, or Native Americans, lived in the area. Most lived west of the Cascades.

The treaties negotiated by territorial governor Isaac I. Stevens tried to place all Indians on reservations. After a decade of wars, the government finally succeeded. Most reservations were much smaller than the territory the tribes had originally inhabited. Often reservation land was poor because white settlers wanted the good farmland for themselves, but some included fishing grounds, timber, or farming areas. Under federal government agencies, reservation Indians were expected to prepare to enter a white culture. They had little opportunity to handle their own affairs.

Many children were taken from their families and sent to boarding schools. Others left reservations to take jobs and make homes among the general population. They often shed aspects of their Indian heritage to seek social acceptance. Thus many Washington Indians either became part of the mainstream or remained forgotten and ignored on reservation lands.

The civil rights movement of the 1960s encouraged a new generation of Native Americans to take pride in their culture and demand rights. Thus young adults, including women, often became tribal leaders. Some tribes sought lawyers' help in reinterpreting their treaties. This effort finally resulted in the lawsuit in which federal judge George Boldt upheld treaty fishing rights.

Indians quarreled with state officials over the use of their lands. Tribes such as the Puyallup, Colville, Quinault, and Makah began to exert control over their reservations. Frequently whites who lived or ran businesses on reservations had to give up leases or limit their activities. Tribal laws and courts began to replace state laws and courts on reservations.

Although tribes sought and accepted federal funds, they increasingly used such money to become economically self-sufficient. The Lummis, for instance, experimented with aquaculture techniques to raise and harvest salmon and shellfish in well-equipped facilities. The Quinaults expanded logging and milling operations north of Grays Harbor. Several tribes made money selling untaxed liquor, cigarettes, and fireworks in reservation stores. A number operate casinos or tourist facilities. An overall reawakening to Indian culture and Indian rights and capabilities became evident.

Many Native Americans sought to rekindle interest in their traditional cultures. They built modern tribal centers. Older people began to teach young children skills that had long been ignored. Members of the Makah tribe encouraged and participated in the study of the buried Indian village near Lake Ozette. A large museum with archaeological laboratories was built on tribal land at Neah Bay to preserve and display findings from the dig. Tribal elders worked to restore nearly forgotten languages that the government had tried to suppress. In 1992, for instance, only three Quileutes still remembered their ancient and complex language. Assisted by anthropologists, they taught language classes to children, made tape recordings and videotapes, and helped publish a dictionary to preserve their language. Throughout the state, Native Americans took steps to protect places of spiritual importance and ancient burial sites.

In Seattle, Indians secured part of an unused government fort to establish Daybreak Star Center for urban Indians. The Puyallup secured a former hospital building located on tribal land in Tacoma.

The Yakama Nation Cultural Center in Toppenish houses a museum, library, theater, and research center.

A museum in the Yakima Valley illustrates the lives of Indians of the Inland Empire and central Washington.

The number of Indians listed in the census has increased as counting procedures have improved and as more persons identify themselves as Indian. In 2000, 93,000 persons, about 1.6 percent of the total state population, were listed as Indian. Almost 22,000 live on the twenty-seven reservations. Most of these are located in western Washington, although the two largest—Yakama and Colville—are east of the Cascades. Several other Indian groups are not listed as tribes by the federal government and are seeking that recognition.

The Yakama Reservation with 6,307 people is the largest in population. In Okanogan County, where the Colville Reservation is located, 11 percent of the population is Indian. Many urban and suburban residents identify themselves as members of various tribes, not all of them from Washington.

Meanwhile, a new generation of Indian leaders emerged, such as Joe DeLaCruz of the Quinaults. These leaders combined a pride and understanding of the Indian heritage with practical skills useful in a society dominated by whites. Billy Frank Jr., a longtime fishing activist and negotiator and a member of a prominent Nisqually family, was awarded the Albert Schweitzer Medal for humanitarian efforts in 1992.

Indians learned the advantage of uniting to gain benefits, to promote their cultural identity, and to educate whites about their cultures and present needs. To assist in this, they established an organization called the United Indians of All Tribes, led by Bernie Whitebear of the Colville tribe. Several tribes publish newspapers. Basic problems that still plague Northwest Indians include heavy unemployment, weak resistance to certain diseases, and a shorter life expectancy than whites.

Northwest Indians have permanently influenced the culture of Washington State. This is evident in art, legend, and architecture, in foods and food preparation, in place names across the state, and in local celebrations and traditions. Many Indian artists produce works treasured by the entire population. One of Washington's most honored writers and filmmakers is Sherman Alexie of the Spokane tribe. He depicts life on the reservation and in towns with an honest, grim, but touching humor.

Horace Cayton Sr., publisher of the *Republican*

## African Americans

African American people are the largest racial minority in most states. This is not true in Washington where there are more Asians. In 2000, 190,267 blacks made up about 3.2 percent of the population. Almost half live in King County, and more than three-fourths live in the two largest counties. About 8 percent of the people of Seattle are African American. Many large towns have few black residents; three counties, all of them rural, have fewer than fifteen.

The first blacks who came to Washington arrived under circumstances different from those that met blacks who entered older states. They came, wrote one historian, not as slaves but carrying the ax of the pioneer, migrating west alongside white pioneers. Expecting equality in Oregon Territory, some were disappointed to learn that although the territory prohibited slavery, it was also anti-black. Laws forbade them to settle. Some, including George Bush and George Washington, crossed the Columbia River into present-day Washington, where they hoped the law would not be enforced.

The number of African Americans in Washington increased slowly, however. William Grose arrived in Seattle around 1859 to become a leading businessman and hotel keeper. He mingled on equal terms with prominent white pioneers such as Arthur Denny and Henry Yesler. From his large landholdings east of town, Grose sold parcels to others. Many were blacks and the future black area of the city began to take shape around his home at 23rd Avenue and Madison Street. But in the early days the few blacks were spread throughout the city.

Both Seattle and Tacoma had early newspapers published by African Americans. Publisher of the *Republican* in Seattle was Horace Cayton Sr., whose wife was the daughter of the first black U.S. senator. The Caytons were active in civic affairs and lived in a wealthy neighborhood. The *Republican* at first did not represent a particularly black point of view. Later, however, Cayton began to report on Southern lynchings and other attacks on blacks. White advertisers withdrew their support, the paper failed, and the family fell on hard times.

Tacoma newspaper editor John H. Ryan served in both the state House of Representatives and Senate during the 1920s and 1930s. He was not the first black legislator. W. O. Bush, son of George

Bush, had been elected to the first state legislature in 1889.

Most early black settlers headed for large cities, but some went to smaller cities and towns. During labor disputes, blacks sometimes were hired as strikebreakers who worked while regular employees were on strike. In the 1880s several hundred came to the coal mines at Roslyn. A few stayed on after the labor troubles ended and made permanent homes there.

Life often seemed good for Washington blacks during the early twentieth century, especially for those who achieved middle-class status. But as more blacks arrived, they became less welcome to the white majority. By the 1920s, Seattle restaurants, which had been integrated, were closed to blacks; movie theaters had segregated seating; and housing was segregated.

The most obvious changes occurred during World War II. War industries drew many workers from out of state, including large numbers of blacks from the South. To many of those who had settled earlier, the newcomers seemed to be a different type of people, with less education, less money, and few cultural and social refinements. Class distinctions developed within the expanding black community as well as between whites and blacks. In Seattle, the black neighborhood fanned south from the area where Grose had once divided up his land. African Americans found it increasingly difficult to obtain housing or financing for homes or businesses outside that area.

A black community in Tacoma grew up the hillside adjacent to downtown, and one in Spokane was south of the business district. Other industrial towns such as Bremerton and Vancouver received large influxes of blacks, as did agricultural areas around Yakima and Walla Walla.

Many blacks came to the Tri-Cities area when construction began on the atomic energy plant at Hanford. Social and economic pressure by whites kept blacks out of the established towns and

A stroll along Seattle's waterfront, about 1900

forced them to settle in East Pasco, just across the railroad tracks from downtown Pasco. Across the Columbia River from Vancouver, Vanport, Oregon, became an instant wartime city of 35,000, many of whom were black. The town and its low-cost homes were destroyed by a flood on Memorial Day weekend in 1948.

Thus the war brought new black neighborhoods and communities into the state. If living conditions were better than those most blacks had left behind, there were disappointments nevertheless. Some housing areas were not open to blacks; certain jobs were never available; salaries lagged; black women were especially discriminated against; and the end of the wartime economic boom closed the best jobs. Various subtle forms of discrimination occurred in neighborhoods, stores, schools, and social and political activities.

The civil rights movement of the 1960s exposed some of these problems. Blacks in Seattle, Tacoma, and Pasco vented feelings in demonstrations that, although less violent than those in other parts of the country, revealed bitterness and frustration. A new generation of African American leaders began to emerge from the churches and from among the young. On the University of Washington campus black students demonstrated against athletic programs, admissions policies, and the lack of academic programs centering on minority culture.

Several outstanding leaders emerged from these struggles. For decades the Reverend Samuel McKinney was the eloquent spokesman for many black Seattleites. Edwin Pratt moved to Seattle and worked to revitalize the Urban League, which worked to improve racial relations. The murder of Pratt on his doorstep on a January evening in 1969 was a reminder that threats of racial violence were real. His killers were never found.

The Central Area of Seattle sent Sam Smith to the state legislature in the 1960s, and later he served six terms as a powerful and popular member of the city council. During the 1990s, blacks held leadership positions in government: mayor, King County executive, fire chief, and school superintendent along with city council member and legislator. A decade earlier, James Chase had become the first black mayor of Spokane. After developing a widely respected self-help program among Pasco blacks, Arthur E. Fletcher held several state and federal offices including chairmanship of the federal Commission on Civil Rights. Under President Bill Clinton,

the Office of Management and the Budget was headed by Franklin D. Raines from Seattle, one of the most powerful blacks in the government. Jack Tanner of Tacoma served many years as a federal judge beginning in the late 1970s.

In 1980, the selection of Harold Reasby as superintendent of the Edmonds public schools signaled that a black leader could be accepted in a heavily white middle-class suburb. Similarly, the selection of Ivory V. Nelson to head Central Washington University marked the first time that an African American was appointed to the presidency of a major college.

Other Washington blacks became prominent in the professions and in arts, entertainment, and sports. James Washington's works established him as an important sculptor, and Jacob Lawrence was a nationally honored painter. University of Washington professor Charles Johnson won the National Book Award for *The Middle Passage*, a novel about life on a slave ship. The famous black author, Alex Haley, who wrote *Roots*, frequently stayed and wrote in Seattle and died there in 1992. Over the years, followers of the Seattle SuperSonics basketball team acquired a whole galaxy of black heroes, including coaches Bill Russell, Lenny Wilkens, and Nate McMillan and players Spencer Hayward, Fred Brown, Slick Watts, and Gary Payton. In 1980 Maury Wills was manager of the Seattle Mariners, the second black manager in major-league baseball. Harold Reynolds and Ken Griffey, Jr., have been celebrated Mariners, and former University of Washington star Warren Moon quarterbacked the Seattle Seahawks.

Singers Ernestine Anderson and Ray Charles, composer-arranger Quincy Jones, and rock guitarist Jimi Hendrix were Seattle blacks who became major personalities in the field of popular music. In 1980 when the Miss America pageant had its first two black finalists, one was a Tacoma music student.

## Hispanic Americans

Persons of Hispanic origin may be of several racial groups and thus not technically one racial minority. Yet culturally they are a distinct group and are counted separately in the U.S. Census. Numbering about 442,000 persons in Washington, they view themselves as an ethnic group and are often treated as a minority. Many live in agricultural areas. Yakima County has 79,905 Hispanic residents, over one-third of its population. These figures increased rapidly during the 1980s and 1990s.

Most Hispanic persons in Washington have Mexican backgrounds. But their various origins are reflected by different terms. Mexican or Mexicano refers to persons directly from Mexico. Chicanos are those with roots in the part of the southwestern United States that belonged to Mexico before the war between those two countries in the 1840s; Chicano implies some Indian blood. Mexican American is an older term similar to Chicano and emphasizes roots in Mexico. Latino is a broad term that recognizes a Latin American background. Hispanic tends to emphasize the Spanish background, but has become a convenient word to cover all groups. Census takers use the term "Hispanic origin" to describe all such persons. For our purposes, Chicano, Hispanic, and Mexican American will be used interchangeably.

The earliest Spanish and Mexican influence resulted from explorations along the coast and on inland waters. Spain briefly settled the first community in Washington, a village and fort at Neah Bay. The Spaniards also left a sprinkling of Spanish place names, especially in the San Juan Islands.

Later, Mexican Americans came to Washington as migrant field workers who did not intend to stay. A few entered Washington Territory as early as 1870 to work in mines. Twenty years later an irrigation developer in the Yakima Valley hired Mexican laborers, and farmers began hiring more for field work.

Washington fields became stops on an annual migration route of seasonal workers and pickers through the valleys of California, Oregon, and Washington. Washington continues to be the most northerly U.S. stop for a wave of migrant workers originating in Texas.

Workers came for several weeks each harvest season. They lived in tiny, cramped, often unsanitary sheds alongside the orchards and fields where they toiled. The job over, they would pack their few belongings and move to the next area of work. Pay was meager and the whole family worked, from young children to grandparents. Many circumstances forced the migrants to keep moving: only residents could obtain welfare, agricultural work was seasonal, and winters in eastern Washington were severe.

During the World War II labor shortage, the United States and Mexico created a bracero program that permitted up to 50,000 Mexicans to

Alfredo Arreguín's paintings are composed of intricate, colorful designs.

enter this country for as long as six months each year. After the war ended, the agreement continued, encouraged by farmers and land owners who paid Mexicans lower wages than local workers would accept. The pattern became fixed. Some towns in the Yakima and Wapato areas and western Washington farming communities such as Burlington came to develop a Mexican American character. Under pressure from the media and legislators, employers improved migrant camps and housing.

Some Hispanics headed for larger cities and the general work force. In 2001, 95,000 lived in King County, and 39,000 in Pierce County.

Meanwhile, more migrants began to settle permanently in the areas where their families had worked. Gradually they found regular jobs and bought homes. In the Yakima area particularly, Mexican Americans have succeeded in farming and business and several hold public offices. In larger cities, Hispanics have become well known as public school and university educators, as business and professional people, as artists, and as professional athletes. Among the more prominent are Tom Flores, onetime coach of the Seattle Seahawks, and Seattle Mariner Edgar Martinez. Alfredo Arreguín is an artist with an international reputation.

## Asian Americans

In most states, Asian Americans are a tiny fraction of the minority population. This is not the case in Washington. Asian Americans in Washington number 322,355, including Chinese, Japanese, Koreans, Asian Indians, Filipinos, Southeast Asians, and Pacific Islanders. They are a rapidly increasing ethnic group.

The Asian tradition in Washington is long and rich. Asian influences abound in architecture, religion, business, clothing styles, and cuisine. The Seattle Asian Art Museum has a major collection of Asian art that includes paintings,

Johsel Namkung poses before one of his nature photographs.

sculpture, and jewelry. Asian Americans have become leaders in politics and business. Governor Gary Locke, whose descendants arrived several generations ago, is the first Asian American to serve as governor of any state except Hawaii. Other prominent figures, past and present, include Seattle City Council members Wing Luke, Dolores Sibonga, Cheryl Chow, and Martha Choe, and King County Council member Ruby Chow.

Frank Matsura photographed scenes around Omak in the early 1900s, and Johsel Namkung is a well-known contemporary photographer. George Tsutakawa was a prominent sculptor, and Paul Horiuchi is a noted painter. Seattle-born Minoru Yamasaki, an architect with national achievements, designed the Pacific Science Center in Seattle. Actor Keye Luke, who for many years portrayed Asians, including detective Charlie Chan, in films, came from Seattle. Bruce Lee, whose kung fu movies made him an international subculture hero, also lived in Seattle. Local writers John Okada and Frank Chin have explored Asian American culture in their work. Already sports stars in Japan, Ichiro Suzuki and Kazuhiro Sasaki became instant local heroes and All-Stars when they joined the Seattle Mariners in 2001. Apolo Ohno of Federal Way was a gold medalist speed skater in the 2002 Olympic Games.

Yet to group all Asian nationalities as if they were the same is inaccurate. Each national group has distinct traditions and has made its own contributions to Pacific Northwest and American life.

## CHINESE

The earliest Asian immigrants to Washington were the Chinese. They labored in mines, logging camps, railroads, and fish canneries. Often they were contracted for by Chinese labor brokers who provided workers for American employers. When major railroad construction ended in the middle 1880s, many unemployed Chinese had no place to go. With few skills or opportunities in a strange land, they drifted about searching for whatever work or housing they could find.

Chinese workers scattered to farms and small communities. Often they were treated as outcasts and met various kinds of racial discrimination. The first serious outbreak of violence by whites and Indians against the Chinese occurred among hop pickers near Issaquah. Similar incidents followed.

Many Chinese drifted toward cities. Willing to take almost any kind of work, they became common laborers and domestics. Working for little pay, they were seen as a threat by other unskilled workers when jobs were scarce. Opposition to Chinese workers created a class consciousness among white laborers. Anti-Chinese attitudes influenced the Knights of Labor, the first important labor union in the region.

Chinese followed customs and practices that many whites considered alien. Whites ridiculed Chinese religion and dress and complained

that the people were dirty and users of opium. Fueled by fiery speeches, riots against the Chinese erupted in Tacoma and Seattle during the winter of 1885–86. The Chinese were driven out of both cities, and there were disturbances in many smaller localities.

Yet, conditions were not bleak everywhere. At turn-of-the-century Port Townsend, the Chinese were valued residents and treated as such. Many leading businessmen were Chinese, as were restaurant and laundry owners, gardeners and vegetable farmers, servants and governesses, and customs house interpreters. Some were highly educated and wealthy. Until economic setbacks caused both whites and Chinese to seek work elsewhere, Port Townsend was a desirable place for Chinese to live.

China was the first nation whose emigrants suffered from U.S. laws to slow or restrict immigration. Beginning in 1882, the Asian Exclusion Acts restricted Chinese and other Asians from entering the United States. Yet many came illegally. Chinese laborers were smuggled in from British Columbia.

Small groups of Chinese gradually returned to Tacoma and Seattle. By the 1920s distinct Chinese districts existed in both cities. Large family organizations, or tongs, regulated the communities; immigrants built churches and other community institutions. Family discipline was strong, expectations were often high, and many of the young began to excel. The Chinese community remained close-knit even while many of the younger generation moved into highly sophisticated fields of endeavor.

When a communist government took over the Chinese mainland in 1949, American ties with China ended. For almost thirty years the United States permitted no formal contact, trade, or travel with the People's Republic of China. The United States confined its relations to the Nationalist Chinese who had established their

A Chinese shop-keeper in Seattle displays his wares, 1909.

government on the island of Taiwan. During these years many persons from other Asian nations, as well as blacks, moved into the former Chinese district in Seattle. The Chinese, many of whom had prospered, moved toward the south end of the city or into suburbs. The original section retained Chinese businesses and interests but was no longer the home for many Chinese families.

During the 1970s, relations between the United States and the People's Republic of China improved. The two nations recognized each other diplomatically in 1979 and resumed trade and cultural exchanges. The Pacific Northwest had the closest mainland ports to China and began to benefit from the new connection.

Chinese officials and other visitors began to arrive. Local Chinese were allowed to visit relatives they had not seen in a generation, and many

tourists from Washington enjoyed visiting China. Northwest business and government delegations regularly visit China to seek business for Washington State. The country has become a leading purchaser of Boeing airplanes. Thus, the Northwest has developed many connections with China and enjoys business and social exchanges with its people.

## JAPANESE

Many Japanese Americans have settled on the western coast of the United States. The original immigrants call themselves Issei, while the first generation born in America are called Nisei, and their children are Sansei. Washington has slightly more Japanese than Chinese. They are also more dispersed throughout the state even though many live in the largest counties and cities.

Japanese experiences in Washington have been

affected by national and state policies. These include a "gentlemen's agreement" between the United States and Japan in 1907 which limited immigration; the Asian Exclusion Act; the 1921 Alien Land Law of Washington, which prohibited Japanese from owning land in the state; and the evacuation of Japanese Americans from coastal areas during World War II. Nevertheless, Washington's Japanese Americans have attained high levels of educational and professional success and significance.

The empire of Japan had no trade or regular contacts with most of the world until an expedition led by Commodore Matthew Perry "opened" the islands in 1853. Japan then moved rapidly into a growing position among world powers. Poverty and overcrowding in the islands caused many young men to emigrate, often to America. Some went to Hawaii, but others continued on to California, Oregon, and Washington. Many expected to return to their homeland one day.

Even while immigration laws tightened, the number of people of Japanese descent in Washington increased dramatically. Only 390 lived in the state in 1890; twenty years later there were 13,000. Immigration laws allowed Japanese— but not Chinese—women to come. "Picture brides" began to arrive, known to their already-immigrated husbands-to-be only through photographs and letters.

Japanese immigrants took the same kinds of jobs most immigrants found: in lumber camps, in canneries, in fields, and doing domestic work. Many went to farming areas in rural King and Pierce Counties, in the Yakima Valley, and in other parts of eastern Washington. Small Japanese truck farms, often on leased land, became common in valleys near Puget Sound where fruits and vegetables were raised for city markets.

In the 1920s, immigration laws stopped Japanese from moving into the United States, and

state laws prohibited those already here from becoming citizens or buying land.

Because they could not get land, many people of Japanese descent were forced into cities. Distinct Japanese communities formed in Seattle and Tacoma. In Seattle, 7,000 Japanese lived in Nihonmachi ("Japan Town"), just east of the railroad depot. It became the second largest Japanese community on the Pacific Coast. Here, Japanese American families built shops, theaters, restaurants, clubs, and Buddhist temples. A meeting hall, the Nippon Kan Theater, drew programs and speakers from Japan and the United States and provided a stage for community events. Japanese schools, held after regular school, passed the culture on to the young.

Some Japanese Americans from Washington returned to their homeland. But despite the upward mobility of those who succeeded in the United States, even the successful ones found themselves treated as a segregated group.

The Seattle Japanese community suffered a major loss in the late 1930s. A large portion of Nihonmachi was torn down to make way for the Yesler Housing Project, a planned development of low-cost housing.

By 1941, as Japan and the United States were heading toward war, almost 15,000 Japanese Americans lived in Washington. Then, on December 7, Japanese planes attacked Pearl Harbor, Hawaii. Federal agents quickly arrested a hundred or more Japanese suspected of aiding their mother country. The next spring the army, under a presidential order, removed all those of Japanese descent, including many American citizens, from the West Coast. Their communities, homes, businesses, and farms were deserted or taken over by neighbors. The removal affected only those living west of the Cascades, and for a while families were allowed to move voluntarily. Some relocated in eastern Washington, and Spo-

Many Japanese women immigrated to Seattle in the early 1900s as "picture brides," known to their future husbands only through photographs.

kane received its first sizable influx of Japanese Americans. Other families were taken to the Puyallup fairgrounds (renamed Camp Harmony) and then shipped to detention camps outside the region.

After the war ended in 1945 and relocation orders were lifted, some Japanese Americans returned to their former localities. Receptions were sometimes unfriendly. The overall Japanese American population dropped between 1940 and 1950. Meanwhile, the military occupation of Japan after the war resulted in marriages between many American servicemen and Japanese women. A new wave of war brides arrived to make homes in Washington.

As more Japanese Americans returned, many settled in urban areas. In Seattle, many moved south into the Rainier Valley or east toward Lake Washington. In Tacoma, a small core remained near the business district, but many dispersed throughout the city and its suburbs. Second- and third-generation Japanese generally did well academically and in business and the professions.

Chided because his generation rarely joined other minorities in civil rights protests during the 1960s and 1970s, one Seattle-born Nisei pointed out that their professional success and acceptance was a quiet form of protest. Japanese Americans have become leaders in the professions, have obtained distinction on university and college faculties, and have gained recognition as artists and writers.

In 1966 voters repealed the Alien Land Law, easing the long restriction on the right to own property. By the 1970s, the Japanese experience was changing once more as increasing investments from Japan went into lands and businesses. Not surprisingly, economic downturns in Asia during the late 1990s affected the Washington economy as well.

Japan has long been the country with which Washington ports have the most trade. One example of business ties occurred when Japan's Nintendo Company set up American headquarters in Redmond and its owner purchased a majority share of the Seattle Mariners. Colleges in both countries have sister schools in the other. As early as 1958, such social and economic ties were highlighted when two similar port cities—Kobe, Japan, and Seattle—became "sister cities." Thirty-two Washington cities and ports including Spokane, Tacoma, Bellingham, Moses Lake, and Camas have Japanese sister cities.

## FILIPINOS

Filipinos did not enter the United States as foreigners but from the Philippine Islands, an American territory between 1898 and 1946. Thus, immigration laws did not affect them at first. While Chinese and Japanese immigration declined, Filipino immigration increased. But their status as American nationals did not spare them from having to accept menial jobs in cities, as farm hands, or in canneries.

During the Great Depression, American labor leaders grew antagonistic toward Filipino workers who accepted low wages and undercut union organizing efforts. Outbursts occurred against Filipinos in several Northwest towns. In the Yakima Valley, mobs threatened them, forced some out of towns, and turned to arson and dynamite bombings. In 1934 Congress promised the Philippines independence at a future date, but it also assigned Filipinos immigrant status like other nationalities. This drastically reduced Filipino immigration until after World War II when many American servicemen brought Filipina brides home with them.

The 65,000 Filipinos make up one of the largest Asian groups in the state, and most live in the three largest counties. Sixty percent of them live in King County. Other concentrations of Filipinos are in Bremerton and in the Yakima Valley where many own farms. Filipinos in Wapato, in particular, keep alive the cultural traditions and holidays of their homeland.

In recent years, close to a thousand Filipinos have entered the United States annually through the Port of Seattle. Some moved elsewhere but many remained in the area. Although many of the newcomers are well educated and were professional people at home, they have experienced difficulty obtaining professional certificates and jobs.

Some Filipinos have become labor leaders (they organized the Cannery Workers Union) and some are prominent in the arts. A celebrated Filipino short-story writer and poet, Carlos Bulosan, lived for a time in Seattle. Two high-ranking political officials of Filipino descent have been Dolores Sibonga and Velma Veloria. Sibonga served a dozen years on the Seattle City Council, and in 1992 Veloria became the first Asian American woman elected to the state legislature.

State Representative Velma Veloria of Seattle addresses the legislature.

Often Filipinos have found that white Americans confuse them with immigrants from the Asian mainland or Latin American countries. They feel they are not always recognized as a distinct nationality.

## THE AFTERMATH OF ASIAN WARS

The end of World War II in 1945 did not bring peace in Asia. In the early 1950s, the small, divided nation of Korea was torn by war. American troops went in. As in previous times, war brides came to the United States—this time from Korea.

In the years that followed, South Korea developed a strong economy, but people lived in crowded conditions, often under harsh dictators. Thousands of Koreans emigrated to the United States. The number of Korean Americans in this country more than quadrupled during the 1970s, for instance. Many were students and professional people in Korea who often had to accept jobs as manual laborers when they arrived.

About 47,000 Koreans now live in Washington, mostly in the larger cities, although distinct Korean neighborhoods are rare. Many operate small businesses or are engaged in the profes-

sions. Often they were Christians before coming to America, and their activities center around Protestant churches. In 1992, Paull Shin, a community college professor, was elected to the state House of Representatives, quite likely the first Korean American in the legislature of any state. He became a state senator in 1999.

The Vietnam War wracked Southeast Asia during the 1960s and early 1970s. The war and its aftermath prompted large numbers of people to flee their ravaged homelands. Often the ones able to escape were the wealthier and better educated. Many were "boat people" who made a desperate flight in small vessels and rafts hoping to be picked up. Families were often separated.

In 2000, 46,000 Vietnamese lived in Washington, the majority in King County. Many Vietnamese, Cambodian, Hmong, and Laotian immigrants were sponsored by churches and service organizations. They helped the newcomers locate homes, learn the English language, secure job training and employment, and assimilate into the society.

Some refugees found employment in skilled or semi-skilled professional positions, but their arrival at a time when unemployment was high and government aid was being cut created additional problems. Meanwhile, aspects of their own culture, especially their cuisine, have added a new Asian dimension to life in the Pacific Northwest.

## Multi-Ethnic Persons

Increasingly, traditional racial, national, and ethnic definitions do not describe everyone. Many people are a blend of several backgrounds. For instance, a person whose father is Caucasian and mother is Chinese shares the rich heritage of two cultures, often mixing appearance, language, religion, and customs. Because parents may also have mixed heritages, a person can easily be a combination of black, Hispanic, Indian, and Caucasian. A famous example, although not from Washing-

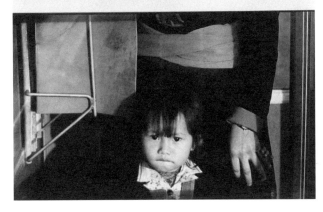

A recently arrived Hmong uses a public telephone for the first time.

ton State, is the golfer Tiger Woods. His heritage includes African American, Thai, Chinese, Native American, and Caucasian. He is thus racially and culturally a mixture of them all. Multi-ethnic persons may or may not wish to identify themselves with any one group. The 2000 census allowed people to indicate if they were members of more than one racial/ethnic group; 214,000 did so. It will be interesting to see how these multicultural combinations affect the life and culture of the state and how Americans come to think of different ethnic groups.

## Women

Native American women traditionally played particularly important roles in their tribes. A new husband often moved in with the family of his wife. Indian women gathered roots, berries, and other foods, and kept the home. Some were honored as shamans, basket and blanket weavers, and as persons who passed along legends, dances, and songs.

But the Indian woman most identified with early Northwest history was from the northern Plains. Captured from her own people as a girl, Sacajawea was the wife of a French-Canadian trapper employed by Lewis and Clark. Early historians exaggerated the extent to which she actually guided that expedition, but her value was great. Her knowledge of nature and of clues to the best routes aided the leaders. When the expedition encountered her brother among a group of Shoshone, she gained allies and advice that saved the party from starvation as they crossed the Rocky Mountains. Sacajawea, carrying a baby on her back, has become a Pacific Northwest legend immortalized in place names, statues, and stories.

Although women are not a minority group in Washington, they have often been treated as if they were. About 25,000 more women than men live in the state. This majority has not always existed. In the earliest days of settlement there were far more men than women. The arrival of the first white women in frontier areas has been glamorized in books and films, and some actual events are as interesting as fiction.

In the 1860s Asa Mercer brought about one hundred women to Seattle by boat in two trips around Cape Horn. He did so to provide wives for the many lonesome males in the region and to help create some permanence in the new city. All but one did marry local men. Mercer himself married one of them. For many years thereafter these "Mercer girls" had a special status among Seattle women.

Missionary women gave aid, comfort, and education to local Indians and traveling whites. Narcissa Whitman is the best known early missionary woman. She and Eliza Spalding were the first white women to come overland to Washington, and her murder at the mission near Walla Walla was a frontier tragedy.

One of the most impressive pioneer women was a Catholic nun of the order of the Sisters of Providence. Arriving with four other nuns at Fort Vancouver in December 1856, Mother Joseph established there the first hospital—a four-bed building—and one of the first schools in the Pacific Northwest. An attic was converted into their first convent.

In her concern for people in need, Mother Joseph proved to be hard working and demanding. She possessed many skills and talents necessary to develop a frontier. From Vancouver her work extended to other parts of the Pacific Northwest. She drew up plans, did architectural drawings and carpentry, and supervised building projects for a variety of institutions. Searching for support and funds, she visited mining camps and isolated villages, traveling on horseback and in canoes. Her knowledge, persuasiveness, and toughness gave force to her causes.

She began the Providence Academy in Vancouver and is recognized as the first architect of the Northwest. By the time she died in 1902 at the age of seventy-eight, she had established eleven hospitals, seven academies, five Indian schools, and two orphanages in the Northwest. Almost eight decades after her death, a bronze statue of Mother Joseph was placed in the Capitol Building in Washington, D.C., honoring her as one of two representatives of Washington State. Dr. Marcus Whitman is the other.

Just getting to the Pacific Northwest was a test of strength for pioneer women. Many left behind

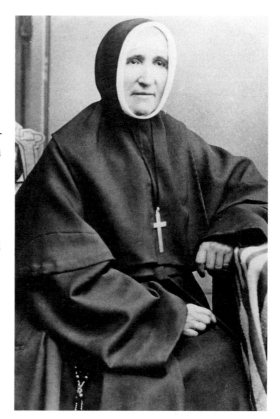

Mother Joseph of the Sisters of Providence

security and comforts to come to an unknown region. They had little awareness of or preparation for what lay ahead. Many shared their husbands' desire to find adventure and opportunity in the opening West.

Pioneer women drove wagons, taught school, prepared meals out of whatever food was available, cared for the sick and dying, and met other crises that came up along the trail west. Many hunted and fished, prepared wagons, and helped to construct new homes. They cleared land, planted, and harvested once they reached their destination.

Women who bore children along the route and immediately picked up to continue the journey are Oregon Trail legends with some basis in fact. Once families became settled, women were occupied with such traditional roles as housekeeping, child rearing, and farming. Some experienced intense loneliness and suffering, feeling out of place and unappreciated in a land that seemed to favor the men.

But many women also threw their energy into new opportunities. The presence of women in a new community signaled stability and permanence as they started homes, planted gardens, and added niceties. They often took the lead in establishing schools, churches, libraries, music and art groups, and service clubs, and in meeting various community needs. Women frequently ran boarding houses in towns that had many single males and little housing. Some began to enter the professions of teaching, nursing, law, and medicine.

### May Arkwright Hutton

May Arkwright Hutton was one of the great personalities of the Pacific Northwest, a character whose activities touched many facets of the role women play in newly settled lands. Born in 1860, she spent her childhood in an Ohio coal-mining town. As a teenager, she cared for her blind grandfather.

In 1883, lured by rumors of exciting growth in the Far West, May Arkwright joined a group of Ohio miners heading west. On the train she met Jim Wardner, who bragged of the mining town he was building in the Coeur d'Alene area of Idaho. He gloried in his town and the riches sure to come. With women scarce, he needed a cook for the only restaurant in town—actually one corner of a saloon. Arkwright left the train in Idaho and became his cook.

The town of Wardner was rugged and turbulent. The new cook proved to be a sympathetic listener and warm friend to disgruntled miners. They complained of long hours, low wages, and unsafe working conditions in mines controlled by distant owners whose search for profit over-

May Arkwright Hutton

rode the needs of employees. Anyone belonging to the miners' union was fired. May eventually married Levi (Al) Hutton, an engineer on a train between Spokane and the Idaho mines.

Tension among the miners led to violence. One night a group of union members took over Al Hutton's train, filled it with dynamite, and blew up a company building, killing one man. Hutton was jailed but convinced authorities that he had been forced to go along. At that time, few convictions were possible in a community where most jurors sympathized with the defendants. From these experiences May Arkwright Hutton wrote a book about the Coeur d'Alene mining wars. She took the miners' side and harshly denounced mine operators.

The Huttons themselves bought a small share in a mine, the Hercules, and began searching for silver. When a rich strain of silver was found in 1901, they became wealthy. Within months, these two workers who had struggled all their lives became millionaires. They moved to Spokane, where they built a mansion that she furnished extravagantly. Al quietly ran his businesses in the background while May became a local whirlwind celebrity. Middle-aged, short, and weighing over two hundred pounds, she lavished money on expensive and flamboyant clothes.

Despite her wealth, May Hutton was snubbed by Spokane's society. Local women viewed her as crude, earthy, unrefined, and comical. Furthermore, her heart remained with the downtrodden and poor, the exploited and friendless. She poured money and energy into hospitals, a children's home, a home for unwed mothers, and a hall for organized labor. She worked for almost any cause that favored poor and working people. Her combination of wealth, energy, and dedication made her someone who could not be ignored.

## WOMAN SUFFRAGE

A growing concern was the fight over woman suffrage. In 1883 the territorial legislature had granted women the vote, and they participated in several elections. Women also sat on juries. Just four years later the territorial supreme court threw out the conviction of a Tacoma gambler accused of swindling a newcomer because women had served on the grand jury that indicted him.

Since jurors were chosen from lists of voters, this verdict effectively ended political participation by Washington women. When the state constitution was adopted in 1889, women were not allowed to vote or serve on juries.

By early 1910, an active campaign was underway for Washington women to regain their voting rights. Several other states were having similar campaigns. May Hutton, who had voted while an Idaho resident, threw her energies into the campaign in eastern Washington. Since women could not vote to give themselves the vote, she and her followers went beyond traditional women's groups to talk to labor unions and others who might be convinced to support women. They also put pressure on the legislature.

West of the Cascades, the campaign was led by two somewhat more sedate women, Emma Smith DeVoe and Dr. Cora Eaton. They concentrated on contacts with women's groups and legislators, wrote notes, and held teas. They considered Hutton and her followers embarrassingly coarse and aggressive. The factions often quarreled, but they cooperated when necessary to reach their common goal.

They finally succeeded. In 1910 an amendment to the state constitution ensured that women could vote, sit on juries, and hold public office. Washington was the fifth state to give women the vote, following Wyoming and other western states. When the federal constitution was amended in 1919 to allow woman suffrage nationally, Washington was the fifth state to ratify the amendment.

Nevertheless, women did not soon acquire major political importance, although many worked effectively in local communities. Most frequently they performed volunteer services that reflected the concerns women had traditionally held, such as schools, home, health, unwed mothers, and honest government.

## WOMEN IN POLITICS

Bertha Landes became the first woman to lead a major American city when she was elected mayor of Seattle in 1926. Landes was a homemaker and active club woman when several groups encouraged her to run for the city council. She was one of the first two women elected to that body. As council president, she occasionally served as acting mayor while the mayor was out of town. On one such occasion Landes authorized the investigation of a police scandal and fired the police chief who was permitting corruption. The mayor scurried home before she could take her reforms further, but Landes gained publicity and praise as an upright leader who would clean up a city wallowing in corruption.

After becoming mayor, she remained true to these efforts. She generally administered city affairs effectively and also encouraged the development of the City Light hydroelectric project on the Skagit River. But efforts to economize forced the layoff of many city employees, and many voters blamed her. When Landes ran for reelection in 1928, she was defeated. She continued to serve on city boards, committees, and in clubs for several years. She died in Michigan in 1943.

A number of other Washington women have held political offices beginning with Lizzie Ordway, a "Mercer girl" who was Kitsap County school superintendent from 1881 to 1889. Josephine Preston and Pearl Wanamaker each served as state superintendent of public instruction, and

Women actively campaigned for the right to vote.

Belle Reeves was a newspaper publisher who was twice secretary of state. The first mayor of Richland was Patricia Morrell.

During the 1960s, two of Washington's seven representatives in Congress were women. Julia Butler Hansen of Cathlamet spent fourteen years in Congress (1960–1975), and Catherine May of Yakima served twelve (1959–1971). From 1977 to 1981, Dixy Lee Ray, a former University of Washington professor and chairperson of the Atomic Energy Commission, was governor.

In 1980 Barbara J. Rothstein was appointed a federal judge in western Washington. The next year Carolyn Dimmick became the first woman justice on the state supreme court; in 1984 she became a federal judge. A decade later Barbara Durham became the first woman chief justice of the state supreme court.

In recent decades, women have been increasingly active in government. They have been judges at all levels of the court system and have served prominently as state legislators, county officials, city council members, and mayors. By the late 1990s, almost half the members of the state legislature were women, more than in any other state. Many held positions of leadership. For several years, six of Seattle's nine city council members were women. Both Spokane and Tacoma had women mayors, as did many smaller cities.

The election year of 1992 was dubbed "The Year of the Woman." In Washington as in several other states, women candidates and workers seemed more active than ever before. Twelve Washington women were nominated by the two major parties for state or national offices, led by Patty Murray of Shoreline, who was elected to the U.S. Senate. Three of Washington's nine representatives in Congress were women. Often both major party candidates for state offices may be women, as in 1998 when Congresswoman Linda Smith unsuccessfully challenged Senator Murray

in her bid for reelection. Two years later, Maria Cantwell of Edmonds was elected to the Senate. Cantwell was a former member of the House of Representatives who had become wealthy in the software business. With her election, Washington became one of three states to have both its Senate seats held by women.

Women can also claim achievements in business. Dorothy Bullitt founded and ran the KING Broadcasting Company, a regional communications company with headquarters in Seattle. Women head school districts and several of the state's colleges and universities. Many women have achieved prominence in the arts, entertainment, writing and journalism, and sports. The Seattle Reign and the Seattle Storm have played professional women's basketball.

The state's attitude toward the role of women was demonstrated by support for the Equal Rights Amendment, the proposed 27th Amendment to the United States Constitution. It was approved by the legislature in March 1973 with little opposition. State voters had already added a similar equal rights amendment to the state constitution. This committed the state to equal rights between the sexes even though the federal amendment failed to be ratified before the required deadline. Meanwhile Washington was the first state to ensure that women receive fair and equal treatment when applying for credit and insurance.

## Education

Early in Washington's history, the Hudson's Bay Company and then missionaries started schools for both white and Indian children. Early schools were usually small and they varied greatly in quality and offerings. Although they often had encouragement from local communities, many lasted only briefly.

In the early 1880s, a territorial law required the larger towns to provide children with at least

University of Washington students on the steps of the territorial university building

three months of school a year. Some persons and businesses, however, opposed this because they thought it was more important for children to work. A few wealthy parents sent their children to private, often church-sponsored, academies.

In 1895, state representative John R. Rogers, later to become governor, pushed the Barefoot Schoolboy Law through the legislature. This required that each year the state would provide six dollars toward the education of each child in the state. It firmly established that Washington would have free public schools for all children and a continuing statewide school system.

In the years since, the school system has grown and now serves about a million students. Each district in the state, ranging from the smallest rural one to the huge Seattle School District, provides education in its community for children between kindergarten and grade twelve. Some parts of the curriculum are required by state law but much is optional or is influenced by college admission requirements. Teacher preparation has become standard and school finances rely heavily on statewide funding. Special programs seek to meet the needs of vocational students, the handicapped, the gifted, and others. Each year the state's high schools graduate about 70,000 young men and women.

Washington has several private schools, most of which are or were originally affiliated with religious denominations. The Lakeside and Bush Schools in Seattle, the Annie Wright and Charles Wright Schools in Tacoma, and Gonzaga Preparatory School in Spokane are well-established private schools. A number of private schools for elementary and secondary children have been established in recent years. About 7 percent of all students attended private schools in the late 1990s.

Higher education was encouraged by the first territorial legislature, which secured federal lands for a university. A single white-columned building was erected by the townspeople on a ten-acre hillside tract overlooking Seattle. With a limited staff and small student body (mostly grade-schoolers), the pretentiously named University of Washington struggled through its early years. But before the new century the university had outgrown its original location and moved to its present site.

The grounds of the 1909 Alaska-Yukon-Pacific Exposition left a nicely designed campus for the university. The university grew and changed significantly as it rounded out its first century with many departments and colleges, including a medical school. It has become one of the largest state universities in the United States with approximately 35,000 students enrolled each year. There are branch campuses in Tacoma and Bothell.

Statehood meant that federal money would be available for an agricultural college. This school was to be located somewhere in eastern Washington, the choice soon narrowing to Yakima, which railroad interests favored, and Pullman. Residents of this tiny farm town in the Palouse Hills used the effort to secure the college as a way to publicize their town. They offered 160

acres for the campus. To their surprise, the Pullman offer was accepted.

The first structure at Washington State University was a red brick building on a lonely wind-swept hillside. Opened in 1891, it remained primarily an agricultural college for many years. Research, experimentation, and instruction served the farming needs of the region. Over the years Washington State University has expanded its programs in many directions and has branches in Spokane, Richland, and Vancouver. With approximately 20,000 students, it is the second largest state-supported university in Washington.

Public four-year colleges also include Western Washington University at Bellingham, Central Washington University at Ellensburg, Eastern Washington University at Cheney, and The Evergreen State College at Olympia. The first three opened as "normal schools," or teachers' academies, soon after statehood. Their programs now include many areas besides the preparation of teachers. They offer several graduate degrees.

The Evergreen State College opened in 1971 as an experimental school with flexible programs to serve a diverse student body. It has achieved a national reputation.

In addition, thirty-four community and technical colleges in towns across the state enroll a quarter of a million students. The oldest still operating is Centralia College, which opened in 1925. Mostly two-year institutions, these schools meet the needs of varied types of students. Some are seeking personal or vocational skills, some are preparing for transfer to four-year degree programs, and others seek to benefit from the enriched education and cultural offerings that such colleges can offer a community.

Although some of the colleges have specialized programs, their major purpose is to serve the people in the community. They offer Associate Arts degrees. They make courses available on the Internet and have other programs for persons distant from the campus. They also offer adult basic education programs and courses in English as a second language.

The oldest private college in the state is Whitman College in Walla Walla, chartered in 1859 by associates of the recently murdered Marcus and Narcissa Whitman. Originally a seminary, it has become a well-regarded liberal arts college. Seattle University in Seattle and Gonzaga University in Spokane are institutions of the Jesuit Order of the Roman Catholic Church, while Saint Martin's College at Lacey is of the Benedictine Order. Schools that specialize in religious training include Northwest College (Kirkland), the Lutheran Bible Institute of Seattle (Issaquah), and the Puget Sound Christian College (Mountlake Terrace).

Cornish College of the Arts in Seattle was established in 1915 to teach the arts and offers a four-year program. Heritage College in Toppenish especially provides educational opportunities for minority students. City College in Seattle provides college programs to working persons who cannot attend full-time. Other schools offer specialized or technical training, and branches of national colleges offer local programs.

Other well-established four-year colleges include Seattle Pacific University, the University of Puget Sound (Tacoma), Pacific Lutheran University (Parkland), Whitworth College (Spokane), and Walla Walla College (College Place).

## Religion

Although missionaries helped to pioneer the Pacific Northwest, Washingtonians have generally appeared to be less involved in churches than people in older parts of the nation. The people of Washington are relatively "unchurched." Only a third to half are members of religious bodies or regularly attend services at churches or synagogues. This is one of the lowest percentages of any state. Among those who do belong to religious bodies, there is a great diversity of religions. Rural eastern Washington has the highest percentage of churchgoers, King County the lowest. Enjoying natural surroundings and recreational opportunities, such as skiing, fishing, boating, and golfing, has become as much an established weekend activity as church-going. A large part of the population is not religious at all. Nevertheless, nine of every ten persons questioned in a survey several years ago expressed a belief in God.

No one church dominates. Since the early days of white settlement, Washington has had a wide variety of religious groups. The beliefs of Native Americans tended to center around nature and great spirits. Roman Catholic missionaries founded early churches throughout the region. Then migration from eastern and midwestern states brought many Protestant believers. These groups set the pattern of religious practices.

Methodists founded the first permanent church at Olympia in 1851, followed by establishments at Steilacoom, Seattle, and Walla Walla. More than any other individual, the Reverend John DeVore was the great church builder in early Washington. This pioneering minister traveled widely to spread the Methodist influence and to start churches. He worked alongside congregation members as they constructed buildings.

Within a few years, Presbyterians led by the Reverend George Whitworth were starting churches in eastern and western Washington. As Scandinavian groups settled around Puget Sound, Swedish, Norwegian, and Danish people set up branches of Lutheran churches. Congregationalists, Baptists, and Episcopalians established churches in many communities. These various Protestant denominations retain their influence throughout much of the state.

Today about one of every ten persons is Roman

Catholic, making this the single largest denomination. Catholics are active in most communities, especially in urban areas. They have built private schools and colleges. In the late 1800s a small Jewish congregation was started in Seattle and in the new century more Jews came to the Northwest from various European communities. The tiny settlements of Home in Pierce County and Republic in northeastern Washington attracted many Jews.

The Church of Jesus Christ of Latter Day Saints, or Mormons, spread out of Utah in its early days into nearby parts of Oregon and Idaho but had never quite penetrated Washington. Many Mormons have recently moved into the Pacific Northwest, and an extensive missionary program has attracted converts. Temples in Bellevue and in the Spokane Valley serve several hundred thousand Mormons throughout the state and northern Idaho.

Chinese and Japanese communities in Seattle, Tacoma, and other towns formed Buddhist churches. The arrival of persons from Asia plus a new interest in Asian religions have increased the number of these religious bodies. There are Muslim mosques in several cities.

In pioneering days, churches and church members often tried to bring reform to the violent and bawdy frontier. They hoped to be a force for good in the midst of what they saw as evil. To an extent, this feeling has continued. When local governments or politicians have grown corrupt, churches have become a rallying point for efforts to clean them up. This is demonstrated dramatically in the career of the most famous Washington minister, the Reverend Mark Matthews, pastor at the First Presbyterian Church of Seattle from 1902 until his death in 1940.

Matthews was the dominant and most socially involved churchman in the Northwest in the early 1900s. He served on various boards and committees locally and nationally. His strong,

DR. M. A. MATTHEWS (44)
Dr. Matthews is pastor of the First Presbyterian church. His church is always filled to the doors, because he has a reputation of saying what he thinks, and thinking some things which are decidedly novel.

Cartoon of the Rev. Mark Matthews in a characteristic pose

fiery sermons, his great moral sense, and his heavily publicized criticisms gave him a powerful voice. Matthews campaigned against vice and corruption, against alcohol, against woman suffrage, against all activities he considered degrading for the people or the community. And he was certain that others should believe in his causes as strongly as he did. Outraged at the corrupt administration of Mayor Hiram Gill and his police chief, Matthews led a successful campaign to recall Gill in 1910. He strongly supported Prohibition in the 1920s.

Matthews was not typical of the ministers, priests, and rabbis of the Northwest, although a few others did enter the political scene. Some ministers championed the cause of minority groups and civil rights during the 1960s, and many opposed the Vietnam War.

In the 1980s, organized church groups demonstrated against the Trident submarine missile system, nuclear weapons, and abortions. Seattle's Roman Catholic Archbishop Raymond Hunthausen withheld a portion of his income tax to protest military spending. Church buildings and members provided sanctuary and help to refugees fleeing Central American dictatorships as well as to local homeless persons. A notable change in old attitudes was displayed in 1987 when the Seattle Council of Churches wrote a letter professing respect for Native American spiritual practices past and present. The Council apologized for past attitudes and actions taken against native religions.

Over the years, individual church leaders have taken stands on such social issues as housing, education, human relations, and welfare. Fundamentalist congregations attracted new members during the 1980s and 1990s, focusing their attention on abortion, education, and family values. Their congregations also had considerable political influence through several candidates and officeholders. The typical church leader in Washington mixes social concerns with meeting the varying demands of his or her local church body and parishioners.

## Recreation and Sports

Outdoor recreation is part of life in a region that abounds in lakes, mountains, rivers, beaches, and other natural attractions in a mild climate. Native Americans enjoyed games and boat and horse races. To the first whites who arrived, hunting, fishing, hiking mountain or wilderness trails, and boating were necessary for existence. But at some point in the development of settlements, people have enough leisure time to engage in such activities for pleasure. This search has become an important part of life for most Washingtonians.

### The Mountains

An early attraction was the mountains. Most spectacular is the highest mountain, Rainier, once called Takhoma or Tacoma. From Fort Nisqually in 1833, Dr. William Tolmie of the Hudson's Bay Company was attracted to the peak that towered above nearby foothills. Indian guides led him up the Carbon River and its tributary streams until he reached the top of a high ridge. Closer to Rainier than any European had yet come, he looked with awe but turned back. His was the first known approach to the mountain.

Many years later, Hazard Stevens and P. B. Van Trump made the first recorded ascent of the 14,410-foot mountain. An Indian guide took the party into the foothills but was held back by the ingrained fears and warnings based on the beliefs of his people. The other two men continued on alone, through the snow fields and glaciers on the southern face of Rainier, to reach the summit on August 17, 1870.

Other early ascents followed several routes, made dangerous by crevasses, avalanches, and sudden storms. In time good roads, visitor facilities, mountain climbing training, and guide services seemed to bring Rainier closer. Today a climb to the summit is commonplace for hardy mountaineers and a proud accomplishment of many others. About 10,000 climbers head for the summit each year, half of them completing the climb. Most often it is a two-day effort up the southern side of the mountain from Paradise Park, with an overnight stay at Camp Muir at the 10,000-foot level before the final early morning ascent. On the slopes of Rainier, Jim Whittaker trained for the first American ascent of Mount Everest in the Himalayas.

But tragedies have mingled with accomplishments. On August 27, 1981, eleven climbers were killed by an icefall on Ingraham Glacier. It was the worst climbing accident in United States history. A few days later, a party of disabled

A climber surveys the view from a peak in Mount Rainier National Park.

climbers reached the summit in a well-recorded display of courage and stamina.

Each of the other major Cascade peaks—Baker, Glacier Peak, Adams, and St. Helens—has an individual fascination and character. Many hikers take to mountain and forest trails each spring, summer, and fall. Some follow the Washington portion of the Pacific Crest Trail that stretches from the Canadian to the Mexican border.

The Olympics are not as high as the Cascades, but saw-toothed ridges and sharp valleys make them difficult and dangerous to climb. Not until 1890 when a Seattle newspaper sponsored a competition did climbing parties successfully cross this range. Now, modern roads and accommodations make the Cascades and Olympics accessible for hiking, camping, climbing, or leisurely touring.

In winter the mountains attract skiers and lovers of snow sports of all ages and skills. Northwest skiing began among Norwegians and other Northern Europeans who took to the mountains, often using homemade or improvised equipment. During the 1930s and after World War II, skiing became a major winter recreation.

Several Northwest skiers have gained national and international repute. Gretchen Fraser of Vancouver, who won the women's slalom in 1948, was one of the first women to win an Olympic gold medal. Phil and Steve Mahre, twins from White Pass, have won world championships and Olympic medals. In the 1984 Winter Olympics, Washington-trained skiers won half of the United States' medals.

### Ocean, Lakes, and Streams

At lower elevations, hunting and fishing are major activities in season. Deer, elk, and bear are found in high elevations with smaller game and birds in lower areas. The Okanogan Highlands and the Blue Mountains are favorite hunting areas. Fishing varies from stream and lake fishing to ocean salmon trolling. Deep-sea fishing is an important pastime and recreational industry, with many charter boats going into the Pacific Ocean from Westport, Neah Bay, Sekiu, Ilwaco, and other locations along or near the coast.

Seattle has a proud reputation as the small-boat capital of the nation. Boats range from small dinghies, canoes, and sailboats to large, comfortably furnished yachts. Launching areas and moorage basins dot Puget Sound and the larger lakes. Sailboat races take place throughout much of the year. Each May the Seattle boating season officially opens when a parade of colorfully decorated boats passes through the Lake Washington Ship Canal. Protected from severe storms and full of coves and inlets, Puget Sound is an ideal boating area.

East of the mountains, boaters, water skiers, and wind surfers can choose between rivers and artificial lakes like Lake Roosevelt or natural ones such as Lake Chelan and Moses Lake. The Columbia River near White Salmon has become a popular spot for wind surfing.

Annual events like the Port Townsend Wooden Boat Festival attract builders and connoisseurs of top-quality boats. For some, building the boat is part of the sport.

Enthusiasm for boating helped create an interest in hydroplane racing. During the 1950s, Seattle automobile dealer Stanley S. Sayres set world records and won the Gold Cup with his "Slo-Mo-Shun" boats. The beaches along Lake Washington provided a natural amphitheater for spectators to watch the big boats race. The Northwest quickly developed a fever for the sport, which drew tens of thousands of fans to the lakeside and to television screens. Since that time, Seattle, Wenatchee, and the Tri-Cities have hosted major hydroplane races. They draw the largest, fastest, and best-known boats into Northwest competition.

## Other Outdoor Sports

Swimming, tennis, golf, and running take advantage of the mild weather from spring through autumn. Spokane's Bloomsday Run is often the largest road race for runners in the country, attracting over 50,000 participants each May. Swimming champions have come from the state. In 1932 Helene Madison of Seattle became the state's first Olympic gold medalist; indeed, she won three gold medals in swimming events. Local swimmers and boaters are often among Olympic contenders and medalists. For instance, Puyallup high schooler Megan Quann won two gold medals in the 2000 Olympics.

Spectator sports are also popular. Early spectator sports centered on town, school, and college teams in softball, baseball, basketball, and football. Rivalries among teams became fierce. Victories and championship seasons occasioned great celebrations; stores and schools sometimes closed so that townspeople could attend tournaments and cheer on their teams.

High school athletics remain an essential part of the school program. Programs have extended beyond the older "major" sports to include track and field events, cross-country runs, golf, soccer, tennis, hockey, wrestling, volleyball, swimming, and skiing.

Colleges and universities also provide opportunities to display regional loyalty. Along with the small college conferences, University of Washington and Washington State University PAC-10 teams have attracted support from fans beyond student body and alumni groups. For many years Seattle University received national recognition in basketball.

At the University of Washington, crew racing set national and international standards. U.W. crews have competed internationally, including at several Olympic Games, and they won the gold medal in 1936.

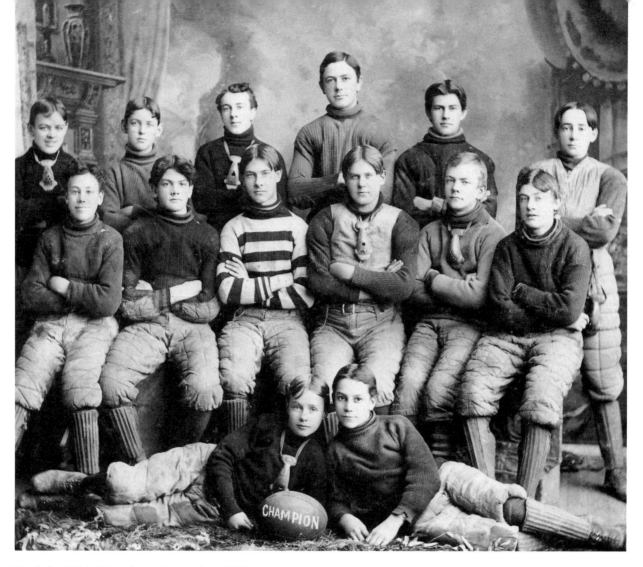

The Ballard High School football team about 1900

University of Washington football teams often rank nationally and win post-season Bowl games. After an undefeated 1991 season, the Huskies earned a national co-championship. A cross-state football rivalry between the University of Washington and Washington State University is renewed with the Apple Cup game every November.

Horse racing was the first sport in the state that might truly be called professional, with tracks in Spokane, Yakima, and Auburn and for fifty years in Renton. Betting is regulated by the state. Semi-professional and minor league sports teams developed in large and middle-size towns. Seattle, Tacoma, and Spokane had teams in the

Pacific Coast Baseball league in the mid-twentieth century and sent players on to the major leagues. Seattle also had a semiprofessional football team called the Ramblers for many years.

Seattle was the center of boxing attention on a balmy June evening in 1938 when Al Hostak of that city challenged Freddie Steele of Tacoma for the world middleweight championship. Hostak won the title with a first round knockout.

Not until the 1950s did major-league professional teams expand to the West Coast, coming to California. Seattle's first major-league team, the SuperSonics in basketball, began in 1967. Gate success, spectator enthusiasm, the expansion of the Seattle Center Coliseum and the

Seattle Mariner Ichiro Suzuki starts his run to first base after a hit.

building of the Kingdome, and local promoters and investors all helped Seattle acquire other major-league teams: the Pilots and the Mariners in baseball and the Seahawks in football. The Tacoma Stars played major-league indoor soccer. Women's basketball teams have included the Reign and the Storm.

For several seasons, Seattle had professional tennis, soccer, ice hockey, and volleyball teams. These have stimulated pride among sports fans well beyond Seattle itself and created a multitude of local sports heroes. The peak of success for professional Seattle teams occurred in 1979 when the SuperSonics won the National Basketball Association championship. The construction of the Tacoma Dome, the conversion of the Coliseum

into Key Arena, and the replacement of the King- dome with the Safeco baseball stadium and a football stadium seem to assure up-to-date venues for professional teams in the Puget Sound area.

## The Arts

In 1940 the famous British orchestra conductor Sir Thomas Beecham remarked that Seattle was thought of as an "aesthetic dust bin." Audiences and reviewers, he complained, lacked a real appreciation for the arts and provided few opportunities for artists. In an isolated corner of the nation, off the itinerary of many touring artists, the Northwest has sought to develop a cultural climate that Beecham might have admired.

The symphony he conducted has become increasingly professional. Under longtime conductors Milton Katims and Gerard Schwarz, the orchestra has brought outstanding guest artists, has toured Europe to critical acclaim, and has made recordings. The symphony has played in communities throughout the state and to schoolchildren. In 1998 the symphony moved to an elegant new concert hall downtown.

Seattle also has an opera company with a strong community relationship. Outstanding guest performers and imaginative staging convinced many Puget Sound residents that opera is an exciting, vital medium of expression. Productions of Richard Wagner's *Ring of the Nibelung* operas brought world attention and acclaim.

A strong jazz movement engulfed Seattle a generation ago. Rock and other pop musicians from Seattle have set national trends, with Jimi Hendrix foremost among them. During the 1990s, Seattle influenced popular music and life styles under the general label of "grunge." Such groups as Nirvana and Pearl Jam developed worldwide followings. Rock culture is celebrated in the Experience Music Project museum in Seattle.

Many communities have built auditoriums,

theater complexes, and cultural centers which enable them to stage concerts, ballets, and other performances. Seattle and Spokane hold concerts in halls built for the world's fairs of 1962 and 1974. Yakima and Tacoma are among cities that have renovated classic old theaters for the performing arts. It is not unusual for a community to have a local symphony, choral group, community theater, youth symphony, or dance group. Nor is it difficult to attract leading performers to towns with facilities and appreciative audiences.

Many towns have amateur or semi-professional theatrical groups. Northwest schools, such as the University of Washington School of Drama and Cornish College, teach music, the fine arts, and drama. Several prominent dancers and choreographers got their start in Washington, particularly Robert Joffrey and Mark Morris of Seattle, and Merce Cunningham, from Centralia.

Asian influences have been important in regional art. In the 1930s, a Seattle doctor and his mother contributed their collection of Asian art, which formed the basis of the Seattle Art Museum. Located for many years in a neighborhood park, the museum moved downtown in 1991 to a dramatic new building above the waterfront; its former home became the Seattle Asian Art Museum. One painter who taught at Cornish for a time and went on to international fame was Mark Tobey. Tobey developed a style of painting known as "white writing" that was influenced by Asian calligraphy. Starting in the late 1930s, he was associated with Morris Graves, Kenneth Callahan, Guy Anderson, and other painters in what national reviewers saw as a "Northwest school" of art. They used muted colors and nature themes associated with the region. A more recent painter of distinction was Jacob Lawrence, whose bold shapes and bright colors depict African American themes. An artist in a different medium who is renowned around the world is Tacoma-born glass artist Dale Chihuly. He has built a flourishing industry around his studios in Seattle.

## Literature

Before there was a written literature of the Northwest, Indian legends and history were passed along by storytellers. Their tales concerned the land, animals, and plants around them. Indians viewed themselves as caretakers of the earth, responsible for the nature that they and every other living thing were a part of. They often attributed human characteristics to animals. The Raven was clever, the Coyote was tricky, the Thunderbird was powerful. Indian stories explained why and how mountains, rivers, and lakes developed as they did. They told of the spirits that lived there. Passed by word of mouth through many generations, these legends form the basis of a Northwest literature that concerns humankind's relationship to the land and natural surroundings.

Workers developed their own stories. Best known are the tales about the giant woodsman Paul Bunyan. First told in forests of Maine and then of Minnesota, Paul Bunyan stories accompanied the American lumberjack across the continent. His strength and skills and his faithful Blue Ox Babe became part of Northwest lore. The tongue-in-cheek legends explain how the woodsman built mountains, scooped out Puget Sound, and cleared forests. Several Northwest writers wrote down the stories that loggers had long retold among themselves. James Stevens, a lumber industry publicist, viewed the Bunyan legends as an important part of that industry.

Stevens was one of several writers who adopted Northwest themes for novels and poetry. Their works were set in woods and logging camps, along the Sound and waterfront, and in the desert land east of the mountains.

Lumberman Paul Bunyan and his Blue Ox Babe became Pacific Northwest legends.

Many wrote primarily for regional readers, but Stevens, Stewart H. Holbrook, Robert Cantwell, and a few others had national reputations in the 1930s and 1940s.

One extremely popular book that shaped thinking about Washington was never thought of as important literature. *The Egg and I*, by Betty Mac-Donald, was a simple, humorous account of life on a backwoods chicken ranch near Port Town-send. It spawned other books and a movie series about the Kettle family. Similarly, earlier stories abut Tugboat Annie (based on Thea Foss of Tacoma) had a popular appeal. Other popular writers living in the Northwest write mysteries set in spots familiar to local readers.

A number of Washington authors have become nationally prominent. Ernest K. Gann of San Juan Island was a major adventure writer who concentrated on aviation and pilots. Frank Herbert of Port Townsend was a significant science fiction writer and futurist known for his *Dune* books. Tom Robbins of La Conner is a major novelist whose themes run to flights of fancy in a modern environment. Ivan Doig has won acclaim with autobiographical works and novels that capture the spirit of Northwest life. University of Washington professor Charles Johnson has written highly praised novels based on the black experience in America.

Mary McCarthy became a prominent writer of short stories and novels, some based upon her Seattle youth. Influential poets from the University of Washington faculty have included David Wagoner and Pulitzer Prize winner Theodore Roethke. Carolyn Kizer, originally from Spokane and later Seattle, won the 1985 Pulitzer Prize for poetry.

Some Pacific Northwest writers have made significant contributions in academic fields. The University of Washington has housed innovative thinkers. Early in the twentieth century, Professor J. Allen Smith wrote an economic interpretation of the U.S. Constitution that helped shape the thinking of Progressive Movement reformers. About the same time, English professor Vernon Louis Parrington made a three-volume study of American literature that influenced attitudes toward American intellectual development.

A recent assessment of Pacific Northwest writing indicates that more may be flourishing currently than at any past time. Some writing remains primarily for readers interested in and familiar with the Northwest, including that of excellent local historians and journalists. Yet, several Washington authors have reached beyond regional limits to national significance.

Original, creative thought is found along with writing and the arts. Scientists and theoreticians have clustered around the atomic energy plant at Hanford. The Battelle Memorial Institute has a "think tank" in Richland where people with varied interests and expertise join together to speculate about a variety of concerns. Colleges, businesses, and government have cooperated to form a technological research institute in Spokane. A cluster of hospitals on that city's South Hill is a center for medical research and treatment of patients. Medical centers such as the Hope Heart Institute and the Fred Hutchinson Cancer Research Center are affiliated with Seattle hospitals. These and other medical centers have made significant contributions to research.

## Architecture and Town Planning

Natural surroundings and the way people live affect the plans of buildings and towns. The first Northwest builders were, of course, the Indians. The cedar longhouses on coastal beaches and the pithouses and portable structures of inland Indians fit their needs and used materials close at hand.

The first white settlers built mainly out of necessity. Their primary purpose was to get something up in a hurry. Small cabins of logs or rough-hewn timbers were built in village clusters or forest clearings. Shakes, shingles, and cut lumber from early mills gave a more finished look to some houses. Having little training, fur traders, missionaries, and early settlers built simple structures with available materials.

The arrival of military forces and then railroads opened a new phase. Forts and depots usually followed standard designs used in older areas. In towns, these buildings—along with government buildings, schools, and business blocks—were often designed and located to convey dignity and importance. Some were massive. The Northern Pacific headquarters and Union Station in Tacoma, the Spokane County court-house, and other county courthouses are existing examples.

Business districts were laid out in simple grid patterns with streets going north and south,

east and west, and intersecting at ninety-degree angles. Many wealthy families built large and elaborate houses that displayed their prominence. They followed the patterns of grand homes in eastern states, with little local originality. The earliest tended to be interspersed among plainer homes, but in time many were grouped in the most desirable locations.

By the early 1900s, growth was rapid on both sides of the Cascades. Many cities endured fires that destroyed parts of the business district. This provided the opportunity to rebuild with better, stronger materials and more modern designs. Street and building arrangements were also improved. New business blocks were usually built of brick or stone, and buildings had a uniform height of three or four stories. Such buildings are still prominent in older districts in Seattle, Tacoma, Bellingham, Port Townsend, Yakima, and Spokane.

About this time, some city fathers were thinking seriously about planning streets, business districts, and parks for future growth. Several hired planners such as the Boston firm of Frederick Law Olmsted. As early as 1873, Olmsted proposed a plan for Tacoma and later for Seattle and Spokane. These included wide, tree-lined boulevards and parks placed along natural ravines and hillsides. Buildings would be in harmony with their locations. Residential roads were likely to curve gracefully along natural contours instead of marching in straight lines. A critic of the Tacoma plan complained that "blocks were shaped like melons, pears and sweet potatoes."

Some areas were to be left natural, although Olmsted preferred smooth, formal parks with fine landscaping and flower beds rather than recreational areas or native trees and plants. These plans affected later thinking but in the short run were forgotten as developers rushed to acquire lots and start building.

In the 1920s, Longview became the most con-

Many Washingtonians past and present have lived in such homes as these: a pioneer house, a bungalow, a "classic box" from early in this century, and a more recent suburban split-level home.

spicuous newly planned town in the state when lumber interests designed it. Diagonal streets intersected at a city center and a large park was included.

A department of architecture was established at the University of Washington in 1914 under Carl Gould, who was responsible for many Northwest buildings of the period. This new center of ideas greatly influenced regional architecture as prominent architects and designers emerged from among faculty and students.

## CHANGES IN THE TWENTIETH CENTURY

Washington and its cities grew rapidly during the early twentieth century. Tall new buildings towered above rows of old business blocks. New materials, including structural steel, made this possible, along with elevators, complex wiring, plumbing, and telephone systems. Some had imposing shapes and created irregular but interesting city skylines for the first time. The 42-story Smith Tower in Seattle, finished in 1914, was the most dramatic of these buildings. For many years, it was the tallest building west of the Mississippi.

Distinct residential areas grew up. The very wealthy could afford to build impressive, often secluded mansions on South Hill in Spokane, on lots overlooking Commencement Bay in Tacoma, or in the park-like neighborhood of The Highlands north of Seattle. Prosperous citizens favored the classic two- or three-storied box style. The one- or one-and-a-half-story bungalow on a narrow lot was a more modest house type.

The Great Depression and World War II slowed building. Then the postwar boom arrived, bringing a large-scale move to suburbs. A new generation of innovative architects and designers planned whole neighborhoods with winding streets and cul-de-sacs. Suburban developments were often criticized for their monotony, although uniform styles are also characteristic of the classic box or bungalow neighborhoods of the past.

Most houses used open space and wood construction and showed a regard for the outdoors. Many were nicely set among trees and gardens. The view from street side was often that of a two-car garage, a landscaped patch, and a hidden entrance.

Ramblers and split-level homes of wood and glass fit in with the casual life developing in suburbs and small towns. Some designers began to develop a distinct regional look using open wood beams, natural stains, and sometimes an Asian or Native American motif. The damp climate inspired the use of cedar shakes and siding, which would not rot, and sloped roofs. Views of water, mountains, and valleys became important.

Suburban development also prompted a new kind of place—the neighborhood shopping mall. This business complex contained a variety of shops often clustered around a branch of a metropolitan department store. The Northgate Shopping Center in north Seattle started the trend, but soon shopping centers and malls were commonplace. Buildings were likely to be low and sprawling, surrounded by parking areas.

During the 1980s downtown city districts tried to attract shoppers, office workers, and visitors back from the suburbs. Civic leaders, architects, planners, and investors promoted the advantages of living and working close to the center of urban activities. They sought to increase services and make downtown areas more appealing. Some older buildings were restored and new ones were built. Central business districts took on new looks and started to thrive once more. Tiny parks and plazas, sculptures, fountains, and artwork appeared beneath new high-rise office buildings and hotels.

Reflective glass and concrete became popular building materials. Architects competed to come up with the most unusual colors and shapes for new office towers. In Seattle, the 76-story Bank of America building stretched above a sky-

For many years, the Smith Tower loomed above the Seattle skyline. Today the Smith Tower is dwarfed by the Bank of America Tower and other downtown high-rises.

line of recently built high-rises. But Seattle voters passed an initiative limiting building heights.

The buildings left by the Seattle and Spokane world's fairs, new stadiums, halls, museums, a convention center in Seattle, the Tacoma Dome, and structures on college campuses throughout the state provide examples of architectural growth and maturity in Washington.

## A PLURAL POPULATION

The people of Washington differ from place to place just as the geography does. They are a mix of several races, and they live in large cities, small towns, and rural areas. Occupations range from persons who work close to the land, the sea, the forests, and other resources to those in urban factories, stores, and offices. Yet they share much in common.

Lines between social classes are less rigid than in some areas of the nation. Poverty and homelessness exist for too many citizens. At the same time, people with modest incomes are likely to own boats or vacation houses and enjoy leisure time activities. Several years ago, cultural historian Raymond Gastil compared the Pacific Northwesterner with residents of midwestern states. He concluded that a person who lives in the Northwest "is probably somewhat more likely to have what passes for a general education, less likely to attend church, more likely to spend his time in outside, participant sports or camping, less likely to be a spectator."

## Centennial Hall of Fame

A group of historians compiled this list in the late 1980s to honor the 1989 state centennial. Some of the names might be quite familiar today, and many may be unknown. Other Washingtonians might have been little known in 1989 or had not yet made their significant contributions. A few such persons could include Bill Gates, Paul Allen, Daniel J. Evans, Jimi Hendrix, and Jacob Lawrence. Who are some others?

Glen C. Adams (1912– ), Fairfield, book publisher

Arthur R. Anderson (1910–1995), Tacoma, civil engineer

Eva Anderson (1899–1972), Douglas County, educator, legislator, writer

Bob Barker (1923– ), Darrington, quiz show host, animal rights activist

William E. Boeing (1881–1956), Seattle, founder of Boeing Airplane Company

George Boldt (1908–1984), Tacoma, federal judge, administrator of price and wage controls

Dr. Walter Brattain (1902–1987), Walla Walla, professor, 1956 Nobel Prize winner for physics, inventor of transistor

Edna Breazeale (1895–1987), Bayview, teacher, environmentalist

Enoch Bryan (1855–1941), Pullman, Washington State College president

Dorothy Stimson Bullitt (1892–1989), Seattle, radio and television executive

Thomas Burke (1849–1925), Seattle, territorial chief justice, property developer

Russell S. Callow (1890–1961), Mason County and Seattle, rowing coach

Dudley E. Carter (1892–1992), Bellevue, wood sculptor

Joseph Cataldo (1837–1928), Spokane, superior of Jesuit missions, founder of Gonzaga University

Horace Cayton (1860–1940), Seattle, publisher

Ralph Chaplin (1888–1961), Tacoma, labor editor and poet

Dr. Wilbert McLeod Chapman (1910–1970), born Kalama, fisheries expert

Hiram O. Chittenden (1858–1917), Seattle, U.S. Army engineer

Barney B. Clark (1921–1983), Normandy Park, dentist, artificial heart recipient

Anna Herr Clise (1886–1936), Seattle, benefactor, founder of Seattle Children's Orthopedic Hospital

Giovanni Costigan (1905–1990), Seattle, history professor, supporter of liberal causes

Harry Lillis "Bing" Crosby (1903–1977), born Tacoma, Spokane, singer and actor

Imogen Cunningham (1883–1976), Port Angeles, Seattle, photographer

Merce Cunningham (1919– ) Centralia, choreographer

Edward Curtis (1868–1952), Seattle, photographer of Northwest Indians

Francis W. Cushman (1867–1909), Tacoma, U.S. representative

Kirtland Cutter (1860–1939), Spokane, architect

Emma Smith DeVoe (1848–1927), Parkland, woman suffrage leader

Sonora S. Dodd (1882–1978), Spokane, poet, originator of Father's Day

Lauren R. Donaldson (1903–1998), Seattle, fisheries professor

William O. Douglas (1898–1980), Yakima, U.S. Supreme Court justice

John Fluke (1911–1984), Seattle, electronics manufacturer

Thea Foss (1857–1927), Tacoma, tugboat company owner

Richard E. Fuller (1897–1976), Seattle, founder of Seattle Art Museum

Albert S. Goss (1882–1950), Benton County, master of National Grange

Captain William Gray (1845–1929), Pasco, river navigation pioneer

Dr. Erna Gunther (1897–1982), Seattle, Bainbridge
Island, anthropologist

Julia Butler Hansen (1908–1988), Cathlamet, U.S.
representative

Raymond A. Hanson (1924– ), Spokane,
constructor of heavy machinery

Samuel Hill (1857–1931), Goldendale, industrialist

Gordon Hirabayashi (1918– ), Seattle, Japanese
American who resisted internment

James Wong Howe (1899–1968), Pasco,
cinematographer

Fred Hutchinson (1919–1964), Seattle, baseball
player and manager

May Arkwright Hutton (1860–1915), Spokane,
woman suffrage leader

Henry M. Jackson (1912–1983), Everett, U.S.
senator

Robert Joffrey (1930–1988), Seattle, choreographer

Eric Johnston (1895–1963), Spokane, business and
government leader

Quincy Jones (1933– ), Seattle, composer,
conductor, musician

Wesley L. Jones (1863–1932), Yakima, U.S. senator

Mother Joseph of the Sacred Heart (1823–1902),
Vancouver, established schools and hospitals

Dr. Trevor Kincaid (1873–1970), Seattle, zoologist

Carolyn Kizer (1925– ), Seattle and Spokane,
Pulitzer Prize–winning poet

Frank H. Lamb (1875–1951), Hoquiam, forest
products machinery manufacturer

Bertha Knight Landes (1868–1943), Seattle, mayor

Raphael H. Levine (1901–1985), Seattle, rabbi and
civic leader

Dr. Dora S. Lewis (1892–1982), Olympia, educator
and author

Mary McCarthy (1912–1989), Seattle and Tacoma,
literary critic, novelist

Warren G. Magnuson (1905–1989), Seattle and
Bainbridge Island, U.S. senator

Edmond S. Meany (1862–1935), Seattle, historian
and author

Ezra Meeker (1830–1928), Puyallup, publicizer
of Oregon Trail, pioneer hop farmer

Patrice Munsel (1925– ), Spokane, opera singer

Edward R. Murrow (1908–1965), Blanchard, news-
caster and commentator

John W. Nordstrom (1866–1963), Seattle, founder
of retail clothing store

Elizabeth (Lizzie) Ordway (1828–1897), Seattle and
Port Gamble, "Mercer girl," educator

James E. O'Sullivan (1876–1949), Ephrata,
promoter of Grand Coulee Dam

Clyde Pangborn (1896–1958), Wenatchee, aviator

Vernon Parrington (1871–1929), Seattle, author
and historian

William H. Paulhamus (1864–1925), Puyallup,
farmer, promoter of Western Washington Fair

Stephen B. L. Penrose (1865–1947), Walla Walla,
president of Whitman College

Edwin T. Pratt (1931–1969), Seattle, civil rights
leader

Dixy Lee Ray (1914–1994), Tacoma, Seattle,
Fox Island, zoologist, head of Atomic Energy
Commission, governor

Mark E. Reed (1866–1933), Shelton, lumberman,
financier, leader in Washington State Legislature

Theodore Roethke (1904–1963), Seattle, Pulitzer
Prize–winning poet

James D. Ross (1871–1939), Seattle, promoter
of hydroelectric power

Richard Scobee (1939–1986), Cle Elum and Auburn,
astronaut

Dr. Belding Scribner (1921– ), inventor of kidney
dialysis improvements

Henry Sicade (1866–1938), Puyallup Indian tribal
leader

Smohalla (c. 1815–1907), Wallula area, prophet
of Wanapum people

Anna Louise Strong (1885–1970), Seattle, labor
journalist and correspondent in Russia and China

Sulkthscosum (Chief Moses) (1829–1899), eastern
Washington, influential Indian chief

Henry Suzzallo (1875–1933), Seattle, University of Washington president, president of Carnegie Foundation

James Gilchrist Swan (1818–1900), Port Townsend and other, author, artist, museum collector

E. Donnall Thomas (1920– ), Seattle, medical professor and researcher

Mark Tobey (1890–1977), Seattle, artist

George Tsutakawa (1910–1997), Seattle, sculptor

Archie Van Doren (1906–1986), Wenatchee, father of controlled-atmosphere apple storage

Orville Vogel (1907–1991), Pullman, agriculturist, developer of wheat strain

Jonathan M. Wainwright (1883–1953), Walla Walla, World War II general

Pearl Wanamaker (1899–1984), educator, government official

James Washington Jr. (1909–2000), Seattle, painter

Evan M. (Ed) Weston (1895–1969), Black Diamond and Seattle, labor leader

John Philip Weyerhaeuser Jr. (1899–1956), Tacoma, lumber executive

Jim Whittaker (1929– ), Seattle, mountain climber

Reverend George Frederick Whitworth (1816–1907), Tacoma and Spokane, minister, educator

Oscar Wirkkala (1880–1959), Naselle, logger and developer of aerial logging equipment

Rufus Woods (1878–1950), Wenatchee, newspaper publisher, booster for Grand Coulee Dam

Walt Woodward, (1910–2001), Bainbridge Island, newspaper publisher, advocate for interned Japanese Americans

Ambrose B. Wyckoff (1848–1922), Bremerton, naval officer, hydrographer, promoter of naval shipyard

Minoru Yamasaki (1912–1986), Seattle, architect

# Chapter 11 Review

**1.** Identify the following people. Tell why each is important to Washington State.

William Grose
Sherman Alexie
Horace Cayton
W. O. Bush
Edwin Pratt
James Washington
Lenny Wilkens
Quincy Jones
Alfredo Arreguín
George Tsutakawa
Minoru Yamasaki
Sacajawea
Mother Joseph
May Arkwright Hutton
Emma Smith DeVoe
Cora Eaton
Bertha Landes
Dixy Lee Ray
Patty Murray
Dorothy Bullitt
John R. Rogers
John DeVore
Mark Matthews
Jim Whittaker
Stanley Sayres
Gerard Schwarz
Mark Tobey
James Stevens
Betty MacDonald
Frank Herbert
Frederick Law Olmsted
Carl Gould

**II.** Define the following words and terms. Relate each one to Washington State.

White Anglo-Saxon Protestant (WASP)
Native American
Indian reservations
Chicano
Bracero agreements
Asian Exclusion Act
Tongs
Nisei
Issei
Alien Land Law
Picture brides
Upward mobility
Nihonmachi
Woman suffrage
Equal Rights Amendment (ERA)

**III.** Each question below should call your attention to factual information in the chapter. Try to answer each one. Then look back in the reading to check your answer, correct your understanding, and find answers you do not know.

1. What was the population of Washington in 2000? What was the percentage increase from the 1990 national census?

2. About what percentage of Washington's population lives in the Puget Sound Basin?

3. What percentage of the population is classified as white?

4. Which part of the United States did people who settled Walla Walla and Port Gamble come from?

5. Many settlers in Ballard, Poulsbo, and Gig Harbor came from a particular part of Europe. Which part of Europe is that?

6. What events in the 1960s encouraged Indian groups to seek changes for themselves? Give three examples of advances Indian groups have made in handling their own affairs.

7. How many Indian reservations are there in the state of Washington?

8. About what percentage of the people in Washington are black? Where do most of them live?

9. What circumstances in the 1940s drew large numbers of blacks to Washington?

10. Describe the backgrounds of the new black leaders who emerged during the 1960s.

11. Identify six prominent blacks who lived in or came from Washington.

12. Which county has a population that is one-third Hispanic?

13. Describe the life and work style of the early Chicanos who came to Washington.

14. Identify three prominent Asian Americans who came from or are associated with Washington.

15. How were many of the Chinese employed who came to Washington in the late 1800s?

16. What happened to the Chinese residents of Tacoma and Seattle in the mid-1880s?

17. After World War II, what events in China interrupted relations between that country and the United States?

18. What did the Pacific Northwest gain when relations opened with China?

19. Why did many early Japanese settlers live in cities?

20. How did Japanese Americans keep their culture alive in the United States?

21. What happened to the Japanese Americans on the Pacific Coast during World War II?

22. How did the background of Filipino immigrants differ from that of other Asian immigrants?

23. What events since the 1950s caused many Southeast Asians to move to Washington?

24. Who were the "Mercer girls"?

25. Name four institutions established by Mother Joseph.

26. When did women first gain the power to vote in Washington? How was it lost? In what year did they regain the right to vote?

27. Identify three women who have held high elected offices in Washington.

28. What action did the Washington State Legislature take on the Equal Rights Amendment?

29. Who started the first schools in Washington?

30. What important event took place on the present University of Washington campus in 1909?

31. What did the town of Pullman do to acquire Washington State University?

32. How many state-supported four-year colleges and universities are there in Washington? Name three private colleges or universities in Washington.

33. What Protestant denomination founded the first churches in Washington?

34. What is the largest single religious denomination in Washington today?

35. Which two small towns had large Jewish populations?

36. Who were the first persons to climb to the summit of Mount Rainier?

37. Name two important sport fishing towns.

38. What was the first major-league professional sports team to come to Washington?

39. Describe the main characteristics of the Northwest style of art.

40. Name the legendary woodsman who is associated with Northwest forests.

41. What is the name of the famous "think tank" located in Richland?

42. What planned town was constructed by a lumber company in the 1920s?

43. What style of house is typical in many older Washington neighborhoods? What is the typical style of many more recent suburban homes?

44. Which areas began to attract businesses after World War II?

**IV.** Think about, discuss, and answer the questions below.

1. Several communities in Washington State were settled mainly by persons from a single nation. If there are such communities near you, learn about one community and its heritage. How do the residents keep such influences alive? What signs or symbols of this heritage are evident in the town? An Indian reservation might also be investigated in this manner.

2. Who are some women in your community who are prominent in political, business, and social affairs? Is it still more difficult for a woman to succeed in these fields than for a man? What are some reasons for this? Interview or do a biographical report on a woman who has had an unusual achievement.

3. Make some predictions about how people will be living in Washington in another fifty years. Consider the style of life, the kinds of people, and the various racial and ethnic groups

that will be here. How will this influence the total life of the state?

4. Many people who live in Washington State were born elsewhere. Talk with relatives, neighbors, and friends to find out where they came from. Why did they come? In what year did they arrive? Perhaps you and other members of the class could categorize the reasons given. A chart might display different reasons why people came during different periods of time.

5. What does the term "plural population" mean? How accurately does it describe the population of Washington? For what other states or places that you know about would it be more accurate or less accurate? How accurately does it describe the town or neighborhood where you live? What are some of the advantages and problems of being part of a plural population?

6. Some readers may have noticed two different spellings for what seems to be the same name: Yakima and Yakama. Can you explain the difference? Do you know of similar instances? Why is this important?

# Chapter 12   Governments in Washington

On January 10, 2001, Governor Gary Locke is sworn in for his second term by State Supreme Court Chief Justice Gerry Alexander as First Lady Mona Locke looks on.

*S*tate Capitol Building, Olympia, January 10, 2001. On this comfortably warm winter day, this massive granite building teems with excitement. Dignitaries and regular citizens crowd the marble halls surrounding the rotunda beneath the high dome. Many are of Asian descent. They have come for the second inauguration of Governor Gary Locke, the first governor of Chinese ancestry in the history of the state and the nation.

Just before noon, the doors of the thickly carpeted House of Representatives chamber open and the governor, a few days away from his fifty-first birthday, is escorted in. A short man with a mop of black hair, he is no stranger here. For a decade, he represented Seattle citizens in the legislature. An expert on state finance, he became influential and powerful. He gained a reputation as a "workaholic," a serious, knowledgeable person who concentrates on details.

Then he became King County executive and ran the state's largest county.

Four years ago, many prominent figures sought to become governor. Along with Locke, they included the mayor of Seattle, a former congressman, the King County prosecutor, several leaders in the state legislature, a prominent businesswoman, and a longtime adviser to previous officeholders. That November Locke won the general election with 60 percent of the vote. Running for a second term, he defeated a well-known radio talk show host and political activist.

Many Americans follow unusual paths to prominence, but Locke's was unique. For decades, the Chinese were denied basic opportunities in America and in Washington State. During this time his family arrived. Locke's great-grandfather lived briefly in California but returned to China.

Early in the twentieth century, his grandfather worked as a houseboy for an Olympia family just a few blocks from here. His father, raised in China, had a restaurant and then a grocery store in Seattle. Gary Locke attended Seattle public schools. He was an honor student and student body president at Franklin High School, a member of the choir and the track team, and an Eagle Scout. He went to Yale and then earned a law degree from Boston University. Back in Seattle, Locke entered Democratic politics. Politics and government appear to be his main interests, along with household chores like plumbing and tinkering with automobiles.

He is married to Mona Lee Locke, a former Seattle television reporter. Today his wife is seated behind the podium, but Emily and Dylan, their two small children, remain at the red brick governor's mansion next door. The Lockes' parents and several dozen members of their two large families watch from the gallery. Other spectators represent all segments of state government. Seven other elected state officials have come to take office. Members of the state legislature fill the floor. The Senate is controlled by Locke's Democratic Party, but the House of Representatives is, for the second time in a row, equally divided between Democrats and Republicans. State supreme court judges have come from the nearby Temple of Justice, and consuls representing other nations are present. The atmosphere today is friendly.

Shortly after noon, Gary Locke raises his right hand as State Supreme Court Chief Justice Gerry Alexander gives him the oath of office. As he did four years earlier, and as twenty others have done over the past 120 years, Gary Locke swears to carry out the duties of governor, enforce laws, and uphold the constitutions of the United States and Washington State. After widespread applause, he delivers a brief speech.

Four years ago, he had recounted the history of his family and others present, "whose ancestors dreamed the American Dream and worked hard to make it come true." Then he urged citizens to carry out the values that sus-tained his family: "get a good education, work hard, and take care of each other." Today, he briefly introduces family members. Then the reelected governor discusses four basic issues that his government must deal with: transportation, education, clean water, and sufficient power. He only hints at how to achieve such goals, but he stresses that needs are urgent and he impresses people by the strength of his appeals.

This scene in Olympia is repeated frequently in state capitols, city halls, and county buildings across the nation as officials assume office. In ten days, at a similar ceremony in Washington, D.C., George W. Bush will be inaugurated as president of the United States. The orderly transfer of responsibility and power from one person or party to another is an important American tradition. It brings together various branches, departments, interests, and philosophies of government. Rarely is political authority in the United States transferred amid gunfire or bitterness.

This evening, 4,500 elegantly dressed celebrants from across the state will crowd Olympia buildings for a festive inaugural ball. Happening every four years, it is this small city's most glittering event. Tonight, though, it is slightly dimmed. An energy crisis along the West Coast demonstrates the need to conserve electric power. Three miles of twinkling lights strung along Olympia streets and throughout the Capitol Building will remain unlit. The great capitol dome will be dark. But nothing dims the excitement inside. The celebration will stress the diverse population of Washington. There will be a Chinese lion, Native American dancers, a mariachi band, and Filipino dancers, along with dance bands.

Governor Locke's Chinese ancestry has been stressed both in this country and in China. He and his wife were hailed as celebrities when they visited the ancestral homes of their families. But that is only the background for his true role. More important, he is a born Washingtonian, elected to serve as governor of people of all backgrounds. Tomorrow the festivities will be over. Gary Locke will resume his duties as the governor of the state of Washington.

# The Idea of Government

Wherever and however people live, they must make decisions and get things done. That is what government is all about. Some kinds of government are very structured and some are loose.

Speaking broadly, government may be as informal as two or three people deciding together where to go shopping, what rules to follow in a game, or how to spend an evening. There are different rules and expectations for different situations. A person acts differently with a best friend than with an elderly grandparent, or with a group of buddies, or on a job, or in a class, or on a sports team, or on a picnic, or at church, or in a library, or at a party. Most people generally understand what they should do and not do in each situation.

Although we rarely think of the family as a unit of government, it is the one closest to most people. The family makes many important decisions and sees that rules are carried out. Some families operate in a loose, almost anarchistic manner: members make their own decisions and go their separate ways. Others are formal but democratic: each member contributes to plans and decisions and then follows the majority opinion or consensus. Some families operate in an authoritarian atmosphere: one member, usually a parent, makes and enforces decisions.

Realistically, most families combine all these characteristics. There are times when each person might have considerable freedom of choice, times when general discussions and agreements are necessary, and times when authoritarian rules prevail. We practice these procedures so commonly with generally understood rules and codes of conduct that we do not think of them as a means of governing people. But they are.

Generally, however, government means something much more formal. Corporations, churches, and organizations usually write basic rules and ideas into charters or constitutions. Bylaws establish ways to handle day-to-day procedures, and officers perform assigned duties. Other governments are public—such as school districts, towns and cities, counties, states, national governments, and international organizations.

In the United States, all of us live under many government units. Most of us live in a school district, a water district, a public utility district, a hospital district, a port district, or other small, specific governments. Each of us lives in a county. Most of us live in incorporated towns and cities. The fifty states each have their own constitutions, and differences exist among them. The national or federal government affects the lives of all citizens.

This chapter will describe how these governments operate in the state of Washington.

## The Federal Government and the States

The national, or federal, government is derived from the United States Constitution. The men who wrote the Constitution in 1787 had strong ideas about the kind of government they wanted. Those ideas were based on practices in England, on various philosophical writings, and on their experiences during the American Revolution. Eleven years earlier, the Declaration of Independence had established our separation from England. The thirteen states created their individual constitutions. Thus the idea of separate states is older than the Constitution of the whole United States.

By the end of the Revolutionary War, individual states had become so strong that Congress could not enforce its rulings. The Constitution tried to correct some of these problems and to place stronger national controls over the states.

The Constitution mentions states in many places. Article Four is about the role that states play in the federal government. Washington, like all of the states, must abide by rules set out in the federal Constitution.

## THE LEGISLATIVE BRANCH
*Article One*

The first article of the Constitution deals with the legislative branch, a Congress that makes laws. Congress consists of a House of Representatives and a Senate. The House of Representatives has 435 members, with the number from each state based on its population. Thus large states have more representatives than smaller ones do. California, the largest state, has fifty-three representatives while seven states have only one each.

When Washington first became a state, it had three representatives. As the population grew, the number of representatives gradually increased. The 1980 census gave Washington eight representatives and the 1990 census nine. Despite the greatly increased population by 2000, the number of representatives did not change: it remained at nine.

Washington is divided into nine congressional districts, each of which elects one representative. Approximately 655,000 people live in each district. The most thickly populated districts are smallest in area. The 1st Congressional District, which includes parts of King and Snohomish Counties, and the 7th District, which includes much of Seattle, are small in area but densely populated. On the other hand, all of eastern Washington is divided into two very large districts.

A representative must be at least twenty-five years old, a United States citizen for seven years, and elected by voters of the district. The general election is held on the first Tuesday after the first Monday in November every even-numbered year. Terms last two years.

The Constitution requires every member of Congress to reside in the state that he or she represents. State law requires representatives to reside in the district they represent and thus be chosen by members of their own communities. Although this may seem natural, it is not the case in Canada, Great Britain, and many other nations.

Most representatives enter Congress after experience in other areas of government. Recent representatives from Washington State have held other elected offices in the state legislature or county government; several were aides to congressional representatives or senators in Washington, D.C.

If a representative dies or resigns from office, the position remains vacant until the governor calls an election to fill it. This rarely happens. Most recently, in 1977 Representative Brock Adams resigned, and his brief replacement lost an election to Mike Lowry, who later became governor.

Every state has two U.S. senators who serve six-year terms. Before 1911, U.S. senators were selected by the state legislature. Much time and energy were spent choosing a senator during a legislative session. The Seventeenth Amendment to the Constitution changed this practice, so that senators are now elected by voters. There are no senate districts; both candidates for senator are voted upon by the entire state. Senators must be residents of the state, at least thirty years old, and a citizen of the United States for nine years.

For almost thirty years, Washington's two senators were Warren G. Magnuson and Henry M. Jackson. Magnuson served six terms between 1944 and 1981. Jackson served from 1953 until his death in 1983. In the early twenty-first century, Washington's two senators are Democrats: Patty Murray, first elected in 1992, and former representative and high-tech executive Maria Cantwell, elected in 2000.

Article One of the Constitution also lists some things that individual states may not do, that only the federal government can do. Some stem from problems that occurred before the Constitution. For instance, states cannot tax goods imported from other states. They cannot make a treaty with another state, country, or Indian tribe. They cannot make war unless they are invaded or are in imminent danger of invasion. They cannot establish their own money system. Like the federal government, the states cannot pass laws that interfere with the constitutional rights of an individual.

## THE EXECUTIVE AND JUDICIAL BRANCHES
### Article Two

Article Two describes the executive branch, which is responsible for carrying out, or executing, the laws passed by Congress. Its top official is the president.

The states take part in electing the president. Each state has the same number of presidential electors as it has members in Congress. Washington, with nine representatives and two senators, has eleven electors. These electors cannot be officeholders but they are usually active in their political party. During a presidential election year, each party selects possible electors at its state convention. At the November general election, voters act as if they are voting for president but are actually choosing a set of electors. The electors' names are not on the ballot in Washington, however.

If the majority of voters in the state choose the Republican presidential candidate, that person has won the popular, or people's, vote, and the Republican electors cast the electoral vote for the state. If the Democratic candidate carries the state, the Democratic electors vote. It is possible, though not likely, for a minor party to receive the electoral bid.

On a Monday in December, the chosen electors meet at the Capitol Building in Olympia and cast the official electoral ballot for Washington. The electors almost always vote for the candidate of their party, although this is not required by law.

The ballots are then sealed in a box and sent to Washington, D.C. There the electoral votes from all fifty states are opened and counted in front of Congress. Then the winner of the presidential election is officially declared. The president is inaugurated on January 20.

The 2000 presidential election was unusual. The winning candidate, George W. Bush, received the most electoral votes following a disputed count in Florida. But Democrat Al Gore had more popular votes, including Washington's. Gore received Washington's eleven electoral votes.

### Article Three

The third article of the Constitution concerns the judicial, or court, system. The federal court system handles all cases which involve federal laws—laws passed by Congress. Kidnapping, bank robbery, counterfeiting, and crimes committed on federal property are some of these.

Federal trials must be heard in the state where the alleged crime took place unless the defendant requests a change. The federal courts also hear cases in which a state is involved or in which citizens of several different states are involved. Thus, no state can exert judicial control over another. Disputes between the state of Washington and Indian tribes are heard in federal courts.

Washington is divided into two federal court districts with eleven judges holding court in major cities. These judges are appointed by the president and confirmed by the U.S. Senate.

### Article Four

Article Four is about the states. Here the federal system is described. The national government and the various state governments share control, each having jurisdiction over certain matters. The Constitution requires every state to treat the acts, records, and court proceedings of other states with full faith and respect. Even though states can write different laws and apply them differently within their own borders, all states are equal in the eyes of the United States. Neither a wealthier nor a larger nor an older one can interfere in the affairs of another state.

Sometimes a person commits a crime in one state and flees to another. In that case, the governor of the first state may request officials in the other state to return the suspect. This process is called extradition. A governor can refuse to honor the extradition request. For example, some states have used extremely severe punishments for minor offenses, or they have treated minority prisoners harshly. Governors have refused to return fugitives into such conditions, especially for a minor crime.

Occasionally, wanted persons raise families and establish reputations as respected, productive citizens in their new state. The governor might reason that no good would be accomplished by returning the person and would thus refuse extradition. This has happened in Washington and in other states.

New states can be admitted to the Union; Washington is one of thirty-seven that have been added since the Constitution was adopted. A general pattern was established even before the Constitution. Territories hold an election, draft a state constitution, elect potential officials, and apply to Congress for admission. Only Congress has the power to admit a state.

No state, however, may be created out of another state or be combined with another state unless the legislatures of every state involved consent. An exception was West Virginia. During the Civil War, the state of Virginia left the Union to join the Confederacy. But several western counties remained loyal to the United States. They formed the state of West Virginia and entered the Union in 1864. Another exception is Texas, which joined the Union with the right to divide at will into as many as five states. That is still possible.

Every so often, someone suggests that eastern and western Washington are different in so many ways that the state should be divided along the crest of the Cascades. Many people in eastern Washington resent the fact that the more populous west side has greater representation in the state legislature and Congress. One recent proposal was to create a new state named Lincoln in the eastern portion.

Earlier a mayor of Spokane had suggested that eastern Washington, the northern Idaho panhandle, and western Montana should separate from their states and join together to form the fifty-first state. These areas have much in common with each other, more perhaps than each has in common with the rest of its state. Such proposals would require long and complicated negotiations by the people of the affected states and the national government.

The Constitution requires each state to have a representative form of government in which people are represented by officials they have chosen. If a governor or another person should attempt to set up some form of dictatorship—to close down the legislature or courts, for example—federal troops could move in to stop this.

The national government will also protect a state against foreign invasion and incidents of violence within the state. A governor can request National Guard or army troops to restore peace and order. Troops were called up in Washington during territorial days because of riots against the Chinese in Tacoma and Seattle. During the civil rights and anti-war movements of the 1960s, governors of several states requested and received federal help to put down disturbances. National Guard troops came in during disturbances surrounding the World Trade Organization meeting in Seattle in December 1999. Following the terrorist attacks on the East Coast in September 2001, National

Guard troops stood watch at major airports and other locations in the state.

## OTHER CONSTITUTIONAL MATTERS

States have a part in amending the federal Constitution. Customarily, amendments are passed by Congress and then sent to the states to be approved, or ratified, by their legislatures. After the legislatures of three-fourths of the states have ratified the proposed amendment, it becomes part of the Constitution and is binding on all states. Debates over amendments sometimes become intense in election campaigns and during sessions of the legislature.

There are now twenty-six amendments to the Constitution. During the 1970s, a twenty-seventh amendment passed in Congress. This Equal Rights Amendment (ERA) would have guaranteed equal rights to all persons without regard to gender. It was a highly emotional issue for people on both sides. Washington had recently added a similar amendment to the state constitution, and the legislature approved the federal amendment. But the ERA did not become part of the Constitution because too few states approved it.

Article Five makes clear that the Constitution and all laws and treaties made under it are the supreme law of the land. Early in our national history, the Supreme Court established that if a dispute arose between conflicting laws, the federal law must prevail over the state law. Federal treaties are also supreme over state laws. The Boldt fishing decision of 1974 illustrated this by holding that rights granted to Indian tribes in treaties overrode state fishing laws.

## The Federal Government in the State of Washington

The federal government plays a major role in every state. Many federal matters affect daily life for everyone. These include the post office,

the highway system, federal law enforcement and courts, and federally funded programs in health, welfare, and education. Because Washington is bordered by Canada and by the Pacific Ocean, there is greater federal involvement in customs, defense, and transportation concerns than in inland states.

The federal government provides funds for state programs through grants and the sharing of federal money. About one-fourth of the state's revenue comes from the federal government. Most of this federal money goes into various kinds of education and human resources. Sometimes these funds have "strings" attached: in order to obtain and spend such money, the state must perform certain duties or comply with certain laws.

The federal government also owns much property in Washington. Several years ago, the *Seattle Times* reported that "Uncle Sam is the biggest landowner in Washington State. One of every three acres is his. The mark of federal ownership might be a picnic bench in a national park, a foot-worn hiking trail high in a wilderness shadow, a Columbia River dam, or a tree in one of the millions of acres of national forest."

The federal government owns 15 million out of over 42 million acres of land in the state. This is an area larger than Denmark, the Netherlands, or several eastern states; it is almost as large as West Virginia.

About nine million acres of this federal land are in national forests. There are six national forests in the state; another overlaps from Oregon. Much of the timber from these lands is sold to private companies. Another million acres of federal land are wilderness and 250,000 acres are held by the Bureau of Land Management. Two and a half million acres are controlled by the Bureau of Indian Affairs. Almost two million acres are in the three national parks—Mount Rainier, Olympic, and North Cascades—

and several smaller recreational areas and monuments.

Other federal properties include dams, hydroelectric projects, and irrigation districts. The Hanford nuclear plant and reservation comprises 570 square miles. Over a thousand square miles—650,000 acres—are controlled by the Defense Department. Fort Lewis, McChord Air Force Base, the Whidbey Island Naval Air Station, the Puget Sound Naval Shipyard at Bremerton, Fairchild Air Force Base, and the Bangor Naval Submarine Base are among the largest military and naval bases.

Small but highly significant federal properties include office buildings, hospitals, and varied institutions in urban areas. Radar and radio installations monitor and transmit from several spots in Washington. Yet for all this, the federal government owns less land in Washington than it owns in other western states.

Land ownership often allows considerable influence over legislation and people. Workers on the land and income from it add to local payrolls and thus affect the economy. The federal government is important in Washington because of its presence here. In some places this is particularly evident. Drive along Interstate 5 between Tacoma and Olympia and note the varied activities of the military; cross through the eastern part of the state and look for dams, power lines, and irrigation canals; circle the Olympic Peninsula and see the federal government working in forests, parks, shorelines, and Coast Guard stations; consider the number of federal personnel in the atomic city of Richland; note the 37-story Jackson Federal Building on the Seattle skyline. Or look in a telephone book for listings under "United States Government." Whether it is the Seattle phone book with twenty-four columns of federal telephone numbers or that of a medium-size town, the number and range of federal activities they represent may surprise you.

## The Washington State Constitution

The Washington State Constitution was written in 1889 after Congress passed an Enabling Act that allowed residents to plan a government. Seventy-five delegates from throughout the territory came to Olympia for the six-week constitutional convention. Many were lawyers and businessmen, but there were farmers and members of other occupations. Differences within the state created a need for compromise.

The constitution they wrote is much longer than the United States Constitution and goes into greater detail. It has been amended ninety-three times by the legislature and the voters. (Constitutional amendments require a public vote.) The first amendment came in 1894 when the state was only five years old; it concerned the investment of school funds.

The government of Washington is patterned after that of the United States. There are three branches. A legislative branch makes laws; this is the state legislature consisting of the House of Representatives and the Senate. An executive branch carries out the laws; this is the governor and eight other elected officials plus many who are appointed. A judicial branch, or court system, makes the final interpretation of laws.

### THE LEGISLATIVE BRANCH

The state legislative branch makes laws. It consists of a two-house, or bicameral, legislature: the House of Representatives and the Senate. These bodies meet in opposite wings of the statehouse, the large domed building in Olympia that is often called the State Capitol. Members have offices in nearby buildings.

The state is divided into forty-nine legislative districts. Two members of the House of Representatives and one senator are elected from each district.

The populations of the forty-nine districts are supposed to be approximately equal. Yet rapid

A color guard brings the state and national flags into the Legislative Chamber to open the 2002 session.

growth and population shifts in the twentieth century resulted in more and more persons being packed into urban areas. A large rural district with few residents would have two representatives and one senator. A small, crowded urban district would also have two representatives and one senator. City people began to complain that rural parts of the state were overrepresented in the legislature and urban areas were underrepresented. This was happening in many states besides Washington.

States regularly redraw legislative boundaries to make districts more equal in population. Each district today has about 12,000 persons. The task of adjusting district boundaries in Washington is handled by a commission appointed to do only

that. After the 1990 census, such a commission redrew old boundaries and also created the new 9th Congressional District between the Olympia and Tacoma areas. After the 2000 census, no new congressional district was added but boundaries were redrawn for both Congress and the state legislature.

### The Two Houses

The state House of Representatives consists of ninety-eight members, two from each district. Representatives must be at least twenty-one years old, citizens of the United States, and residents in the state of Washington and their district. They serve two-year terms.

The Senate has forty-nine members, one from

State legislative districts

each district. Their four-year terms are staggered so that half of the terms end at each two-year election.

The presiding officer of the House of Representatives is called the Speaker of the House; the Senate is presided over by the lieutenant governor of the state as president of the Senate. Both leaders have considerable power over the members and over legislation. They can recognize or not recognize speakers, call members to order, and help appoint committees and chairpersons. After each election, members of the House of Representatives elect a Speaker for the next two years. Usually the Speaker is the leader of the

party that is in the majority. Since the lieutenant governor is not a member of the Senate, he or she cannot speak on an issue or vote except to break a tie.

The House of Representatives has a clerk and the Senate a secretary to keep records of debates, proposed bills, and other materials. Each house has a sergeant-at-arms and doorkeeper to maintain control and handle visitors. Staffs made up of lawyers and clerks help to write and prepare bills—making certain that the language follows correct legal forms—and to advise committees. Each committee has a staff. And each legislator has an office and money for a personal staff to

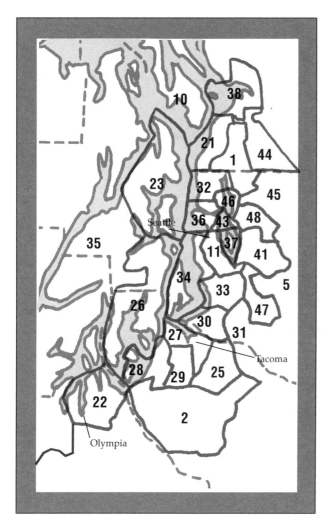

Detail of the thickly populated legislative districts on Puget Sound

or permanent committees in the House and fifteen in the Senate. Each committee deals with a particular concern such as education, agriculture, or fisheries. Committees usually divide into subcommittees which handle more specific topics. The House Transportation Committee, for instance, may be divided into subcommittees to deal with such concerns as mass transit, marine transportation, and highways. These committees do much groundwork studying and investigating bills for the full House.

Members of the major political parties organize themselves in each house. A party leader helps set party policies, promotes bills favored by the party, and tries to get members to follow party lines. The party with the most members in each house is the majority party and will probably try to enact specific programs. The minority party may serve mainly in opposition. Chairpersons of committees are from the majority party; that party will also have more members on each committee. An unusual situation occurred between 1999 and 2001, when each party had an equal number of representatives. There were cospeakers and co-committee chairs. Efforts at real cooperation sometimes faltered.

Members of the governor's party generally try to support and push the governor's program. They are not necessarily in the majority. Most of the twelve years that Republican Daniel J. Evans was governor, the legislature was controlled by Democrats. For two years, Democratic governor Gary Locke faced a legislature controlled by Republicans. Even when the governor and the legislative majority are from the same party, they do not always cooperate well.

Until 1979 the state constitution required the legislature to meet at least once every two years in January following the election. A session could not last more than sixty days. As the state grew and issues became more complex, the legislature rarely finished its business in this time.

help gather information, handle correspondence, and maintain contacts with the people in the district.

Teenage pages work as messengers in the legislature for one week each session. Various clerks, secretaries, custodians, and other employees are needed for the great activity of a legislative session. It costs about $42,000 each day the legislature meets during the regular session.

Each member of the legislature serves on one or more committees. There are nineteen standing

Two teenagers who serve as pages are flag bearers to open a daily session of the legislature.

Lawmakers devised ways to spend more time in session. One method was to "stop the clock." Clocks in the legislative halls were literally stopped on the sixtieth day of the session. Members continued to meet and pretend that the sixtieth day had not ended. Sometimes the legislature adjourned on time and the governor called them back into session. This created problems and was not always dependable.

A constitutional amendment passed in 1979 requires the legislature to meet every year. A 105-day session in odd-numbered years sets the state budget and deals with other matters. A sixty-day session meets in even-numbered years. Also, the governor or two-thirds of the members of each house can call a special session at any time; this is limited to thirty days.

## A Bill Becomes a Law

The principal tasks of the legislature are to make laws and to set the budget. The process in Washington is similar to that in the national government. A bill is a proposed law. To become a law, it must pass both houses of the legislature with a simple majority—at least one more than half the votes cast—and be sent to the governor. The governor has several options: to sign it, to allow it to become law without signature, to veto it, or to veto parts of it. The legislature can override a veto with a two-thirds majority vote. Voters can also make laws through the initiative process with the legislature playing no part at all.

Ideas for bills come from various sources. Some are required by the state constitution, and many arise from the need to run state business. If laws did not authorize and budget money, none could be obtained and spent. Some bills are requested by the executive branch.

Governors often propose a full program involving many bills to meet varied state needs. Other officials and agencies make requests. Bills concerning education may originate in the Office of Public Instruction, for example, or those dealing with insurance in the Insurance Commission. Business groups, professional organizations, labor unions, and private citizens often suggest laws.

Wherever the idea for a bill may have originated, it can be introduced into the House of Representatives or the Senate only by a member. Usually a bill introduced by one legislator is also sponsored by others to show wide support. The legislative staff phrases the actual wording so it is in correct legal terminology. The bill is given a "first reading" when it is introduced and is then numbered and sent to be published. The presiding officer refers it to whatever committee seems appropriate.

Committees do much work on bills. A committee gathers information about a bill and studies it closely. The committee will invite interested persons to testify at hearings. Other state officials might speak before the committee on the need for the bill, or object to all or parts of it, or suggest changes. Organizations affected by the bill may send a spokesperson to hearings, and interested citizens may also speak.

Some testimony is presented in writing, and all is recorded so that it will be available for later review. Committee members are likely to ask questions or debate with persons who testify. Often several bills on a common topic are considered together in the same hearings.

Some hearings continue over several days. Then committee members discuss various aspects of the bill and make their decisions. They may amend bills or combine features of several bills into one. Finally the committee members vote,

Two representatives from different parties discuss an issue before the House of Representatives: Democrat Mike Cooper of Edmonds and Republican Brad Benson of Spokane.

recommending either that the full House pass or reject the bill. In both the House and the Senate, bills go first to a Rules Committee, which sets the schedule by which the full membership of each house considers the bill. The Rules Committee can virtually kill a bill by not placing it on the calendar or by delaying it until an inconvenient time.

The bill gets its second reading before the full House or Senate. Private citizens do not take part, but legislators may read their views into the record. Debates follow regular procedures, though the style may be informal. Members may question one another. Amendments can be proposed and discussed.

In both the Senate and the House, bills are sent back to the Rules Committee to be scheduled for a final vote.

Voting is usually simple and short. Amendments are voted upon first and then the final bill, including any amendments that have passed. Senators vote by responding individually to a roll call. House members vote with push buttons on their desks. Votes are then recorded electronically on a large board behind the Speaker's

Representative Bill Fromhold of Vancouver addresses the House of Representatives.

podium. After a moment for changes and corrections, the results are locked in.

Most bills go through this procedure. In the Senate, appropriations bills go through the Ways and Means Committee. Bills that involve spending money are reviewed with more than usual care. The full Senate can change the amounts of money appropriated, but this is purposely made difficult to do.

After passing one house, the bill goes to the other house. Here a similar procedure occurs. Usually, committee hearings in the second house are not as intensive as those held in the first, but the second house will review what has been done. If a bill is defeated in the second house, it is dead for the session. A bill may be amended by the second house and then go back to be reconsidered by the first one. It must come out of both houses with exactly the same wording.

Some changes in a bill are accepted with little opposition. When two versions are very different, a conference committee consisting of interested members from both houses may be set up. These usually include sponsors and opponents of the bill or members of the committees that studied it. The conference committee is a temporary committee established specifically to work out differences in one particular bill. Members try to reach a compromise that they believe both houses will accept. If they succeed, the bill goes back to the two houses for votes, and if both approve, the bill moves on to the governor.

If the governor signs the bill, it becomes law. If the governor does not sign the bill, it nevertheless becomes law in thirty days if the legislature is meeting, or in ten days after the end of the session. Allowing a bill to become law without signing it permits the governor to express disapproval without blocking the bill or bringing about a quarrel with the legislature.

Representative Cathy McMorris, of northeastern Washington, addresses the House of Representatives.

Senator Rosa Franklin of Pierce County discusses issues with a constituent.

The governor can also veto a bill. A veto is a formal message to the house where a bill originated that explains the governor's objections. In Washington, part of a bill can be vetoed; this is called an "item veto." In this case, the rest of the bill becomes law.

The legislature must consider whether to try to force a vetoed bill through over the governor's objections. Usually a veto stands and the bill or rejected portion does not become law. Occasionally but rarely, the legislature successfully overrides a veto with a two-thirds vote in each house. Such a confrontation draws firm lines between the governor and the legislators, and it often signifies major differences between them. If the governor and the legislators who vote to override are members of the same political party, it implies a serious division within that party.

Most often, legislators try to work out a compromise or amend a vetoed bill into something they believe the governor will accept. If it is changed, the bill returns to the governor for action. In politics, compromise is an important way to get things done.

While a bill is being considered, legislators may receive political pressure, and advice may come from many sources. Individuals and groups contact their legislators, committee chairpersons, and key members to express views on bills of particular concern. Toll-free hot lines allow citizens to telephone messages to a legislator at any time. A single legislator may receive several hundred messages a day by letter, telephone, e-mail, or fax. Some come from the constituents in his or her district, and many come from various other groups in and outside of government. They may be received at the legislator's home, business, or Olympia or local office. Members often meet with individual constituents and groups in Olympia or during visits to their home districts.

Legislators often "trade" votes. A member who desires support for something important to his

# HOW A BILL BECOMES LAW

**1.** Bills are introduced by legislators in either the House or the Senate, given a number (HB No. _____ or SB No. _____), and assigned to a specific committee.

**2.** The committee studies the bill, often holds public hearings to seek citizen input, considers amendments, and determines whether or not the majority of the committee recommends passage. The bill dies here if the committee recommends against passage.

**3.** If the committee recommends passage, the bill goes to the Rules Committee, which determines when and if it gets presented to the full House or Senate. The Rules Committee can stop a bill from being presented on the floor.

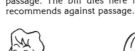

**4.** When a bill reaches the floor of the House or Senate, it is debated. It may also be amended on its second reading. If the bill is amended, it returns to the Rules Committee for scheduling of a third reading. If the bill reaches the floor, a vote may be taken and the bill either accepted, rejected, or referred back to committee.

**5.** The same process must occur in each house for a bill to become a law. If the Senate and House versions differ, conference committees may try to resolve the differences. The conference comittee report is accepted or rejected by each house. If rejected, the bill can die.

**6.** Once a bill is approved by both houses, the Speaker of the House and the President of the Senate sign it and send it to the Governor. The Governor may veto all or any section of the bill. A two-thirds vote in both houses is needed to override a veto. If the Governor neither signs nor vetoes a bill, it may become a law without signature.

From their desks, representatives can vote "yea" or "nay" on a bill or excuse an absence. The member can also call a page, address the rostrum, or make a phone call.

# An Idea Becomes Law

As the mother of two teenagers, State Senator Tracey Eide of Federal Way had personal concerns about the driving habits and abilities of young people. Even the best of kids seemed to have problems when driving, sometimes resulting in deaths. After gathering information on the topic, she proposed an "Intermediate Driving Law" that was similar to laws already existing in thirty-four other states. It required a person under the age of eighteen to successfully pass through several phases in order to receive a permanent driver's license.

In January 2000, Senator Eide introduced her bill in the Senate. Twelve other senators joined her as co-sponsors. Each new bill is assigned a number; this one became Senate Bill 6264 and was immediately sent to the Senate Transportation Committee. That committee studied the bill and held a hearing where private citizens could express opinions. Fourteen persons spoke in favor of it, including representatives of the Automobile Association of America (AAA), the insurance industry, the state patrol, school groups, and organizations concerned with traffic safety. They showed that similar laws had dramatically reduced accidents and fatalities in other states. Nobody spoke against the bill. The Transportation Committee made some minor changes and recommended the bill to the full Senate, which voted on it a month after Senator Eide had first introduced it. Forty-three senators favored it, with five opposing and one absent.

SB 6264 was then sent to the House of Representatives and its Transportation Committee. The House made an amendment that would allow a permanent license if the driver had no violations during the first year. Then the amended bill was approved by the Transportation Committee as well as the Rules Committee, which oversees all bills. There was some opposition in the House, but it passed 66 to 31 with one absent. Next the bill was returned to the Senate, which agreed with it as it had been amended.

While this process was going on, citizens sent their views about the bill to legislators. It was discussed in newspapers and other media. Several teenagers explained how the requirements would place a hardship on their driving to and from school, jobs, and recreation events, and some complained that it unfairly lumped all drivers—good and bad—together. Others thought it was a good idea even if inconvenient. A state patrol officer who was also a member of the House of Representatives wrote an editorial arguing that it would save lives. During this time, several well-publicized traffic deaths drew particular attention to the need for safety measures.

On March 24, Governor Gary Locke signed SB 6264 and thus made it the law. The new driver would need a learner's permit and have to pass a road test and driver's education test. In addition, new drivers would need to accumulate fifty hours of supervised driving experience, including night time. Then he or she would receive an intermediate license for six months, but during that time could not have passengers under the age of twenty in the car, except for family members. The driver could not drive between midnight and 5 A.M., except under special conditions. If the driver committed an offense during this time, there would be strict penalties. Although the law would not go into effect for a year, educators and the licensing bureau prepared for the time when it would.

An idea grown of need and personal experience had passed through the two houses of the legislature. It had been the subject of discussion and study in the legislature and in the media, and had been altered in the process. The final form of the bill was then approved by both houses and signed by the governor. SB 6264—known as the Graduated Licensing Law—provides an example of how an idea can become the law of the state.

Representative Phyllis Gutierrez Kenney speaks during an Asian Pacific Day rally in Olympia.

or her own district may gain support by agreeing to vote for a measure affecting another district.

Although the public has many contacts with lawmakers, each one ultimately makes his or her own decision on each bill and takes responsibility for that decision.

Lobbyists play an important part in passing bills. Lobbyists are officially recognized representatives and spokespersons for organizations, business concerns, and specific groups of persons who share a particular interest. Labor unions, large corporations, professional groups, service organizations, and other special interest groups all send lobbyists to Olympia. Individuals may also try to influence legislation.

In the 2001 session, there were five times as many registered lobbyists as legislators. They represented almost a thousand groups and organizations. Most are well-informed individuals with special knowledge and statistics at hand that may help the legislator. Yet legislators rec-

ognize that each lobbyist has a particular point of view to promote, while the lawmaker is responsible for understanding differing views in order to achieve good legislation.

Most bills are not controversial. Many housekeeping chores are necessary to carry on the work of government. Individual items may affect only a particular area of the state or meet a particular need and yet be acceptable to most legislators and presumably to many citizens. The bills that attract media coverage and arouse discussions and controversy are those likely to bring significant changes or affect large numbers of people. These controversial bills are comparatively few out of the three or four thousand items introduced in a session.

Ordinarily, only about one in every six bills introduced actually becomes a law. In one regular and three special sessions of the legislature in 2001, a total of 2,513 bills were introduced, 1,230 in the Senate and 1,283 in the House of Representatives. Only 379 of these passed both houses and were sent on to Governor Locke. He vetoed nine. The other 370 became law either with or without his signature, although Governor Locke vetoed parts of twenty-seven.

As soon as one session of the legislature ends, work begins on the next one. Many bills that failed will be reintroduced in the next session in the same form or with changes. Between sessions, legislators go home to their constituents but they keep in touch with one another. Committees and subcommittees meet and prepare for the next session. The process of making laws never ends.

### Direct Legislation

A few laws are voted upon by the people themselves. The Progressive Movement in the early 1900s tried to bring government closer to the people. Progressives introduced direct legislation, which included the initiative and the referendum.

Behind the scenes, security guards observe various parts of the Capitol Building on television monitors.

Adopted in Washington and other states, these gave people a direct part in making laws.

The referendum is a process in which a bill is "referred" from the legislature to the voters. The subject may be one of such great concern that legislators believe the public should vote. Having passed a bill, they vote to send it not to the governor but to voters at the next general election. Or, if many citizens oppose a bill the legislature has passed, such groups may petition for a public vote on it. If 4 percent of the number of persons who voted for governor in the last election sign referendum petitions, the measure is placed on the ballot. It has been "referred" to the people. A referendum approved by a simple majority at the election is as firm a law as one that goes through the normal process involving the legislature and the governor.

An initiative never passes through the legislature at all; it is "initiated," or started, by the people. A group of interested citizens, often an established organization, proposes a law and collects signatures of enough registered voters to have it placed on the ballot. If passed, it becomes law even though neither the legislature nor the governor took part.

A few initiatives pass even though they call for actions that run counter to the state or federal constitution. These do not become law, but they do indicate the attitudes people have. Sometimes people cast "advisory" votes that show officials how the public views an issue. In 1998, for instance, residents of southern Puget Sound and the Olympic Peninsula voted to favor building a second Narrows Bridge between Tacoma and the peninsula. This had no legal force, but officials learned what people wanted.

An example of the use of initiatives occurred in the election held in November 2000. Along with candidates for president and other offices and local issues, voters had six initiatives to consider. Three concerned schools. One would reduce class sizes, extend training programs, expand teacher training, and construct facilities. The measure also told where the funds would come from. Another would give annual "cost of living" salary increases to teachers and some other school and community college employees. That is, their salaries would increase automatically as the cost of living increased. Both of these passed, the second by a large majority.

A third school measure was defeated. If passed, it would have allowed school districts and public universities to establish "charter schools" that would be somewhat independent and not required to follow all state school laws. Those who favored it believed it would give greater choice to students and parents and improve schools generally. Opponents argued that some choices were already available and

Governor Gary Locke wears a false goatee to honor Olympic gold medalist speed skater Apolo Ohno.

this could destroy the public school system.

Three other initiatives in 2000 had various topics. One tried to deal with the state's transportation problems by requiring that 90 percent of transportation funds be spent on roads and highways. It failed, but if passed it would have slowed efforts to provide mass transportation. A successful initiative made it a misdemeanor to use certain kinds of traps or poisons to capture an animal. Another eliminated recently passed taxes and required a vote on many future tax increases. Two years earlier, initiatives concerned an even wider range of social issues: abortion, marijuana use, affirmative action programs, and a minimum wage. These initiatives demonstrate

how people can use their votes to shape the outcome of a variety of issues that directly affect many lives.

In 1999 voters approved the very controversial Initiative 695. It did two things: it reduced the fee for automobile license tabs to thirty dollars for every car and it required that the people vote on most tax increases. The state supreme court, however, ruled that dealing with two separate issues made the initiative unconstitutional. The initiative was thrown out. Soon after, license fees were reduced anyway, but the second issue remained. Some agencies quickly increased taxes and fees before the I-695 rules went into effect. So in 2000 the sponsors of I-695 came back with

## Governors of Washington

### Territorial Governors
### (appointed by the president)

| | | | |
|---|---|---|---|
| Isaac Ingalls Stevens (D) | 1853–1857 | Clarence D. Martin (D) | 1933–1941 |
| Fayette McMullen (D) | 1857–1859 | Arthur B. Langlie (R) | 1941–1945† |
| Richard D. Gholson (D) | 1859–1861 | Mon C. Wallgren (D) | 1945–1949 |
| William H. Wallace (R) | 1861 | Arthur B. Langlie (R) | 1949–1957 |
| William Pickering (R) | 1862–1866 | Albert D. Rosellini (D) | 1957–1965 |
| George E. Cole (R) | 1867 | Daniel J. Evans (R) | 1965–1977 |
| Marshall F. Moore (R) | 1867–1869 | Dixy Lee Ray (D) | 1977–1981 |
| Alvin Flanders (R) | 1869–1870 | John Spellman (R) | 1981–1985 |
| Edward S. Salomon (R) | 1870–1872 | Booth Gardner (D) | 1985–1993 |
| Elisha P. Ferry (R) | 1872–1880 | Mike Lowry (D) | 1993–1997 |
| William A. Newell (R) | 1880–1884 | Gary Locke (D) | 1997– |
| Watson C. Squire (R) | 1884–1887 | | |
| Eugene Semple (D) | 1887–1889 | | |
| Miles C. Moore (R) | 1889 | | |

§Note that governors are elected in November but take office the following January. Thus the election year is one year earlier than the date given here, with the exception of the first governor, Elisha P. Ferry, whose election took place before Washington formally became a state in 1889.

*John R. Rogers was elected in 1896 as a candidate of both the Democratic and Populist parties. Reelected in 1900 as a Democrat, he died the following year.

**Samuel E. Cosgrove was very ill when elected but came to Olympia for his inauguration. Immediately he asked for a leave of absence in order to try to regain his health. This was granted. He left the next day for California, where he died two months later. He had served as governor for less than one day, January 27, 1909.

†Arthur B. Langlie was defeated by Mon C. Wallgren when he ran for reelection in 1944. Four years later, he defeated Wallgren and returned to the governor's office. He was elected to a third term in 1952.

### State Governors (elected by voters)

| | |
|---|---|
| Elisha P. Ferry (R) | 1889–1893§ |
| John H. McGraw (R) | 1893–1897 |
| John R. Rogers (P,D) | 1897–1901* |
| Henry McBride (R) | 1901–1905 |
| Albert E. Mead (R) | 1905–1909 |
| Samuel E. Cosgrove (R) | 1909** |
| Marion E. Hay (R) | 1909–1913 |
| Ernest Lister (D) | 1913–1919 |
| Louis F. Hart (R) | 1919–1925 |
| Roland H. Hartley (R) | 1925–1933 |

another initiative to nullify or throw out those increases and limit most property tax increases to 2 percent a year. This passed.

Amendments to the state constitution also have to be approved by voters. One proposed in November 2000 would permit certain state funds to be invested for persons with developmental disabilities. It passed and became part of the state constitution.

Some persons believe that we turn to initiatives and referendums too frequently. They argue that making laws is the responsibility of legislators and that those officials dodge their duties when the task is passed on to voters. Also, it is argued that the people cannot always understand the details and often unclear legal language that go into proposed laws. And sometimes the "titles" of these measures are so confusing that people are not sure what they are voting for. Nevertheless, they do provide ordinary citizens an opportunity to make laws.

The recall is a third form of direct legislation. Voters can petition a recall election against public officials who have not carried out their obligations. If they get the required number of signatures on the petition, an election is held at which voters decide whether the official should remain in office or be removed. Recall elections have most often occurred at local levels of government.

## THE EXECUTIVE BRANCH

Members of the executive branch carry out laws passed by the legislature and supervise most areas of state government. Each of the nine elected state officials serves a four-year term. All campaign as candidates of a political party except for the superintendent of public instruction, who is elected as a non-partisan official, that is, one not affiliated with a particular political party.

### The Governor

The chief executive officer of the state is the governor. The governor supervises the executive branch, sees that laws are carried out, and plays a direct part in enacting laws. As a participant in lawmaking, the governor makes specific requests for laws, uses or threatens to use the veto, and can call special sessions of the legislature.

The governor can issue executive orders that have the effect of law. Some may proclaim special events or direct how government matters are handled. In 1997 Governor Locke issued an order canceling seventy-five very old executive orders that had become obsolete. The power to appoint heads of agencies and members of boards and commissions that affect most state affairs is an important part of the job. The governor can call out the National Guard and assume control of state functions in emergencies.

More than any other person, the governor is the symbol of the state. He or she is its chief representative and spokesperson, especially in contacts with federal and other officials and with the general public.

### Other Elected Officials

The lieutenant governor has only two major functions: to preside over the Senate and to act as governor when the governor is out of state or unable to perform duties. Three lieutenant governors have succeeded to the highest office when the governor died, but none since 1919. Unlike the vice president and the president of the United States, the lieutenant governor is elected separately and may be of a different party from the governor.

Some governors have been extremely cautious about leaving the state in the hands of a lieutenant governor, who assumes full executive powers when the governor is away. In the early 1930s, Governor Clarence D. Martin made a rushed flight home from the East Coast after learning that Lieutenant Governor Vic Meyers was about to call the legislature into special session. Because he distrusted Meyers, Martin never left the state again during his two terms in office.

The secretary of state is the chief record keeper. A major part of the secretary's job is administering elections. This includes filing of candidates, receiving and certifying petitions, handling the election itself, and validating results. This office also publishes a voters' pamphlet shortly before each election. Mailed to every registered voter, this booklet provides information about candidates and arguments for and against measures on the ballot.

The secretary of state registers and verifies official acts of the legislature, and as keeper of the official state seal, affixes it on necessary documents. Records of corporations and of codes and licenses for businesses and professions are maintained by this office.

The 278-foot dome of the Legislative Building, commonly called the State Capitol, is the fourth largest dome in the world and it dominates the Capitol Campus in Olympia. The building was constructed during the 1920s and completed in 1928. Offices of the governor and other state officials are in this building along with reception rooms. The chamber of the House of Representatives is on the west (left) side of the building and the Senate on the east. Other buildings, moving clockwise from the upper left, are the Temple of Justice, home of the State Supreme Court; the Insurance Building; the John A. Cherberg Senate Office Building; the State Library; the John L. O'Brien House Office Building; and, partly obscured by trees, the Executive Mansion, home of the governor.

The state auditor and treasurer deal with money. The treasurer receives, keeps, and disburses all state funds that are not the responsibility of some other official. The auditor watches over financial records to make certain that funds are used according to legal procedures and for the purpose intended. The auditor regularly checks smaller government units and financial systems throughout the state so that public money is handled properly.

The attorney general is the chief legal adviser and attorney for the state. The attorney general advises state officials, including the governor and members of the legislature, county prosecutors, and smaller local governments, about points of law concerning their duties. These are the opinions of a lawyer rather than the final decision of a judge, but they carry much weight.

Although most criminal investigations and prosecutions involving state laws are conducted by county officials, the attorney general may participate. When the state is involved in legal action, including suits, the staff of the attorney general represents the state. In the 1970s Attorney General

Slade Gorton personally defended state actions concerning the Boldt Indian fishing decision before the U.S. Supreme Court. Divisions within the attorney general's office handle specific legal concerns, such as education, corporations, and consumer protection.

The commissioner of public lands heads the Department of Natural Resources and supervises 3.5 million acres of land, mostly forests, that are controlled by the state. The use and leasing of such lands and the handling of timber and minerals are among the responsibilities of this department.

The insurance commissioner supervises and regulates the insurance industry, making certain that companies doing business within the state are financially sound and follow legal procedures. The commissioner is also the state fire marshal.

The superintendent of public instruction supervises the public schools. The office is non-partisan. The superintendent is involved with school funding and provides leadership and guidance to the school districts concerning curriculum and programs. Private schools and four-year colleges are not within the jurisdiction of this department.

### Appointed State Officials

In addition to offices filled by elections, about 150 administrative departments, boards, commissions, and committees are appointed either by the governor or by a specific commission. A few titles and functions will illustrate some of their activities. The Department of Ecology is concerned with numerous environmental matters. The Department of Transportation deals with highways, bridges, and the ferry system, and it regulates commercial vehicles. The Department of Motor Vehicles registers vehicles and licenses drivers. The Department of Social and Health Services supervises institutions such as prisons and state hospitals, and administers welfare pro-

grams. The Department of Licenses supervises persons who need licenses to do business within the state such as physicians, pharmacists, and barbers.

The executive branch of Washington State government thus involves a number of offices with varied responsibilities and more than 2,000 employees. Most have headquarters in Olympia and other offices throughout the state. In any community, a look in the telephone book under "Washington, State of" is a good clue to the local activities of state government. In the Aberdeen-Hoquiam area, for instance, there are over sixty local listings of agencies and departments to serve about 70,000 people.

State government does not exist only in Olympia but operates all around us. Much that we do daily—whether we drive the highways, build a house, fish and hunt, have our hair cut, attend school, or buy insurance—is directly affected by our state government.

## THE JUDICIAL SYSTEM

The courts ultimately interpret or decide what a law means and whether it has been broken. But a basic idea in our government is that the judicial system must be entirely separate from the legislative and executive branches. The courts are not made up of the same officials who write and carry out the laws.

The state court system has several levels. Each has its own jurisdiction, which defines the kinds of cases the court can hear. Some courts were created by the state constitution. Others have been added since. Most local judges in Washington are elected, and all the positions are non-partisan.

### Local Courts

Closest to the people are municipal courts and district courts. They hear cases involving relatively minor offenses and violations of local laws. About nine of every ten cases in the state are handled by these courts. Many municipal judges are appointed; others are elected on a non-partisan basis.

Municipal courts are not technically a part of the state court system, for they are established by towns and cities to handle violations of local ordinances. Sometimes they are called police courts.

There are forty-nine district courts in sixty-one locations in Washington. Every county is divided into districts with a district court and at least one judge. They have jurisdiction over traffic cases and minor offenses or gross misdemeanors, those for which the maximum penalty is a thousand-dollar fine, a year's imprisonment, or both. These courts also can hear civil cases—actions relating to contracts, damages, or injuries—involving less than $50,000.

Jury trials may be requested in district and municipal courts; if so, a jury of six or fewer persons is impaneled. If no jury is requested, the judge gives the verdict.

### Superior Courts

Cases involving more serious offenses are tried in the superior courts; there is no limit to the kind of case they can hear. Most counties have one or more superior court positions. A few small counties are joined into one judicial district. King County has fifty-one judges.

The superior courts are courts of record and have original jurisdiction. In other words, most of the criminal cases that people hear about, such as those for robbery and murder, are first tried in superior court. Here evidence is presented, witnesses testify, the defense is given, a verdict is delivered, and a sentence is imposed.

Defendants in criminal cases have a right to a jury of twelve persons, although the defendant may give up that right and have the judge alone decide. Juveniles—persons under eighteen years

of age—are tried in these courts, although procedures are different than in adult cases. In some counties, one judge may specialize in handling juvenile cases. Civil cases including divorces and lawsuits involving more than $50,000 are also heard in superior courts.

Superior court judges are elected to four-year terms. Occasionally reelection campaigns have been hotly contested because judges are often in the public eye during well-publicized cases. Several judges who have appeared to the public to be "soft" or "unfair" have been defeated in recent elections.

### Courts of Appeals

A person who loses a criminal or civil case in superior court has the right to appeal to a higher court. Appeals may also be made from district and municipal courts to the superior courts, in which case an entire new trial is held. All appeals used to go directly to the state supreme court, but in 1969 the legislature created a court of appeals.

The state is divided into three appellate divisions. Division I includes the populous northwest region of the state and has ten judges. Division II (which includes Pierce County, the southwest corner, and the Olympic Peninsula) has seven judges, and Division III (all of eastern Washington) has five. Judges are elected from districts within their own divisions for six-year terms, staggered so that not all leave office at the same time.

Judges sit in banks of three to hear appeals. They do not hear new evidence. Instead they review transcripts and listen to attorneys debate whether a lower court handled the case properly. If they find errors, the case can be sent back for retrial or it can be dismissed. If the judges determine that the case was properly handled, the lower court decision stands, but the loser may still appeal to the state supreme court.

### The State Supreme Court

The highest state court is the supreme court in Olympia. The Temple of Justice is directly opposite the legislative statehouse, or Capitol Building. Built in 1910–12, this is the oldest public building on the capitol campus. Nine supreme court judges, called justices, serve six-year overlapping terms so that three judges are elected every two years. The judges select one of themselves every four years to preside as chief justice and to handle administrative matters.

The supreme court hears appeals from lower courts, although it may refuse to consider them after a brief review. Some cases bypass the courts of appeals to reach the supreme court directly. These include cases that involve a state official, those with broad importance to the public, those in which the constitution may have been violated, and those that involve conflicting ordinances or rules of law.

All members of the supreme court sit together, or *en banc*, to hear cases by reviewing the transcript of earlier trials and listening to presentations by attorneys. Like the appeals court judges, they may send a case back to a lower court for retrial or dismiss it. Supreme court decisions help guide future decisions in the lower courts.

### The United States Supreme Court

As far as state laws are concerned, the state supreme court is the highest court in Washington. There remains one other possible court of appeal. The courts considered so far are state courts, dealing with Washington State laws and practices. The federal system is separate and different. But a person who loses a case before the state supreme court may appeal to the U.S. Supreme Court in Washington, D.C. The case must concern an important issue that is directly related to the Constitution of the United States.

Even then, the U.S. Supreme Court may refuse to consider the case.

Such a case from Washington reached the U.S. Supreme Court in the 1990s. A new state law prohibited physicians from assisting a terminally ill person in committing suicide. Opponents appealed, and the case reached the U. S. Supreme Court. After hearing all sides, the justices upheld the state's ban, but they allowed doctors to prescribe medicines to reduce pain, even if such medicines might hasten death.

The justices are not obligated to hear every case appealed to them. If they do hear a case, it will be to review lower court actions and hear brief pleadings from attorneys. The U.S. Supreme Court does occasionally overturn an action of the state courts. But this is unusual. Almost always, the state supreme court is the last resort for court actions in Washington State.

### Other Judicial Matters

There are other parts of the Washington court system. The state's supreme court oversees lower courts. The Washington Judicial Council is made up of court and legislative officials and a few other prominent citizens. The council does research and offers advice on administrative problems before the courts. In some counties, court commissioners have been appointed to handle routine matters such as adoptions, uncontested divorces, name changes, corporate dissolutions, and some minor offenses such as traffic violations.

Court administrators work to improve the overall operation of the courts. They try to maintain communication and seek uniform decisions among the various courts. Officials such as bailiffs, clerks, probation officers, and court reporters enable the judicial system to function in Washington. Many cases are heard and judged by jurors. These are private citizens drawn at random from voters' lists to serve for short, specific times.

## County Government

Washington has thirty-nine counties. When Washington was part of Oregon Territory, all of it was divided into two counties: Lewis in the farthest western portion, and Clark. By the time the state constitution was written in 1889, there were thirty-four counties. These were recognized as legal subdivisions of the state, and the constitution specified how new counties could be added. Five have been added since that time, but none since 1911 when Pend Oreille County was formed out of Stevens County. Four years later, Chehalis County was renamed Grays Harbor County.

In the early 1980s, some residents on the Olympic Peninsula urged that a new county be created in the far northwest corner out of Clallam and Jefferson Counties. Nothing was done. Also, some people living in the rural parts of King, Pierce, and Snohomish Counties in the 1990s started movements to separate from the urban, usually western, areas. None of these efforts has succeeded.

King County, with 1,685,600 people in 2000, is the largest county in population; Garfield, with 2,300, is easily the smallest. In area, Okanogan County is largest with 5,281 square miles, more than three eastern states. San Juan County has only 179 square miles, all on islands.

Headquarters for the county government is in a town selected to be county seat. Bitter rivalries sometimes erupted between towns competing to become county seat. The town that won was assured of increases in residents, businesses, property values, and revenue. In Pacific County in 1892, South Bend residents rowed into the county seat of Oysterville in the dark of night and stole county records in their successful effort to become county seat. Similar contests occurred in Clallam County between Port Angeles and Dungeness; in Snohomish County between Everett and Snohomish; in Lincoln County between Sprague, Davenport, and Harrington;

and in Spokane County between Spokane and Cheney.

The state constitution indicates the kind of government each county may have. Counties are divided into ten classes according to population. Most have three county commissioners who together set basic policies and make decisions. Other officials are prosecuting attorney, treasurer, sheriff, clerk, assessor, and auditor. Some counties have home rule; that is, they can adopt a charter with their own plan of government.

Counties can do what is necessary to carry on government. They can enact laws and govern their affairs, make contracts, raise money, and sue and be sued. They also are a local arm of state government to enforce laws and prosecute cases, hold elections, maintain records, and handle such concerns as health care and roads.

Counties that have commissioners are divided into three districts; a commissioner candidate is nominated by voters in each district and voted upon by the entire county. Commissioners pass laws and carry them out. They adopt the county budget, levy taxes, engage in lawsuits, and appoint some officials. They provide such essential services as maintaining roads and highways, jails, courthouses, and garbage systems.

Counties collect and handle property taxes for several governmental units. The county assessor regularly evaluates real property, including land, houses, and other buildings. The amount of tax due is based on the evaluation and is set by the commissioners and approved by the voters.

The county treasurer collects taxes, disburses money, and handles accounts for all small districts in the county that receive tax funds. These include school and hospital districts.

The sheriff is responsible for law enforcement including crime prevention, investigation, and the confinement of prisoners. The sheriff also may handle some civil procedures such as serving court orders and summonses, collecting cer-

Counties and County Seats

tain fees, and selling properties that have been seized. Many sheriffs also are responsible for emergency services. The prosecuting attorney is the county's chief adviser in legal matters and prosecutes cases before the courts. The coroner is responsible for investigating deaths, and the clerk maintains county records, including those of the courts.

Under the "home rule" amendment, four large counties—King, Whatcom, Snohomish, and Pierce—have adopted charters to establish their own forms of government. Instead of commissioners, these counties are governed by an elected county executive and a council consisting of members elected from districts. The council makes laws. The executive carries them out and administers the government much like a governor or mayor. The county executive may also appoint officials, such as the sheriff, coroner, and clerk, positions that in other counties are filled by elected officials. Many persons consider this form of government to be more reliable and efficient because it clearly fixes who is responsible for different aspects of government. Gary Locke is one of three county executives who later became governor. Clallam County also has adopted its own county charter, but has three commissioners rather than a county executive.

## MUNICIPAL GOVERNMENTS

In 1854 Steilacoom in Pierce County became the first town to incorporate. Incorporation is the process by which voters in an area can create a municipality that is a corporate body, able to handle many local affairs, levy taxes, and spend funds.

Well over half the people in Washington live in incorporated towns or municipalities. Over a third live in the twenty largest cities. The 280 incorporated cities range in size from Seattle, with over half a million people, to Krupp in Grant County, which has only sixty persons. Spokane and Tacoma—both with over 190,000 people—and Vancouver and Bellevue are other cities with populations over 100,000. During the 1990s, thirteen new cities incorporated, all of them in the Seattle-Tacoma area. Three of them, Federal Way, Lakewood, and Shoreline, were immediately among the state's fifteen largest cities. In 2001 Liberty Lake, east of Spokane near the Idaho border, became a city with about 3,200 residents. The next year, an adjacent city tentatively called Spokane Valley was formed.

There are three basic forms of city government. The mayor-council form is easily the most common. Elected council members, who represent different districts within the city, make laws. An elected mayor carries out laws, appoints leading officials, administers city business, and can veto ordinances. Some large cities have full-time mayors. In smaller towns the mayor and council are part-time officials who can appoint officials but receive little or no salary.

In 1948 Sunnyside in the Yakima Valley became the first city to adopt a council-manager system of government. Now forty-eight cities have them, including Spokane, Tacoma, Richland, and Yakima. Here an elected council sets policies and appoints one of its members to serve as mayor. The mayor presides over council meetings, represents the city, and performs ceremo-nial duties, but the person holding this office has limited power. City business is actually run by a full-time manager who is hired and can be fired by the council. Usually this person is profession-ally trained in government and public manage-ment. Many people consider this the most efficient form of city government. Others object on the grounds that control is no longer in the hands of a local citizen elected by the people.

Wenatchee and Shelton are the only cities with a commission form of government. Three elected commissioners divide the major functions of government, pass local ordinances, and appoint other city officials.

The state constitution allows cities some choice of government depending on their population. Cities with more than 10,000 persons at the time the city was organized can adopt a government of virtually any description by electing freehold-ers to draft a city charter. If approved by voters of the city, it then goes into effect.

A city can pass ordinances and provide facili-ties for water, streets, fire protection, sewage dis-posal, and the like. It can set punishments for crimes within certain limits, although major crimes come under state laws. Much money is raised from taxes on properties, but cities can adopt several other forms of taxes including a sales tax. Various licenses and permits provide additional funds. Cities also receive money from state and federal governments.

## INDIAN TRIBAL GOVERNMENTS

An important unit of government in many states including Washington concerns Native Ameri-cans, their tribes, and their reservations. Attitudes toward Indians have been confusing and compli-cated ever since whites took over the land. At various times Indians have been treated by the national government as the enemy, as primitive peoples, as foreign governments, as conquered people, as children who needed to be looked

Wilferd Yallup, former chairman of the Yakama Nation Tribal Council, recalls as a child hearing tribal elders discuss the need for leadership.

after and cared for, and as people who should be assimilated as part of the broader American culture.

The federal government in 1924 recognized Indians, both on and off reservations, as American citizens who could vote and hold office. By 1949 all of the states guaranteed these rights. Indians today may be called into military service, and they pay state and federal taxes on income from sources off the reservations. Reservation schools are part of the state public school system. Some reservations have their own school districts while others are part of a larger district. Reservation schools receive federal and state funds according to the number of Indian students in the school, and they are also eligible for money from the Bureau of Indian Affairs (BIA).

Reservations were established by treaties between 1850 and 1871. The Allotment Act of 1887 reduced the size of reservations and allowed white settlers to homestead on most of the land taken away. The BIA administers most of the remaining reservation land. During the 1930s, the federal government began to give Indian tribes more control, or sovereignty, over their own affairs. Tribes could write constitutions and organize councils to conduct business and write laws affecting their people. Traditionally, native decision-making had been based on consensus, with everyone having the right to participate. The council form of government was modeled on United States political bodies that had elected representatives who made decisions for the group.

Even with tribal councils, Indian self-government was limited. The BIA could veto decisions made by tribal councils. Disputes arose over when the state or federal government and their agencies had authority and when tribes did. For instance, many non-Indians lived or operated businesses on reservations and thousands more passed through. Were they subject to laws enacted by the tribal councils? And who had control over tidelands, waterways, and natural resources on reservations? Could state environmental laws be enforced?

In 1953 Congress passed Public Law 280, which took a big step toward ending tribal self-government. The intent of the law was to help assimilate Indians into non-Indian society. It allowed each state control over many affairs that affected Indians. Washington enacted laws to give the state, rather than the tribes, authority to handle such things as compulsory school attendance, child support, mental illness, and the operation of motor vehicles. Some—but not all—of the tribes and reservations were brought under these state laws.

How Indians and non-Indians are affected by these laws and changes is often determined in court. The United States Supreme Court and lower courts have often defined which agencies have authority or jurisdiction. Generally, tribal authorities have sovereignty in matters that affect only Indian people. For example, in the case of Oliphant versus the Suquamish Tribe, the U.S. Supreme Court ruled that tribal officials could not prosecute a non-Indian who had been arrested for assaulting an officer on the reservation and then resisting arrest. This ruling set a legal precedent that further reduced Indians' control over their reservations. Nevertheless, tribes do have the right to sell such products as liquor, cigarettes, and fireworks tax free to Indians on reservations; non-Indians must pay taxes on these items.

Sovereignty versus assimilation was once again the issue in 1975 when Congress passed the Self-Determination Act. Since then the BIA and the Indian Health Service have transferred more and more services to tribal control. In 1988 a small group of tribes was awarded federal grants to design social programs without having to follow guidelines established by other agencies. The self-governance program began with only four tribes (three of them in Washington State). By 1993 thirty tribes (six in Washington) enjoyed this responsibility. These tribes are exercising more sovereignty over their affairs than at any time in the past.

Currently decisions in the United Nations support sovereignty and human rights for indigenous (or native) people in all parts of the world. Decisions in the future may greatly affect the role of tribes and their governments.

## SPECIAL DISTRICTS

One other unit of government remains. Special districts handle particular functions, usually within small local areas. They include school districts, public utility or power districts, water districts, port districts, fire districts, park districts, hospital districts, and library districts. Most are governed by a board of three to nine members elected by voters. The board members appoint (and can dismiss) another official to administer their program and assume responsibilities for it. These districts can do the things that most corporations do, such as raise and pay out money, construct buildings and facilities, and make rulings concerning district affairs.

Most common of these special districts are the school districts in the state. Many spread beyond town limits or encompass several towns. Washington school districts are completely separate from the governments of their towns and cities. Edmonds School District #15, for instance, is the sixth largest in the state, serving over

21,000 students. Its governing board has five citizens who are elected for staggered four-year terms and receive no salary. The area covers much of south Snohomish County and is largely suburban. (A few school districts, such as the neighboring Northshore District, cross county lines.)

Within the Edmonds School District, more than 150,000 people live in five incorporated cities and large unincorporated parts of the county. The board of directors appoints a super-intendent of schools, principals, teachers, and staff members: over 2,100 employees. It operates on a $137 million annual budget. It is the fourth largest employer in Snohomish County.

The district owns properties, including many buildings, a stadium, play fields, a bus garage, buses, other facilities, and a large amount of equipment and materials. Within state laws, the board and the superintendent are responsible for meeting the needs of kindergartners through twelfth graders, although they have some flexibility in what they may do.

Some districts also have adult education programs, although many have been taken over by local community colleges. The activities and responsibilities of the Edmonds School District can serve as a clue to what other special districts do.

## PAYING FOR OUR GOVERNMENTS

We want and expect many services from our state government and other governments. These services cost money. Each state budget is for a two-year period and hovers around $20 billion. By far the largest expenses are for education from kindergarten through college and for various human services.

To pay for this, we pay taxes. Much revenue is from the sales tax that is familiar to all of us when we purchase items. Businesses also pay special taxes, and licenses are required for many professions. Citizens pay state taxes on such items as automobiles, gasoline, and liquor. In addition to the state itself, counties and cities and special districts must raise funds for the services they provide. Most often these are taxes on property or additional sales taxes.

Real Estate Excise 4%
All Other 10%
Property 12%
Retail Sales 56%
Business and Occupation 18%

Source: Washington State Office of Financial Management, 2002

Where Washington State Gets Its Tax Dollars

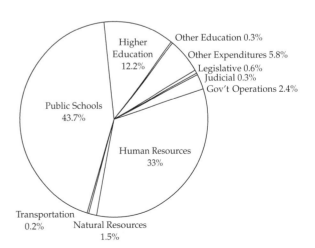

Higher Education 12.2%
Other Education 0.3%
Other Expenditures 5.8%
Legislative 0.6%
Judicial 0.3%
Gov't Operations 2.4%
Public Schools 43.7%
Human Resources 33%
Transportation 0.2%
Natural Resources 1.5%

How Washington State Spends Its Money

## Elections and Voting

In Washington, as in all states, voters must be eighteen or older, U.S. citizens, and legal residents of the state. They must register in their local precinct, which covers roughly the neighborhood. Two regular elections—a primary and a general—are held each election year. At the primary election, held on a Tuesday in September, voters narrow the field of candidates to one from each party, or two in each non-partisan race. The winner will be chosen in the general, or final, election in November.

An unusual feature of voting in Washington has been the open, or blanket, primary. Voters could cross party lines to vote for the candidate of their choice. As a result, political parties in Washington are fairly weak, and one strong or popular candidate may not carry fellow party members along to victory. But the U.S. Supreme Court has ruled that such primaries must end, that only voters who consider themselves of a certain party should choose that party's candidates. Thus Washington must change its primary election procedure. Voters will most likely express themselves as supporters of a particular party and choose only among the candidates of that party in the primary election.

Voters also have the opportunity to write in names of candidates who are not printed on the regular ballot. "Write in" candidates rarely receive many votes, but an exception occurred in Washington in 1994. That September, enough Republicans wrote in the name of state senator Linda Smith that she won the primary election for U.S. representative. She was elected to Congress that November and served two terms.

Small political parties may put candidates on the November ballot by holding a nominating convention in September. Whereas the Democratic and Republican parties try to appeal to a wide number of voters, some small parties, such as the Socialist, Green, Libertarian, Natural Medicine, Prohibition, and American Heritage parties, take strong stands on very specific issues. Often these parties do not appeal to large numbers of voters, but they strongly promote a particular point of view.

Sometimes these "third" parties gain widespread support and elect candidates. Examples in the early twentieth century were the Populist

Cherry blossoms frame the Legislative Building, commonly called the State Capitol, on a spring day in 2002.

and Progressive parties. Occasionally a candidate will run as an Independent with no support from an organized political party. For instance, H. Ross Perot won 24 percent of the vote in Washington during his independent campaign for president in 1992.

One thing must be certain. There is no such thing as *the* government. We live among many governments serving many functions and administered in many ways. We encounter them in a wide variety of our own activities. Sometimes the maze of governments may seem confusing. To get a job done—to build a house, for instance, or to open a small business—often requires following rules set by a number of different governments. The alternative, however, is probably worse: to be under the total control of one central government with all others serving as its agents.

The American system of government involves many layers and units, but clearly the division of responsibility among several powers serves people while it protects our freedoms.

Campaign signs for local as well as state and national candidates become familiar in Washington towns each election year.

## Chapter 12 Review

**I.** There are many government officials or leaders with whom you should be familiar. Several are listed in the questions at the end of chapter 9. Find out the names of the current United States senators and the members of the House of Representatives from Washington. Learn about the representative from your congressional district. Know the present governor of Washington and other officials in the executive branch. Know the leaders in the Washington State legislature and the senator and two representatives from your district.

**II.** Define the following words and phrases. Relate each one to Washington State.

Government
Federal government
Constitution
Legislative branch
Executive branch
Judicial branch
Popular vote
Electoral vote
Federal system
Extradition
Amendment
Rules Committee
Veto
Item veto
Direct legislation
Referendum
Initiative
Partisan
Non-partisan
Recall
Appeal
Criminal cases
Civil cases
General election

**III.** Each question below should call your attention to factual information in the chapter. Try to answer each one. Then look back in the reading to check your answer, correct your understanding, and find answers you do not know.

1. Why is it incorrect to think that we live under only one government?

2. Give three sources of the ideas in the United States Constitution.

3. Which article in the United States Constitution concerns the role of states in the federal government?

4. How many representatives does Washington State have in the U.S. House of Representatives?

5. What are the requirements to be a member of the U.S. House of Representatives?

6. How many U.S. senators does Washington have?

7. Name four things the United States Constitution says that states cannot do.

8. How are presidential electors chosen?

9. How many federal court districts are there in Washington?

10. What does the United States Constitution require each state to do with regard to other states?

11. List the steps by which a territory may become a state.

12. When might federal troops be brought into a state?

13. What part do states have in amending the United States Constitution?

14. Which is stronger, federal law or state law?

15. About what percentage of the state's revenue comes from the federal government?

16. About what percentage of the land in Washington State is owned by the federal government? Give some examples of land owned by the federal government.

17. When was the constitution of Washington State written?

18. What is a bicameral legislature?

19. How many legislative districts are there in Washington State?

20. How many representatives to the state legislature are elected from each legislative district? How many senators?

21. Who presides over the state House of Representatives? Who presides over the state Senate?

22. What are the duties of a leader of a political party in the state legislature?

23. How often does the legislature meet?

24. What steps must a bill pass through to become a law?

25. What choices does a governor have after receiving a bill passed by the legislature?

26. What is an executive order?

27. What do lobbyists do?

28. List four duties of the governor.

29. What is the major duty of the lieutenant governor?

30. What is the major responsibility of the secretary of state?

31. Which official advises other officials on legal matters?

32. Which elected official supervises a particular industry?

33. Which official is elected as a non-partisan?

34. List three agencies or departments whose heads are appointed by the governor.

35. Which courts handle about nine out of every ten cases?

36. Which courts hear those cases that we usually think of as crimes?

37. What is the difference between criminal cases and civil cases?

38. If a defendant loses a case in superior court, where is the first place to appeal?

39. What is the highest court in the state?

40. What kinds of cases might go from state courts to the United States Supreme Court?

41. How many counties are there in Washington?

42. The town that has the headquarters of state government is called the capital. What term is used for the town that has the headquarters of county government?

43. What responsibilities do county commissioners have?

44. Name three forms of city government.

45. What may large cities do to select their own form of government?

46. Identify several federal laws that have changed the way Indian reservations are governed.

47. List five examples of special districts.

48. What is the legal voting age? What steps must a person take in order to vote?

**IV.** Think about, discuss, and answer the questions below.

1. Check through your local telephone book (possibly in the blue pages) to find all the different

government agencies in your community. Make a list of services they provide or concerns they handle. Notice which are local units, which are state, and which are federal government agencies.

2. For one week, keep a record of all the government agencies that you come into contact with. Don't forget to include such everyday, simple things as the post office, federal roads, school lunch programs, school classes, etc.

3. Washington's executive branch of government consists of nine officials who are elected by voters. In some states, voters elect only the governor, who then appoints and can fire other officials. Which do you think is the better method? Give some arguments for both points of view.

4. What are some ways that the federal government can influence or put pressure on state and local governments? Why might the federal government do this? Do you approve or disapprove? Discuss.

In 1984 Congress passed a law intended to curb drunken driving. The law threatened to hold back money for building highways from states that did not set the minimum drinking age at twenty-one. What is your opinion of this law? What is your opinion of this method of influencing state laws? Is it a good way to get worthwhile laws passed? Or is it an interference in state matters by the federal government?

# Suggested Reading List for Students

This brief list includes a varied group of books that students might find enjoyable for perusing, reading, or researching.

Alt, David D., and Donald W. Hyndman. *Roadside Geology of Washington*. Missoula, MT: Mountain Press Publishing Co., 1984.

Alwin, John A. *Between the Mountains: A Portrait of Eastern Washington*. Bozeman, MT: Northwest Panorama Publishing, 1984.

Ambrose, Stephen E. *Undaunted Courage: Meriwether Lewis, Thomas Jefferson, and the Opening of the American West*. New York: Simon and Schuster, 1996.

Armbruster, Kurt E. *Orphan Road: The Railroad Comes to Seattle, 1953–1911*. Pullman, WA: Washington State University Press, 1999.

Beal, Merrill D. *"I Will Fight No More Forever": Chief Joseph and the Nez Perce War*. Paperback edition. Seattle and London: University of Washington Press, 1966.

Belyea, Ed. *Columbia Journals: David Thompson*. Paperback edition. Seattle and London: University of Washington Press, 1998.

Blair, Karen J., editor. *Women in Pacific Northwest History*. Revised edition. Seattle and London: University of Washington Press, 2001.

Brewster, David, and David M. Buerge, editors. *Washingtonians: A Biographical Portrait of the State*. Seattle: Sasquatch Books, 1988.

Clark, Norman H. *Mill Town: A Social History of Everett, Washington, from Its Earliest Beginnings on the Shores of Puget Sound to the Tragic and Infamous Event Known As the Everett Massacre*. Seattle and London: University of Washington Press, 1970.

Clark, Norman H. *Washington: A Bicentennial History*. New York: W. W. Norton and Company, Inc., 1976.

Crowley, Walt, and the HistoryLink Staff. *Seattle and King County Timeline*. Seattle: HistoryLink, 2001.

Dietrich, William. *The Final Forest: The Battle for the Last Great Trees of the Pacific Northwest*. New York: Simon and Schuster, 1992.

Dietrich, William. *Northwest Passage: The Great Columbia Basin*. Seattle and London: University of Washington Press, 1995.

Dorpat, Paul, and Genevieve McCoy. *Building Washington: A History of Washington State Public Works*. Seattle: Tatu Publications, 1998.

Egan, Timothy. *The Good Rain: Across Time and Terrain in the Pacific Northwest*. New York: Knopf, 1990.

Fargo, Lucile F. *Spokane Story*. New York: Columbia University Press, 1950.

Ficken, Robert E. *Washington Territory*. Pullman, WA: Washington State University Press, 2002.

Ficken, Robert E., and Charles P. LeWarne. *Washington: A Centennial History*. Seattle and London: University of Washington Press, 1988.

Harris, Stephen L. *Fire and Ice: The Cascade Volcanoes*. Seattle: The Mountaineers, 1976.

Hughes, John C., and Ryan T. Beckwith, editors. *On the Harbor: From Black Friday to Nirvana*. Aberdeen, WA: The Daily World, 2001.

Kirk, Ruth. *Sunrise to Paradise: The Story of Mount Rainier National Park*. Seattle and London: University of Washington Press, 1999.

Kirk, Ruth, and Carmela Alexander. *Exploring Washington's Past: A Road Guide to History*. Revised edition. Seattle and London: University of Washington Press, 1995.

Kirk, Ruth, with Richard D. Daugherty. *Exploring Washington Archaeology*. Seattle and London: University of Washington Press, 1978.

Kirk, Ruth, with Richard D. Daugherty. *Hunters of the Whale: An Adventure of Northwest Coast Archaeology*. New York: William Morrow and Company, 1974.

Lavender, David. *Land of Giants: The Drive to the Pacific Northwest, 1750-1950*. Garden City, NY: Doubleday and Company, Inc., 1956.

Lee, W. Storrs, editor. *Washington State: A Literary Chronicle*. New York: Funk and Wagnalls, 1969.

LeWarne, Charles Pierce. *Utopias on Puget Sound, 1885-1915*. Seattle and London: University of Washington Press, 1975.

McDonald, Lucile. *Coast Country: A History of South West Washington*. Portland, OR: Binfords and Mort, 1966.

Morgan, Murray. *The Last Wilderness*. Paperback edition. Seattle and London: University of Washington Press, 1976.

Morgan, Murray. *Skid Road: An Informal Portrait of Seattle*. Revised edition. New York: The Viking Press, 1960.

Northwest Environment Watch. *This Place on Earth 2002: Measuring What Matters*. Seattle: Northwest Environment Watch, 2002.

Phillips, James W. *Washington State Place Names*. Seattle and London: University of Washington Press, 1971.

Pitzer, Paul. *Grand Coulee: Harnessing a Dream.* Pullman, WA: Washington State University Press, 1994.

Reyes, Lawney L. *White Grizzly Bear's Legacy: Learning to Be Indian.* Seattle and London: University of Washington Press, 2002.

Schwantes, Carlos A. *Railroad Signatures across the Pacific Northwest.* Seattle and London: University of Washington Press, 1993.

Shane, Scott. *Discovering Mount St. Helens: A Guide to the National Volcanic Monument.* Seattle and London: University of Washington Press, 1985.

Spiedel, William C. *Sons of the Profits, or, There's No Business Like Grow Business! The Seattle Story, 1851-1901.* Seattle: Nettle Creek Publishing Company, 1967.

Taylor, Quintard. *The Forging of a Black Community: Seattle's Central District from 1870 through the Civil Rights Era.* Seattle and London: University of Washington Press, 1994.

Williams, Hill. *The Restless Northwest: A Geological Story.* Pullman, WA: Washington State University Press, 2002.

Williams, Jacqueline. *The Way We Ate: Pacific Northwest Cooking, 1843–1900.* Pullman, WA: Washington State University Press, 1996.

Woodbridge, Sally B., and Roger Montgomery. *A Guide to Architecture in Washington State.* Seattle and London: University of Washington Press, 1980.

In recent years, many printed histories of cities, communities, and even neighborhoods have been published along with videos and CD-ROMs. Readers are advised to check local libraries and historical groups for them.

Many historical and anthropological organizations in Washington have museums and Web sites that provide additional information about the history of the state. The Washington State Historical Society in Tacoma and the Northwest Museum of Arts and Culture in Spokane are the major such groups in the state, but county and local groups often have museums as well. Other museums are dedicated to specific fields of interest such as aviation, telephones, lumber, software, Native Americans, Asians, and the like. A unique organization is HistoryLink, a Seattle-King County interactive group that in 2002 is expanding its focus statewide.

Because Web site addresses tend to change over time, none are listed here, but conventional search engines will lead interested individuals to many of them.

# Acknowledgments

Special thanks and appreciation are extended to:

—the staff at the University of Washington Press, especially Naomi Pascal, Veronica Seyd, and Marilyn Trueblood, who have encouraged and guided this project;

—Lane Morgan, whose extensive knowledge of Washington history and its contemporary scene and whose superb editorial work have diminished errors and enhanced the quality of the book;

—Carolyn Marr for an energetic search for photographs that would not merely illustrate but would also help to tell the story of Washington;

—the staffs of numerous libraries and historical societies and public offices who have found materials and answered questions, with particular thanks to Carla Rickerson and the staff of the Pacific Northwest History Collection at the University of Washington Libraries, and to Al Meinert at Meadowdale High School;

—Robert E. Burke, Carlos A. Schwantes, Dan Peterson, and persons unknown to me who read early drafts of this manuscript—some of them more than once. Their invaluable comments and suggestions have made this a far stronger book than it would have been;

—Vernon A. Carstensen, Joyce Hudemann, Linda Bakken, Tom Stern, Paul Spitzer, Claudia Buckner, and others for help with specific sections and problems;

—former state senator Sue Gould, whose reading of chapter 12 brought practical insights and advice from the perspective of her years of public service; former state representative John Beck, who read the same chapter and provided similar information and insights for the 1993 revised edition;

—administrators and colleagues in the Edmonds School District and Meadowdale High School (especially the lunch bunch) for their continuing interest, encouragement, and support;

—several generations of students upon whom some of the ideas in this book were tried out;

—friends for their interest and for all the things that good friends do;

—Pauline Nelson LeWarne, who once again allowed a book to become part of our lives.

With appreciation for all this, the final responsibility for the book remains my own.

*Washington State* is dedicated to the memory of my parents and to the promise of their grandchildren: To Charlie and Angie, and to Charles, Anne, and David.

The 2003 edition of *Washington State* rests upon the support and help of all those persons listed above and the many, sometimes anonymous, individuals who helped with specific areas, provided information, or answered questions. Special appreciation is also extended to Ruth Kirk, Deb Otterby, Doris Pieroth, and Chuck Richards for reading and commenting upon all or portions of the manuscript. As before, Pauline LeWarne has played an essential part in this undertaking.

Thanks go to Jacqueline Ettinger of the University of Washington Press, who sympathetically and effectively assumed the task of editing this new edition. The 2003 edition is dedicated to a new generation of Washingtonians born in the twenty-first century: To Ava, Charlie, Audrey, Annika, and Jane.

Charles P. LeWarne
Edmonds, Washington
June 1985, March 1993, August 2002

# Picture Credits

# Index